**UNIVERSITY OF**
**WOLVERHAMPTON**
KNOWLEDGE • INNOVATION • ENTERPRISE

Harrison Learning Centre
City Campus
University of Wolverhampton
St Peter's Square
Wolverhampton WV1 1RH
Telephone: 0845 408 1631
Online Renewals:
www.wlv.ac.uk/lib/myaccount

**Telephone Renewals: 01902 321333 or 0845 408 1631**
**Online Renewals: www.wlv.ac.uk/lib/myaccount**
Please return this item on or before the last date shown above.
*Fines will be charged if items are returned late.*
*See tariff of fines displayed at the Counter.*

# THE FAMILY

# SOCIOLOGIE VANDAAG / SOCIOLOGY TODAY

Volume 3

# THE FAMILY

## CONTEMPORARY PERSPECTIVES AND CHALLENGES

### FESTSCHRIFT IN HONOR OF WILFRIED DUMON

Edited by
**Koen Matthijs**
**With the collaboration of Ann Van den Troost**

1425

**Leuven University Press**

Cover: Lejon Tits
Photo cover: L. Oosterlynck

© 1998 Universitaire Pers Leuven / Leuven University Press / Presses Universitaires de
Louvain, Blijde-Inkomststraat 5, B-3000 Leuven/Louvain, Belgium

ISBN 90 6186 926 9
D/1998/1869/74

# Contents

*Contents*

# Prof. Dr. Wilfried Dumon: a portrait

After an academic career of 35 years, most of that time as a full professor, Prof. Wilfried Dumon was given emeritus status in late September 1998. Together with a few others, such as Karel Dobbelaere, Edward Leemans (†), Yvo Nuyens, Jan Van Houtvinck, Frans Van Mechelen and Lode Van Outrive, he was present at the birth of sociology in Leuven during the mid-nineteen sixties. He was there during the development of the required administrative, logistical and academic structures and the mapping out of the areas of research and education in which sociology at Leuven was to specialize. These kindred spirits very soon developed a unique sociological perspective referred to as the 'Leuven Triangle', that is, the integration of sociological theory, methodology and (social) policy. Wilfried Dumon himself preferred to speak of a pyramid, with society forming the base.

The name of Wilfried Dumon is inextricably linked with the sociology of the family or, more broadly, with family sciences. He was without doubt the father of Flemish family sociology. Hundreds of students received from him an unconventional – others might use more colourful adjectives – form of education as regards both form and content. He was directly or indirectly responsible for practically all Leuven family sociology subjects even outside his own faculty; anyone writing a dissertation or doctoral thesis on a subject in any way connected with topics such as marriage, family or sexuality was invariably confronted with his critical analysis and special vocabulary. Wilfried Dumon's academic attention also focused on the flank of the sociology of the family, namely research methods, social stratification and mobility, and demography and the sociology of population. Wilfried Dumon also carried out a very considerable amount of empirical research which, certainly in the early days of Leuven sociology, was not to be taken lightly. After all, the methodological and theoretical fundamentals of empirical sociology had yet to be cast – and on shaky foundations. The academic climate at the time was not exactly well disposed towards the empirical ambitions of a few young academics full of enthusiasm. With the wisdom of hindsight, however, their stubborn adherence to the empirical angle of attack is one of the main explanations for their subsequent success. Besides education and research, Wilfried Dumon's long career also spanned numerous policy assignments, such as editorial secretary or editor-in-chief of periodicals, as head or director of all manner of institutions and as member, manager or (deputy) chairman of a succession of committees and associations – all at national and international level. It is almost inconceivable that anyone could do so much in one human lifetime. Unless, of course, you can count on a healthy and energetic body, on a relativizing and agile mind and on support from the immediate social environment.

A festschrift was compiled to mark the occasion of his retirement. With this initiative, the *Sociology Department* in general, and the *Section of the Sociology of the Family and Population* in particular, wish to express their profound respect and appreciation for their guiding light and pioneer. Apart from the inevitable administrative and logistical pressures that accompany the preparation of such a book, compiling it was a conspicuously easy matter. The reason is simple: Wilfried Dumon had and still has an extensive, close-knit international network of friendly academic contacts all over the world.

Wilfried Dumon was born on 20 January 1933 in Maldegem. In February 1957 he graduated in Political and Social Sciences. With a view to the preparation of a doctorate, he then served for a number of years as a trainee at the Nationaal Fonds voor Wetenschappelijk Onderzoek (National Scientific Research Fund). Following on from the theme of his dissertation, he received his doctorate on 6 March 1963 in the Political and Social Sciences with a thesis entitled, *The middle class as a sociological category: an exploratory examination of the concept of the middle classes*. This study was rewarded with the University Prize from the Ministerie van de Middenstand (Ministry for the Self-Employed). In 1966, Wilfried Dumon was a lecturer at the old Faculty of Economic and Social Sciences and became a full professor in 1968. By now, he was able to spread his mighty international wings as an honorary fellow at the Family Studies Center, University of Minnesota (USA). He worked there alongside, among others, Reuben Hill (†), an eminent colleague whose efforts on behalf the expansion of sociology (of the family) at Leuven were rewarded in 1970 with an honorary faculty doctorate.

At the beginning of his academic career, Wilfried Dumon was passionately involved in the development of the Sociologisch Onderzoeksinstituut (Sociology Research Institute). The roots of this institute stretch back to the Centrum voor Sociale Politiek/Centre de Politique Sociale (Social Policy Centre) established in 1955 – a centre that would, by virtue of its statutes, be involved in research into 'the problems of social life in general'. The expansion of this research structure was a clear sign of the launch of sociological research in Leuven. After one or two academic adjustments and, more particularly, after the dovetailing of the university research institutions into the new structures of the University of Leuven, split in 1970, a new research unit was called into being under the name of the Sociologisch Onderzoeksinstituut. That institute was officially inaugurated on 31 January 1968 by Rector Piet De Somer. Wilfried Dumon was its first director. The institute was placed under the management of a Board of Directors in which the departments and study groups of the day were represented. In this respect, the structure of the Sociological Research Institute was a reflection of the sociology educational initiatives, which offered some guarantee that the university sociological teaching would have the solid backing of research. The first graduate course in sociology began during the 1963-1964 academic year with three specialities: religion, employment, industry and commerce, and family and population. Wilfried Dumon was – needless to say – the first head of the Section of Sociology of Family and Population (later renamed Sociology of Family, Population and Health Care) and would remain in that post until his retirement.

Under the stimulating leadership of Wilfried Dumon, the Sociological Research Institute conducted highly diverse research projects, some with a predominantly social and applied bent, others of a more pure-scientific persuasion – however confusing and ambiguous these terms may be in sociology. Through its research, the Sociological Research Institute was directly involved in the training of sociological researchers, at that time a profession in the making. To support the sociologists' professional interests both physically and symbolically, structures were now required. After all, once a certain size and depth had been attained, well-intentioned voluntarism was no longer enough. The Organisatie voor Vlaamse Sociologie (Flanders Sociology Organization) was set up in 1963, with Karel Dobbelaere as its first director and Wilfried Dumon as co-initiator. The Organization encouraged the professionalization of sociology in word and deed. In 1964, for instance, an initial congress was held in Leuven on the theme of 'Sociology and Society' – you can hardly get more general than that. The Organization also had its own newsletter, which was remodelled in 1972 to become a Sociological Bulletin. It aimed to distinguish itself at international level and, with this in mind, published the *Sociological Contributions from Flanders*, of which three issues appeared. In 1975, the Organisatie voor Vlaamse Sociologie merged with the Belgische Vereniging voor Sociologie (Belgian Sociology Association). However, under pressure from the ongoing cultural/federalization process, the Association was swiftly split up again into a Flemish and a Walloon wing. On 17 December 1975, The (Flemish) Vereniging voor Sociologie was created with Karel Dobbelaere as its first director. The Association founded the non-profit-making *Tijdschrift voor Sociologie*

(Journal of Sociology), the first Dutch-language exclusively sociological journal in Belgium. Wilfried Dumon was its first general editor. The symbolic import of the Association for Sociology and the Journal of Sociology can hardly be overestimated. The temptation to look away from the manifold social responsibilities of sociologists was now, in a manner of speaking, structurally impossible. However, the Association's function was of course first and foremost academic: bridging the academic islands and furthering the cause of inter-university communication and co-operation.

In the mean time, Wilfried Dumon worked, with others, towards close co-operation with Dutch colleagues as regards both institution and content. The avoidance of any intellectual in-breeding was always one of his chief concerns. Co-operation was given a substantial shot in the arm via the Dutch periodical *Sociologische Gids* (Sociological Guide). In 1961, an editorial secretariat was set up for this journal in Belgium, with Wilfried Dumon as its first secretary. The links with the Dutch family sociologists during the late 1970s and the early 1980s were with the so-called 'post-academic family sociology course'. Wilfried Dumon was the person in charge in Leuven. That initiative – primarily intended as an advanced course for graduate family sociologists – laid the foundations for many bonds of friendship that still exist today. The course led to interesting and informative Flemish/Dutch comparisons, a form of comparative sociology that Wilfried Dumon always supported. This, to be sure, is the cure for the mind-numbing *pensée unique.*

To begin with, Wilfried Dumon was principally involved in family sociological policy studies; that is, research with the implicit or explicit expectation of hammering out concrete policy alternatives to (social) problems. One of his early inquiries concerned the employment outside the home of married women – an acute problem in the mid-nineteen sixties that caused considerable social panic. The problem was tackled using a specific research strategy, the so-called situational approach, an angle that was also used in other investigations, such as that into marriages with age dispensation and home-care. The first two doctoral theses supervised by Wilfried Dumon, namely those of Rozemie Bruynooghe (*The social structure of the home-care situation among tenant families and patients,* 1973) and of Edmond Lambrechts (*Female employment in Belgium. An analysis of employment policy with reference to female workers since 1930,* 1975) can be set in that theoretical-methodological context. Wilfried Dumon applied the adopted methodology flexibly to the nature of the research problem. His investigations of the sexual attitudes and behaviour of Leuven university students – several of which were conducted during the nineteen seventies – were first and foremost interactional. Still others – such as various studies of divorce – were system-theoretical or institutional. The doctoral thesis by Thérèse Jacobs (*Divorce. A typological inquiry on the basis of court files in divorce cases*, 1976) is just one example. A combination of a situational approach and development perspective can be found in Mariette Masui's doctoral thesis (*The unmarried mother. Sociological analysis of the genesis process*, 1980). Sybille Opdebeeck's doctoral thesis (*Dependency and the cessation of partner violence*, 1993), for its part contains an interactional perspective on families and family processes. The undersigned graduated under Wilfried Dumon with a study of *suicide and attempted suicide* (1983). The six masters graduates named later all went on to a university or research institution which, in Wilfried Dumon's arithmetic, comes to six out of six.

Regarding divorce, the Section worked intensely for more than a decade on various international projects. The unique longitudinal perspective used in these inquiries yielded a wealth of material. The methodological and theoretical expertise that the Section built up was one of the decisive factors in the organization in Leuven (30 August - 4 September 1981) of the XIXth CFR International Seminar on Divorce and Remarriage. The reactions of the delegates at the conference were genuinely positive; everyone appreciated the professional academic seriousness brought to bear on a socially delicate subject. The participants still remember the seamless organization even today. All these elements must have played a part in the conferment upon Wilfried Dumon of an honorary doctorate by the University of Uppsala (Sweden) in 1983 – surely one of the high points of his academic career.

Wilfried was President of the Sociological Research Institute at the time when the so-called Nationaal Onderzoeksprogramma in de Sociale Wetenschappen (National Social Sciences Research Programme) was launched. This National Research Programme in the Social Sciences also included a family sociology strand, entitled *Prevention of structural marginalization of non-traditional families*. This initiative by the Ministry of Science Policy had a dual purpose: firstly, to give the social sciences a substantial economic boost to remedy their position of relative neglect – with hindsight, this was indeed a stimulating position of neglect – in relation to other areas of science and, secondly, to encourage utilitarian policy studies, not only studies, but action too. Through its breadth and depth – expectations were high and there were ample funds – this programme gave the social sciences in Belgium a much-needed impetus, particularly through a more professional approach. For the first time, it was now possible, using representative samples, to collect relevant information concerning the state of social play and the situation throughout Belgium. For the first time, the data thus collected could now be subjected to multivariate analysis. The relevant methodological and technical expertise had in the mean time been acquired – mainly in the USA. In the first phase (1975-1978), these projects identified and took stock of problems. During the second phase, the accent was more on the transfer from research findings to policy. That was and still is symbolically important, because the partnership between science and policy was thus given structural support. Informal science education had to be broken down in favour of concrete policy commitment.

The Section of Sociology of Family, Population and Health Care has always devoted particular attention to (foreign) immigration which, naturally, is connected with the quantitative-demographic and with the qualitative-sociological importance of this phenomenon. Since 1973, the Organization for Economic Co-operation and Development (OECD) has published an annual report on immigration: *Système d'Observation Permanente des Migrations* that draws on national information provided by the correspondents from the participating member states. Wilfried Dumon was Belgian correspondent from 1975 to 1979. Also at the request of the OECD, a report was drafted in 1987 on the school situation and education of children from immigrant families. To remain in the same field, Wilfried Dumon was general editor from 1982 to 1991 of the leading periodical *International Migration*, published by the International Organization for Migration (Geneva). According to an impartial observer, Wilfried Dumon raised this publication to *a leading journal in the field*. In this line of work, as in others, Wilfried Dumon did not shirk his local responsibilities: addressing himself to a wide audience, he wrote a book on the social and cultural difficulties and the delicate problem of immigration and immigrants.

Mention has already been made of the peculiar triple perspective, typical of Leuven sociology, with policy as one of the supporting pillars. Wilfried Dumon still holds this perspective, but seems to have taken it to even more to heart in the last ten years of his academic career – for him, it had a firm link with family policy. In the beginning, it was a matter of national initiatives, such as the projects concerning international adoption and medical school visits but, gradually, the international card was also played. At the request and with the financial support of the European Union, (Directorate-General of Employment, Industrial Relations and Social Affairs), Wilfried Dumon spent the past few years on a number of international social-scientific research projects in preparation for social policy, which occasionally resulted in direct policy plans. It is mainly as a result of his efforts towards the European Observatory on National Family Policies that his name is permanently linked to European family policy. The European Observatory on National Family Policies then consisted of twelve national correspondents, one from each member state. The intention was that each independent correspondent would collect and publish the necessary data on the basis of a common questionnaire featuring aspects such as taxation and the family, family allowances, social security and the family, family and employment, home-care, family law, family therapy, violence in the home and related topics. On the basis of these national reports, a coordinator would then compile a summary report for subsequent discussion in the workshops. Wilfried Dumon was the European coordinator for this important initiative between 1989 and 1993. Evidence that he has not the least intention of ceasing his academic activities after retirement is revealed by the fact that he is the Belgian expert for the European Observatory for the period 1998-2004. A clearer indication of his love of the subject would be hard to imagine.

His function as European coordinator exacted a heavy psychological price from Wilfried Dumon because his input had to be mobilized – I shudder at the thought – under very difficult personal circumstances. Christiane Bauwens, his wife and the mother of their four children, died on 10 April 1994; the children now all had to catch their father's international bug. With her typical modesty, Christiane Bauwens was a key figure in Wilfried Dumon's academic career. She was, after all, literally and figuratively his right hand, his diary and organizer. With her equally typical subtle assertiveness she led Wilfried Dumon's near legendary gaucheness along socially acceptable channels – almost within the bounds of the possible. How she managed to make Wilfried Dumon's head, heart and hands operate in harmony is something of a mystery to anyone who knew the Dumons at all well – fortunately.

For over two decades, Wilfried Dumon was the driving force behind the *Gezinswetenschappelijke Documentatie* (Family Sciences Documentation), an impressive reference work – in Wilfried Dumon's university terminology, a "piece of knitting" measuring 78 cm and weighing 24 kg – that climbed to the top of the Flemish family sciences network. Number 23 of this series appeared in 1998. The non-profit organization publishing the work - GIDS, or Gezinswetenschappelijke Informatie, Documentatie en Serviceverlening (Family Sciences Information, Documentation and Service Provision) – is without doubt the intellectual child of Wilfried Dumon. GIDS is an institute within an institute, the Family Science Documentation is a series to be treated with due reverence. The Section recounts the achievements of GIDS with vicarious pride. All these initiatives are in fact the material expression of Wilfried Dumon's enthusiasm for the social and cultural characteristics of and changes within marriage and the family. By logical extension, it should come as no surprise to hear that he played a key role in the formulation of the content of the International Year of the Family in 1994. His efforts on behalf of the Year were, incidentally, rewarded by a Medal of Honour from the United Nations. A spin-off of the International Year of the Family is the International Family Policy Forum (headquarters in Montreal, Canada). Wilfried Dumon is a Member of the Board of Directors.

Wilfried Dumon also had great respect for the difficult work of interest protection associations. He supported them not only with words, but also with action, as shown by his contributions to the International Union of Family Organizations. He contributed to the organization of various world congresses of the International Union and was active serving on its various commissions, such as the Commission on Family Housing, the Commission on Education and the International Commission on Marriage and Interpersonal Relations. At present, he is chairman of the Demography and Housing working party and is charged with the task of drawing up the *Leuven Standards* on family and accommodation. In the same context, he was recently co-organizer of the Family, Demography and Accommodation symposium (Leuven, March 1998). Wilfried Dumon gave his social commitment concrete form in all manner of fields. He was chairman of Trefpunt Zelfhulp (Self-Help Centre) from 1988 to 1993, chairman of the Federatie van Consultatiebureaus (Federation of Consultancies) from 1983 to 1994 and, from 1990 to 1994, first chairman of the Vormingscentrum voor Consulenten (Consultants' Training Centre) – incidentally also founded by him. He was formerly also President of the Hoge Raad voor Volksopvoeding (Supreme Board for Popular Education) as well as of the Commissie voor Culturele Centra (Cultural Centres Commission).

Meanwhile, Wilfried Dumon also arranged, or, more precisely, accumulated all kinds of national and international policy tasks. After his directorship of the Sociological Research Institute, he became Dean of the Faculty of Social Sciences in 1981 (until 1984). Various economies – there is nothing new under the sun – made this a difficult period at times. After all, no over-hasty measures were to be taken, yet the requirements of the academic authorities still had to be met, of course with as little human damage as possible and as little scientific sacrifice as possible. In this period, Wilfried Dumon laid the foundations for all kinds of faculty initiatives that still exist today. This is nothing unusual: Wilfried

Dumon was and still is a system-person who thinks in the long term, not someone who trusts in instant assessment.

That general profile is also abundantly clear from his many and various activities outside his own faculty. Shortly after his deanship, he moved his academic ambitions once and for all to the world outside Belgium. He had previously paved the way as visiting professor at several universities, including Minnesota, Notre Dame, Uppsala, Paris (Sorbonne), Antwerp (UFSIA), Salzburg (Seminar in American Studies). Later, he was a visiting professor at universities all over the world. He lectured from 1965 to 1979 at the Hoger Instituut voor Gezinswetenschappen (Institute of Further Family Sciences Studies) (Brussels, Bond van Grote en Jonge Gezinnen (Association of Large and Young Families). In 1992, Wilfried Dumon became a member of the board of professors of the Stichting Benelux-Universitair Centrum (Benelux University Centre Foundation), where he held the chair in demography. From 1968 to 1972, he was Secretary and, from 1972 to 1977, President of the Instituut voor Familiale en Seksuologische Wetenschappen (Institute of Family and Sexual Sciences). He was Executive Secretary of the Committee on Family Research of the International Sociological Association from 1974 to 1982. In 1998, he was elected member at large for a period of four years. He was member of the Executive Committee of the International Sociological Association from 1982 to 1986.

With such a curriculum vitae, it was not long before he received a top appointment. Thanks to his numerous international contacts, his unflagging hard work and his organizational talents, 1986 saw him elected to serve for a period of four years as Vice-President of the International Sociological Association (ISA), the world association of sociologists. In terms of his logistical services to sociology, this is a peak in his career. In the USA at the time he was Chairman of the Membership and Finance Committee. He was jointly responsible in that capacity for the organization of two world congresses: in 1986 in New Delhi and in 1990 in Madrid. Similarly, from 1986 to 1990, he was a Member of the Publications Committee of the International Sociological Association and Editor of the Sage Studies in International Sociology. He could draw on his long and intense experience as an editor: from 1969 to 1979 he was Associate Editor of the top family sociological publication *Journal of Marriage and the Family*, Associate Editor of *Sage Family Abstracts* from 1978 to the present and, from 1980 to 1990, member of the editorial board of *The International Journal of Sociology and Social Policy*. It is no exaggeration that, between 1980 and 1990, Wilfried Dumon was one of the most important ambassadors of the sociology of Leuven, even of Belgium. However, that was certainly no reason to cast off his local duties. He was a long-serving member of the editorial staff of the Dutch-Flemish series *Sociologische Monografieën* (Sociological Monographs) and of the Leuven-based series *Sociologische Verkenningen* (Sociological Explorations) and *Sociologische Studies en Documenten* (Sociological Studies and Documents). He spent years working on the editorial staff of a paper jointly published by the Centrum voor Bevolkings- en Gezinsstudiën (Centre for Population and Family Studies - CBGS) and the Nederlands Interdisciplinair Demografisch Instituut (Interdisciplinary Demographic Institute of the Netherlands), two institutions he often supported in word and deed. From 1970, he was a member of the Wetenschappelijke Raad (Scientific Council) and of the CBGS Jury voor Aanwerving en Bevordering (Recruitment and Promotion Jury). Following the structural adjustments within that body, he rejoined the Wetenschappelijke Raad (Scientific Council) and the Raad van Advies (Advisory Board) of the periodical *Bevolking en Gezin* (Population and Family) in 1997.

In the field of educational services, mention should also be made of two further important initiatives. From 1986 to 1992, Wilfried Dumon played a key part in the academic development and logistical execution of a sociological education programme set up in Flanders (especially at the Katholieke Universiteit Leuven) for (lecturers from) the University of Bandung (Indonesia). At local level, he was the initiator within the School of Social Sciences and the architect of the specialist course *Master in Comparative European Family Studies,* an academic postgraduate course uniting the K.U.Leuven and six other European universities.

A glance through the chronological bibliography – which is included at the back of this book – points to a dual thematic movement in the thinking and in the fields of interest of Wilfried Dumon, with 1980 as a watershed: from national to international and from family theory to family policy. Both developments run parallel and reinforce each other; a clear evolution is evident in Wilfried Dumon's publications from a predominant interest in national (especially Flemish) issues to a pronounced leaning towards international (especially European) family policy. In addition, various other temporary staging posts are visible, with divorce, social stratification and (foreign) immigration as the most obvious. These, however, never received the same attention as Wilfried Dumon's pet subjects: family theory, family problems and family policy, preferably with the prefix 'macro-'. He wrote on the subject with the flair of an original, creative, concise thinker. With a feel for understated humour, oblique observation and well-planned hidden meanings, he offers an unorthodox, sometimes even recalcitrant vision of the sociology of the family, without paying too much respect to modern sociological fashions and populist trends. In his own inimitable way, he combines the qualitative solidity of demography with the qualitative creativity of sociology, nonetheless with a preference for the latter discipline. At the end of the day, this characteristic is more important than statistics. Wilfried Dumon does, in point of fact, have a strong predilection for pure disciplines and does not conceal his contempt for derived knowledge. With a certain feel for provocative cynicism, he once described the interdisciplinary approach with which some are so obsessed as cumulative incompetence.

Wilfried Dumon was and still is a steadfast observer of family and population developments in the second half of the 20th century. In the midst of his flourishing academic career, there was no shortage of social dynamism and change; never before had there been such intense change within the space of one or two generations. Wilfried Dumon was passionately interested in these post-war developments and this comes across loud and clear in his publications. At the beginning of his career, the family cycle was still fairly immutable: people married soon after the onset of adulthood, getting married was the socially accepted transition from the family of reference to the family of procreation; children soon followed in a family where the husband/father/man of the house provided the income while the wife/mother/woman of the house saw to the cooking and childcare. That was thoroughly modern in its day, even though it was a 19th-century invention. Most followed this classical family cycle without alien structures such as women outside home, marriages within walking distance, latchkey children, divorce and step-relations. How women especially felt in all this is difficult to imagine but, with hindsight, it seems that they – sometimes with support and sometimes despite opposition from the male onlookers – swiftly drew up a new social blueprint under the heading of social emancipation and female liberation – a subject on which Wilfried Dumon wrote several original papers. One of his central questions was how we are actually supposed to study all these developments from a sociological perspective. That resulted in 1975 in the volume *Woman and Family. Relevance of certain family sociology studies to the question of women.*

From the 1960s and 1970s onwards, the division between instrumental-male jobs and expressive-female domestic tasks – even the terms themselves! – was assailed from all sides, frequently with much lip-service, sometimes with resolute action. For many, sexual segregation stifled women, their subjective identities, personal lifecycles and social possibilities. Some hitched up their grievances to a feminist bandwagon, still others found an ideological accommodation in one or other social or ecological movement. Be that as it may, there was now sufficient ammunition for a protracted war of attrition between the sexes which is still far from over – on the contrary. The core question is not simple either: how, in a post-modern society – or should that be in a pre-technological society? – do we settle male-female conflicts that are rooted in the industrial society? Many problems revolve around the dislocation of parenthood and partnership, two models of social relationships that constantly recur in Wilfried Dumon's publications, even when later he focuses on family policy.

The above developments have deeply affected at least one dependent group, children, in many ways, and this did not escape the sociological gaze of Wilfried Dumon. His writings show a latent concern for the future of the upcoming young generation, since little is known about the question of what the new social teaching environment might mean in the long term. Meanwhile, for parents and children alike, the semi-institutionalized standard life is being replaced by a variety of plural and multiple lifecycles where a large measure of individual interpretation is involved. Some see this as an erosion of crucial family and social values, a process of social defoliation taken as symptomatic of general social malaise. Families look to themselves as to an unsolved problem. Others take the view that the modern societal situation is anything but a threat, rather a normal adaptation of the private life to the needs and requirements of post-industrial society.

Wilfried Dumon reviews the social changes and their various interpretations with passion and amusement. With hesitation and reluctance, he employs semi-classical terms like informalization, privatization and individualization, three wonderfully nebulous, ambiguous concepts that, with some goodwill, refer to the erosion and dismantling of strict social buttresses and prestructured social arrangements and to the expansion of greater individual autonomy, more space for personal decision-making and freedom of action. Whether or not you now marry, cohabit or have children, all these semi-private decisions now involve – besides continued social standardization – greater individual choice. Does this spell the switch from a standard personal and family life to an individual choice life? Large groups do not in fact follow the standard lifecycle any more and gender roles and identities are no longer so hard and fast. That creates the space for a shift from formal rules to informal discussion, from an ordered to a negotiated household. This leads to fresh tension between the social and the individual: the greater the uncertainty regarding (the future of) the social commitments we enter into, the more we ourselves are responsible for them.

As already mentioned, Wilfried Dumon is a keen student of all developments and their associated sociological issues. The search for a theoretical thread is a futile enterprise. His thinking is not readily boxed in the traditional academic pigeon-holes or in one or other sociological paradigm. He is too deep and too headstrong for that. Some would even say too muddled-headed, but those who know him well know better than that. His headstrong nature is revealed, among other things, by the fact that his most characteristic publications contain hardly any footnotes and/or endnotes and/or bibliographical references. He was after all never one eagerly to seek the advice of others. As an original thinker within the real meaning of the word, he never allowed his mind to be diverted by the pronouncements of the sociology pundits.

Wilfried Dumon's thinking marries the Durkheimian social fact and the Weberian economic theory. It contains snatches of both individual and collective exchange theory and of the fine-mesh interpretations and readings of phenomenology and symbolic interactionism. He was just as flexible on the level of theory as in the field of methodology. But there is always that Dumonic twist. Wilfried Dumon accepted that much was possible in theory provided it was not too psychological. If we must have a pigeon-hole for his thinking, why not 'macrosociological systems theory'? This is the only intersection between the dual challenge of sociology as a behavioural science and as a social science. It is a framework for thinking and analysis where the influence of one of his first teachers, Reuben Hill, lives on. Wilfried Dumon expressly chooses not to subscribe to the philosophical and psychological excursions from this systematic thought because, with a measure of exaggeration, we might suppose that he had little confidence in or tolerance for behavioural sciences outside sociology. Only sociology gave him intellectual release.

Acknowledgements
Although the texts were all prepared by others, compiling them into a book, was no easy enterprise. In just a few weeks, Margot Van Baelen and Chris Vander Hulst have again shown that they can make the impossible happen. On behalf of the Department of Sociology and of the Section of Sociology of Family, Population and Health Care, I offer them my sincerest thanks.

Koen Matthijs
27 September 1998

Family Theory

# The changing concept of fatherhood

JOAN ALDOUS
NOTRE DAME, USA

Human families are generally thought to consist of at least two generations of parents and children usually in some form of cohabitation arrangement. And though it is necessary for a woman and a man to come together in some fashion to produce their offspring, there are a variety of partnership forms that result in children (Ingoldsby, 1995). Regardless of the form, however, the mother's identity is clear at the child's birth, but the identity of the father is not so apparent. This truism has led to many strategies among the male-dominated societies of the past and present to ensure that the infant has a recognized father as well as a mother. Otherwise, the child was labeled as illegitimate and a bastard. The infant had a mother who was able to feed it and care for it. But it took the presence of a male who admitted to being the father to give the newcomer a legitimated status in society.

My article concerns how the prescriptions for being this important personage have changed over the centuries. Given the central importance of the father position in the family with respect to its recognition in society, there is surprisingly little literature on fathering. For example, I took two books off the bookshelf when beginning my research whose titles looked promising on the subject. One book was Daniel J. Levinson's (1978) *The Seasons of a Man's Life*. There was nothing on fathers or mothers and very little on parenting. The second book was an edited collection of articles titled *Themes of Work and Love in Adulthood* (Smelser & Erikson, 1980) that came out about the same time. Again, there was nothing on fathers. Parents' roles, fathers or mothers, did not seem a part of 'love' among adults.

I then turned to my own bibliographic work. For the years 1900-1964, there were some 12,850 references my colleagues and I found on marriage and the family. Of these, only 302, two percent, had anything to do with fathers (Aldous & Hill, 1967). The years 1965-1972 showed a quickening of interest in marriage and the family. There were more references for those seven years, 12,870, than the 12,850 references from the previous 64 years. But, as in the earlier years, just a small number, 286, two percent, had to do with fathering (Aldous

& Dahl, 1974). However, I am happy to report that in recent years there has been a marked upsurge of interest in fathers and fathering. One recent estimate based on references on the World Wide Web lists about 2,000 references with the interest beginning in the 1980s. However, the majority of publications have come out as recently as the mid-1990s (Pickard, 1998). Consequently, there is much material to draw upon to get at present prescriptions for fathers, but comparatively little on fathering in the past.

In this article, I shall draw upon the limited historical material on fatherhood to describe its earlier forms. There will also be a discussion of the possible reasons for changes in the prescriptions for fathering over time. This survey of the standards set for fathers is largely limited to research on United States' fathers. However, the starting place of my historical review is Europe, especially England and Wales. It was there that the ancestors of the earliest immigrants to America developed their ideas about paternal behaviors. Before 1776, the start of the War of Independence from Great Britain, the majority of early colonists came from there (Cremin, 1970: 123).

There is some suggestion that the patriarchal power of men in families was strengthened during the period of European state formation. It was between the eighth and fifteenth centuries, that rulers were attempting to consolidate their own power. The rulers had to weaken men's allegiance to their kin groups and shift it to themselves in order to create a united country. To do this, it was in the would-be ruler's interest to have men assume some of the kin group's authority over women and children as well as land (Muller, 1977). The assumption was that heads of nuclear households would support the authoritarian ruler. Benefiting from the deference shown to them as heads of their households, they supposedly would show the same to the king. Thus, rulers saw patriarchal nuclear families as sources of strength. These same rulers and their governments discouraged extended kin-centered families, viewing them as threats to the growing power of the centralized states (Stone, 1975). Fathers who were household heads came to represent their families in these states (Fox-Genovese, 1977).

This development of the public role of fathers was furthered by British philosopher, John Locke's argument that political authority came from the individual. Locke justified limiting political authority to male individuals by making families a private world. Families, were the area of women and children, and were set apart from public politics. Fathers as heads of families dealt with interchanges between families and the outside world. The ideology of individualism thereby further strengthened fathers' family power after the centralization of state authority (Fox-Genovese, 1977). Thus, one of the central roles of fathers still common today, that of public figure, who is the link between families and the broader world, came into being. But this brief summary of the effect of the development of central governments on fatherhood alerts us that much of what we know about fathers in the past describes the better-off and more powerful. The lives of peasants and laborers are not a part of early family-life accounts. For this reason, my discussion refers to middle-class fathers. They and their families have always possessed 'substantial social and ideological (even if not always economic) influence' in the US, and their way of living has been held up as the model for other groups (Rotondo, 1987: 65). What writers of the various periods reported about them tells us what fathers did or wanted to do, depending upon their social class.

The period in the early 1600s first saw English women and men leave their native land to make their homes in the new territories. They were neither from the well-born nor from those without skills, but people in between. This middle group provided the first comers to America. The prescriptions for being a good father with which these early settlers of the American colonies were familiar appeared in royal edicts. The emigrants from Britain came from a country in which fathers and mothers were urged by Royal Injunctions to ensure that their children and servants learned some occupation, husbandry or craft. This was to prevent children and servants from falling into idleness. The lack of a useful activity could lead the individual to become a beggar or a thief (Cremin, 1970: 120). Parents, especially fathers, were the central figures in seeing that youngsters became worthy adults.

The middle-class fathers in the colonial period (1620 to about 1800) were towering authority figures in their families. This position came from their family responsibilities and from their ownership of the land. Families were the basic economic units in which every member worked. Subsistence farming was how most families made their livings. Fathers were the production chiefs, and supervised the contributions of every member. Mothers and daughters joined fathers and sons in working the land. The men were more often in the fields while the women took care of the 'barnyard, cattleyard, pigpen, garden and orchard' (Cremin, 1970: 127). What little was left over from meeting family needs could be traded to others in the small agriculture villages.

Fathers' leadership roles as managers of the household economy and landowners were strengthened in New England by the settlers' religion. They were Puritans, followers of John Calvin (Morgan, 1966: 8). Fathers were the moral leaders in their families. They monitored the behavior of their children, both daughters and sons. Fathers were the teachers and disciplinarians who were to guide their children on the paths of righteousness. In serving as the instructors of morality, fathers depended mainly on persuasion and sympathy. Contrary to what we might expect of such powerful men in their role as disciplinarian, they only used corporal punishment 'as a last resort and even then in moderation' (Rotondo, 1987: 66).

Fathers' relationships with their sons and daughters differed. Young children regardless of gender were left to their mothers to feed, care for and love. When children reached the age of three, fathers became the moral teachers of their children. These early colonists, especially in Puritan New England, believed that too much affection would spoil their children and so lead to the ruining of their characters. Since men were supposed to be able to control their emotions better than women, they were to set an example of self-restraint for their children. They were rather distant, aloof figures who expressed satisfaction and dissatisfaction with their children rather than love and anger. When they did show affection, it was largely limited to their daughters. They received paternal love for their good behavior. This love was conditional on proper behavior, and fathers threatened to withdraw affection from disobedient daughters. Thus, fathers were both teachers of morals and disciplinarians for sons and daughters, but they showed more tender emotion to their daughters (Rotondo, 1987). To the extent of their own literacy, fathers were also responsible for teaching their sons and daughters the rudiments of reading and writing (Demos, 1982).

Children in that period were expected to receive vocational training in a family setting. But this parental training was assigned to parents on the basis of their children's gender. Fathers were responsible for sons; mothers trained daughters. Although fathers were moral models and teachers of right character besides being instructors in basic literacy to both sons and daughters, it was only with sons that fathers served as teachers of vocations (Rotondo, 1987). While little girls were largely limited in their vocations to housewifely arts, there was more of a range of occupations available to sons in the early years of colonial settlement. Thus, fathers also were influential in their sons' occupational choices. Puritan parents' fear of ruining their children's moral development through giving them too much affection also played a part in fathers' role as vocational teachers. Young teenagers, accordingly, both girls and boys were sometimes placed in the homes of other families. Supposedly, the girls could better learn housekeeping skills and the boys a trade from teachers who were more objective than their parents. Even when fathers had the necessary skills to teach sons the vocation fathers felt appropriate, they still might choose to send them for instruction to other men. These adolescents would become adults in families other than their own, as apprenticeships began generally at 14 years of age and lasted for seven years (Morgan, 1966: 68, 76-77).

Because of the colonial fathers' ownership of the family property, usually in the form of farming land, they could control whom and when their children married. They were matchmakers, as it was fathers who decided which individuals were suitable to wed their offspring. Property considerations determined fathers' decisions as to which men were eligible to marry their daughters and the women their sons should court. Fathers played the role of benefactors to the young couples whose formation they had encouraged (Demos, 1982: 427). Fathers allotted portions of their land to sons and provided dowries to daughters whose marital choices they promoted. I should add that fathers were not, despite their authority, supposed to force children into marriages with persons they disliked (Morgan, 1966: 84). After all, in making marital arrangements for their children, the father's goal was to ensure the new couple's economic well-being but also their getting along together.

Since fathers were so active in their children's upbringing, they were the family members held responsible for proper child care. Contrary to the situation after 1800 and continuing into our own age, books with child-care prescriptions were directed to men, not women. Men were supposed to be superior to women in domestic matters as well as in other areas. Men, it was thought, generally benefited from receiving more reason from God than did women. Fathers, as a result, were better able to avoid temptation and to serve as models of approved behavior. Moreover, being less subject to their emotions they could serve as better teachers of deportment. As a consequence, fathers, not mothers, received advice about childrearing (Demos, 1982: 427-428).

At this time when families were the units of production, fathers were also a visible part of the everyday lives of their children living at home. Fathers and sons worked together on their farms as did the few artisans and tradesmen. Fathers were also part of the daily lives of daughters, busy with their mothers in making their own contributions to the family economy. Thus, fathers at this time were a constant presence in their children's lives as work supervisors, teachers, moral models, property givers, and disciplinarians. All these roles stemmed from their position as family patriarch, as well as being physically in the family household. Fathers may have been emotionally distant particularly with their male offspring, but this distance had nothing to do with geography. They were always present in their children's lives adding the role of companion to their more awe-inspiring roles (Demos, 1982: 429).

The great power middle-class fathers had over their children's futures coupled with their many responsibilities in their upbringing began to wane during the second half of the eighteenth century. Their authority for the fathering roles they played depended upon their control of property. Due to population growth in the small farming communities near the Atlantic coast, men came to own less land. Fathers were losing the economic means to control their children's behavior. They had less property to pass on to their sons and to contribute to the dowries of their daughters. This gradual shift in the economic value of paternal approval led to a modification in the standards set for fathers' child care. The new parental norms downplayed rigid authority while maintaining the emphasis on fathers and mothers as moral teachers (Rotondo, 1987: 67).

During this period of the family patriarch's ebbing power, the view of mothers was changing. The decline in paternal authority was accompanied by an upturn in the reputation of mothers as child-care authorities. They, not fathers, were now judged as better able to nurture children. In sharp contrast to the past, mothers were thought to be fundamentally 'moral, more spiritual, and more tender than men' (Rotondo, 1987: 167). As a consequence, in the popular view mothers took on more importance. This period in the first half of the nineteenth century was also one in which middle-class individuals centered their attention on family life. In this development, families were always on display. Their suitable performances depended upon a parental division of labor. If fathers were the producers of the family 'drama', mothers were its directors (Gillis, 1996: 76). And with middle-class men's shift from farming to buying and selling the products from the country outside the growing commercial towns and cities, fathers were no longer a part of their children's everyday lives. These urban businessmen, lawyers and clerks were leaving home each morning and not returning until evening. Their labor took place in offices away from their children. No longer was the family a production unit in which every member participated under the father's overall direction. In the 1800s, the emerging commercial economy was based on business partnerships and in the latter part of the century, corporations. Fathers were the producers for families in this extra-familial world. At the same time, they were performing their other function as public figures, representatives of their families in the outside world. Mothers and children were 'purely domestic beings' whose comings and goings from the family did not count (Gillis, 1996: 95).

The Industrial Revolution in the middle of the nineteenth century completed the severing of economic production from the middle-class family's functions. Fathers' roles that demanded their physical presence with children were gone while others were strengthened. His work outside the family determined its social status. He might have been a self-made man, but in the process he also made the social place of his wife and children. His paternal role as breadwinner was joined to that of determining the family's social class. Fathers were less often matchmakers as family connections and family property played a diminished part in young people's marriage decisions. With economic production no longer a family matter, sons no longer looked to fathers to learn a vocation. With the heavy emphasis on individualism in commercial capitalism where success was presumably based upon a man's abilities and energy, sons sought to out-do their fathers. Unlike the previous two centuries, when sons depended upon the power, property and often teaching of their fathers for their own occupational achievements, fathers and sons were now competitors (Rotondo, 1987: 68).

However, fathers' daily absences from home strengthened their role as moral teacher and with it their role as disciplinarian. Fathers in their time at home led families in prayer and were responsible for Bible readings. This moral training by fathers included moral preachments about wrongdoing. These were more directed to sons than daughters. Getting ahead in the world of business demanded close attention and much effort. Fathers as moral teachers and examples were to train their sons in the qualities needed to succeed (Rotondo, 1987: 69).

While fathers when present in the family were to set the ways children were to behave, mothers supplied the love and affection that encouraged children to obey. Alexis de Tocqueville, the 21 year-old French nobleman, who visited the United States in 1831, wrote of the democratic family. Based on his observations, he believed fathers in the new nation were allowing their children more freedom and granting their wives more authority in household matters than was the case in France. Mutual love and more equality characterized these marriages, along with a concern about the upbringing of children (Mintz & Kellogg, 1988:

45). But fathers were too invisible during the day to be the intimate companions mothers were. Fathers, as in the past, continued to be rather distant figures to their children, more feared than friends (Rotondo, 1987: 69). Fathers made the final decisions concerning discipline. Mothers monitored children's behavior and warned unruly children, 'just wait until your father gets home.' And as the upholder of behavioral standards, fathers continued their role as moral leaders (Demos, 1982: 432). Unlike the past, however, they were largely absent from their children's daily lives.

Fathers in the middle and later 1800s did perform some roles that indicated to their children their humanity. Middle-class fathers, after they got home from the office at night, not only administered discipline, but also were known to play with their children. When fathers were too tired or too formal for these 'romps' on the parlor floor, they might serve as friendly observers of their children's play. In either case, they were playing the role of occasional companions to their children whether as fellow playmates or friendly audience. And, even though fathers had the final say as to discipline, their daily departures from home necessitated their role as moral support for wives' parenting efforts. Their part-time fathering also modified paternal roles as counselors and models (Demos, 1982). They were just not present to be able to provide advice to children or serve as exemplars in touchy situations.

In fathers' relations with their sons, even if less a continuous daily experience, they were the ones responsible for inculcating in sons the characteristics of hard work, the wise use of money and the ethics of getting ahead in the business world. To do so, sons needed fathers' advice on their education outside the home. Fathers might no longer be able to train sons in a vocation, but as education counselors they could point sons to appropriate occupation mentors. And fathers continued as major role models with respect to their sons' future achievements. In rural areas, sons were still expected to work for their families even if their fathers were storekeepers or lawyers. Fathers made arrangements for the sons' jobs and often supervised them, punishing their sons for failure to follow rules (Rotondo, 1993: 48). Whether in the country or the city, fathers were the parents prepared to show sons how to maneuver in the worlds of politics and finance from which women were barred (Rotondo, 1987: 69).

However, as father/husband and thereby household head, a middle-class man's most important role was that of economic provider for his family. Although this role earned him power and respect within the home, it also made him vulnerable. It was not easy for a man to make a living in the nineteenth century. Opportunities were limited, but successful men were supposed to be self-made. If they failed, and many did during the 1930s Great Depression, it was a reflection on their own efforts and abilities, not the absence of opportunities. They saw themselves as failures, and their families along with outsiders were likely to share this judgment. Thus, the power and respect fathers gained from being their families' providers could easily be placed in jeopardy through job loss (Demos, 1982: 435).

Moreover, the requirements for being family providers presented men with difficult choices. There was usually a conflict between what a father's employment demanded and the attention he should give his wife and children. Was there enough time for him to complete his job responsibilities and also to play his domestic roles? This was a problem with no easy answers. His job and role as provider clearly took priority. But the job and family time conflict raised such issues as just what duties should a father perform and which should he ignore, given the limited time he could spend with his family. Also, the style of interaction and the character of qualities called for on the job could not be transferred to the family setting. It was appropriate for men to be ambitious, clever and aggressive as well as manipulative to make their way in the competitive corporate world. The behaviors these characteristics inspired could not be displayed at home without creating serious difficulties. Men seemed to have to choose between doing well on the job or in the family. For many men, it was easier to choose to concentrate on work and public affairs rather than on paternal and partner roles (Demos, 1982: 436-437).

But men's single-minded devotion to their jobs created controversy. True, it helped them to provide for their families despite difficult job situations. But observers at the end of the nineteenth century were increasingly concerned that the absence of fathers from home resulted in sons becoming feminized. While a century before in the late 1700s patriarchal fathers were ever visible to teach proper behaviors to sons, mothers were now in charge. What did they know, critics charged, about inculcating manly characteristics in little boys? And school teachers, being poorly paid, were usually women. There was a fear that breadwinner fathers were producing weakling sons through a failure to give attention to them. Mothers had the gentle qualities advantageous for child nurture, but they were unable to prepare their sons for the rough and tumble of the business world (Hantover, 1978). Fathers, therefore, started the twentieth century with two fundamental threats to their family position. They could fail at making a living for their families, and they could fail at training their sons to be capable men. The time demands required to get along in their jobs made it difficult if not impossible for fathers to perform their paternal roles with sons.

Another irony stemming from the absence of men from the domestic scene was that they became competitors with their children for their wives' attention. I have already noted that in training their sons in the characteristics needed on the job and counseling them as to the kind and amount of education they needed, fathers created sons as economic competitors. But, also, due to a shortage of time in their families, fathers when home, instead of seeing their offspring as the fulfillment of family existence, could resent the care mothers directed to children. In the skimpy time budget fathers allotted to families, they could feel that children were competitors for their wives' attention. After all, fathers might reason, we are putting food on the table with our hard work and long hours on the job. Don't we merit special treatment and having our wants attended to by our wives before they serve the children? Such paternal expectations and demands contributed to the view of other family members that fathers were somewhat set apart from the domestic circle and were rather demanding intruders in it (Demos, 1982: 442).

But other trends were softening the image of fathers as distant disciplinarians in families. Though their repertoire of fathering roles was considerably diminished from the 1700s, advice givers and some fathers were not willing to accept the largely absent model of fatherhood. Writers of child-care books extolled the virtues of patience and affectionate persuasion that were supposedly a part of women's natural heritage. At the same time, these writers urged fathers more used to the order-giving atmosphere of the job to follow women's examples and instructions concerning childrearing (Demos, 1982: 437). This might well have been a hard piece of advice for a majority of men to follow. It involved turning to women, lower-status individuals, for counsel concerning the world of families, almost by definition one less important than the world of masculine affairs. Matters of domesticity were left to mothers, since fathers had to go outside the home to earn the family's living.

Yet there were some fathers who refused to separate themselves from the daily goings on in families. They were willing to give up their pretentions to patriarchal authority, in order to play paternal roles consistent with the democratic family Tocqueville described early in the nineteenth century. These few middle-class fathers were happy to depart from the distant disciplinarian model of fatherhood and experiment with new roles. They were companions to their children, playing with them in their times together. They also tried to be affection givers to their children, supplementing the love mothers gave as emotional centers of the family (Rotondo, 1987: 71). They were seeking to shift from being family patriarch to family participants. But these fathers remained few in numbers.

By the middle of the twentieth century, during the late 1940s and the 1950s, men were confronting different family and occupational situations. After World War II, many fathers were forced to become more involved in child care. This was the case despite their feeling that it was mothers' work. Because the G.I. Bill subsidized war veterans to obtain advanced educations, men were postponing entering the labor force. Families were also having more children in what resulted in the postwar baby boom. Some of these college students who became fathers had wives who held jobs in order to supplement the government payments. These fathers necessarily were forced to perform child care tasks in their wives' absences while getting the training to become more successful breadwinners (Parke & Stearns, 1993: 149). However, most of these fathers, like their predecessors in the previous century, perceived these child care roles as temporary and as ones to be relinquished as soon as they started their careers.

Despite this firm conviction, men continued to face conflicting pressures concerning fatherhood. On the one hand, post-war prosperity brought demanding but well-paying jobs. As family breadwinners, fathers put in long hours at work with little time left for families. On the other hand, in some postwar families the trend for more paternal involvement in families accelerated. Fathers were adding to their disciplinarian, playmate and affection-giving roles. Some were keeping down their hours on the job in order to perform tasks like feeding and dressing their children. This care of children deepened fathers' emotional ties to children. Even fathers concerned about maintaining their status as household heads became closer to children especially sons through performing the role of coach for children's amateur sports (Rotondo, 1987: 72). These Little League games enabled dads concerned about maintaining their traditional masculine separateness from family matters still to perform some role in childrearing. Such activities provided a sort of 'neutral ground' on which fathers and sons could meet as equals, not competitors or rivals. Fathers as chums of daughters and sons enabled the two generations to do things together as comrades (Demos, 1982: 443).

If fathers in the middle years of this century wanted to be active in childrearing, they received little support from child-care experts. In the 1946 first edition of Dr. Benjamin Spock's book on childrearing, he devoted a scant nine pages to fathers' roles (Parke & Stearns, 1993: 153). Moreover, beginning in the nineteenth century and continuing until today, the 'tender years' doctrine when couples split up led judges usually to assign child custody to mothers. The legal community was thereby adding its considerable influence to the belief that raising children was the concern of mothers, not fathers. This, of course, was a departure from the eighteenth century and earlier when fathers were the unquestioned primary parent and so automatically received custody. The reason for the custody shift to mothers, given as early as 1810 by a Pennsylvania court, was that children of 'tender age' required the kind of assistance which could be 'afforded by none so well as a mother' (cited by Demos, 1982: 439). Fathers had changed over the nineteenth century from being all-knowing and very visible patriarchs to part-time family members. Fathers then and in the first half of the present century were so seldom active players in the family drama that they often lacked the skills and know-how to get along there. Returning home tired from a long day at the office, fathers were likely to be impatient and overly harsh in their dealings with fretful children. Such behaviors further contributed to their reputation as unneeded bit players in family activities (Parke & Stearns, 1993: 151; Demos, 1982: 442). Their fathering roles were limited, and many fathers continued to use their reputations for ineptitude as a good excuse for not taking on tedious and tiring child-care duties.

There were sizeable exceptions to this trend. Not all men wanted to be outside the main events in their children's lives. Several studies in the 1980s documented this concern of some fathers. Researchers, for example, found that 74% of their male respondents would prefer to be on a so-called daddy-track job where they could spend more time with their children than on a 'fast-track' to success requiring long hours away from home (McEnroe, 1991: 52). Another study found that 48% of the fathers deliberately shortened their working hours in order to have more time with their children. There were also 23% of them who gave up promotions for the same reason (Griswold, 1997: 85).

The intellectual, political and economic climate outside the family has also been changing in the last third of this century in ways that encourage active fathering. Let me begin with the intellectual changes. During the first 60 years of this century, Freudian psychology was dominant in child-development thinking. It supported the notion of mothers' biological superiority in child care. According to Freudian doctrine, the feeding situation of infants and young children determined the child's 'social and emotional' development. Mothers were the initial feeding sources for infants which seemingly supported their primacy in child care. But research has failed to demonstrate a link between infants' feeding contexts and their social relationships. Infants establish attachments to fathers as well as to mothers, so that fathers also are 'vital social contributors even in the child's infancy'. Other studies show that fathers can be as skillful as mothers in caring for newborns (Parke & Stearns, 1993: 158-159). Thus, the notion that there is a biological necessity for mothers' childrearing roles, a notion a knowledge of history would have discounted, was discredited.

Politically, the women's movement of the 1960s and 1970s weakened the view that fathers are observers and not participants in family matters. Women were drawing upon the biological evidence to press their case for seeing women and men in terms of cross-cutting similarities and not stereotypical differences. Gender, they argued, is socially constructed (West & Zimmerman, 1987). Women had identities apart from families and men had identities within families. As history and research demonstrated, the existing division of household labor had more to do with custom and male power than with innate desire and natural ability. Thus, feminists added their support to the concept of fathers being child caretakers and homemakers.

Most influential in the changing world of accepted family roles for men was the steady increase in the number of mothers in the paid labor market. A substantial majority of women, even those with infants under one year of age, are now performing the role of breadwinner. Mothers are no longer as financially dependent upon men, and fathers' role as breadwinner is no longer enough to legitimate their parental status in families. At the same time, mothers continued to perform the roles involved in child care with only limited participation from most fathers (Aldous, Mulligan & Bjarnason, 1998). But whether fathers chose to be more active in child care or not, the pressure from harried wives, child development professionals and the minority of active fathers was there for men to play more childrearing roles. These egalitarian voices expressed an ideology that is a central element of the US conscience. It should grow stronger as women's economic status approaches that of men's (Griswold, 1997: 85).

Here are some of the roles fathers are being urged to perform. There is a continuing emphasis on fathers being emotionally closer to their children. This affection-giving role is associated with a departure from the distant disciplinarian role. Mothers are to assume more of this role instead of leaving it, at least in public discourse, to fathers. The roles of playmate and chum have also been modified. There is more concern that fathers encourage cooperative rather than competitive interchanges in their children. Fathers as play partners seem to be especially effective in teaching children how to govern their feelings in dealing with their friends (Parke & Stearn, 1993). Thus, fathers can play the role of interpersonal counselor.

Fathers after leaving their children to mothers to raise a century and a half ago are also now reentering children's lives in other ways than through play.

There is a blurring of gender distinctions. Fathers are urged to be involved in the actual physical care of children along with serving as their comforters. This means that men have to undertake new ways of feeling and how they display their emotion, probably considerably different from the ways *their* fathers felt and behaved. This intergenerational division is accompanied by a shift in intragenerational relations. In becoming more a part of their children's lives, fathers have had to 'surrender substantial authority to their wives' (Rotondo, 1987: 75). No longer the family patriarch or when that position was lost not even the family disciplinarian, men now have greater freedom to create closer relations with their children and in the process to expand their role repetoires as fathers. But being active fathers goes against the definition of traditional masculinity. Giving up authority to wives, taking on dirty, demanding and unpleasant chores of child care and losing leisure time are all aspects of current prescriptions of fatherhood that make it hard for most men to conform. Job demands also continue to limit fathers' family time as well as providing a convenient excuse for fathers to maintain a distance from the younger generation at home.

Thus, in this brief discussion of the history of middle-class fathering we have seen a shift from a period when fathers were all in the family to one where fathers were largely invisible powers. Presently, we appear to be in a time of flux. There are strong forces often backed by organized religion urging a return to fathers as family patriarchs who do not participate in the daily tasks of child care or homemaking (Blankenhorn, 1995; Popenoe, 1996). And middle-class men generally are in occupations they enjoy, occupations with never-ending time demands. Yet the intellectual, political and economic changes that created the contested issue of fathers' roles have not stopped. The major difference today from previous years in the century is that women presently are increasingly joining men in such occupations. Active fathers are still in the substantial minority, but they set an example for their children and for other men that is impossible to overlook or to ignore. The increasing calls for fathers to be partners in childrearing will not go away, and loving fathers will want to heed them.

REFERENCES

Aldous, J. & N. Dahl (1974). *International bibliography of research in marriage and the family, Volume II, 1965-1972.* Minneapolis, MN: University of Minnesota Press.
Aldous, J. & R. Hill (1967). *International bibliography of research in marriage and the family, 1900-1964.* Minneapolis, MN: University of Minnesota Press.

Aldous, J., G.M. Mulligan & T. Bjarnason (1998). Fathering over time: What makes the difference? *Journal of Marriage and the Family, 60*(4), 809-820.

Blankenhorn, D. (1995) *Fatherless America: Confronting our most urgent social problem.* New York: Basic Books.

Cremin, L.A. (1970). *American education: The colonial experience, 1607-1783.* New York: Harper & Row.

Demos, J. (1982). The changing faces of fatherhood: A new exploration in American family history. In: S.H. Cath, A.R. Gurwitt & J. M.Ross (Eds.). *Father and child: Developmental and clinical perspectives.* Boston: Little, Brown & Company, p. 425-445.

Fox-Genovese, E. (1977). Property and patriarchy in classical bourgeois political theory. *Radical History Review, 4* (Spring/Summer), 36-59.

Gillis, J.R. (1996). *A world of their own making: Myth, ritual and the quest for family values.* New York: Basic Books.

Griswold, R.L. (1997). Generative fathering: A historical perspective. In: A.J. Hawkins & D.C. Dollahite (Eds.). *Generative fathering: Beyond deficit perspectives.* Thousand Oaks, CA: Sage, p. 71-85.

Hantover, J.P. (1978). The boy scouts and the validation of masculinity. *Journal of Social Issues, 34*(1), 184-195.

Ingoldsby, B.B. (1995). Marital structure. In: B.B. Ingoldsby & S. Smith (Eds.). *Families in multicultural perspective.* New York: Guilford Press, p. 117-137.

Levinson, D.J., C.N. Darrow, E.B. Klein, M.H. Levinson & B. McKee (1978). *The seasons of a man's life.* New York: Alfred A. Knopf.

McEnroe, J. (1991). Split-shift parenting. *American Demographics, 13*(2), 50-52.

Mintz, S. & S. Kellogg (1988). *Domestic revolutions: A social history of American family life.* New York: Free Press.

Morgan, E.S. (1966). *The puritan family: Religion and domestic relations in seventeenth century New England.* New York: Harper & Row.

Muller, V. (1977). The formation of the state and the oppression of women: Some theoretical considerations and a case study in England and Wales. *Review of Radical Political Economics, 9* (Fall), 7-21.

Parke, R.D. & P.N. Stearns (1993). Fathers and child rearing. In: G.H. Elder, Jr., J. Modell & R.D. Parke (Eds.). *Children in time and place: Developmental and historical insights.* New York: Cambridge University Press, p. 147-170.

Pickard, M.J. (1998). Fatherhood in contemporary society. *Family Relations, 47*(2), 205-208.

Popenoe, D. (1996). *Life without father: Compelling new evidence that fatherhood and marriage are indispensable for the good of children and society.* New York: Free Press.

Rotondo, E.A. (1987). Patriarchs and participants: A historical perspective on fatherhood in the United States. In: M. Kaufman (Ed.). *Beyond patriarchy: Essays by men on pleasure, power, and change.* Toronto: Oxford University Press, p. 64-80.

Rotondo, E.A. (1993). *American manhood: Transformations in masculinity from the revolution to the modern era.* New York: Basic Books.

Smelser, N.J. & E.H. Erikson (Eds.) (1980). *Themes of work and love in adulthood.* Cambridge, MA: Harvard University Press.

Stone, L. (1975). The rise of the nuclear family in early modern England. In: C.E. Rosenberg (Ed.). *The family in history*. Philadelphia: University of Pennsylvania Press, p. 13-57.

West, C. & D. Zimmerman (1987). Doing gender. *Gender & Society, 1*, 125-151.

# Family and democracy

JACQUES COMMAILLE
CEVIPOF, FRANCE

The vocation of the sociology of the family has traditionally been to study family behavior and its transformations (even if the greatest sociologists, starting with Emile Durkheim, never dissociated the study of the family from that of the organization of society). Still we find that social science research applied to the family increasingly involves a political component, including those studies, precisely, which belong to sociology of the family.

This increasingly present political component in analyses of the family is what we intend to examine in the present essay.[1] Of course taking into account the political dimension of the family allows us to understand how the political sphere contributes to structuring the family (if only through public policies known as 'family policies'), but the angle we will mainly adopt here, in a reversal of perspective we are performing, will be to remember that 'the family also structures the political sphere'. The family reveals essential aspects of the political sphere and the changes that occur within it, as well as certain issues it is confronted with. If democracy is indeed in a crisis, as many political analysts maintain, the hypothesis we make is that this crisis can also be detected in the forms in which the individuals that make up society organize themselves and function within it, and the ways in which states and political forces contribute to the proper functioning of this private life, and more broadly, to individual welfare.

## THE FAMILY AS THE FOUNDATION OF POLITICAL AUTHORITY

Analyses devoted to the history of the family, family behavior and changes occurring in it suggest a separation from politics, in other words there is a gradual move away from the vision according to which the family is indissociable from the political realm and vice versa. It is this conception of the family that political or philosophical rhetoric sometimes is nostalgic for, particularly when it calls for the reinstatement of the status of father, of 'the Father', since, precisely, the traditional stratified political order was consubstantial with a patriarchal model of the family. It should not be forgotten that this model was particularly widespread in the 'golden age of the paternal monarchy' that was expressed in the 18th century with the 'natural' filiation between the male head of the family, the soverign and God (Delumeau & Roche, 1990).

The nostalgia that transpires in certain political speeches is not a nostalgia for the traditional family in itself, but for a political society built on the idea of the family. The preoccupation of the 19th century 'reactionaries' was, moreover, no different. Their aim was to reestablish an integrated conception of the political and the family sphere that had been devalued by the French Revolution and the development of economic liberalism. The 'private' sphere had become autonomous with respect to the 'public' and was relegated strictly to the realm of interpersonal relations. By advocating a return to the patriarchal family, the goal was to make the family once again 'the only material and primary institution (...) ensuring the ascendency and the primacy of the social sphere over the individual' (Dupaquier & Fauve-Chamoux, 1992). Louis de Bonald, crusader of the French Restoration, celebrated family ties and property ownership and outlined a theocratic, Christian conception of economic and political life. In his view, 'the nation appears as a big, hierarchically organized family in which the king is father; the head of state, the father of the family and all other intermediary authorities, each in his rank, representing the image of the heavenly Father; paternal authority emanates from the supreme divine paternity' (Deniel, 1965).

In this perspective, family members – father, mother, child – belong to domestic society only as actors in a political society that is 'naturally' unequal and stratified. This is why, for Louis de Bonald, it is preferable to replace 'the physical and specific denominations of father, mother and child' with 'the moral and general expressions of power, minister, and subject' (de Bonald, 1830).

The structural homology between the family order and the political order was all the more emphasized since this reasoning was part of a long tradition in which the family was held up to be an expression of the basic laws of the universe after which political society itself should model itself. The power of the father thus was part of the 'natural authorities', to use Frédéric Le Play's (1879) expression, resurrecting in the 19th century some of the ideas Bossuet had already put forth in the 18th century when he asserted that 'the first idea of command and human authority came to men from paternal authority' (Bossuet, 1864; Brechon, 1976).

The family thus constitutes the genesis of political authority. The stratification that 'naturally' organizes it places political power itself in its natural dimension and justifies it as a 'natural' fact. The reference associating the family with the idea of nature poses the very question of the justification of power and political authority. This question takes root and feeds on a lack of differentiation between the family and the political sphere, and their indissociability, which is cultivated so that individuals themselves will interiorize this lack of differentiation.

Nothing better illustrates the confusion maintained between the two registers than the question of citizenship. The family is a productive element of the political sphere to the extent that what happens within it is indissociable from what happens in the political realm. Private behavior is of the same 'essence' as political behavior. As it was stipulated in article 4 of the preamble to the Constitution of Year III (under the French Revolution) stating the rights and duties of men and citizens: 'No one is a good citizen if he is not a good son, a good father, a good friend, a good husband.' A direct causality is established on the principle of reciprocal functions, so to speak, that is contained 'in the very term of citizen, if one goes back to the etymology of the word. It in fact refers to both those who 'share political rights' and who participate in the 'family circle" (Benvenist, 1969).

The use of metaphors is common practice when constructing any representation of the political sphere that manifests itself in 'imagery and symbolism' such as those images meant to portray the Republic in France.[2] Speeches aiming to celebrate politics or define its forms or principles have constantly used and abused the family metaphore throughout history. For Jean-Jacques Rousseau in the *Social Contract*, 'The family is (...) the first model of political societies, the oldest and the most natural: the head of state bears the image of the father, the people the image of children.' In the 16th century, Jean Bodin maintained that 'proper government of the home [is] the true model for the government of the Republic.' In a brilliant analysis, we can see how the use of the family metaphor in the political field endeavors to establish this lack of differentiation between the family order and the political order that we have pointed out, their interchangeability so to speak (Borgetto, 1983). This is how one arrives at 'the analogy of the king and the father, the people and children, the kingdom and the family' (Borgetto, 1983). To evoke the idea of homeland, reference is made to the 'loving mother' or even the 'big brotherly family' (Borgetto, 1983).

Using the family to symbolize the political sphere – do we not speak of 'political family'? – thus has multiple reasons. There is no better way to celebrate patriotic duty as attests the 'nation's schoolmaster', Lavisse, in his civics manual first published in 1884: 'By defending France, we are being good sons. We fulfill our duty unto our fathers' (Cicchelli-Pugeault & Cicchelli, 1998: 28).

Lastly, the reference to the family suggests a vision of the political sphere and its functioning inspired by the myth of the happy family. In response to the antagonistic approach according to which conflict is the driving force for the functioning of society, the family reference is partly an attempt to impose a consensualist approach according to which conflict is a pathology that must be overcome, an accident. In this way, the family metaphor serves a vision of the political sphere that is in search of a lost paradise, one that is supposedly represented by the 'community', in other words a society in which the virtues (closeness of its members, their 'familiarity', the solidarity they show towards one another, the ability to settle their conflicts or transgressions internally, etc.) are indeed those… of the family. The family metaphor, 'by postulating […] unity and brotherhood in the imagination […] not only has the advantage of unifying political, administrative and social structures; its continued use can also be explained by its aptitude if not to obscure, at least to present as secondary, the conflicts that run through society' (Borgetto, 1983). And, for instance, the words Edouard Balladur pronounced when he was French Prime Minister not so long ago – 'we are, all of us, sons and daughters of the same fatherland. What brings us together is infinitely more important than what divides us. And our differences are infinitely less important than our resemblances' (Tournier, 1997) – echo those of the republican patriot Crémieux who in 1848 declaired: 'All class distinctions are erased before equality. All antagonisms settle and disappear in this holy brotherhood which makes the children of the same fatherland the children of one family and makes all peoples allies' (Borgetto, 1983).

Making family relationships and political relationships homologous produces 'ideological profits' (the idea of consensus and social integration) by associating social relations with 'kin relationships (that sort of warm, limitless fraternity that can be called 'communitarian') rather than with economic relations in capitalist societies' based on calculations and the quest for material interests, and with political relations based on the quest for power through power struggles (Lenoir, 1985: 47).

The family imagery as a space of love for one's fellow man, illimited generosity, solidarity, affective and material reciprocity, a meeting of souls, in other words as a space that has a potential for universality and sublimation of differences, thus serves to construct an image of politics that is always present, at least in the form of nostalgia: that of a bygone past, or a utopia, a future to attain. The family thus functioning as a founding myth of politics goes much further than the one that refers to forms of organization of private life within which functions useful for society take place and which, in this respect, the family serves to regulate. The ambivalences of the political sphere with regard to the family, its hesitations and its contradictions, beyond party cleavages, will be better understood if we keep in mind the issue that the family is likely to constitute in structuring the political sphere and the central place it occupies, at least in its origin or how its origin is represent. And the family remains an issue whether it is a matter of founding a political authority in which the 'Father's reason' would legitimate the existance of a 'leader', or establishing a positive representation of any political order, including the most democratic one.

Of all we have just reviewed with regard to relationships between the family and politics, we could say that the family order is indissociable from a certain order in the world, and this holds true for all of its features: political, of course, since the essence of politics is family-like; economic, (as attests question of property transmission which formally comes under the 'civil order'. Alexis de Tocqueville (1993: 96-99) pointed this out when opining that inheritance laws 'should be placed at the head of all political institutions' and that they were indeed 'part of the public order'; social, since, according to Frédéric Le Play (1878), the social order obviously flows from 'the proper organization of the family'. This ideal-type of relationships between the family and politics reveals a veritable fusion of the private and the public sphere.

## THE FAMILY AS A POLITICAL OBJECT

The advent of the modern state marks the beginning of a dissociation between the private and the public sphere that manifests itself by the latter's concern for no longer simply seeking the source of its legitimacy in the family but by taking an interest in the family's contribution to maintaining the social order. In this context, as Michel Foucault (1986) noted, the family 'disappears as a model of government'; the model instead becomes 'the preferred instrument for governing populations.'

The family sphere turns into a locus of incompetence or, at least, a place of real or potential weaknesses that the State should remedy. In the name of hygienism, an idea of public hygiene that appeared at the end of the 18th century, a doctor was qualified to 'supervise the body' which is the same as 'supervising' souls. In the name of an 'intimate link between the physical and the moral', medical competency was broadened: 'Doctors are assigned the task of determining the rules by which the physical and mental health of individual, biological bodies will be maintained, just like the social body treated in the same fashion. It is with science's assent that they thus become responsible for defining the rules of private and public life' (Cicchelli-Pugeault & Cicchelli, 1998: 8) Thus medicine became a science of the social sphere, an instrument to rationalize family life.

The institutionalization of education and its expansion under the aegis of the State are part of the same logic. Families no longer have a monopoly over education. The values they handed down, the socialization function they fulfilled can only contribute to the common good in a world where the private sphere was indissociable from the public. The autonomization of the private sphere under the influence of individualism and the realization of its deficiencies justify the State's taking over for families to insure the inculcation of general values that supposedly ciment national unity. In a traditional conception, 'the matching of pedagogical aims and national and republican principles also helps to underline the necessity of maintaining both stratified values and the feeling of respect owed by young generations for their elders. By educating the families' children, public school helps nourish vertical social ties. The need men have to rely on a symbolic order that structures their relations is thus met' (Cicchelli-Pugeault & Cicchelli, 1998: 28).

In the 19th century, the development of individualism and the socioeconomic transformations provoked by the industrial revolution convinced social thinkers and, later, sociologists, of the need for a means of organizing society that no longer made the family the natural instrument for preserving social order but an authority whose deficiencies could threaten the pursuit of this vital aim. The idea of community remained in the back of people's minds, as an absolute reference to an enchanted world: in a world where there is no differentiation between the family, the social and the political sphere, the question of social ties need not even be posed.

The issue with which industrial society was confronted in fact flowed from a decoupling of social and family relationships which required the public authorities to look into the latter. The family was likely to be the weak link in this new society, basically a market society that challenged the traditional structures and highlighted or emphasizing inequalities among individuals. The 'major transformation' that Karl Polyani (1983: 182) analyzes is thus characterized by a 'dual tendency': one being the 'principle of economic liberalism', the other being 'the principle of social protection'.

The advent of the State and its development accompany, foster and compensate for the effects of the autonomization for the private sphere with regard to the public sphere and its errors. Political authority is no longer an extension of family authority as it once was with the *lettres de cachet* that allowed a father to have his offspring put in prison if he deemed it necessary (Farge & Foucault, 1982).

In the traditional conception, the one that continues to want to make the family an essential cog in the wheel of society and its political structure, the problems encountered in certain families, or the 'disorders' that appear, justify State intervention. The lack of education or care for children, or inadequate living conditions of the mother or the family in general are not so much a problem because of the *inequalities* they indicate than because of the social disorders they are likely to portend. If a child's or a mother's fate preoccupies the public authorities, it is not because they are individuals exposed to specific inequalities. It is because they are part of an institution – the family – and that in this manner, just like poor families, they must elicit mobilization of the State, whose mission is to insure their protection, in the name of a social order that requires families precisely to fulfill their functions in the service of society.

## THE FAMILY AS AN ELEMENT OF DEMOCRACY

The history of the family exhibits another conception of the relationships between family and politics, this time with a strong link to the democratic ideal. In his time, Alexis de Tocqueville (1993: 266 ff.) made the distinction between democratic society and aristocratic society by referring to the ways families are organized. In aristocratic society, the father is the spokesman, the political relay: 'Among aristocratic people, society only actually acknowledges the father. It only holds the reins by the father's hands; it governs him and he governs them,' this in the name of a 'political right to command' that he is given. In a democratic society, 'there is no need for such an intermediary' and the conditions for a relative 'equality between the father and his children gradually sets in.'

In the context of this side-by-side examination of the family and democracy, the question is whether democracy is a sort of replica in the political order of an equality of its members that are in the familly, this 'miniature Republic' or 'miniature democracy reflecting the big one: political democracy'.

That is a philosophical tradition that has not disappeared and is even fairly topical. For some, in fact, the transformations in private life that have occurred in recent decades do not mean the end of the family institution but the reconfiguration of this institution in a more democratic and horizontal fashion. In the 'new' family, identities are constructed in a more egalitarian relationship and thus depart from the bonds of privileged and stratified statuses and roles. We can speak, in that case, to echo Anthony Giddens (1992), of a process of democratization of the private sphere. Anthony Giddens underlines the connections between transformations in the private sphere and the public sphere, the inter-action between the construction of political democracy and the democratization of the private sphere. In reference to David Held (1986), the principles of democracy can be compared to those that are established in the private sphere. These principles are based on the idea of autonomy, free and equal relationships, the capacity of individuals to be self-reflective and self-determined, in a position to weigh, judge, choose and follow different possible courses of action. These principles are precisely those that have contributed, in the public sphere, to the renewal of political rights and obligations, those no longer founded on tradition, status or prerogatives derived from property ownership.

Everything that constitutes the elements of a new relational economy in the private sphere, including what Charles Taylor (1992) calls 'the ideal of authenticity', thus echoes what should define an individual's individuals and his relations in the political world. Far from the pessimist views that hold that transformations in the private sphere are part of an inevitable rise of individualism in the sense of egoism, the conception that is put forth here is one of social relations put into practice on egalitarian bases by autonomous, self-determined individuals, both in their private lives as well as in the political sphere that they help structure as active citizens and actors.

### The problem of unequal financial resources

'Detraditionalization', as Ulrich Beck (1992) calls it, is potentially a process of positive social transformation involving both the private and public spheres. The problem in that case would be not so much what Alexis de Tocqueville (1993: 266 ff.) feared at the time: passive citizenship, but, precisely, the possibility of achieving this full and total citizenship likely to emerge as much in the private sphere as in the political arena. From this standpoint today's situation exposes a contradiction. On one hand, the evolution of private lifestyles can be seen as an emancipation, a liberation of the individual from the constraints that the traditional family, the family environment and the forms of kinship imposed on him, with what this implies in terms of confinement into prescribed roles, particularly by gender. We are observing the development of a family based on the fulfillment of the individual and his identity within the chosen family network in which the 'principle of autonomy' reigns. This development would indeed mark the consecration of a 'positive individualism' and a 'democratization of personal life' (Giddens, 1992).

But such an evolution is thwarted by unequal access to this 'detraditionalized' form of family due to unequal resources that allow individuals to be part of this type of family or expose them differently to the risks that it implies, this depending on social class, age bracket or gender.

The universalist vision of the family or the enchanted vision suggested by the democratization of private life should not let us forget that the family remains an institution that helps produce social inequalities or perpetuates them on the basis of the 'capital' it has or doesn't have at its disposal. The family continues to participate effectively in the reproduction of a stratified and unegalitarian social order, in the 'reproduction of structural factors of the global social context' (Schultheis, 1977) and it does so in several ways: in the socialization process it performs, the strategies it develops to help guarantee the children's scholastic 'career', the solidarities it mobilizes among kin, the forms of which will vary depending precisely on the wealth it possesses (Attias-Donful, 1995).

The analysis of the social functions fulfilled by the family are there to remind us that the democratization of private life in no way implies an autonomization of the family with regard to the social sphere and the inequalities that go with it. The way a family assumes its social functions depends on the position it occupies in the social sphere as well as the conditions in which it assumes them. The effects of exercising these social functions themselves result from the social position the family occupies. The democratization of private life is likely to correspond actually to a gain in freedom for individuals, to greater emancipation... but it is thwarted by the inequalities that are produced or reproduced, maintained or sometimes reinforced.

The risk of reinforcement is moreover all the greater since European countries are confronted with a resurgence of the social question. For example, there has been a rise in the rate of relative poverty in the European Union, in other words an increase in income inequalities related, of course, to the spreading of unemployment. The occurrence of unemployment in a family is not only synonymous with financial difficulties but of disorganization in the exercise of family and social roles, their transmittal and consequently their perpetuation. Unemployment can also weaken the very substance of the family, perturb it severely in its most basic practices: forming a couple, dissolving it, having children. The increase in social risks is also likely to interact with family risks in such a way, for instance, that the effects of disunion can take a very heavy toll on certain social categories or on certain women (the problems encountered by single-parent families illustrate, for example, the greater vulnerability of women with regard to the democratization of private life given the specific inequalities that they face) (Martin, 1997).

The social situation of some women after the break-up of a couple particularly well illustrates the importance of this question of unequal resources. In fact, women risk being doubly exposed to these inequalties; as productive members of society, of course, like any individual on the job market, but also because their greater investment than men in the family to which they are attached exposes them to specific forms of inequality on the job market and in their attempts to reconcile family life and commitment to salaried employment (Bihr & Pfefferkorn, 1996). This inequality of resources that is specific to women, likely to thwart the democratization of the family in a structural manner, has been reinforced by the employment crisis that insures more than ever the primacy of the law of the Market over individual's aspirations, especially women's.

So, although we are prepared to adhere to the idea of a positive interaction between democratization of private life and political democracy, if the inequality of financial resources are not taken into account, of which we have just briefly outlined the main manifestations, they could well turn the representation of a positive individualism, of which the private sphere would be one of the places of expression, into a 'negative individualism', represented by isolated, disunited, excluded individuals who are supposed to bear the responsibility for their misfortune or unhappiness. This would make the unequal resources that certain people are victim of, in terms of social class, age bracket or gender, lose their dimension of collective or political problem. In that case, there could be a great temptation to perceive the modernization of private life as a risk as well as a threat for the entire society.

Subscribing to the relation between democratization of private life and political democracy and thus breaking from a conception in which the family can only be at the basis of traditional political authority definitely assumes for us that certain problems usually treated separately must be treated simultaneously and jointly: the question of the family (as individuals's forms of organization of their private lives), that of gender (the types of social relationships between men and women), and that of the social sphere (in the sense of public compensations set up or not to alleviate the differences in resources among individuals). Such an option in fact imposes itself when considering a political ideal such as democracy by relating it to the realm of private life implies the principle of equality: between the sexes (assuming that the gender question is treated), among social categories (assuming that the question of social welfare is treated), all this together with the question of the family, which, itself, does not exhaust the problem of equality or even, on the contrary sometimes serves as a pretext to avoid treating it.[3]

NOTES

1   A recently published work, in conjunction with Claude Martin: *Les enjeux politiques de la famille*. Paris: Bayard Editions, coll. Société, 1998, inspires the study of the family's political dimension to which this article is devoted.

2   Our point here is based on an analysis already developed in J. Commaille 'Les sciences du politique' in F. de Singly (Ed.) (1991). *La famille, l'état des savoirs*. Paris: La Découverte.

3   It is on the basis of this conception of the relationships between private life and the political order that the types of public intervention should be reexamined depending on the country (i.e. the typologies of welfare states) and the ways political forces grapple with the question of family. On these points one can refer to J. Commaille & Martin, Cl., *op. cit.*.

REFERENCES

Attias-Donful, Cl. (Ed.) (1995). *Les solidarités entre générations*. Paris: Nathan, coll. Essais & Recherches.

Beck, U. (1992). *Risk society. Towards a new modernity*. London: Sage.

Benvenist, E. (1969). *Le vocabulaire des institutions indo-européennes*. Paris: Ed. de Minuit, Vol. 1, p. 335-337, quoted by R. Lenoir (1991). Politique familiale et construction sociale de la famille. *Revue Française de Science Politique*, 41(6), 791.

Bihr, A. & R. Pfefferkorn (1996). *Hommes/femmes, l'introuvable égalité. Ecole-travail-couple-espace public*. Paris: Editions de l'Atelier.

Borgetto, M. (1983). Metaphore de la famille et idéologies. In: Coll., *Le droit non civil de la famille*. Paris: PUF.

Bossuet, F. (1864). Politique tirée des propres paroles de l'Ecriture sainte. In: J.-B. Pélagard. *Œuvres complètes*. Vol. XIII, 1st ed. 1709, quoted by V. Tournier (1997). *Le politique en héritage? Socialisation, famille et politique: bilan critique et analyse empirique*. Grenoble: IEP. Doctoral thesis in political science [this dissertation provides a very clever analysis of the ideas that justify this structural homology between the family and politics].

Brechon, P. (1976). *La famille, idées traditionnelles, idées nouvelles*. Paris: Le Centurion.

Cicchelli-Pugeault, C. & V. Cicchelli (1998). *Les théories sociologiques de la famille*. Paris: La Découverte.

de Bonald, L. (1995). *Démonstration philosophique du principe constitutif de la société*. Paris: Vrin, 1st ed. 1830; quoted by Boltanski, L. & L. Thévenot (1991). *La justification. Les économies de la grandeur*. Paris: Gallimard, p. 125.

Delumeau, J. & D. Roche (1990). *Histoire des pères et de la paternité*. Paris: Larousse.

Deniel, R. (1965). *Une image de la famille et de la société sous la Restauration*. Paris: Les Editions ouvrières.

de Tocqueville, A. (1993). *De la démocratie en Amérique*, I. Paris: Gallimard, Folio Histoire, vol. 2.

Dupaquier, J. & A. Fauve-Chamoux (1992). La famille. In: J.-F. Sirinelli (dir.). *Histoire des droites en France*, 3, *Sensibilités*. Paris: Gallimard.

Farge, A. & M. Foucault (1982). *Le désordre des familles. Lettres de cachet des Archives de la Bastille*. Paris: Gallimard-Julliard.

Foucault, M. (1986). La gouvernementalité, Leçon au Collège de France (February 1978), *Actes*, 54.

Giddens, A. (1992). *The transformation of intimacy. Sexuality, love and eroticism in modern societies*. Cambridge: Polity Press.

Held, D. (1986). *Models of democracy*. Cambridge: Polity Press.

Lenoir, R. (1985). Transformations du familialisme et reconversions morales. *Actes de la Recherche en Sciences Sociales*, 59, 47.

Le Play, F. (1878). *La Réforme sociale en France*. Paris: Mame.

Le Play, F. (1879). *La méthode sociale*. Paris: Méridiens Klincksieck, 1st ed. 1879.

Martin, Cl. (1997). *L'après-divorce. Lien familial et vulnérabilité*. Rennes: Presses Universitaires de Rennes.

Polyani, K. (1983). *La grande transformation*. Paris: Gallimard.

Schultheis, F. (1977). La contribution de la famille à la reproduction sociale: une affaire d'Etat. In: J. Commaille & F. de Singly (Eds.). *The European family*. Dordrecht: Kluwer Academic Publisher.

Taylor, C. (1992). *Grandeur et misère de la modernité*. Montreal: Bellarmin.

# Intergenerational relationships and solidarity within the family*

JENNY DE JONG GIERVELD
NEDERLANDS INTERDISCIPLINAIR DEMOGRAFISCH INSTITUUT,
THE NETHERLANDS

## INTRODUCTION

As economic welfare increases in more and more countries in the western indus-trialised world, there is increasingly less need for people to share their homes and be part of the same household. Ongoing improvements in social security provision are also enabling increasing numbers of older and younger people to embark on independent living arrangements and lifestyles. These socio-cultural changes which are typical features of the processes of secularisation and individualisation cause people to move away from the more rigid and traditional patterns of social behaviour to the sorts of norms and values typical of small groups. The importance of social institutions and the social conventions associated with being part of a community become less and less pronounced.

These changes affect demographic behaviour. The result is a trend away from the multi-generational households which still dominate the picture in certain regions of Southern Europe, towards living alone, cohabitation, informal parenthood and the complex step-family structures characteristic of Northern and Western Europe. The average number of household members has fallen sharply over the past century, and the lifestyles of those who continue to share the same household have become increasingly individualistic, with adult members having full- or part-time jobs outside the home or working flexible hours which clash with those of other members of the household, pursuing different

*   This paper is partly based on data collected in the context of the research pro-gramme 'Living arrangements and social networks of older adults', which is being conducted at the Departments of Sociology and Social Science Methodology, Faculty of Social Cultural Sciences of the Vrije Universiteit in Amsterdam, and at the Netherlands Interdisciplinary Demographic Institute in The Hague. The research is supported by a programme grant from the Netherlands Programme for Research on Ageing (NESTOR), funded by the Ministry of Education and Science and the Ministry of Welfare, Health and Cultural Affairs.

leisure activities and participating in different networks of social relationships dictated by personal preference.

The key research question in this article is what effect these trends will have on intergenerational relationships and solidarity within the family. Will personal care be available when it is needed?

Intergenerational relationships differ according to the phase of life of the parties involved. The main preoccupation of a young family is the care parents provide for young children. A key preoccupation in older age categories is 'the care arrangements younger generations make with older persons who need help with day-to-day activities'.1 This is the issue that will be addressed in this chapter.

Before addressing the research question I will begin by summarising a number of changing characteristics of older persons and addressing some common misconceptions about older persons and about ageing.

I will then deal with the issue of (numerical) availability, i.e. how many of the younger generation are available to care for the older generation. This is followed by a section on the willingness of the younger generation to support the older generation. In this section special attention is given to a recent analysis of survey data about the mutual support provided by older persons and their children in which the quality of the lifelong relationship between parent and child will be seen to be of primary importance.

## CHANGING CHARACTERISTICS OF OLDER PERSONS

In the first half of this century older cohorts of men and women and their life courses could fruitfully be described by referring to the 'standard biography' (Liefbroer & de Jong Gierveld, 1993). This standard biography consisted of: leaving the parental home to marry, followed shortly afterwards by the birth of the first child. When women married, they left the labour market in order to raise their children and take care of the household. Parents stayed together until death. The bereaved older person (usually the woman) would continue life as a widow or widower living with their children or in a one-person household. Nowadays, the co-residence of older and younger generations is virtually unheard-of in the western and northern countries of Europe (the Netherlands: 2%, Denmark: 4%), in contrast to the patterns of co-residence still found in Greece (39%), followed by Italy (34%) and Spain (30%) (Commission of the European Communities, 1993).

Nowadays, marital status is no longer the most reliable indicator of the household or partner status of men and women aged 55 and over in Western and Northern European countries, as will be illustrated by data from the

NESTOR-LSN survey. In the NESTOR-LSN survey on 'Living arrangements and social networks of older persons', 4,494 respondents, aged 55 to 89, were interviewed in 1992. They constituted a random sample of men and women living in the western, northern and southern regions of the Netherlands (Broese van Groenou, van Tilburg, de Leeuw & Liefbroer, 1995). These data revealed that of the ever-married, the largest category were those who were in their first marriage and sharing a household with their partner; the percentage for the ever-divorced (10%) was not negligible, as was the proportion of those cohabiting and those engaging in a so-called LAT (living apart together) relationship (see Figure 1). The percentage of ever-divorced (Dykstra, 1998) and cohabiting (de Jong Gierveld, 1995) men *and* women was higher amongst the younger cohorts. Approximately 48% of the ever-divorced men, and 30% of the ever-divorced women, went on to remarry. At the time the interview was conducted, approximately 12% of the ever-divorced men were cohabiting outside of marriage, and 16% were engaged in a LAT-relationship, i.e. had a partner outside the household. Approximately 7% of the ever-divorced women were cohabiting and 4% were engaged in a LAT-relationship (Dykstra, 1998).

The options open to older persons are therefore becoming increasingly characterised by a 'choice-led biography' which replaces the standard biography of the past.

## Changes in the need for care

It is a common fallacy to equate old age with frailty and infirmity. Nowadays, most older persons, particularly those under 75 years of age, are in fairly good health. The vast majority of the elderly population live independently and are capable of looking after themselves. With advancing age, and particularly as people reach their mid-seventies and early eighties, the likelihood of developing diseases and functional incapacities increases. A number of 'modern' diseases is on the rise, particularly chronic, degenerative diseases and handicaps (e.g. heart diseases, cancer, cerebrovascular disease). The prevalence of physical handicaps increases with age: about 25% of men and women aged between 65 and 74 report an inability to perform at least one of 14 physical or functional daily activities, whereas amongst those aged 85 and over, 80% are unable to perform one of these activities. Multiple morbidity is another characteristic of old age. Moreover, the elderly are not a homogeneous group. There is little point discussing the physical capabilities of 'the elderly in general': we should focus instead on differences in their capabilities. Here we see the usefulness of the concept of 'differential ageing', which takes into account not only the vast differ-

Figure 1. Partner status and partner history according to marital status of men and women born between 1903 and 1937

| Marital status | Partner in the household | Partner outside the household | No partner |
|---|---|---|---|
| In 1st marriage 55.6% (N = 2272) | 54.1% (N = 2207) | 1.5% (N = 65) | |
| In 2nd (3d) marriage after widowhood 2.2% (N = 90) | 2.2% (N = 90) | | |
| In 2nd (3d) marriage after divorce 2.1% (N = 87) | 2.1% (N = 87) | | |
| Not married after widowhood 28.3% (N = 1190) | 1.1% (N = 43) | 1.3% (N = 52) | 26.9% (N = 1095) |
| Not married after divorce 5.2% (N = 212) | 0.8% (N = 31) | 0.7% (N = 28) | 3.7% (N = 153) |
| Never married 5.4% (N = 230) | 0.2% (N = 10) | 0.2% (N = 7) | 5.2% (N = 213) |

(Ever-)married 94.6%

Never married 5.4%

ences in the physical and functional capacities of the elderly but also the opportunities and restrictions they may be confronted with.

Elderly persons, including the very old, are showing an increasing inclination towards maintaining and continuing their 'personal life-strategies',
including the deeply-felt wish to remain independent for as long as possible.
They want to attend to their own daily needs and be responsible for their own
decisions and consequently refuse to become part of the households of their
children (and/or other relatives) or move into institutions for the elderly. Even
after the loss of a partner, the younger old as well as the older old and the very
old prefer to remain independent and would rather live in a one-person household than live elsewhere, given that their health and their financial situation
make their independence a realistic option.

As far as the financial situation of older persons is concerned, the percentage
of older persons active in the labour market after the age of 65 is minimal in
most European countries and continues to decline (Kinsella & Gist, 1995). It is
well documented that labour income decreases with age and that financial transfers replace this source of income. As a result, the average disposable income of
the elderly is lower than that of younger age groups. But various factors have to
be taken into account when considering the financial situation of older persons
and here again, we see the relevance of 'differential ageing'.

Generally speaking, there is a large discrepancy between the incomes of older
persons in the different European countries. Countries with the highest GDP per
capita also spend the greatest proportion of GDP on social security in the form
of old-age benefits, with Portugal, Ireland, Spain and Greece at one end, and
Denmark at the other end, of the spectrum (Kinsella & Gist, 1995). In most of
the countries which have state-funded old-age pension schemes, there is also a
facility for additional earnings-related pensions schemes to supplement the basic
state pension: so-called private, occupational or supplementary pension
schemes.2 Approximately a third of the labour force in OECD countries is covered by occupational pension plans. The number of contributors to private pension schemes is on the increase in most European countries, and in France and
Switzerland (whose governments have made occupational pension schemes compulsory) all private-sector workers contribute to a private pension scheme. The
economic resources of older persons are also affected by the wealth they accu-
mulate during their lifetime. Home ownership, for example, is one aspect of
wealth. In most European Union countries, owner-occupation is the dominant
status with the proportion of older people who own their own houses ranging
from 80% in Ireland to 50% in Denmark, France and the UK. The major excep-

tions to this picture are Germany and the Netherlands where only one in three older people are owner-occupiers (Walker, 1993).

The main issue on the policy agenda is guaranteeing the financial stability of pensions and social security systems in the face of pressure caused by the ageing of the population. Most countries have relied on a combination of the state-funded pension and private, supplementary pensions to guarantee stable, or perhaps even rising, living standards. This raises the concern that policy-makers may focus their attention exclusively on those who have recently retired or on the aggregate data and so neglect the characteristics of differential ageing, more particularly the persistence of long-term poverty amongst various categories of older persons. It is important to remember that older people's living standards are particularly susceptible to changes in public policy and that old age is still a significant indicator of poverty. National reports from countries in Europe reveal 'a continuing problem of poverty amongst specific categories of older persons', with the size of these categories varying considerably between countries.

There are signs that poverty in old age is increasingly becoming a situation which predominantly affects women. Older women, particularly widows and divorced women, are among the poorest and most socially excluded groups in the European Union. These gender differences are not simply a function of the greater longevity of women as compared to that of men. The main causal factors are that the employment patterns of women (part-time work, shorter contribution period; Dykstra & Fokkema, 1998) differ from those of men, and crucially that the majority of pension schemes in the EU are based on an employment testing and/or earnings equivalence requirement (Gonyea, 1994; Groves, 1993; de Jong Gierveld, 1997; Starrels et al., 1994; Walker, 1993). As such, occupational pension schemes, which provide an important part of retirement income in several countries, indirectly discriminate against women in general, and women who work part-time in particular. Governments should therefore pay special attention to assisting these categories by providing pension income which is above poverty level. An income level above the poverty line would enable older persons to purchase additional types of external support when it was needed. Social security and private pension schemes in the countries of the European Union therefore play a major role in providing income for the elderly and can provide the means for ensuring that older persons can continue to lead independent lives which have quality and which are governed by their own personal preferences.

In a Eurobarometer survey carried out in 1992 in the twelve member states of the European Union, people were asked about their attitudes towards the financial situation of older persons. On average just under half of all citizens saw financial problems as the main problem facing older persons although there were wide variations between the different countries. Interestingly, younger people tended to put financial problems first whereas older people were more likely than younger people to mention loneliness or social isolation. But it was only in four member states that older people were found to be satisfied with their pensions. The countries in which older people were most adamant that their pensions did not provide the living standards they desired after a lifetime of contributions were, in descending order, Greece (66%), Portugal (56%), Italy and Spain (42%) and the UK (41%). The remarkably high level of consensus with the statement that 'those in employment have a duty to ensure, through contributions or taxes, that older people have a decent standard of living', suggests that the informal social contract is still emphatically endorsed (Commission of the European Communities, 1993).

With advancing age, elderly persons living alone (especially the never-married and divorcees) are over-represented amongst the elderly persons applying for domiciliary and residential care when their health deteriorates and specialist (medical) care is required (de Jong Gierveld & van Solinge, 1995; de Jong Gierveld & Dykstra, 1997). However, the 'majority of older persons do not need formal care'; support available from informal sources is sufficient for most older persons, even for the oldest old.

The availability of domiciliary and institutional care for the elderly population differs from region to region and is evaluated in different ways by the local population. It is reported that Greek families, particularly the elderly themselves, are resistant to the idea of residential care as an option because they prefer to receive assistance from the family; as a result, less than 1% of the elderly population in Greece currently live in institutional care facilities. The use of residential care is more widespread in Western and Northern European countries; approximately 5 or 6% of people aged 65 and over in these countries live in institutions. The use of residential care is regarded as a last resort in the event of deteriorating health. Faced with this situation, most elderly persons in Western and Northern Europe prefer institutional support to dependence on their children (de Jong Gierveld & van Solinge, 1995).

As a result of these trends, the elderly population tends to live either in two-person households (in the case of married couples), or alone (in the case of widow(er)s, older divorcees and the never-married). Living alone in a one-person household is predominantly a female phenomenon, but in the near future more and more older men are expected to be confronted with the prospect of living in a one-person household. Needless to say, elderly persons who live alone are the first to need 'support from outside the household', if care is needed. This brings us back to the central research question: will intergenerational informal care be available for older persons who need help?

## THE CARE POTENTIAL AMONG YOUNGER GENERATIONS VIS-À-VIS THE OLDER GENERATIONS

As mentioned above, the socio-structural and socio-cultural environment of the family in Europe is changing: ongoing and radical developments in the economic and labour market structure, in medical care and in the system of core social values and norms have given rise to important and unforeseen trends in demographic behaviour. The first trend is the continuing decline in the fertility rate which began in the nineteenth century and which (for more than twenty years) has resulted in under-replacement fertility levels in many European countries. This is evident from the total period fertility rates for the countries. In 1960, this rate was higher than 2 or even 3 in every country, but in 1994 the fertility rate for every country was lower than 2 (Bosveld, 1996).

A second trend is the spectacular increase in the life expectancy of both men and women. The average life expectancy for men in the Netherlands, for example, has risen from 47 years in 1900 to 74 years in 1994 (Van Poppel et al., 1996). In 1994, the life expectancy for men in the member states of the European Union was between 70.6 (Portugal) and 75 years (Greece), and for women between 77.8 (Portugal and Denmark) and 81.5 years (France) (Council of Europe, 1995).

These two trends in demographic behaviour have resulted in a dejuvenation and ageing of the population. There will be a shift in the age distribution: the number of older persons is increasing in both absolute terms and relative to other generations. Between 1950 and 1995, the relative share of the elderly population aged 65 and over in Europe increased from 8.2 to 13.8%, primarily at the expense of the youngest generation (0-14 years) which decreased from 26.2 to 19.1% over the same period. According to the average variant contained in the 1996 revision of the UN population projections, the proportion of older persons in Europe will increase further to 24.3% by the year 2040.

Although the process of ageing is taking place all over Europe, substantial differences exist between regions. These differences largely reflect the different timing and intensity of the fertility decline in the various regions. The decline in fertility in the northern and western regions of Europe began much earlier and manifested itself more gradually. In the southern and eastern regions this trend is a much more recent phenomenon and the drop was dramatic. In 1996 the lowest (period) fertility rates of Europe were reported in Italy (1.22) and Spain (1.15). Ireland's fertility rate had followed a different pattern for some time but as a result of an extraordinarily rapid decline, Ireland reached sub-replacement fertility in the early nineties (Ditch et al., 1996). The total fertility rate of Ireland is 1.91 in 1996.

## The very old

Within the group of elderly persons, the group of the very old (80 years and over) is growing most rapidly. In 1995 Europe had a total of 21.7 million persons aged 80 or over. By the year 2040, the European population will include almost 44 million people who fall into the oldest age category (UN, 1994). This represents an increase of more than 50%. Progressive ageing has affected, and will affect, all regions in Europe, and the age category of 80 years and older is growing faster than the total group of people aged 65 and over (double ageing). It is anticipated that Southern and Western Europe will experience the sharpest increase in the oldest segment of their population (in both absolute and relative terms). Southern countries are expected to have nine times as many very old people by the year 2040 as there were in 1950. The 65 years and older category will increase in every region over the next decades, although not as spectacularly as the 80-plus age group. By the year 2040, the 65 years and older age category is expected to be three to four times larger than it was in 1950.

## Changes in family support ratios

The need to adapt to an ageing society will inevitably have far-reaching repercussions on family life as well as in other areas.

Firstly, it is useful to consider the marital status of older persons because it provides an indication, at aggregate level, of the potential sources of support available in the event of increasing dependency and the need for help. It has been frequently noted that 'spouses' provide the main support for vulnerable elderly persons in need of care ('for better and for worse'). The combined effect of higher life expectancies and the younger age at which women marry mean that widowhood is more commonly experienced by women than men (Dooghe & Appleton, 1995). For example, in the Netherlands in 1994, the proportion of women aged 75-79 who were widowed was 54%, whereas the proportion of men who were widowed at that age was only 17%. Being (very) old is therefore very different for men and women. For women, it generally means having no partner, i.e. having to turn to others when they are no longer able to fend for themselves. For men, it generally means being attached, i.e. having a spouse available for assistance and care. Due to the rising life expectancy of both men and women, the chance of ageing 'together', as a couple, is increasing in most countries in Western and Northern Europe. But the effect of this trend is partly nullified by the incidence of divorce which is still on the increase, even amongst those in the higher age categories.

Generally speaking, single, widowed and divorced older persons are considered more likely to need assistance and advice from their children or other relatives and, eventually, to need public assistance.

Table 1. Composition of the kin network of female elderly in the Netherlands, 1939, 1984 and 2035

| Average number of: Year/age | Sisters | Daughters | Grand-daughters | Brothers | Sons | Total |
|---|---|---|---|---|---|---|
| **1939** | | | | | | |
| 60 to 64 | 1.4 | 1.7 | 1.2 | 1.3 | 1.7 | 7.3 |
| 65 to 69 | 1.2 | 1.7 | 1.8 | 1.1 | 1.7 | 7.5 |
| 70 to 74 | 1.0 | 1.6 | 2.3 | 0.9 | 1.7 | 7.5 |
| 75 to 79 | 0.8 | 1.6 | 2.6 | 0.6 | 1.7 | 7.3 |
| 80 and over | 0.5 | 1.5 | 2.8 | 0.3 | 1.6 | 6.7 |
| **1984** | | | | | | |
| 60 to 64 | 1.2 | 1.3 | 1.2 | 1.1 | 1.3 | 6.1 |
| 65 to 69 | 1.1 | 1.3 | 1.5 | 1.0 | 1.3 | 6.2 |
| 70 to 74 | 1.0 | 1.3 | 1.6 | 0.8 | 1.3 | 6.0 |
| 75 to 79 | 0.9 | 1.3 | 1.6 | 0.6 | 1.3 | 5.7 |
| 80 and over | 0.6 | 1.2 | 1.6 | 0.3 | 1.3 | 5.0 |
| **2035** | | | | | | |
| 60 to 64 | 0.7 | 0.7 | 0.4 | 0.7 | 0.8 | 3.3 |
| 65 to 69 | 0.6 | 0.7 | 0.5 | 0.6 | 0.8 | 3.2 |
| 70 to 74 | 0.6 | 0.7 | 0.5 | 0.5 | 0.8 | 3.1 |
| 75 to 79 | 0.5 | 0.7 | 0.5 | 0.4 | 0.8 | 2.9 |
| 80 and over | 0.3 | 0.7 | 0.5 | 0.2 | 0.8 | 2.5 |

Source: Bartlema et al. (1986).

The overall decline in mortality has led to the survival of increasing numbers of generations within families, particularly in those countries where the age of the mother at the birth of the first child is fairly low. At the same time the decline in fertility has depressed the numbers of same-generation kin at any given time.

Bengtson et al. (1990) refer to this as the 'beanpole family'. The resulting changes in the composition of the kin network of older women in several birth cohorts is illustrated in Table 1. The consequences of these developments at family level can also be illustrated by using family support ratios which indicate the relative size of two cohorts: the cohort of older persons and the cohort of the children born to them. Based on these ratios, one can conclude that the intergenerational care-providing 'potential' within the family has been decreasing rapidly since 1950. In that year, an average of roughly 6 to 7 potential care-providers were available for each person aged 80 or over. This number has fallen to roughly 3 to 4 in 1995 and will decline further to roughly 3 by the year 2020.

CARE WILLINGNESS AMONGST THE YOUNGER GENERATION VIS-À-VIS THE OLDER GENERATIONS; THE FACTS ABOUT SUPPORT

Surveys conducted in European countries (and in North America) consistently report a high degree of willingness to provide care for older disabled family members where it is required. Children state that it goes without saying that they will step in to take care of their handicapped and frail mother or father because 'the child is duty bound to the older generation', and because of the affection and love shared with the parent, the life-long historical bond between the parent and child, and other more practical reasons, such as not living too far away from the parent, and (grand)children having left the parental home and therefore being in a better position to care for someone outside the home. These and other motives lie behind the finding that 60 to 80% of all Alzheimer's patients in the Netherlands are cared for and supported by their family members and that less than 40% of all severely handicapped Alzheimer's patients are registered in formal care institutions (Duijnstee, 1996).

Informal family care generally means care provided by women since women are traditionally the main providers of services within the family. Middle-aged women therefore have to combine their involvement with the family and the labour market with care for their children, grandchildren, parents and parents-in-law. This frequently takes up a large proportion of their leisure time, particularly when regular assistance is needed. Their brothers tend to provide help sporadically, usually limiting themselves to specific tasks such as financial assistance or household repairs (Matthews & Rosner, 1988).

The findings of the 1994 European 'Community Household Panel' revealed that there was a high degree of involvement by adult children in the informal care of the older generation. The predominant carers were women, but men also put up a good show in certain countries. In a recent NIDI report, Dykstra (1997) stated that an average of roughly 10% of all European adults between the ages of

35 and 64 were involved in providing daily, unpaid care to members of the older generation. Women accounted for approximately 14% and men 6% (see Table 2).

Table 2. Percentage of men and women aged 35-64 involved in the care of older adults in selected European countries

|  | 35-44 | 45-54 | 55-64 | All |
|---|---|---|---|---|
| The Netherlands |  |  |  |  |
| Men | 3 | 7 | 8 | 6 |
| Women | 11 | 15 | 13 | 13 |
| Belgium |  |  |  |  |
| Men | 3 | 8 | 8 | 6 |
| Women | 9 | 15 | 14 | 13 |
| Denmark |  |  |  |  |
| Men | 3 | 5 | 3 | 4 |
| Women | 7 | 11 | 8 | 9 |
| Italy |  |  |  |  |
| Men | 8 | 11 | 10 | 9 |
| Women | 18 | 22 | 16 | 19 |
| Europe (12 countries) |  |  |  |  |
| Men | 5 | 7 | 8 | 6 |
| Women | 11 | 16 | 14 | 14 |

Source: ECHP, 1994.

Moreover, the older the generation of care-providers becomes, the greater the number of hours per day they are involved in providing care. Approximately 13% of adult women in the Netherlands provide informal care for older adults, with 7% of these devoting more than four hours a day to the task. The 45-54 age group was found to be particularly active in this area. These data were, however, based on a one-off survey and are therefore an underestimation of the number of adults who might at some point in their lives be involved in providing informal care for the older generation. Figures from the United States show that 55% of women should expect to be asked to provide informal care for older adults at some point during their lives.

But whether or not parents can actually count on receiving support from their adult children when they have problems depends on a great many factors, including their children's geographical proximity and how many of them are still alive. But one particularly important factor in this respect – an often neglected one – is what type of 'strategies' the older and younger generation have – and had in the past – for sustaining their relationship with one other, i.e. for fostering a sense of closeness and reciprocity. If, for example, the younger generation's relationship with its parents had been one of friendship, mutual respect and encouragement, then there is a very realistic chance these children would offer support when it was needed. But a different strategy can produce different results, as in the case of children who found their parents to be critical or uncaring. Parents who had exhibited deviant behaviour – alcoholics, for example – would often have to manage without informal help from their adult children (Umberson & Terling, 1997). One would also expect to find altered relationships between the generations in situations where parents had caused sweeping, 'discontinuous changes' in the lives of their children. To disentangle the effects of the factors in play, one needs micro-data analysis based on data from a large-scale survey research project. This is borne out by the findings of recent Dutch research into older mothers and fathers who had required informal care due to physical disabilities (de Jong Gierveld & Dykstra, 1997). The support received by widows and widowers, and parents still in their first marriage, was found to contrast sharply with that of ever-divorced parents (see Table 3).

Table 3. Sources of help received by older adults aged 55 and over, with surviving children and with limitations in activities of daily living, by sex and partner history (in percentages)

| | In first marriage | | Ever-widowed | | Ever-divorced | |
|---|---|---|---|---|---|---|
| | M | F | M | F | M | F |
| *With partner:* | | | | | | |
| Received help from: | | | | | | |
| – partner | 62,5 | 63,1 | 54,3 | – | 47,1 | 73,1 |
| – children living outside the household | 25 | 25,3 | 22,9 | – | 0 | 15,4 |
| – formal care/social services | 8,1 | 14,2 | 17,1 | – | 5,9 | 11,5 |
| *Without partner:* | | | | | | |
| Received help from: | | | | | | |
| – children living outside the household | – | – | 46,5 | 52,6 | 12,5 | 23,1 |
| – formal care/social services | – | – | 31,7 | 30 | 18,8 | 33,3 |

Source: NESTOR-LSN, 1992.

The most striking feature in Table 3 is the virtual non-participation of children in support arrangements for older ever-divorced adults, and ever-divorced men in particular: only 13% of male, and 23% of female, ever-divorced respondents without new partners said they received support from their children when they needed it, compared to 47% of widowers and 53% of widows in the same situation, which would suggest that widowed adults are able to rely on their children for support more readily than ever-divorced adults can. The findings also suggest that the group most likely to become estranged from their adult children are ever-divorced men. The obligation these children feel to support their ever-divorced fathers appears to become marginal once they reach adulthood and they appear to take few opportunities to provide support (cf. Cooney & Uhlenberg, 1990; Rossi & Rossi, 1990).

The children of widowed parents were found to 'intervene' when their partnerless parents needed help, in contrast to the children of ever-divorced parents who tended not to become involved in providing care. The lion's share of support for older ever-divorced parents with ADL limitations was provided by any new partner they had, and where there was no new partner either within or outside the household, ever-divorced mothers, and in particular ever-divorced fathers, received very little informal help. But did those who received no informal support receive formal support?

Interestingly, Table 3 also indicates that of all the categories of men and women not in their first marriage, ever-divorced men, either with or without partners, were the group least likely to receive formal help. In other words, the percentage of those who receive no support at all, whether formal or informal, is highest amongst ever-divorced men. Nor did the findings indicate that groups who were less likely to receive informal support were more likely to receive formal support. In fact, they indicated the reverse: that a 'high' reliance on informal support went hand in hand with a 'high' reliance on formal support, with widows being a case in point. One obvious explanation for this would be to attribute these findings to the relatively favourable health status of (younger) ever-divorced men who would presumably have little need for informal (or formal) support and would therefore receive little. But further multivariate analyses have revealed that health is not a significant predictor of the uptake of care amongst ever-divorced men. An alternative explanation could lie in the relationship between ever-divorced fathers (and mothers) and their children, and the premise that the relationship requires nurturing. If this relationship is disrupted by divorce or non-residential parenthood, it is more likely to lack intrinsic and reciprocal rewards. The number of children from marriages which had ended in divorce was found to be an important factor in terms of the care provided to ever-divorced fathers and mothers but one which affected the two groups in different ways. The number of children ever-divorced fathers had from previous marriages was found to be a significant predictor of their uptake of formal care and the amount of informal care they received. The more children ever-divorced fathers had from previous marriages, the less likely they were to make use of formal care. But in the case of ever-divorced mothers, there was a negative correlation between the number of children they had from a marriage which had ended in divorce and their likelihood of making use of formal care. These findings reflect predominant practices in custody arrangements whereby most children live with their single mothers after a divorce but they also reflect the different likelihood of men and women remarrying after divorce. Moreover, the findings suggest that most ever-divorced men fail to develop explicit strategies for maintaining good relationships with their children from a previous marriage and are more able to invest in the relationships with their children from subsequent marriages. Having said that, the mean number of children from subsequent marriages is relatively low, which suggests that the risk of ever-divorced men having gaps in their social networks is fairly high. But there are obviously a great many factors which determine whether or not children choose to be involved in providing care for their parents, such as their geographical proximity to one another, and the income and employment status of sons and daughters.

Further studies should be carried out to examine the scope for substituting a lack of informal care with a specific strategy whereby savings are used to buy care and other services, thereby enabling older adults to maintain their independence and well-being.

In summary and based on the above-mentioned research findings, it can be said that the vast majority of frail, non-institutionalised over-80s who receive assistance either in terms of the self-care activities of daily living (ADL) or the home-management activities of daily living (IADL) receive this assistance either from their spouse (if they have one), or from their children (primarily the daughters). There is a very strong correlation between the number of children and both the giving and receiving of most forms of support. However, where only a small number of children is born to these parents so that few children are available, each of them will take turns to provide the parent with the necessary support, although the mean amount of support per capita provided by these children exceeds the mean amount of support provided by children who have a larger number of (surviving and available) siblings (Dykstra & van Tilburg, 1994).

Although informal networks respond to the increasing incapacity of the older parent by broadening the scope of assistance that can be provided, there is a point at which the needs of the older adult exceed the resources of the network. Generally speaking, the need for, and importance of, formal care services increases as elderly persons get older. Empirical research findings suggest that formal help to supplement informal support is only enlisted as a last resort. Ideally, the provision of informal help should be combined with a wide range of community-based services such as home help, meals-on-wheels, emergency alarm systems and day care for disabled older adults as well as respite help for caregivers and temporary admissions to nursing homes. Services of this kind would increase the effectiveness of informal care. Caring for disabled elderly relatives will not become a realistic option for many family members until financially affordable formal services are available to supplement and support informal caregiving.

Family policies should provide incentives to family care-providers in the form of tax advantages or tax exemptions. Government policies should also provide more opportunities in the workplace to encourage men to adopt a more active role in terms of sharing the burden and rewards of caring for ageing parents with women. The idea of a 'time account' from which workers could draw flexibly over their working life is a good example of a possible new measure in this area. And older adults would find it easier to accept long-term informal help if they knew that the family members providing care were being supported and assisted by a system of formal help provided by the community. Elderly persons are extremely reluctant to put strains on their family relationships, such as the strain associated with the imbalance of exchanges that can arise in a caregiving situation.

These findings contrast with the notions of those who claim that mutual support is virtually non-existent in modern industrialised societies and who idealise rural, traditional societies where mutual support is governed by strict norms and obligations. One of the drawbacks of this second support system is that there is no choice whatsoever in terms of who has to look after the elderly, whether in financial or emotional terms. This support system also has enormous implications for the number of offspring that are needed to guarantee a minimum level of security in old age. Being part of a more modern system of relationships appears to put older persons at a disadvantage when they reach dependency. Whether or not they will be provided with the kind of support they need will depend on the quality of their social network which in turn will depend on their explicit life strategy as well as on proximity, mutual interest and personal preference. We would like to point out that a more voluntary style of modern relationships also has its advantages. Older adults are more free to choose the people they want to have as support-providers. In fact, the willingness of younger generations in European countries to provide care is generally greater than the willingness of elderly family members to accept such care. The reluctance stems from a desire to remain self-sufficient and the fear of being a burden to others.

## Notes

1  When we use the concept older persons, we are talking about a category that is not clearly defined. Not only does the minimum age fluctuate – 55, 60 or 65 – but various classifications are used within the group as well. In this article we concentrate on persons aged 65 or over; persons aged 80 years or older are referred to as 'the very old'.

2  The main characteristics of occupational pension schemes are that they are employer-sponsored (employer and employee contributions set aside) and 'fully funded' (enough assets are accumulated to cover the value of future payments owed to the participants in the pension system).

## References

Bartlema, J., N. van Nimwegen & H. Moors (1986). Kleinere families, verdwijnende verwanten en de zorg voor bejaarden. *Demos, 2*(5), 33-36.

Bengtson, V.L., C. Rosenthal & L. Burton (1990). Families and aging: Diversity and heterogeneity. In: R.H. Binstock & L.K. George (Eds.). *Handbook of aging and social sciences.* California: Academic Press, p. 263-287.

Bosveld, W. (1996). *The ageing of fertility in Europe: A comparative demographic-analytic study.* Amsterdam: Thesis Publishers.

Broese van Groenou, M.I., T.G. van Tilburg, E.D. de Leeuw & A.C. Liefbroer (1995). Data collection. In: C.P.M. Knipscheer, J. de Jong Gierveld, T.G. van Tilburg & P.A. Dykstra (Eds.). *Living arrangements and social networks of older adults.* Amsterdam: VU University Press, p. 185-197.

Commission of the European Communities (1993). *Age and attitudes: Main results from a Eurobarometer Survey.* Brussels: EC-Dir V.

Cooney, T.M. & P. Uhlenberg (1990). The role of divorce in men's relations with their adult children after mid-life. *Journal of Marriage and the Family, 52,* 677-688.

Council of Europe (1995). *Recent demographic developments in Europe 1995.* Strasbourg: Council of Europe Press.

de Jong Gierveld, J. (1995). The collection of survey data on household structures. In: E. van Imhoff, A. Kuijsten, P. Hooimeijer & L. van Wissen (Eds.). *Household demography and household modelling.* New York: Plenum Press, p. 137-162.

de Jong Gierveld, J. (1997). Armoede en isolement: oudere alleenwonende vrouwen in Nederland. In: G. Engbersen, J.C. Vrooman & E. Snel (Red.). *De kwetsbaren; Tweede Jaarrapport armoede en sociale uitsluiting.* Amsterdam: Amsterdam University Press, p. 177-193.

de Jong Gierveld, J. & P.A. Dykstra (1997). The longterm consequences of divorce for fathers. In: *International Population Conference, Beijing, China,* International Union for the Scientific Study of Population, Volume 2, p. 849-866.

de Jong Gierveld, J. & H. van Solinge (1995). *Ageing and its consequences for the socio-medical system.* Population Studies, No. 29. Strasbourg: Council of Europe Press.

Ditch, J., H. Barnes, J. Bradshaw, J. Commaille & T. Eardley (1996). *A synthesis of national family policies 1994, European Observatory on Family Policies.* University of York: Social Policy Research Unit.

Dooghe, G. & N. Appleton (Eds.) (1995). *Elderly women in Europe: Choices and challenges.* Brussel: CBGS.

Duijnstee, M. (1996). *Het verhaal achter de feiten. Over de belasting van familieleden van dementerenden.* Nijkerk: Intro.

Dykstra, P.A. (1997). *Employment and caring.* The Hague: NIDI, Working paper 1997/7.

Dykstra, P.A. (1998). The effects of divorce on intergenerational exchanges in families. *The Netherlands' Journal of Social Sciences, 33*(2), 77-93.

Dykstra, P.A. & T. Fokkema (1998). *Partner en kinderen: belemmerend of bevorderend voor beroepssucces? Intragenerationele beroepsmobiliteit van mannen en vrouwen met verschillende huwelijks- en ouderschapscarrières.* Paper presented at the conference of the European Science Foundation 'European societies or European society?'. Castelvecchio Pascoli, Italy, 3-7 april 1998.

Dykstra, P.A. & T.G. van Tilburg (1994). Steun voor ouderen [Elderly support]. In: N. van Nimwegen & G. Beets (Red.). *Bevolkingsvraagstukken in Nederland anno 1994.* Den Haag: NIDI, p. 189-208.

Gonyea, J.G. (1994). The paradox of the advantaged elder and the feminization of poverty. *Journal of the National Association of Social Workers, 39*(1), 35-42.

Groves, D. (1993). Work, poverty and older woman. In: M. Bernard & K. Meade (Eds.). *Women come of age: Perspectives on the lives of older women.* London: Edward Arnold, p. 43-62.

Kinsella, K. & Y.J. Gist (1995). *Older workers, retirement, and pensions.* Washington: US Bureau of the Census.

Liefbroer, A.C. & J. de Jong Gierveld (1993). Veranderingen in de overgang van jeugd naar volwassenheid. Een vergelijking van cohorten geboren tussen 1903 en 1965. In: M. du Bois-Reymond & J. de Jong Gierveld (Red.). *Volwassen worden.* Boekuitgave Mens en Maatschappij 1993, p. 17-35.

Matthews, S. & T.T. Rosner (1988). Shared filial responsibility: The family as the primary caregiver. *Journal of Marriage and the Family, 50,* 185-195.

Rossi, A.S. & P.H. Rossi (1990). Of human bonding, parent-child relations across the life course. New York: Aldine de Gruyter.

Starrels, M., S. Bould & L.J. Nicholas (1994). The feminization of poverty in the United States: Gender, race, ethnicity, and family factors. *Journal of Family Issues, 15*(4), 590-607.

Umberson, D. & T. Terling (1997). The symbolic meaning of relationships: Implications for psychological distress following relationship loss. *Journal of Social and Personal Relationships, 14*(6), 723-744.

Van Poppel, F., E. Tabeau & F. Willekens (1996). Trends and sex-differentials in Dutch mortality since 1850: Insights from a cohort- and period-perspective. *Genus, 52*, 3-4.

Walker, A. (1993). Living standards and way of life. In: A. Walker, A. Guillemard & J. Alber (Eds.). *Older people in Europe: Social and economic policies.* The 1993 Report of the European Community Observatory, Commission of the European Communities, p. 8-34.

# The family in Europe: A mediterranean perspective

SALUSTIANO DEL CAMPO
UNIVERSIDAD COMPLUTENSE MADRID, SPAIN

Comparative research focusing on social trends in industrial societies suggests a growing move towards convergence in many domains: religion and secularization, education, employment, conflict resolution and others. The same applies to the family field even though as Caplow, Mendras, and other authors observe divergences and singularities (Langlois, 1994). For the purpose of analysis we use the geographical sorting of European countries in three clusters: Sweden, Norway, Finland and Denmark in the north; Greece, Italy, Spain and Portugal in the south; and the central EU countries.

Based on a matrix analysis of some 78 trend reports for fhe first four societies - included in the Comparative Charting of Social Change Project (CCSC) - Forsé and Langlois (1994: 19) stated: "most often, classic comparative analyses of social change conclude, in a more or less embarrassed way, that there is a certain mixture of convergences and divergences in the processes studied. The reason for this confusion is that strong divergences between industrial societies are exceptional and absolute convergence is even rarer. Most often the differences mask resemblances or, what comes to the same thing, similarities mask divergences. This is what we call a singularity. It is possible to understand this phenomenon only if one systematically restituates each analyzed element in a substructure."

As Theodore Caplow and Henry Mendras (1994: 19-20) rightly note "the concept of singularity help us to visualize the subtle balance between convergence and divergence", yet it does not always predict the responses to given trends in any particular society. Take, for example, fertility decline in European societies during the sixties. Generally this process tends to be associated with the same set of causal factors: improved contraception, the entry of married women into the labor force, the equalization of the sexes, the legitimation of consensual unions, the shift from blue-collar to white-collar work, the emergence of a feminist movement, which encouraged the employment of women, the postponement of marriage, the increase of divorce and illegitimacy, and the growing incidence of abortion and sterilization, among others. There is no way to assign a relative weight to these factors or to assess the complementary influence of mutually reinforcing trends. Although it is sure that each of the above mentioned changes were present in all four societies, their interactions were and are not identical, but differ from one society to another. As a consequence, the convergence of trends that we observe in European societies does not imply that they will experience an identical future, since their differences are inextricably linked to what they have in common. They simultaneously converge and diverge and singularities emerge.

The application of this framework to the European family should start remembering the pioneering contribution of Louis Roussel (1992: 133-152), who in 1992 compared fertility, nuptiality, divorce, and age at marriage indicators for 16 contries. His main conclusion was that everything seemed then to announce the general triumph of the Parsonian type of family: medium sized, stable, asymmetric and highly institutionalized.

Yet this was an illusion and in fact the differences observed circa 1988, especially those concerning cohabitation, were large between the southern countries, the northern countries and the western and central countries. Comparing the southern and the nordic countries he found that Spain, Italy, Portugal and Greece were low in fertility, divortiality, cohabitation and births out of marriage, while in Denmark and Sweden fertility was relatively high, divortiality and cohabitation were high and births out of marriage strong or medium. For the rest of the countries (western and central) the corresponding indicators were more mixed. However, between 1965 and 1988 this situation tended toward convergence, as was the case for fertility decrease, nuptiality decrease, divortiality increase and births out of marriage increase.

He also pointed out that the new patterns of behavior are the result of national processes and that their diffusion started in the Scandinavian countries and had advanced faster towards the south than in any other direction. The later collection of a number of family indicators around 1994-1995 shows that the differences persist although they are not the same as before.

As shown in Table 1, the largest differences today are related to employment and unemployment which are lower as to the former and higher as to the latter, in the southern countries. Noteworthy is the unfavourable situation of Mediterranean women, having lower employment and higher unemployment rate as well as less part-time jobs. These facts bring to our attention the inequality of Mediterranean women vis-a-vis men, in contrast to the more equalitarian gender situation enjoyed by Nordic women. In Southern Europe women roles are still rather different from men's and women are still assigned to lower posi-

Table 1. Demographic and employment variables (EU 15)

| Variables | X̄ | SEC | NEC | D |
|---|---|---|---|---|
| **1. Age structure of the population** | | | | |
| < 15 | 17 | (15-18) | (18-19) | (-) |
| > 60 | 21 | (20-22) | (20-22) | |
| **2. Activity rates** | | | | |
| Men | 66 | (62-70) | (65-72) | (-) |
| Women | 45 | (35-49) | (55-59) | (- -) |
| **3. Employment rates (15-64)** | | | | |
| Men | – | (61-73) | (62-81) | (-) |
| Women | – | (32-54) | (58-69) | (- -) |
| **4. Part time workers** | | | | |
| Men | 5 | (3-5) | (8-11) | (- -) |
| Women | 31 | (13-17) | (16-40) | (- - -) |
| **5. Involuntary part time** | | | | |
| Men | 27 | (15-52) | (12-35) | (- -) |
| Women | 17 | (23-34) | (15-44) | (- - -) |
| **6. Unemployment rates** | | | | |
| Men | 10 | (6-18) | (5-15) | (-) |
| Women | 13 | (8-30) | (7-16) | (- -) |
| **7. Long-term unemployed** | | | | |
| Men | 46 | (46-64) | (22-41) | (- -) |
| Women | 50 | (54-67) | (16-31) | (- - -) |
| < 25 years | | | | |
| Men | 37 | (37-63) | (6-13) | (- - -) |
| Women | 41 | (40-66) | (8-13) | (- - -) |

X̄: Average; SEC: Southern European Countries; NEC: Northern European Countries; Differences: Small (-); Medium (- -); Large (- - -); –: no data.

Source: Eurostat: *Living Conditions in Europe. Selected Social Indicators, December 1997*, Luxemburg, 1998.

tions, despite the progress they have made in recent decades. As a matter of fact, the place of women in society is not as much a subject for debate in the Scandinavian countries as it is in the Mediterranean ones. In Spain, for instance, more than half of the inactive women would like to work and feel deprived by not being able to do so, whereas in Denmark inactivity is the result of an option rather than a condition women are obliged to accept willy nilly.

All this suggests that when the roles of men and women become similar, fertility and other family characteristics change. The new understanding of reproductive behavior carries with it a change in the concept of masculinity and of femininity too, mainly because the modern contraceptive techniques introduced in the sixties are controlled by women while their job opportunities are either scarce or inadequate. Perhaps it is not fully inappropiate to name this association of variables as the *Lysistrata effect* because of its impact on conception, although not necessarily on sexual intercourse, as in the old Greek comedy of Aristophanes.

If we now turn our attention to the family and household variables included in Table 2 we can also see many differences between southern and northern countries. The average number of persons per household is the lowest in the northern ones (Sweden= 2,1), whereas Ireland, Greece, Spain and Portugal all exceed three persons per household. Accordingly, the proportion of one person families is three times as high in Sweden as in Spain, Greece and Portugal. As fertility continues to decline, however, these figures are converging in Europe.

Information about households taken from the European Conmunity Household Panel (ECHP) reveal that single adults over 65 are much less frequent in Greece, Spain, Portugal and Italy (3-4%), than in Denmark, Sweden, UK and Germany (8-11%). The same observation applies to young and mid-aged singles. Even couples with one person over 65 are less frequent in the South and Ireland. In contrast, the category extended households, including three-generation families and households including other relatives or persons living in, are much more frequent in the South, but are extremely rare in Denmark, Sweden, the Netherlands and Finland.

These data indicate that households in the southern countries incorporate a larger part of young adults as well as the elderly generation. It is to be expected that these members of the enlarged household often have relative low income or pensions, or are often in education or exposed to unemployment. In these cases the extended family in the south serves as a support. By contrast, in the north we find much lower shares of young adults living with their parents and moving out happens at a certain age, relatively independent of job and family. In the South the move is closer related to job, income and family formation, and occurs much later.

And now a few lines by way of conclusions. The matter is not so much whether the stated differences between Southern and Northern European countries will persist or not. The most important thing is that we do not really know what these differences really mean. We observe them, but we cannot predict reli-

Table 2.  Household and family variables

| Variables | X̄ | SEC | NEC | D |
|---|---|---|---|---|
| 1. Average household size | | | | |
| 1985 | 2,6 | (2,9-3,0) | (2,2-2,6) | (-) |
| 1995 | 2,6 | (2,7-3,2) | (2,0-2,3) | (- -) |
| 2. One person households (%) | 13,2 | (5,4-9,1) | (16,8-22,5) | (- - -) |
| 3. Marriage | | | | |
| 1970 | 7,6 | (7,5-9,4) | (5,1-7,9) | (- -) |
| 1995 | 5,1 | (5,0-6,6) | (3,8-6,6) | (-) |
| 4. Cohabitation (%) | – | 2,3 | 25 | (- - -) |
| 5. Divorce | | | | |
| 1970 | 1,0 | (0,1-0,4) | (1,7-2,5) | (- - -) |
| 1995 | 1,8 | (0,5-1,2) | (2,5-2,7) | (- - -) |
| 6. Contraception (%) | | | | |
| Total | – | 59 | 78 | (- -) |
| Modern | – | 38 | 71 | (- -) |
| 7. Fertility | | | | |
| 1960 | 2,6 | (2,3-3,1) | (2,2-2,7) | |
| 1995 | 1,4 | (1,2-1,4) | (1,7-1,8) | Reversal |
| 8. Births outside marriage (%) | | | | |
| 1970 | 6 | (1-7) | (6-19) | (- -) |
| 1995 | 23 | (3-19) | (33-53) | (- - -) |
| 9. Mean age of women at child-bearing | | | | |
| 1970 | 27,5 | 28,3 | (26,7-27,1) | (-) |
| 1995 | 28,9 | (28,1-29,7) | (29,2-29,3) | (-) |
| 10. Single-parent families (%) | | | | |
| 1980 | – | (4,4-11,6) | 18,1 | (- - -) |
| 1990 | – | (5,7-12,5) | 20,8 | (- - -) |
| 11. Children living with one parent (%) | 9 | (4-7) | 8 | (- - -) |

See Table 1 for footnotes and sources

able conclusions from our observations. Of the three major types of families present at the end of the xxth Century - the conjugal family, the lone parent family and the stepfamily - only the first is far more frequent in Southern Europe.

The other two types plus cohabiting couples and single person households are more frequent in the North.

A final remark: during the decades dealt with in this paper the European family has been converging in general, but simultaneously diverging in some respects. Exceptionally a reversal of patterns has happened also, to the effect that currently Spaniards and Italians are behaving fertilitywise the way the Swedish did thirty years ago. Whether the present singularities will decrease or become permanent or increase, no one can tell for sure, but at any time the picture of the European family will always be incomplete unless we not only consider convergences but also divergences and singularities.

REFERENCES

Caplow, T. & H. Mendras (1994). Convergence or divergence? In: S. Langlois (Ed.). *Convergence or divergence? Comparing recent social trends in industrial societies.* Montreal: Campus Verlag. McGill. Queeńs University.

Forsé, M. & S. Langlois (1994). Comparative structural analysis of social change in France and in Quebec. In: S. Langlois (Ed.). *Convergence or divergence? Comparing recent social trends in industrial societies.* Montreal: Campus Verlag. McGill. Queeńs University.

Langlois, S. (Ed.) (1994). *Convergence or divergence? Comparing recent social trends in industrial societies.* Montreal: Campus Verlag. McGill. Queeńs University.

Roussel, L. (1992). La famille en Europe occidentale; divergences and convergences. *Population*, 1.

# Negotiation strategies in modern families: What does it mean for global citizenship

Manuela du Bois-Reymond
Rijksuniversiteit Leiden, The Netherlands

## Introduction

In December 1994, I attended an international conference 'Families as Educators for Global Citizenship'.[1] It was at this conference that I met Wilfried Dumon for the first time. There were many stimulating discussions, sometimes somewhat confusing and chaotic because the members who attended the symposium came from all over the world and from various scientific disciplines. Everybody tried to contribute to the topic from the viewpoint of her or his expertise as best as she or he could. Wilfried Dumon did so with an admirable erudition and subtle humour. Robert Rapoport of the Institute of Family and Environmental Research, London, and Imre Kovách of the Institute of Political Science of the Hungarian Academy of Sciences in Budapest who convened the conference, suggested at the end a publication and asked the participants for contributions. The book never materialised.[2] But when I was asked by Koen Matthijs and Ann Van den Troost to write a piece for an English liber amicorum for Wilfried Dumon, vivid memories on those days and discussions in Budapest entered my mind and I decided to put the never published contribution in this book. Apart from updating the references, I did not alter the text.

In social sciences, we go to pains to learn how to negotiate systematically between macro and microprocesses. However, it has always been unwise to confront 'Society' and 'The Individual' as antagonistic figures and to separate one from the other in the cognitive process, as criticised often and most sharply by Norbert Elias (Elias, 1983; also cf. Bertaux, 1994). In fact, this separation may nowadays be more of a barrier to the acquisition of knowledge than ever before, for societies in modern times are at the same time societies of highly individualised people and mass societies which can no longer be grasped adequately within traditional national boundaries. Individualisation and globalisation are totally inseparable; no individual, no family, and no inhabitant of a city or rural area can live or be imagined without some connection to world processes. In what follows I explore what relationships there might be between negotiation strategies in the family on the one hand – a microprocess – and the notion of global citizenship on the other – a macroprocess. When I talk about the family, I refer to societies in Central and Western Europe (and, less directly, to North America). My own research on family communication was and is carried out in two countries with similar structures: the Netherlands and Germany.

Inasmuch as the concept of 'global citizenship' is not yet unambiguously used in political-scientific discourse, thoughts about it are open to critique, and I want to stress at the outset that I am fully aware of that. I can only hope that the reader is willing to follow my arguments, even if he or she disagrees with some or all of them.

First, I shall point to various influences modernisation at all levels of society has on the family. Even though they are units which can be localised concretely, families take part in global processes (section 2). Second, I shall direct my attention to the areas of relationships between the genders and generations, which in the last decades have changed familial life substantially in all Central and West European countries and also outside these regions (section 3). Third, I shall deal with some of our own studies, in which we have discussed familial communication within the perspective of modernisation theory (section 4). I conclude by taking the liberty of speculating about the context of familial negotiation and 'global citizenship', suggesting some recommendations for further research on the matter (section 5).

## FAMILY AND MODERNISATION

The great social changes of recent decades have altered European families very profoundly, both structurally and emotionally. This process is often referred to as modernisation. Mass education in the Western European post-war societies made it possible to postpone starting a family and extended woman's social role. Secularisation weakened traditional values, morals, and duties and opened up new repertoires of action. Medical technology allowed birth control, and thus tore apart the relation between reproduction and sexuality. Family sizes have decreased to the modern ideal family which consists of two parents and two children; childless marriages and unmarried partners nowadays no longer are taboo. Courses of life become de-standardised: the gender-specific normal biography is not the only socially sanctioned form of life any more, but becomes just one among many others possible. At the same time, courses of life come under the influence of standardised education careers, jurisdiction of the welfare state and mass consumption (Blossfeld, 1995).

More open concepts of life for men and women (particularly for women) do not affect in any way the desire to have a family and have not eliminated families. But family expectations are transformed, at least for the adults, from a compulsory community to a community of choice: opting out and starting anew are permitted and practiced on a mass scale. In all western (and increasingly also in ex-communist) countries, the divorce rates have been rising since the end of the 1960s. Currently, they have reached a level of approximately one third of all marriages in Europe. Pluralised families are the consequence: children from two or more marriages or partnerships, together with biological and non-biological parents and brothers/sisters, form new family constellations (Ditch et al. 1998). Extended opportunities for choice for men and women within and outside the family make family life more intimate, especially within marriages taking place according to choice and not duty, and with couples having the few children they choose to have instead of the many children they were 'supposed' to have. A child is more and more a product of the parents' love and desire to have children, and thus an object of emotional investment (Eurobarometer, 1993: 57). The great majority of children may well be living in two-parent families, but in Sweden, an example of an advanced society, approximately 10% of all school-age children live in families with so-called 're-made' couples, i.e. adults other than the child's parents (Therborn, 1995: 292).

These major social trends, which are made up of so many different components, affect family life by changing the development of family members' abilities and desires. Collective and traditional practices are forced into the background. In comparison to former family life, the balance of power between the parents/partners and between parents and children has shifted: women have gained an increasing amount of power in their relationships with men, and children today have more influence on their own and the family's life than ever before. At the same time, modernised gender and intergenerational relationships, often in combination with poverty, create new problems and risks. They are manifest in the mass phenomena of single mothers, teenage pregnancy (particularly in the USA; hardly at all in European countries), neglect or abuse of children, or also of fathers deprived of their rights who fight for custody of their children after a divorce. The modern family in most European countries has turned from an authority-oriented family to a negotiating one. Modern families communicate and quarrel about desires, needs, conflicts, plans and frustrations, about education careers, household organisation and family duties, about buying of consumer goods and where the holidays are spent; about how to bring up the children, partnership and custody, and about leisure time arrangements and divorce plans. Compromises are looked for, found, rejected, re-negotiated. Balancing out the power between man and woman and parents and child requires verbal skills, an awareness of and planning for the future, aptitude for reflexion and tolerance, and the capacity to deal simultaneously with limits in an atmosphere of openness and freedom of choice.

Not every one has the opportunity to learn and develop these qualities and strategies of acting, yet they become ever more indispensable for coping with increasing complexity in personal and social life.

The negotiating family has become a mass phenomenon, despite the individual differences in the way it looks and functions. It incorporates new values of upbringing which, in contrast to universal values of duty and obedience and christian morals, prefers particularist individual values and tolerates the most various ideologies: christian, non-christian, feministic, hedonistic, humanitarian – and all kinds of blends. The main idea is to allow and hope for a child to become an individual, a distinct personality, independent and prepared to realise what might be called a choice-biography (du Bois-Reymond et al., 1998). The child is supposed to be able to react flexibly to unpredictable circumstances, as the world is unpredictable, whatever degree of far-sightedness parents may want to put into their planning.

In answer to the question which qualities the family environment should seek to encourage in children, the values indicated most frequently by Europeans are: a sense of responsibility (56%), tolerance (50%), good manners (40%), self-reliance (29%) and love of life (28%). In these values, traditional and modern elements blend, with modern elements dominating the more, the younger the Europeans are. Which means that future parent generations will regard individual values very highly (Eurobarometer, 1993: 81-83; see also Wilkinson, 1997).

It is beyond doubt for researchers of modernity that the changes in social and familial life outlined here are irreversible. Therefore, there will be no return from individualised (western) societies which are open and linked to the world back to local, self-contained small worlds with collective forms of living. This may block off certain nostalgic and moral argumentation (back to comprehensible local worlds in the sense of Tönnies *Gemeinschaft*; the intact family as a cornerstone of human social life, etc.). But in what direction the journey of modernisation is going to lead man and woman, child and parents, is yet open.

## FAMILIAL BALANCE OF POWER

Even though in social sciences, including women's studies, there is an agreement that the balance of power between men and women and between parents and children in their mutual roles is much more equal than one or two generations ago, there is as much uncertainty and disagreement concerning the evaluation of this development than among those personally affected in everyday life (Ambert, 1994; Gerhardt et al., 1995). Family sociologists specialising in modernisation theory are inclined to see the development as positive on the whole. They point out a large number of studies in European countries, both East and West, which indicate that children and adolescents are satisfied with their parents, put them in first place as confidants, and do not want to imagine their own lives as adults without a family (European Values Group, 1992).

A meanwhile immense mass of studies, also carried out in many countries, deals, in the face of new role expectations and professional demands of women, with the question in what way increased and still increasing labour market participation of mothers is affecting the family (Oppenheimer, 1994; Desplanques, 1993; Henkes et al., 1993; Kempeneers & Lelievre, 1993; van Praag & Niphuis-Nell, 1997; Niphuis-Nell, 1997; Näsmann, 1995). Discussion of such matters in scientific, public and private life is increasingly shifting from the question of sole responsibility of women to that of shared responsibility of men and the state in order to make 'child and profession' compatible. That a woman and mother should limit herself (once again) completely to her role and tasks at home – this opinion has no place in a modern world any more, even if in actuality, women run the risk of being driven out of the labour market rather than men in times when work is in short supply.

Educationalists and developmental psychologists are rather more inclined than sociologists to warn about the negative consequences of women in employment for mother, child and family life. It is also clear that teachers have a much more critical view of the modern family and the modern child than sociologists. They are concerned about the effects of being a single child on social development; they complain that the latest generation of children shows weak concentration and insufficient willingness to adapt. They also criticise a predominance of the new values of upbringing: are children not brought up to be too individual instead of becoming social beings? Is their happiness not emphasised too much instead of a feeling of responsibility? But also: with so many rights to have a say in family matters and the pressure to do well outside, does the modern child have enough opportunities and space to be 'a child' (Elkind, 1981; a critical opinion: Qvortrup, 1995)?

Emancipation between genders is a process and reality which children participate in, as it takes place in the family to a great extent. Children watch and listen when their parents negotiate power and discuss (incompatible) needs. Already at an early age, they nowadays often take part in separation affairs and the 'managing' of divorces, by, e.g., being allowed to have a say in arranging vis-

iting dates. At the same time, they themselves are active participants in negotiating the balance of power between the generations. There is no doubt that in
the course of the last few decades, children have gained power and influence
over their parents; they have turned from recipients of orders into young partners in the family. The extension of the school career is primarily responsible for
this. Pupils remain children or adolescents for a longer time, and students stay
at home for longer and delay joining the labour market. They thus develop an
extra-familial life which encourages their independence and gets them away
from their parents' control. Secularisation and democratisation of overall social
circumstances have also increased their degrees of freedom and demands for
independence, along with increasing their strong needs for emotional intimacy
and care in the family.

## FAMILY NEGOTIATION

In several projects we have addressed the research questions of the way modern
parents and children deal with one another in everyday life, in what areas of life
they negotiate power, and what are the results. On the basis of empirical data,
we have developed a typology of styles of communication between parents and
children. The results could be positioned on a 'trajectory of modernity' whose
one end represents the type of traditional authority, and whose opposite end
represents partnership negotiation.

In an oral history study of urban childhood in two Western European cities
(Leiden, the Netherlands, and Wiesbaden, Germany) around 1915/1925, we
did not find any negotiating households at all. It was not possible to determine
empirically in this project to what degree the upper classes already then showed
an orientation towards the negotiation type – there were no cases for this in our
sample. But we found beginnings of modern values of upbringing in middle-
class families and in some working-class families with prospects for social climb-
ing (du Bois-Reymond & Jonker, 1988). Through this study, we became interested in the value of cross-cultural comparative studies, in order to detect
synchronous and diachronous developments in the European modernisation
process.

In a Dutch longitudinal youth study we systematically varied social class and
style of upbringing and family communication, and we also interviewed the parents.[3] For the parent generation (born around 1940/45), we found a clear predominance of authoritarian styles in all social milieus; negotiating styles were a
great exception in the times when today's parents were young (the exceptions
could be found in the upper social milieus). On the whole, children in the

1950's were in no way brought up with a negotiation orientation. These findings correspond to the overall conditions of society which were then still in a state of pre-modernity or just on the verge of becoming modern in the sense outlined above.[4]

A shift in the balance of power between the generations and genders happened in the Netherlands just as in other West-European countries at the end of the 1960s and in the 1970s. The parents interviewed by us therefore belong to a transitional generation which is bridging the gap to modernity in the area of upbringing: brought up themselves to a great extent in an authoritarian style, these parents want to and have to bring up their children tolerantly and with preparedness to negotiate, for them to become mature citizens. And, what is crucial here, adolescents also expect such an open attitude of their parents. Our data show a clearly developed milieu trend: negotiation can be found mainly in the middle and upper cultural milieus (Bourdieu, 1984). But it must be pointed out that also in the lower classes, a negotiating style has become increasingly common since the 1960s/1970s (du Bois-Reymond, 1995a; Rispens et al., 1996; Zinnecker & Silbereisen, 1996; cf. also Boer et al., 1998).

In a project which included three European regions (the regions of Rotterdam/ the Netherlands, Halle/East Germany, and Marburg and Frankfurt/West Germany), we once more examined the question of parents' preparedness to negotiate, children's opportunities to influence familial decisions, and their range of autonomy (du Bois-Reymond, 1995b; Büchner et al., 1998; Torrance, 1998).[5] In all three European regions, despite otherwise different living conditions and national traditions, we found a predominance of negotiating styles; restrictive and authoritarian families were the exception everywhere and can be considered a model which is successively being phased out in the modernisation process.

The children in advanced negotiating families decide about their bedtime (even if the parents think it is too late), friends (even if the parents do not accept them), choice of school (even if the parents would have preferred a different one), and taste in clothes, music style, and room decoration.

It is important to stress that not all children live in such circumstances, not all children are allowed to negotiate with their parents their daily lives and decisions. The point is that 'modern familial education is orientated towards negotiation' and thus sets the guiding standards even for those families which do not follow these new behavioural and communicative standards in all respects.

In the process of balancing out power, younger people have gained power while older people have lost. The older the adolescents get, the more their parents withdraw from making decisions and controlling their children, and the more they limit their attempts at enforcing a conflict-free life within the family and advising their children regarding further education/training and choice of profession (du Bois-Reymond et al., 1998).

A gain of power for younger children against parental authority is also expressed in punishment behaviour of the older generation: while most of our subjects in the oral history project reported physical punishment, this was the exception in the adolescent and child project. Conflict situation management by cooling down (withdrawing to one's own room) replaces the old forms of punishment, e.g. a slap, not allowing the child to go out, no meals, etc.

The fairly great concessions of the more powerful to the younger were clearly not a move to a laissez faire attitude or permissive parenting style in our studies. It is a main characteristic of the modern negotiating family that there is and has to be intensive communication about differing opinions among the family partners to keep situations under control. For example, one mother deals with her twelve-year-old daughter's desire to choose her school by arranging that the daughter has to change schools if her performance does not meet a certain basic standard. The parents of older adolescents do not show an indifferent attitude, either; they are still involved adults who are always prepared to give emotional, practical, and often financial support when their child demands it.

In spite of our findings, however, recent child and family research has not yet answered to what extent laissez faire or neglecting attitudes are present in modern families in different countries (du Bois-Reymond, 1996; Büchner et al., 1998). Cross-cultural research on this question is urgently needed to assess the negative effects of modernisation processes as well as the positive. It might be characteristic of Dutch families within a warm family climate that we did not find cases of neglect in our samples of 'normal' families (i.e. not clinical or therapeutic cases); we did not find those cases in the German sample either.

Parents today find bringing up children difficult and are quite prepared to admit it. They are quick to criticize themselves, even in front of an interviewer, and see their own actions and opinions in relative terms ('I'm not sure if I'm right on this matter', 'I'm not sure whether my child thinks the same about this'). Modern parents have descended from their historically constructed pedestal of infallibility in bringing up children. And it is the case for both generations that with growing communicative competence, the level of reflection also increases. The difference between those who are able to acquire these skills and those who are not is therefore becoming increasingly pronounced.

In cross-cultural comparisons in our studies, more similarities than differences appeared in the familial context of life and upbringing. It appears justifiable to speak of something in the way of 'a European family culture', where, on the trajectory of modernity, the families are moving from the traditional end (traditional authority) towards the modern end (negotiation), even though the movement is not coordinated on a general scale.

## NEGOTIATION AND 'THE GLOBAL'

In this section I will attempt to explore the relationship between the modern negotiating family described above and 'global citizenship'. It seems reasonable to assume a homology: family negotiation partners and their communication strategies are a result of the same modernisation processes which have created interdependencies on a global scale (Lamb et al., 1992). 'Global citizenship' therefore would be a generalisation of the democratised power relations in the family, and the young family member would be a cosmopolitan by implication. Yet modernisation theoreticians point out the dialectics of 'global' and 'local' – 'the glocal' (de Swaan, 1995; Robertson, 1992). By that they mean that local life-worlds intersect with global networks and systems, creating yet another reality that exists between concrete traditional, local surroundings and the abstract principles which govern 'the global'.

It appears to me that this dialectic also applies to family relations and that the homology between the modern family and globalisation/global citizenship remains ambiguous. It seems to be productive to look at the relationship between 'the glocal' and modern families from a generation perspective. We can then state that the older generations do not introduce the younger generations to the world in the old sense by opening it up to them on the basis of their advanced knowledge and experience. Under the influence of globally accessible media for all age groups, 'knowledge becomes less and less hierarchical'. Both the older and the younger generations participate in learning about the world simultaneously (Wilkinson, 1997).

Part of these stocks of knowledge distributed by the media are global problems: war, poverty, gender conflicts, ethnic strife, endangered environment. Certainly adolescents, and even many children, know that adults do not have the power to solve these problems, and this (adult) failing is also discussed explicitly in the media. Parents in former times did not have this power either, but the children thought they did, and they were taught that powerful groups of adults such as politicians, educators and clergymen were in that position. Children and adolescents today know or feel that their parents do not have the power to solve complex problems, so adults find themselves gradually being stripped of their role-model functions in the areas of education and politics. For many adolescents, there are very few truly relevant grown-up persons apart from their parents to whom they can relate and with whom they can or want to discuss problems. Instead, young people 'meet' relevant adults on the television screen. Nevertheless, parents are the most important (real) adult persons to relate to for today's children and adolescents. Nowhere else in the adult world, except in the family, do children experience that they are taken seriously and have some significance as partners. Adolescents rarely have this experience outside the family; they have only marginal influence on goings-on at school, none at all on the labour market, and the same applies for 'top brass politics' (for which adolescents, as surveys show again and again, have no interest), the legal system and many other institutions of society (Jugendwerk der Deutschen Shell, 1997; Helve & Bynner, 1996; Walther & Stauber, 1998; Vanandruel et al., 1996).

An exception to this rule of powerlessness is the consumer-market. Where and how they spend their monetary resources influences what is available and how much it costs. Hence there is an enormous reciprocal impact of youth-cultural products and role models in the consumer arena, such as idols in music, sports, and advertisements, on the lives of young people (Miles et al., 1998).

Parents are of relevance to adolescents within the framework of the family. Everyday life and immediate concerns are negotiated much more than 'the world' and global problems. 'The World' is conquered by adolescents mainly outside the framework of the family, via the grooves of youth culture and lifestyles. Young people produce, receive and participate in some kind of 'global youth culture', and in this dimension, they are as close to 'global citizenship' as they are distant from their parents' local and national politics and traditional values. It is because of that cleavage between unattractive and distant adults, and the attractions of media-transmitted youth cultures, that those adults who are active in the fields of media and culture are most likely to have access to the world of adolescent language and feelings.

To adults, 'global citizenship' is a concept which stimulates them to interpret the world in political and moral ways. To adolescents, on the other hand, 'global citizenship' is a habitualised life-style which approximately manifests itself in the fact that European and American kids recognise each other by their tags and graffiti pieces. Concerning lifestyle, the 'new' children re-educate their 'old' parents without any moral intentions. They demonstrate how important music is in life; how innovations in the field of media can be acquired instantly; that trips are not planned but taken; how to despise stress ('Keep cool, man....'); that the head is not the only part of the body. Without any moral intentions or programs, they demonstrate tolerance. (Projected on the whole young generation, violent skinheads, who are sub-fraction among skinheads themselves, and other violent adolescents are a very small minority, albeit not in poverty-stricken parts of metropolitan areas.) The motto of most adolescents (girls and boys) in Western European societies is: 'LIVE AND LET LIVE'. They respect different cultural styles and class situations, or consider them to be of little importance in concrete projects and encounters.

What families can do for 'global citizenship' must definitely not be posed in too pragmatic and direct a way. It seems wholly inappropriate to the problem if involved educational scientists, teachers and politicians demand or expect that parents should wish to bring up their children to have more of a sense of responsibility, to be more environment-conscious, peaceful and anti-xenophobic. If one sees what has been said so far as correct and symptomatic, one must admit that it is not as simple as that. In this context, it does not appear to me that the numerous recent publications, e.g. *Shared Values for a Troubled World* by Kidder, (1994), are able to grasp the problem situation adequately.

Possibly even more so than the lives of adults, adolescent lives take place at intersections between 'global' (media, travel) and 'local' (place of residence, family, school). It is the young generations who explore those intersections actively, and make intersections of their own (i.e. create their own networks, peer groups, travel routes). But, although I do not believe in moral education to bridge the cleavage between the experiences of the older and the younger generation, I do think that part of the 'glocal' could consist of a new bond between the generations. In a world which is increasingly interdependent and connected by a denser and denser media network, a world with more and more risks, the generations should and could find joint projects for getting closer to the concept of 'global citizenship'. The way towards such 'joint generation projects', if it is to be passable at all, leads along the rails of culture, not along those of politics or pedagogy. Exactly this is the challenge for modern pedagogues, since Montessori, Makarenko and Korczak are no more (Röhrs & Lenhart, 1994).

Much would be achieved already if the generations could come to joint problem definitions, not yet minding about solutions. Why? Because the likelihood of intergenerational consensus on problem definitions is probably greater than intergenerational consensus on solutions. For example, parents and children (partly also teachers) agree that the school as it functions today in modern society is not able to satisfy the needs of either children or adults (parents and teachers); it is, by and large, a much duller place to be than so many other places in society, not in the least because the school is local and not glocal (UNESCO-Kommission, 1997). Yet, a joint problem definition does not necessarily imply the same solution. To arrive at joint solutions, we will need to engage in an 'informed discourse between the generations'. Such a discourse forms, in my view, the basis of 'global citizenship'.

## CONCLUDING REMARKS ON RESEARCH PRACTICE

Children, adolescents and families should be studied no longer only in the framework of nation-states (the 'Dutch', 'German', American' family). Instead, we should learn to look for intersections between 'local' and 'global' concerning intergenerational relationships. It would be worth researching, for example, what parents and children/adolescents know about one another with regard to their ideas and desires for a local and global world that is worth living in. To my knowledge, such research does not exist, neither national nor international. It would be worth researching what a trans-national and 'intergenerational media education' would look like. Adults and children of different nations and cultures could communicate local knowledge about 'hot issues' to their children (such as the causes for local wars; the devastating effects of mass-keeping of cattle, and other environmental issues); are the children in such families closer to the concept of 'global citizenship'? These and similar questions are still of minimal significance in mainstream family sociology, as can be verified by bibliographies (Dumon & Van Acker, 1995) which do not even mention the notion of globalisation in connection with the family.

I have attempted to find connections between family modernisation and globalisation. What becomes clear is how unclear these connections still are to those of us who are right in the middle of this transformation process. To educate modern children and young people for 'global citizenship' is a project that is much more complicated than many of those who either propagate it or are sceptical about it are willing to admit.

## NOTES

[1] The Conference was sponsored by UNESCO, the Commission of the European Union, the Hungarian Soros Foundation, the Johann Jacobs Foundation and the William T. Grant Foundation. It took place in Budapest, 15-18 December 1994.

[2] One of the major reasons were that R. Rapoport died unexpectedly.

[3] The sample of the research consists of 120 young people and their parents. When we interviewed the adolescents for the first time (1988) they had just finished secondary education and were between 16 and 19 years old. Meanwhile we have interviewed

them four times and their parents two times. Main topics are: educational and occupational careers; relationships with peers and parents; expectations for the future in the occupational and private sfeer (genderspecific division of labour concerning work - child-care). We controlled for SES (three levels: high, middel, low).

4 North America was different; there the decisive developments in the direction of modernized family life occurred some decades earlier than in Europe, in the forties.

5 It concerns a longitudinal qualitative study; we conducted biographical interviews with in total 106 families (children and one parent, mainly the mother). The children were at the beginning 12 years old. With a smaller sample we carried the study through to two more rounds (14 and 16 years old). We controlled for SES (three levels: high, middel, low).

## REFERENCES

Ambert, A.M. (1994). An international perspective on parenting: Social change and social construct. *Journal of Marriage and the Family, 56*(3), 529-543.

Bertaux, D.F. (1994). Families and mobility: The European experience. *Innovation. The European Journal of Social Sciences, 7*(1), 89-104.

Blossfeld, H.P. (Ed.) (1995). *The new role of women. Family formations in modern societies.* Boulder/San Fransisco/Oxford: Westview Press.

Boer, F., M. Dekovi, J. Rispens & G.A. Schmid (Red.) (1998). *Vaders,* speciale uitgave *Kind en Adolescent.*

Bourdieu, P. (1984). *Distinction: A social critique of the judgment of taste.* Harvard: Cambridge University Press.

Büchner, P., M. du Bois-Reymond, J. Ecarius, B. Fuhs & H.-H. Krüger (1998). *Teenie-Welten. Aufwachsen in drei europäischen Regionen.* Opladen: Leske & Budrich.

Desplanques, G. (1993). Activité féminine et vie familiale. *Economie et Statistique, 261,* 23-32.

de Swaan, A. (1995). De sociologische studie van de transnationale samenleving. In: J. Heilbron, N. Witterdink (Red.). *Mondialisering. De wording van de wereldsamenleving.* Groningen: Wolters Noordhoff, p. 16-35.

Ditch, J., H. Barnes, J. Bradshaw & M. Kilkey (1998). *A synthesis of national family policies 1996. European Observatory on National Family Policies.* Brussels: European Commission.

du Bois-Reymond, M. (1995a). The role of parents in the transition period of young people. In: M. du Bois-Reymond, R. Diekstra, K. Hurrelmann & E. Peters (Eds.). *Childhood and youth in Germany and The Netherlands. Transitions and coping strategies of adolescents.* Berlin/New York: Walter de Gruyter, p. 73-102.

du Bois-Reymond, M. (1995b). Parent-child relations in Western and Eastern Germany and in the Netherlands. In: M. du Bois-Reymond, R. Diekstra, K. Hurrelmann & E. Peters (Eds.). *Childhood and youth in Germany and The Netherlands. Transitions and coping strategies of adolescents.* Berlin/New York: Walter de Gruyter, p. 127-160.

du Bois-Reymond, M. (1996). Gezin en modernisering. Een problematische relatie voor jongeren? In: W. Vollebergh & W. Meeus. *Psychosociale problemen in de adolescentie.* Themanummer *Pedagogisch Tijdschrift, 21,* 279-293.

du Bois-Reymond, M. & A.E.M. Jonker (1988). The city's public space and urban childhood. In: L. Heerma van Voss & F. van Holthoorn (Eds.). *Working class and popular culture*. Amsterdam: Stichting Beheer IISG, p. 43-58.

du Bois-Reymond, M., Y. te Poel & J. Ravesloot (1998, in press). *Keuzen van jongeren*. Bussum: Coutinho.

Dumon, W.A. & J. Van Acker (1995). *Gezinswetenschappelijke documentatie 20. Jaarboek 1995*. Leuven: Universitaire Pers Leuven.

Elias, N. (1983). *Engagement und Distanzierung*. Frankfurt/M.: Suhrkamp.

Elkind, D. (1981). *The hurried child. Growing up too fast too soon*. Reading, Mass.: Addison-Wesley.

Eurobarometer (1993). *Europeans and the family. Results of an opinion survey*. Brussels: Commision of the EC.

European Values Group (Eds.). (1992). *The European Values Study 1981-1990*. London: The Gordon Cook Foundation.

Gerhardt, U., S. Hradil, D. Lucke & B. Nauck (Hrsg.) (1995). *Familie der Zukunft. Lebensbedingungen und Lebensformen*. Opladen: Leske + Budrich.

Helve, H. & J. Bynner (Eds.) (1996). *Youth and life management*. Yliopistopaino: Helsinki University Press.

Henkes, K., L. Meijer & J. Siegens (1993). The labour supply of married and cohabiting women in The Netherlands, 1981-1989. *European Journal of Population. 9*(4), 331-352.

Jugendwerk der Deutschen Shell/A. Fischer & R. Münchmeier (Hrsg.) (1997). *Jugend '97. Zukunfperspektiven, Gesellschaftliches Engagement, politische Orientierungen*. Opladen: Leske + Budrich.

Kempeneers, M. & E. Lelievre (1993). Women's work in the EC: Five career profiles. *European Journal of Population 9*(1), 77-92.

Kidder, R.M. (1994). *Shared values for a troubled world*. San Francisco: Jossey-Bass Publishers.

Lamb, M.E., K.J. Stenberg, C.-P. Hwang & A.G. Broberg (Eds.) (1992). *Child-care in context. Cross-cultural perspectives*. Hillsdale, NJ/Hove/London: Lawrence Erlbaum.

Miles, S., C. Dallas & V. Burr (1998). 'Fitting in and sticking out': Consumption, consumer meanings and the construction of young people's identities. *Journal of Youth Studies, 1*(1), 81-96.

Näsman, E. (1995). Childhood, family and new ways of life: The case of Sweden. In: L. Chisholm, P. Büchner, H.H. Krüger & M. du Bois-Reymond (Eds.). *Growing up in Europe. Contemporary horizons in childhood and youth studies*. Berlin/New York: Walter de Gruyter, p. 121-131.

Niphuis-Nell, M. (Red.) (1997). *Sociale atlas van de vrouw, deel 4: Veranderingen in de primaire leefsfeer*. Rijswijk: Sociaal en Cultureel Planbureau.

Oppenheimer, V.K. (1994). Woman's rising and the future of the family in industrial societies. *Population and Development Review, 20*(2), 293-342.

Qvortrup, J. (1995). Childhood in Europe: A new field of social research. In: L. Chisholm, P. Büchner, H.H. Krüger & M. du Bois-Reymond (Eds.). *Growing up in Europe. Contemporary horizons in childhood and youth studies*. Berlin/New York: Walter de Gruyter, p. 7-19..

Rispens, J., J.M.A. Hermanns & W.H.J. Meeus (Red.) (1996). *Opvoeden in Nederland*. Assen: van Gorcum.

Robertson, R. (1992). *Globalisation: Social theory and global culture*. London: Sage.

Röhrs, H. & V. Lenhart (Hrsg.) (1994). *Die Reformpädagogik auf den Kontinenten*. New York: Peter Lang/Europäischer Verlag der Wissenschaften.

Therborn, G. (1995). *European modernity and beyond*. London/Thousand Oaks/New Delhi: Sage.

Torrance, K. (1998). *Contemporary childhood: Parent-child relationships and child culture*. Leiden: DSWO-Press.

UNESCO-Kommission (Hrsg.) (1997). *Unser verborgener Reichtum. Unesco-Bericht zur Bildung für das 21. Jahrhundert*. Neuwied/Kriftel/Ts./Berlin: Luchterhand.

Vanandruel, M., P. Amerio, O. Stafseng & P. Tap (1996). *Young people and associations in Europe*. Strasbourg: Council of Europe Publishing.

van Praag, C.S. & M. Niphuis-Nell (Red.) (1997). *Het gezinsrapport*. Rijswijk: Sociaal en Cultureel Planbureau.

Walther, A. & B. Stauber (Eds.) (1998). *Lifelong learning in Europe*. Tübingen: Neuling Verlag.

Wilkinson, H. (1997). Kinder der Freiheit. Entsteht eine neue Ethik individueller und sozialer Verantwortung? In: U. Beck (Hrsg.). *Kinder der Freiheit*. Frankfurt/M.: Suhrkamp, p. 85-123.

Zinnecker, J. & R.K. Silbereisen (1996). *Kindheit in Deutschland. Aktueller Survey über Kinder und ihre Eltern*. Weinheim und München: Juventa.

# The family and the construction of adult identity[*]

JEAN KELLERHALS
UNIVERSITÉ DE GENÈVE, SWITZERLAND

## INTRODUCTION

How do contemporary families contribute to build the adult identity? From a sociological point of view, the question is to know how families integrate and orientate their members into larger social settings and, simultaneously, define the individual's specificity and autonomy. I shall evoke in these pages some hypotheses about this topic. They imply however, as a kind of prerequisite, the dismissal of the common allegation that the agitation consecutive to the 1965's utterly ruined the families' capacity to produce identity and meaning. Some might have seen, in the today well-known demographic *Syndrome* – fall in marriages, swift increase in divorces, decrease in birth-rate together with a progression of dual careers – the triumph of anomia: the family would have lost direction and commit its quite temporary members in a wild whirligig with no rythm or tune. Some pondering opened the way, after such a dramatic view of events, to interpretations that proved nearer to the truth. Sociologists like J.-Cl. Kaufmann, on the one hand, showed that this upheaval corresponded more to a redefining of the first adult ages – an inevitably multishaped time of socialization to others, that often ends with the ranging within rather classic roles – than to a radical break with former institutional contexts (Kaufmann, 1988). On the other hand, various surveys conducted during the 1980's suggest a still classic family scheme – concern to form a monogamous long-lasting couple, and bearing children – even if there is a refusal to identify with the traditional marriage by insisting on un-differentiated conjugal roles, and on the using of institutions by the spouses rather than their subjecting to institutional requirements (Finch

---

[*] This is the text of a Conference pronounced at the Fourth Plenary Session of the Evora Congress of the International Association of French Speaking Sociologists. A version of this text has been published in French in R. Steichen and P. Servais (Eds.) (1997). *Identification et identités dans les familles*. Academia: Bruylant. Translated by Mrs. Catherine Schaichet. I thank very much Mrs. Claudine Burton-Jeangros for her valuable help in finalizing this manuscript.

& Morgan, 1991). The changes that resulted from the 1960's certainly led to vaguer definitions of the family, insisting, on the one hand, upon the opening of the group and, on the other hand, upon the plurality of its structures and functionings.

Regarding first the opening, the growing importance of the affinity (or choice) principle for the definition of the family frontiers has often been underlined. Rather than a plain acceptance as kins – entitled to defined rights and duties – of a whole class of equal others – uncles, aunts, cousins etc... – one tends to acknowledge only such relationships – debts or claims – to those who have been emotionally 'adopted'. Reciprocally, this affinity principle admits the incorporation within the family of external elements, i.e. good friends raised to the rank of relatives through a 'godfathering' bias (Fine, 1994), or stepparents whom no biological link or legal (juridical) legitimation could establish as such (Le Gall & Martin, 1993; Théry, 1993). Theoretically, at least, there exists a porosity and a mobility of the frontiers of the family group, whose official definition is now quite difficult to establish.

Next, as far as structural plurality is concerned, some tend to hold the notion of family life cycle – founded on the existence of regular and standardized phases for each family to go through – is more and more challenged by the notion of trajectory, which tells about plural biographies made either of planified decisions or of events gone through. So much so that some – Cheal (1991) for example – see the contemporary family as a composition of 'interlocking trajectories' rather than as the everlasting identification of individuals to the future of a group, itself ruled by patterned roles and well-tried formulas.

Finally, as for interactional functionings, we can subscribe to the expression of Finch and Morgan (1991: 71): 'Treating domestic life as a process has meant that individuals are seen as active beings who construct their own relationship out of those constraints and opportunities and who may therefore come up with a variety of different forms. The concept of developing different "strategies" has been used widely to express this.'

These ideas of opening, trajectory, 'made up' relationships, have led a few sociologists – like Scanzoni (1987) – to propose giving up the term 'family' – historically too heavily connoted, for him, to build a well-founded sociological term – to take up the word 'primary relationships'. Without going so far, these notions suggest to change the direction of the objection we have just raised, at least as an hypothesis: instead of claiming that – for lack of ready-made patterns and ways – the family can no longer make sense, isn't it possible to hold that, quite contrarily, as it precisely no longer stands there 'ready to go', the family henceforth is led to constitute, or create some meaning? How does the family accomplish it all, and with what convulsions and contradictions? This is what will be considered now.

## BUILDING AN IDENTITY

Sociologists like F. de Singly (1996) – who do not deny the importance of the 'traditional' functions of the family (security, accumulation, socialization etc.) and refuse to roughly oppose the past to the present – see the main function of this group nowadays as a centre for the elaboration of self-identity, the key to the 'self-revelation' process. Let's be more conspicuous. Modern societies offer a quite diversified structure of opportunities to people, and multifarious potential biographies. Besides, group memberships are numerous and sectorial, often cut off from each other. This is the setting for the person to show his/her autonomy, which involves the selection of affiliation and projects and their organization into a hierarchy; and also to elaborate his/her unity. Marriage and family bonds represent the place for these various potential fates and exploded membership to find some unity, a principle of hierarchical organization, a meaningful direction. The family's part stands less as a normed, organized institution than as a domestic space for emotional/affective relationships. It generates 'such an atmosphere for the self to propitiously achieve its triple quest: the discovery of its hidden resources, unity, stability' (de Singly, 1996: 14). Resuming Taylor's argument, de Singly (1996: 15) estimates the family to have, more than previously, an identificational dimension, in other words the vocation to give birth to a 'certain way to be a human-being that is my own, not imitating that of others'. The other becomes the ego's Pygmalion. Here is another development of the nomical construction idea, dear to Berger and Kellner (1988), and in fact already present in the compagnonship notion of Burgess (Burgess, Locke & Thomes, 1963). Expressed in another way – and these are my own words – there exist at least, from the sociological point of view, three privileged modes for constructing an identity (or else three dialectical phases in this construction): one builds identity from Membership (I am what my Blood, my Homeland or my Faith describes/defines), another comes from the Role (I am what my job, my children, my power or my properties tells about me), and the third builds identity from the affective Relation/ Communication; the latter is the very dialectical moment that appears so crucial nowadays. For de Singly, the contemporary society requires from the person an individualism defined as a quest for authenticity or self reference, that is built, for its main constituents, in the relationship with a privileged other. Thanks to the relational work accomplished with one or several close 'friends' – were they relatives or not – the constituents of the identity will 'clot together'. This is a viewpoint close to Luhmann's (1986), who estimated that the progressive systemic differentiation had generated a great variety of specialized structures. As people take part to a great number of them and are no longer pledged to any of them, the results are very specific combinations of experiments that cannot be compared with those of others, and that the person expresses through an acute sense of uniqueness and autonomy. A steady love affair testifies to this unicity, this authenticity, and in a way to this existence (or existential unity); be it for the lovers to mutually confirm their identity, or to build unity within their very relationship. Cheal (1988: 133) complements this perspective on the level of social values. The increasing indetermination of cultural codes within conditions of social pluralism, the potential confrontation between the rights to individual autonomy and the requirements of social solidarity implies that family relationships form a 'moral individualism', that is to say a place where individual autonomy and social responsibility are made concordant through highly sentimentalized ties, themselves creating intersubjective consensuses upon the biographies of the persons involved.

This point of view does not mean that the institution or social statuses are enemies of the identity, or of the intimate self, as de Singly puts it, but it endows them with a specific function of the unification of the self.

'With regard to concubinage', writes de Singly (1996: 227), 'contemporaneous marriage would appear as the indicator of another form of personal commitment, linked to the transformation of identities. It would play a more significant role on the pole "unity" than on the pole "stability" (...).' Close to this perspective, we find J.-Cl. Kaufmann's (1993) idea of subjectivation – when he refers to an actor building his identity/project within the play of constraints and institutional opportunities – a notion that fortunately stands distinctly from certain ambiguous aspects of the concept of 'privatisation', as commonly used in the 80s, which quite bluntly opposes the development of the individual project to the former yoke-like institutions.

## AMBIVALENCES, TENSIONS AND PLURALITY

Characterizing with these words the main function of family and married life in the building of personal identity seems fundamental to me. We must however not fail to perceive first the important ambiguities and tensions of this plan, and secondly the plurality of its mode of expression.

a) A first ambivalence relates to the status of individualism within the family project. Several authors showed rather pessimistic views in this respect. Bellah, for example, stigmatizes negatively the evolution of the family sensibility which, after having been marked by the advent of individualism into the free choice, made in the name of love, of a spouse, hardens nowadays in the form of the research of a personal 'growth', or of a personal opening out, to which the family is only instrumental (Bellah, Madsen, Sullivan, Swidler & Tipton, 1985: 90). This project seems to him a never ending quest that will not necessarily stabilize in strong emotional relationships, or in steady commitments, the latters being only allowed as temporary stages within a research for the itinerary of the self, which may last for a whole life. The danger is that long-lasting relations that only stem from personal preferences, in fact hardly last for a long time, which results in the weakening of engagements, a process that contradicts social solidarity and successful identital construction (Bellah et al., 1985: 275). Popenoe (1988: 329) also assigns to the idea of progress (conceived as an individualist will of self realization) a kind of deterioration of the family, put into evidence in and through the desinstitutionalization of the family bond (lessening of economical interdependence and of the control of the group upon its members), and in a lesser efficiency of the family as far as socialization is concerned, and in the unsteadiness of the family bond, and last in a lesser valorization of the family as opposed to the individual. If this tendency does not reverse, writes Popenoe, the function of the family as a mediator between the individual and the society will be compromised. These pessimistic views offer both a common point and a major difference with the parsonian type of functionalism. To Bellah, as to Parsons, the differentiation process is the key factor that allowed the opening out of individualism. But, on the whole, Parsons considered the disintegrative forces of differentiation to be (coud be) balanced by new forces of integration. It is this view that Bellah and a few others do not share; they doubt a 'wide, open, honest communication' to be able to win over the disintegrating effects of individualism. F. de Singly (1996: 216, 219), if I don't err, is more optimistic. He holds the contemporaneous quest for authenticity and self reference is not so much that of a subject who values independence than of one who values/actualizes autonomy. Among the modes of construction of the personal identity is the meaningful sense of family responsibilities. I think it is quite possible to admit such a view, even if the social conditions which favour disintegration vs. integration are not clear yet, for both the pessimistic and the optimistic theories.

b) A second ambiguity relates to the internal contradictions of the family relational project, that Finch and Morgan (1991: 66), talking about the families in the 80s, summarize under the term of family 'neo-realism'. According to

Morgan, the 80s – unlike the 60-70s that were focused on the 'conjugal conversation' – marked the sudden awareness of three types of tensions within the family relational plan:

– The first is an obvious gap between, on the one hand, the representations and ideals that insist on equality, on the altruistic negotiation of power, and on the other hand the persisting of quite unegalitarian practices, were it in matters of domestic activities or of socialization roles. The great change of the 80s, according to Finch, is the public valorization of fatherhood rather than the actual rising importance of the 'new age fathers'. And a great number of analysts link this apparent steadiness of family behaviours with the persisting of socio-professional disparities between the genders, that affect the management of domestic power all the more so since the latter has lost all legitimating discourse (Dandurand, 1991).

– The second is a tension that opposes the often fusional ideals, of conjugal happiness to the rather individualistic ideas of the person (for whom the clear establishing of his or her rights and autonomy seems a sign of psychic maturity and an evidence of relational success) (Mansfield & Collard, 1988: 180). The setting up of the 'good distance', an essential element to the cohesion of the group (Olson et al., 1983), often appears as conflictual and fragile. One can likewise consider, together with Ashkam (1984), that the concern for security/stability, as much in social life than in relations, often conflicts with the aspiration for identity, perceived as the expression of some authenticity/autonomy which valorizes innovation and change.

– Finally, the gap that exists between the social representations of the family bond and the families everydaylife has often been brought to the fore. We must refer here to the 'hyperreality' mentioned by Baudrillard talking about 'generating models of reality, without origin nor reality, through medias'. Denzin (1987) writes that a large amount of mediatic messages present 'family myths' that, being very far from the intimates' concrete life, are both unable to constitute a guidance for daily activities, and nevertheless disqualify the everyday experience of the family members. Therefore, the 'sense of the family' is to be put together within this kind of fake conscience, and in spite of it. The very same time that sees the family getting free from certain legal yokes, also sees the family permeated with so-called knowledges (aspects of hyperreality as seen by Baudrillard) that are experimented either on the escapist form (one finds shelter in it) or on the disqualification form (one compares one's own 'poor' life to them). 'The post-modern interpretations of romance narratives see them as constituting the "subjectivity" of the individual, or, in other words, as creating the individual sense of self (...). The self, or subject, produced by this complex of experiences is seen not as a coherent, stable essence, but as a fragmented participant in various discourses' (Cheal, 1988: 148). Morin's words could also be repeated, and we could mention 'flickering' identities.

From such a viewpoint, the building of identities through family relations can certainly be marked, to some extent, by dependence, violence, or even total alienation. In other words, the construction of the identity is not always, and by far, a positive, coherent or opening up process. Part of the contemporaneous realism, according to Finch, consists for many women and children, in acknowledging the family to be the most violent group they could belong to. And rather than to account for family violence by individual pathologies, it seems more appropriate to see it as an expression of the social structuring of gender relations (Finch & Morgan, 1991: 70). I think Morgan (1991) is right to insist on the importance of analyzing family life in terms of internal contradictions: dialectics of love and hate, of individuation and fusion, of egalitarism and power; the whole of it is necessary to understand the strategies of construction of meaning and to analyze family 'unseemly' behaviours (violence, breaking off, silence, humdrum, lassitude) as a result of contemporaneous life that is as normal as success is in the assertion of a positive identity. In this respect, the relative de-codification of married or family relations must not only be analyzed as a possibility to discover an authentic self that is respectful of others, but also – as underlined by DuQuai talking about newly established couples – as favouring, in many cases, the transition to relationships that are physically and symbolically violent precisely because there exist only few elaborated codes of exchange (see also, talking of 'good distance', or violence and gender connections, the work of B. Bawin) (Bawin-Legros et al., 1994).

c) Let's turn to the plurality of the construction forms of identity. Seeing in contemporary families an essential work of constructing identities does not mean a one and only approach. I hold it that Commaille (1996) is right in criticizing the reading of one sole kind of family model in modernity. The idea of Young and Wilmott (1974) that tells about a universal diffusing of the 'symmetrical family' is still out of tune. A general survey of the literature allows in fact to draw, as a temporary hypothesis, four ways of accomplishing the work in question:

– The Network form encompasses a widely open definition of the family group. We have here the apex of the affinity (or choice) principle, which selects both within and without the kinship borders. Here, family is made of interlocking trajectories, linked together by the individual. The whole can consist of relations from various origins, i.e. those resulting from the preservation of post-divorce parental relations (logic of complementarity in the sense of Le Gall) (Le Gall & Martin, 1993; Théry, 1993). There is not necessarily any tight connection between the various links, and as a general rule, the organization of the network itself is not very important. Moreover, interactions are not structured according to very differentiated and rigid functions. The network rather stands as a wealth of resources that are sporadically activated by such or such person, depending on his/her needs. The main values for organizing behaviours are autonomy and the stress laid upon dialogue/negotiation. Identity is constructed mainly through communication/confrontation. There is no strong ritualization, which may even be depreciated for more spontaneous expressions.

– On the contrary, the Shelter figure defines a group that is tightly structured around legal biological relationships that clearly mark permanent borders. If need be, the principle of affinity will act, but only within these borders. The group organization is settled upon rather clearly differentiated and steady roles, that constitute social identities. The dominant values are loyalty, solidarity; a closely knit family. The main factor for the construction of the identity is the membership principle (identification to the group), rather than the principle of communication/confrontation. The social environment is not a very significant factor for the constitution of identities. When family reconstitution intervenes, the principle of substitution is more frequent than the principle of complementarity between old and new family relations. A stress is laid upon routines and domestic ritual.

– The 'Community' way suggests, as seen previously, a strong alliance of steady relationships set in a group form rather than in a network form. But in this case, there is a strong connection with the surrounding social sphere. The family bond feeds upon wider belongings (church, political party, social neighbourhood etc.) and the personal identity stems from them. The construction of the identity is not essentially built through the identification to a role or through a communication/confrontation, but rather through the belonging to diverse interlocking groups. Solutions of continuity between the individual and the community are scarce. The communitarian memberships that wrap the individual into successive layers are discussed and expressed within the family. Donati's organic familialism model, that bears a stress upon citizenship, accounts rather well for this procedure of identity construction. The main values are those of responsibility and property (in a patrimonial sense that expresses the identity and allows exchanges with the outside). There is a strong ritualization. The group does not act episodically, but in a rather constant and marked way.

– Last, the 'Providence' procedure does not crystallize any network structuration or a strong group. In a serialized, atomized way, it rather gathers quite bondless persons, who are as ill at ease in communicating as in roles, and who mainly draw their unity/cohesion and their identity from their relations with institutions of social help. The group (if this term is convenient) is rather uncommunicative, with loosely connected and unfrequently activated bonds. Coalitions of limited scope (2-3 persons) and deeply fusional, border on much unsteadier bonds, or on short-lived links punctuated by exchanges with institutions of social help. Fatalism is common. There is, so to speak, a hollow identity, built within the categories established by the services of social help. The way Denzin (1987: 33) describes an important and widespread 'post-modern' American family illustrates the procedure: 'It's a single parent family, headed by a teenage mother, who may be drawn to drug abuse and alcoholism, she and her children live in a household that is prone to be violent'.

d) These various illustrations of the individuation/integration construction are coupled with a variety of subjective managements of time. One might suppose the necessary process of family construction always includes broad concern for a long-term planification or an irrepressible will to bring the course of events under control. However, qualitative studies on the first years of married life show patterns that do not necessarily follow this way. Clark (1991) proposes four of them, but I will mention only three. (1) Among others, he mentions 'drifting', to indicate that many of the couples that have been studied do not see the need/possibility to organize the future. Deadlines, delays, changing course in matter of engagements, or children, or marriage etc. are numerous and hazardous. The professional ambition is no more precise than the family project. The same happens with the management of leisure time, a compound of occasional interests rather than an organized time-planning. The same is true with regard to money. But be careful: 'Drifting should not be regarded as a residual category nor as a negative one; it might rather be seen as a purposive strategy whereby the marital world is constituted in such a way that both emotional and material expectations are limited, kept in check, and shielded against the possibilities of disappointment' (Clark, 1991: 149). (2) The couples characterized by a logic of 'establishing' are wholly different. In their case, the practical organization of the Home seems a focal point of the identity construction, notably through purchases such as furnitures, or lodgings. A long period devoted to saving or to carefully settled plans precedes marriage. No child before financial and professional circumstances allow it safely. The assistance of kins is requested to help with the construction of the family. The spouses reflect things and plans:

'almost a family tradition in the making' (Clark, 1991: 156). (3) The third pattern, 'struggling', shows couples struggling with the hardships of life. The child was born too early, by accident. Unemployment lurks around. Former unextinguished passions haunt the current relationship. Neighbouring families meddle in the couple's private life. It is impossible to plan anything. There are fruitless endeavours at steadying oneself. When there is no way to overcome difficulties, one may get entangled in thoughtless plans or rash financial commitments (debts). 'Violence' is looming ahead.

e) These various individuation/integration pathways depend upon the composition of the social and economic capital of the family members. J.-Cl. Kaufmann shows with relevance how the identification through roles (or identification to a model) is more frequent when social power is weak, whereas the identity construction through negotiation/differentiation is more marked in families with significant social assets. A similar view is held by Commaille (1996: 177-178), who doubts impoverished families to desire/have the possibility to use the 'contractual model' as well-off families do. Our own studies about types of family functioning go along the same lines (Kellerhals, Troutot & Lazega, 1992). This does not imply the general acceptance of the Resources Theory, which assumes that any disparity in resources is to be paid with transfers of power or some forced accomodating attitude. On the contrary, we had the opportunity to show that through their very 'conversation' husband and wife bring various senses to gender discrepancies (Kellerhals, Coenen-Huther & Modak, 1988). Some interpret them in comparative terms, judging their fate not for itself, but in the light of their neighbours' experience; others legitimate disparities into ultimate goals or into superior values (Child's Welfare, social Establishment of the family, Solidarity and intergenerational debts etc..) which makes those seem either logical or unimportant. Finally, others perceive gender discrepancies as the expression of openly assumed gifts and counter-gifts. Thus the couple is giving a meaning to discrepancies, and the theoretical analyses that do not take this point into consideration are unconvincing. More precisely, and in order to constitute their own and collective identity, to work out their rules (or terms) of exchange, both couples and families blend, in varying proportions, three 'languages' borrowed from the social environment: a) the language of the economic 'rationality' that compares costs and benefits, maximizes investments, makes assets profitable; b) the language of the 'institution', where meaning comes from the identification to patterns or pre-existing cultural codes (appealing to the above mentioned superior values); c) the language of the 'relationship', that uses empathy, attention towards others and oneself, and spontaneity of exchanges as the main constituent of the identity construction process. These are like the weberian forms – charismatic, traditional and rational – of legitimation. Lesthaege on the same line examines the different schedules and trajectories of European marriages, and shows that economic perspectives such as Becker's or Easterlin's are not sufficient to explain plurality. Cultural factors, such as religion or political affiliations, play a significant role in the structuring of the family group. However, it must be acknowledged that the rules of this blending are not well enough known yet.

Besides, the present debate cannot be confined to the sole question of the actors, without taking into account macro factors. Interesting studies show how a family construction of the identity organized around such values as autonomy, negotiations, or empathy rather than conformity to some model, is significantly more widespread when the national social policy emphasizes the well-fare state (The Netherlands) than when it is more neutral (Germany) or clearly liberal (United States) (van den Elzen, 1995).

IDENTITY AND MEMBERSHIP

The building of both meaning and identity within the family obviously goes through the affiliation process, which includes two complementary aspects: (1) the integration of the person, through the construction of a family memory, within a family lineage (time orientation) and (2) the establishing, through current groups of relatives and other group memberships, of a continuity between the individual and the community.

Recent research such as by J. Coenen-Huther (1994) provides good landmarks for studying self-construction through family history.

Let us first remark that the use of memory as an identity and project device seems stronger during periods – such as ours? – of uncertainty and anxiety. But the attitude varies significantly from one troubled period to the other. For Hareven and Taylor, the 1860-70s 'memorial mobilisations'- reactions to the spreading of the Industrial Revolution – aim at 'regenerating moral standards by revitalizing family traditions'. This evocation of the past aims at educating new generations by confronting them with '... ancestors of such surpassing merit that they will comparatively discover their own inadequacies, and acknowledge how far they now are from former virtues and values' (Taylor, 1982: 29). Contrarily, the interest for the past that spread during the 30s crisis also stems from a criticism of the present, but it introduces and settles only a nostalgia for a past decidedly beyond reach, that stands as a remedy for the current hard times. There is no thinking of the past as a model for the future.

Finally, progress seen as a disillusion will mark the third phase of the revival in the interest for the family past during the 60s and 70s. According to Hareven, this return to the family past still takes on another meaning. It aims less at gloryfying traditional American culture than at looking for one's individual roots. Everyone tries to define one's own identity, one's difference in a way, rather than one's belonging to the 'melting pot' (Coenen-Huther, 1994: 80).

From these perspectives emerge the three 'operations' of the family memory in matters of personal identity: re-linking, opposing, differentiating. How do these operations come to the fore in the 'memory construction' nowadays? J. Coenen-Huther's research distinguishes relational, statutarian, 'socio-economic' and anomial memories:- Relational memories describe the clan as an expressive group whose cement is Love. The in-group is based on blood-ties. The group is not inscribed in any wider context, and is only narrowly open. The dominant self-perception is characterized by 'existing', rather than 'doing', or 'becoming': everyone is coura-geous, joyful, loving etc.. The evoked personalities embody family virtues; they are models of excellence to be imitated. Finally, there is only little historicity, and the short-term focus on personally known figures obstructs the horizon.

– Statutory memories define the clan mainly as a group whose dominant char-acteristic is instrumental. Its cement is the economic and social patrimony. The values are social success, fortitude, family pride. Links with the social environ-ment are strong: the family partakes of history and contributes to the making of it. A widespread mode of self-perception is 'doing': one tells about one's own realizations, and the star figures of the family saga are public personalities, the founders of 'enterprises' and lineages. Here the question is of a long-termed his-toricity, with a stress set upon continuity.

– Socio-economic memories consider the family is torn apart by misery and fighting for life. The link with the social environment is subjected to fate ('mis-fortune') which eradicates any personal will. The dominant mode of self-per-ception is 'submission' (to the will of others or to the whims of history). There are few family values to identify with or to cling to. Such a tragic life is never-theless experienced through some identification – that can be passive – with the members of the social class one belongs to. The star personalities of the family story are scarce and not very typical; they are hardly models – and may be counter-models. These memories are marked by a strong historicity, but the past is perceived as being over: 'progress' will make it all better.

– Finally, anomic memories do not really leave room for the family's own and proper existence. It rather seems a reunion of ill-assorted individuals, whom no clear common value can bring together or motivate. There is only an undefined and discoloured tie with the social environment. Such a tie does not organize the family, nor does the family have any impact on it.

From this interesting analysis I will draw two important facts. Firstly, most memories proved to be of the relational kind. These describe the internal functioning of the family, together with the attendant kind of feelings, rather than the connection with both the social environment and historical events. For over half of the families, family and historical time are heterogeneous. Coenen-Huther (1994: 247) writes: 'The privatisation of the memory meets that of the family itself: the latter being defined as a space of liberty that is relatively isolated from the outside world'. Furthermore, the predominance of relational stories is higher in families who stand at the bottom of the social ladder, while statutory memories are dominant at the top. We are then led to draw a two-faced conclusion about the role of family memory. On the one hand, and in most of the observed cases, memory construction does contribute to the construction of the identity. But on the other hand, memory construction does not explicitly link the individual to society, nor does it assign the individual any particular task within society.

Let us turn now to the relation between the individual and society through ties existing with the current kinship. Several studies showed that – contrarily to the atomization hypothesis that supposes nuclear families are withdrawn into themselves – a great many ties, both expressive and instrumental, come and go between kinship and family. [1] In many respects, modern families function with the help of kinship. But is this enough to consider that kinship ties constitute a bridge between the individual and its community? According to the surveys led in Switzerland as an example of tertiarized society, the building/constitution of kinship ties obeys the following characteristics (Coenen-Huther, Kellerhals & von Allmen, 1994):

– They are often restricted to 3-5 persons who form some kind of shield for the spouses. As de Tocqueville puts it: 'the family builds its own little society, leaving the larger society to itself'. Which means that a large part of the blood ties potential is left unactivated. The affinity (or choice) principle rules most of the activated blood ties: one sees, or helps, the loved ones, leaving a smallest share to the status principle (that recognizes rights and duties due to all members of a particular kind of blood ties). The selection, however, remains written within the limits of blood frontiers and friends, likewise, do not take over kinship, at least in terms of intensity. With the exception of the emotional sphere, their support or their potential of help (according to the members of the family) is widely inferior to the (potential) contribution of kins (in financial matters, among others, or for a long lasting support).

– The vertical axis of kinship is much more activated than the horizontal. One's normative references and solidarities are more firmly established along generations than among siblings or first cousins.

– As regards its constituting values, the blood tie does not work like a counter-model of society; it is not marked by the sole concern for gratuitousness and utter self-denial. In fact, the blood tie is stretched between a norm of autonomy – rather individualistic: a good family is to manage on its own, and to answer for its members' destiny – and a norm of solidarity – relatives have to help one another. The meeting of these two principles results in the fact that if, when necessary, relatives accept to cut into superfluity to help each other, they are nevertheless quite reluctant to accept either doing without the basic necessities in order to help others or the intruding of some other person into one's own private life. Besides, it is interesting to see how, when families are called to give very substantial help, it often brings conflicts rather than cohesion. But the opposite is true when requested support is only light and temporary.

– The potential resources of the relatives' network is often inversely proportional to the family needs: the lower socio-economic strata have little to offer to their kinship, even though such a support would be quite welcome. In this respect, one can talk of an anti-redistributive effect of family services (Pitrou, 1992; Déchaux, 1990; Martin, 1992a, 1992b).

In all these aspects, if kinship is fundamental in family functioning, it does not bring that much citizenship. As suggested by J.-Cl. Kaufmann (1988), it may even be that family solidarity takes place to the detriment of more open social relationships; in other words there may also be some kind of antinomy between family solidarity and social solidarity. Not to mention that mutual aid in blood ties is in fact often brought by women only.

Finally, this question of citizenship can also be examined through family socialization. How much do contemporary families seek to transmit an 'active' citizenship? Research carried on this topic brings the conviction that parents rather aim at forming an 'efficient cosmopolitean' than a traditional citizen (Kellerhals & Montandon, 1991). They want an independent and responsible person, endowed with an efficient technical equipment (job, language...) and who could 'function' in Asia as well as in the US or in Europe. Compared to this founding ambition, the parents efforts to teach their children attachment to the groups that form the community (country or region, churches, political parties or trade-unions, etc.) are little. A great majority of these parents say they did not start anything concrete in this respect, and do not particularly value this kind of bonds. One even gets a feeling that such bonds would be a constraint, and thus hinder a good personal functioning. It seems better to stand aloof from such constraints: loyalties that get cumbersome when put into practice, but also possible signs that the person may not be independent enough, nor critical-minded, nor objective, or else that he/she is the victim of some sect feeling, or of parochialism.

So does the identity egged on by the parents seem to be constructed – if not against – at least at the border of group memberships rather than by identifying to them. Of course it can be supposed that getting free from 'local' bonds brings about superior values: world-wide citizenship, generalized solidarities etc... But no clues in the parents educative attitude allow us to say such an opening is really put into practice.

In short, if the family actually offers space for the constitution of meaning/identity, there is no certainty so far about wether the family is a good mediator of the relationship between the individual and the community. Besides, this is reflected in the legislative developments commented by J. Commaille (1996): 'If, rather than 'familism', individualisation is to inspire nowadays the laws of family policies, don't we then have the very proof of the henceforth triumphal achievement of a republican doctrine, whose fundamental symbolics is to institute the facing each other between the State and the individual. The former being established as the source of all powers, and the latter being the ultimate grounds for existence of all social bonds.'

CONCLUSION

Any family life is stretched between two poles that can be qualified, quoting Scanzoni's terms, between morphostatism and morphogenetism.

The first establishes distinct internal landmarks (some family tradition, clearly defined roles, a 'family house' etc.) in order to guide and motivate behaviours. Memberships are concentrically organized around some emblematic figure (possibly a collective one). Values of permanence (loyalties, reproduction of the identical) put identities together.

The second founds the tie on 'doing' (activated exchanges) rather than on 'being'. The mobilization of both resources and potentials overrides the matter of frontiers and statuses. Memberships are multifocal and little organized into a hierarchy. Landmarks are mainly external: structures of opportunity, modes, etc. The central value is adaptation: make transitions successful.

Two elements are now clear to me concerning the subject: a) the contemporaneous social context puts a special emphasis on the morphogenetic pole; but b) families cannot possibly be efficient without some morphostatism. The problem is that families often cannot easily turn to former 'traces', and therefore have to forge new ones. Are they always successful in this task? It is my opinion that in three extreme cases, in fact not so seldom, they hardly manage it:

1) When utter un-affiliation, that suppresses all languages, erases all horizons, changes the home into a cacophonous Babel, and ends up in madness;

2) When utter precarity, by suppressing all connection between resources and projects, opens into violence;

3) And when utter fanaticism – were it religious or political – imposes its own dogmas to the relation, and simultaneously prevents the wonderful discovery of the other.

NOTES

[1]   For a synthesis see C. Attias-Donfut (Ed.) (1995). *Les solidarités entre générations.* Paris: Nathan, Recherches.

REFERENCES

Askham, J. (1984). *Identity and stability in marriage.* Cambridge: Cambridge University Press.

Attias-Donfut, C. (Ed.) (1995). *Les solidarités entre générations.* Paris: Nathan, Essais et Recherches.

Bawin-Legros, B. (1996). *Sociologie de la famille.* Bruxelles: De Boeck Université.

Bawin-Legros, B. & A. Gauthier (1994). Relations intergénérationnelles: Vers une typologie des grands-parents. In: P. Pestieau (Ed.). *Héritage et transfert entre générations.* Bruxelles: De Boeck Université, p.129-143.

Bellah, R., R. Madsen, W. Sullivan, A. Swidler & S. Tipton (1985). *Habits of the heart.* Berkeley, CA: University of California Press.

Berger, P. & H. Kellner (1988). Le mariage et la construction de la réalité. *Dialogue*, n° 102. Paris (1ère ed. 1960).

Burgess, E.W., H.Y. Locke & M.M. Thomes (1963). *The family from institution to companionship.* New York: American Book Company.

Cheal, D. (1988). *The gift economy.* London/New York: Routledge.

Cheal, D. (1991). *Family and the state of theory.* New York/London: Harvester Wheatsheaf.

Clark, D. (1991). Constituting the marital world. In: D. Clark (Ed.). *Marriage, domestic life and social change.* London/New York: Routledge, p. 139-166.

Coenen-Huther, J. (1994). *La mémoire familiale.* Paris: L'Harmattan.

Coenen-Huther, J., J. Kellerhals & M. von Allmen (1994). *Les réseaux de solidarité dans la famille.* Lausanne: Ed. Réalités sociales.

Commaille, J. (1996). *Misères de la famille, question d'Etat.* Paris: Presses de Sciences Po.

Dandurand, R. (1991). *Le mariage en question*. Québec: IQRC.

de Singly, F. (1996). Le soi, le couple et la famille. Paris: Essais et Recherches, Nathan.

Déchaux, J.H. (1990). Les échanges économiques au sein de la parentèle. *Sociologie du Travail*, (1), 77-94.

Denzin, N. (1987). Postmodern children. *Society*, 24.

Finch, J. & D. Morgan (1991). Marriage in the 80's: A new sense of realism? In: D. Clark (Ed.). *Marriage, domestic life and social change*. London/New York: Routledge, p. 55-82.

Fine, A. (1994). *Parrains, marraines*. Paris: Fayard.

Kaufmann, J.-Cl. (1988). *La chaleur du foyer. Analyse du repli domestique*. Paris: Méridiens, Klinsieck.

Kaufmann, J.-Cl. (1993). *Sociologie du couple*. Paris: Que Sais-je, PUF.

Kellerhals, J., J. Coenen-Huther & M. Modak (1988). Figures de l'équité. Paris: Presses Universitaires de France, coll. Le Sociologue.

Kellerhals, J., M. Modak & D. Perrenoud (1997*). Le sentiment de justice dans les relations sociales*. Paris: PUF, Que Sais-je?

Kellerhals, J. & Cl. Montandon (1991). *Les stratégies éducatives des familles*. Neuchâtel/ Paris: Delachaux/Niestlé.

Kellerhals, J., P.-Y. Troutot & E. Lazega (1992). *Microsociologie de la famille*. Paris: PUF, coll. Que sais-je?

Le Gall, D. (1993) *Formes de régulation conjugale et familiale à la suite d'unions fécondes. Habilitation à la direction de recherches*. Paris: Université de Paris V-Sorbonne.

Le Gall, D. (1994). *Des recompositions du familial à la suite d'unions fécondes défaites. Situations d'incertitudes et recomposition des identités*. Caen: Travaux et Documents de la Maison des Sciences humaines de l'Université de Caen.

Le Gall, D., C. Martin (1993). Transitions familiales, logiques de recompositions et modes de régulation conjugale. In: M.T. Meulders-Klein & I. Théry (sous la direction de). *Les recompositions familiales aujourd'hui*. Paris: Nathan.

Luhmann, N. (1986). *Love as passion*. Cambridge: Polity Press.

Mansfield, P. & J. Collard (1988). *The beginning of the rest of your life? A portrait of the newly-wed marriage*. London: MacMillan.

Martin, Cl. (1992a). *Transitions familiales*. Thèse pour le doctorat de sociologie, Paris: Université de Paris-VIII.

Martin Cl. (1992b). Support et affection: logiques d'échange et solidarités familiales après la désunion. *Revue internationale d'action communautaire*, (27), 67.

Morgan, D. (1991). Ideologies of marriage and family life. In: D. Clark (Ed.). *Marriage, domestic life and social change*. London: Routledge, p.114-138.

Olson, D. et al. (1983). *Families: what make them work?* Beverly Hills: Sage.

Pitrou, A. (1992). *Vivre sans famille? Les solidarités familiales dans le monde d'aujourd'hui*. Toulouse: Privat.

Popenoe, D. (1988). *Disturbing the nest*. New York: Adline de Gruyter.

Scanzoni, J. (1987). Families in the 1980s: Time to refocus our thinking. *Journal of Family Issues*, (8).

Taylor, Ch. (1982). Summoning the wandering tribes: Genealogy and family reunions in American history. *Journal of Social History, 16*, 21-38.

Théry, I. (1993). *Le démariage*. Paris: Odile Jacob.
van den Elzen, A.(1995). *Family values and welfare state*. Paper presented at the second ESA Conference, Budapest, September 1995.
Young M. & P. Willmott (1974). *The symmetrical family*. New York: Pantheon.

# Caregiving within families

GABRIEL KIELY
UNIVERSITY COLLEGE OF DUBLIN, IRELAND

One of the key functions performed by families both on behalf of individual members and society is that of caregiving. This caregiving occurs primarily, though not exclusively across generations and consists of care by parents for children, the care by adult partners for each other, the care of dependent parents by their children, the care of other dependent relatives by family members and the care of older dependent siblings for each other. This chapter will address some of the issues involved for families as providers of care both for children and dependent older relatives including partners and parents and some of the family policy measures needed to support this caring function.

## DEFINITION OF CAREGIVING

Care provided by family members for each other is for the most part unpaid work. While it overlaps with housework in so far as some housework, such as, the preparation of meals, can be defined as caregiving it is a separate task. A large proportion of housework is not caregiving as for example in single person households. Caregiving is the emotional and physical care given by family members to other family members who may or may not share a common household. This care given for example by grandparents to grandchildren when their parents are at work although not living in the same household is as much caregiving as the care given by adult children to dependent relatives sharing the same household. No distinction is being made between care for children by parents, and care by other family members for family members who are not children.

As the European Commission Equal Opportunities Unit points out in its Final Report (Deven et al., 1997: 1) care is not a single and unitary concept. It includes emotional, financial, practical and physical care and it may be 'continuous or occasional, predictable or unpredictable, direct or indirect'. The focus of this paper is on the care provided by family members to dependent children and to older family members. This is not be suggest that these two types of caring are the same. There are many differences between them, such as the needs of those being cared for and the needs of the caregivers. However, both types of caregiving place a similar demand on family members and have similar policy implications.

ECONOMIC VALUE OF CARING

While most caring provided in the home for family members can be described as a 'labour of love', it should not be forgotten that it is 'labour' and for most people it is unpaid and unrecognised labour. However, like housework it can be traded i.e. someone else can be paid to provide the caring, such as, child minders and home help services. In so far as caring is tradeable it is an economic activity and can be given a monetary value. While the boundary between what is classified as non-economic activities and economic activities in the household can be difficult at times to distinguish, it is clear that much of the caring provided within the household is economically productive (Kiely, 1995a: 99).

Calculations estimate the output of private households as between 30% to 50% of Gross Domestic Product (Keppelhoff-Wiechert, 1993: 9). This consists of all household production including housework and caring. While it is difficult to separate caring from other household production it seems reasonable to assume that it constitutes a substantial portion. It in an earlier study Kiely (1995a: 102) calculated the monetary value of household work carried out by women in Irish homes at 33% of GDP. This calculation was based on the average female industrial wage and the number of hours spend on average by women (based on Labour Force Survey data) on the production of goods and services for consumption by the household within the household.

It is clear from these calculations that apart from the social value of caring provided by family members that caring also has a high monetary value even though it is unpaid work. Placing an economic value on this work simply helps to make it more visible.

EXTENT OF CARING

There are no reliable figures on the number of people providing care for other family members in the home. However, since only 10% of the population in the European Union (EU) living in private household live in one person households and 3% of people living in multi-person households are living with non-relatives it is reasonable to assume that the remaining 87% of the population live in households where there is at least one person in a caring role, (Eurostat, 1995).

In terms of care for children, 65.9% of families in the EU consist of families with children (Eurostat, 1995). The majority of children (91.4%) live in a single family nucleus. This ranges from 82.6% in Portugal to 98% in Denmark. A further 8% live in couple households consisting of more than two generations ranging from a low of 1.9% in Denmark to a high of 17.2% in Portugal. Within households the predominant living arrangement in the EU for children is a couple family household (82.7% of children) (Ditch et al., 1998: 24-25). From these figures it is evident that families continue to be major providers of care for children under the age of 16 years.

In addition to care of children families also provide care for adults. Excluding the mutual exchange of care between adult partners, as in marriage, and between siblings, the family provides care for dependent disabled and elderly family members. Walker (1993: 28) found at a European level that 38% of the population aged 60 and over said that they suffered from functional incapacity. Of the 60 to 64 year olds, 18% said that they had regular assistance with personal care or household tasks while as much as 59% of those aged 80 and over required this assistance.

While many elderly people live independent lives the risk of dependency greatly increases over the age of 80 years (Phillips, 1996: 6) resulting in greater demand for caring within families. Since 1960 the percentage of the population over 80 years has more than doubled in all member states of the EU except in Ireland, (Ditch et al., 1996: 5), reflecting the increased demand for caregiving. In addition to the number of people who are providing full-time caregiving in the home it is estimated that a third of employers in the EU are caring for an adult who is primarily an older person (Phillips, 1996: 50).

Ditch et al. (1998: 9) show that the dependency ratio of people 65 years and over to 15-64 years old has increased for every member state except Ireland in the EU since 1970, with ratios ranging from a low of 18 (Ireland) to a high of 25 (Italy). A true dependency ratio however would have to include children and the number of young adults who continue to be economically dependent on their families because of longer time spend in education and training. It would also have to take account of employment and unemployment rates of men and women and the age at which people retire. While dependency ratios do not represent the demand on caregiving within the family they do however reflect the consequences for families of changing demographic trends.

## WHO ARE THE CAREGIVERS?
Women are the primary caregivers in our society. Every time budget analysis shows that women 'end up doing most of the household chores and childrearing', (Fagnani, 1994: 14). Despite all the predictions of the rise of the 'new age man' there is little evidence to show his willingness to share these tasks with

women. The findings of a Eurobarometer (Malpas & Lambert, 1993) study show that women continue to perform most of the caring tasks associated with the care of children. The trends were similar for all member states of the European Union. The report concludes this part of the study by saying 'the mother remains in charge in all matters relating to the daily care of the child' (Malpas & Lambert, 1993: 99). In addition only 1.1% of the population in the EU live in lone father with children households compared with 8.4% of lone mothers (Eurostat, 1995).

This lack of participation by men in caregiving is further evidenced by the limited use of parental leave by fathers. In Sweden for example, while 45% of fathers take some period of parental leave they only use 10% of the total time available to families (European Commission Network on Childcare 1993: 29). Indeed, this situation has lead to concern that prolonged parental leave can become a trap for women if men and not using it, resulting with women staying at home for a longer time and thus missing opportunities in working life.

Caregiving by family members is cross-generational. It is not just care by parents for children or adult children for dependent or older relatives. It is also care by grandparents for children and by young adult children for grandparents. For example, it is estimated that 14% of women and 7% of men aged over 50 years provide free child-care across the European Union, mostly in the form of care for their grandchildren (Ditch et al., 1998: 8). Children are caregivers too as they often provide care for younger siblings.

In terms of family care for older people Walker (1993: 28) found that two thirds of care being supplied to older people came from within their families. Savage (1995: 36) while noting the absence of surveys based on representative national samples observes that most informal carers in the EU are women. These consist of adult children who represent 40% of carers and spouses who represent 32%. The majority of the adult children are daughters and to a lesser extent daughters-in-law. Phillips (1996: 5) in a study of caregiving in the workplace describes the typical employee with caregiving responsibilities for another adult as female, married, and between 40 to 50 years of age.

While men do provide some caregiving it is significantly less than women. Mostly it is provided to spouses (Savage, 1995: 36). In the case of male employees who are carers they are likely to be carrying out caregiving jointly while defining their role as managing the caregiving. They use more professional assistance than women and provide financial assistance rather than providing personal assistance (Phillips, 1996: 5). There seems to be a certain parallel between the role of men as caregivers in this context and the role of fathers in childcare.

Studies of fathers' participation in childcare show that they are involved primarily in a joint capacity with the other parent and where they do take sole responsibility this tends to be in activities such as providing pocket money and taking children on outings (see Kiely, 1995b).

## THE FEMINISATION OF CAREGIVING

As seen above, women are predominantly the caregivers in families. This situation reflects the traditional division of labour within the home with women continuing to perform an 'expressive' function while men retain an 'instrumental' role. Women are the carers, men are the providers. This situation persists in spite of apparently changing attitudes about the role of men. A Eurobarometer study in 1993 found that 87% of the respondents consider that a father should be very involved in bringing up a child (Malpas & Lambert, 1993: 89). Kiely (1995b: 148) reports a similar finding in Ireland with 80.7% of mothers in the study saying that fathers and mothers should share housework equally.

Clearly, caregiving is feminised. By that is meant that in so far as it is women who provide the care, caregiving is a woman's function. This feminising is a social construction and since men can equally provide care it is not a biological given. The problem with the feminising of caregiving is not just that it increases the number of working hours (unpaid working hours) of women and in particular for caregivers who are also working outside the home, but by extension it feminises occupations that reflect caregiving in the home. For example, 95% of those employed in the care sector are women and these jobs are poorly paid, require little in terms of qualifications or training and have little prospects of career development. In addition, the feminising of caring has been repeatedly identified as a major obstacle to equality between men and women both in the home and in professional life (see European Commission Network on Childcare, 1993).

## CAREGIVING VS EMPLOYMENT

Nora Gilligan (1994: 63) of the European Housewives Association makes the argument that the campaign for equality between men and women throughout Europe has focussed primarily on the removal of obstacles to women's participation in the workforce outside the home. She argues for a similar degree of recognition and support for those women whose main role is working in the home. The issue is about choices. That is, the freedom of both men and women to choose between caregiving and employment and to be able to realistically combine both of these roles.

Across Europe the policy trend has been towards greater reliance on community care, i.e. family care for the dependent older people and on encouraging parents of very young children to provide care for them within the home. In France, for example, there is a parental child-rearing allowance which is a non means tested tax free benefit paid to one parent either mother or father following the birth of the second or subsequent child and provided the parent is not working and is paid until the last child reached the age of 3, (Fagini & Strobel, 1998: 102). In Denmark, there is a paid child care leave of up to 52 weeks for each child up to the age of 8 years for all working parents paid at the rate of 60% of the general maximum rate of unemployment benefit (Bering-Pruzan, 1996: 18). Many member states of the EU have introduced some form of payment for carers of dependent older people (Deven et al., 1998: 7). However, apart from a limited number of initiatives the policy is not matched with the provision of resources. In relation to the care of elderly people a study by the European Foundation for the Improvement of Living and Working Conditions (Savage, 1995: 67) pointed out that: 'There is a need for a much higher level of partnership than currently exists; a realisation that if community care policies are to be anything other than a cheaper alternative to institutional care, the irreplaceable role of families must be acknowledged and their contributions fostered … at present neither elderly people nor their carers have any real degree of choice in terms of what is provided by whom'.

There is some evidence to show that there is a tension for many families in reconciling the needs of caregiving and the need for income security generated by employment. A Eurobarometer study (Kempeneers & Lelievre, 1991: 48) found that a quarter of the female respondents stated that they completely stopped working because of their family life. Family reasons included bringing up children and caring for an adult family member. The same study found that 50% of the women who were in employment expressed a desire to work part-time (p. 113) and that as the number of children increased the proportion of women in part-time employment also increased. An Irish study found that 50% of women in part-time employment indicated that family responsibilities determined their employment options and an additional 29% argued that they did not want to work full-time (Coveney et al., 1998: 3).

Another Eurobarometer study (Malpas & Lambert, 1993: 86) while it found that 92.8% of the respondents considered that having children was not an obstacle to the working life of the man, it also found that 55% considered it was an obstacle for women. A Danish study found that over 40% of parents preferred a reduction of working hours over a choice of several other options in order to reduce the daily pressure on family life (Jorgensen 1990: 99). Interestingly in the same study the least preferred option (1% of respondents) in term of potential employment was for the mother working full-time while the father stayed home to mind the children. Similarly, Norwegian parents of young children prefer the man working full-time and the woman part-time (38%) with only 4% having a preference for both parents working full-time (Deven et al., 1997: 27). The preferred option (38% of parents) was for the father working full-time and the mother part-time. Research seems to show that the parents and other family caregivers are making choices between caregiving and employment not on the basis of real options but on the basis of necessity and what is available.

SOME POLICY CONSIDERATIONS

Caregiving extends across the life cycle of the family from the care of children to the care of dependent elderly people. Measures to support families with their caregiving function should reflect this by an integrated approach. For example, the income foregone by a parent caring full-time for children in the home is no different to the income foregone in caring for an adult dependent family member. The main difference is that the need arises at a different time in the family life cycle.

Equally the difficulties of combining caregiving for children with the demands of employment are the same when the caregiving is for adult family member. Thus, policy measures that support family caregiving, such as, leave for family reasons or compensation for loss of income, should not differentiate between such measures as applied to different caring needs and different demands throughout the family life cycle.

A second policy consideration has to do with the distinction that exists between measures to support caregivers who combine caregiving with employment and full-time caregivers. This distinction is most noticeable in the area of income supports. If official policy maintains that family members are the primary caregivers and that the State should support them in carrying out this function then it should support equally families who provide this on a full-time basis as those who do not. Thus measures such as income tax deductions, parental leave and the provision of child care facilities while of enormous benefit to caregivers who are in employment are of little benefit to those who are not. This is not an argument against these measures, it is simply underlying the imbalance between the two types of caregiving.

The Commission on the Family established in Ireland to make recommendations to the Government on family policy issues in its *Final Report* (1998) set out in detail a number of options on financial support for families with the care of very young children. The options try to promote equity between full-time caregivers and those who combine caregiving with paid employment. While the Commission did not reach agreement on any of the options, the analysis of the options shows the complexity of the issues. However, perhaps more importantly the Commission did adopt what it termed a child and family centred approach with a 'focus on supporting parents with their childcare responsibilities whether their choice is to work full-time in the home or outside the home' (5.12).

A third policy consideration is that choices should be maximised for both the family and the person cared for. This applies to both the care of children and the care of elderly people. A balance, therefore between care in the family and care outside the family such as child care or institutional care needs to be maintained. A carer should not be obliged to undertake a caring role nor should a dependent family member be institutionalised because of the lack of support in the family.

A fourth and final policy consideration is that policies aimed at supporting caregiving in the family should be gender neutral where possible. Not all policies can however, be gender neutral as for example with maternity protection. The trend across Europe in recent years is to gender neutral policies, such as, the provision of parental leave and other similar provisions that are available to both parents. As seen above men continue to play only a minor role as caregivers but if they are to be enabled to participate more then the opportunities for doing so need to be in place. Equal opportunities between men and women is the driving principle behind much of the legislation as women's participation in the active labour force. This principle, if it has any real meaning must also apply to work within the home.

From a policy point of view there are two approaches to caregiving within the family as identified by the OECD (1991) report on models of childcare. The first is what the report calls a 'maximum private responsibility' model. The second, it calls a 'maximum public responsibility' model. In the first model the problem of child care, family life and labour force participation are entirely left up to the individual to solve as the problem is seen as purely a private concern. The second model defines the problem as an important state concern with the state investing heavily in underwriting the costs of childcare while having a policy of equal pay in the labour market. These two models also apply to the wide concern of caregiving including the care of children. While states across the European Union differ in their emphasis none can justify the adoption of the 'maximum private responsibility' model, with the current acceptance of equality as a basic principle of European democracy.

## CONCLUSION

Caring by families for family members is not only a highly valued service but also one of the central functions of families. Support by the State for families should, therefore, reflect the value to the community of this caring through the provision of comprehensive family support services. The reported higher incidence of stress and illness among women perhaps reflects what while they are caring for others they neglect to care for themselves.

Care for family members extends over all phases of the family-life cycle with an increased burden of caring falling heavily on women in the age group 40 to 60 years. Not only are children remaining dependent on their parents into young adulthood and parents living longer but the children are themselves becoming parents while still living with their own parents. Thus we see not just a two or three generational family unit but four generations living together as a single household.

This emerging family type, sometimes called the 'long family' has received very little attention from either family researchers or policy makers. While 91.4% of children in the EU live in households composed of a single family nucleus, 7.9% live in couples households. Across the EU almost 90% of children in couples households are living within extended families in which all household members are related (Ditch et al., 1998: 25). While there has been some focus on intergenerational solidarity the concern has been more with a need to provide family supports for an ageing society than providing supports for the expanding caring functions of the family across the family life cycle.

## REFERENCES

Bering-Pruzan, V. (1996). Denmark: Issues concerning the family in 1995. In: J. Ditch, H. Barnes & J. Bradshaw (Eds.). *Developments in national family policies 1995.* York: European Observatory on National Family Policies, p. 15-24.

Commission on the Family (1998). *Final report.* Dublin: Department Social, Community and Family Affairs (pages numbered by Parts and Sections).

Coveney, E., J. Murphy-Lawless & J. Sheridan (1998). *Women work and family responsibilities.* Dublin: Larkin Unemployment Centre, 87 p.

Deven, F., S. Inglis, P. Moss & P. Petrie (1997). *State of the art review on the reconciliation of work and family life for men and women and the quality of care services.* Final Report for the European Commission Equal Opportunities Unit. Brussels: Commission of the European Community.

Ditch, J., H. Barnes & J. Bradshaw (1996). *Developments in national family policies in 1995*. York: University of York, European Observatory on National Family Policies.

Ditch, J., H. Barnes, J. Bradshaw (1998). *Developments in national family policies in 1996*. York: University of York, European Observatory on National Family Policies.

European Commission Network on Childcare (1993). *Men as carers*. Report of an International Seminar in Ravenna, Italy, May 21-22, 1993, Ravenna 35.

Fagini, J. & P. Strobel (1998). Changes in the field of family policy in France in 1996. In: J. Ditch, H. Barnes & J. Bradshaw (Eds.). *Development in national family policies in 1996*. York: European Observatory on National Family Policies, p. 97-112.

Fagnani, J. (1994). Key-note speech. *Proceedings of the European seminar: Women and families*. Alverca 5-6 December 1994. Coface, p. 14-17.

Gilligan, N. (1994). Round table. *Proceedings of the European seminar: Women and families*. Alverca 5-6 December 1994, Coface, p. 63-65.

Jorgensen, P. (1990). The family with dependent children in Denmark. In: G. Kiely & V. Richardson (Eds.). *Family policy: European perspectives*. Dublin: Family Studies Centre, p. 89-104.

Kempeneers, M. & E. Lelievre (1991). *Employment and family within the twelve*. Eurobarometer 34. Brussels: Commission of the European Communities, p. 173.

Keppelhoff-Wiechert, H. (1993). *Report of the Committee on Women's Rights on the Assessment of Women's Unwaged Work*. European Parliament Session Document.

Kiely, G. (1995a). Paid and unpaid work in families: Ireland. In: T. Willemsen, G. Frinking & R. Vogles (Eds.). *Work and family in Europe: The role of policies*. Tilburg: Tilburg University Press, p. 99-112.

Kiely, G. (1995b). Fathers in families. In: I. Colgan-McCarthy (Ed.). *Irish family studies*. Dublin: Family Studies Centre, p. 147-158.

Malpas, N. & P. Lambert (1993). *Europeans and the family*. Eurobarometer. Brussels: Commission of the European Communities, p. 137.

Phillips, J. (1996). *Working and caring*. Dublin: European Foundation of Living and Working Conditions, 51 p.

Savage, A. (1995). *Who will care?* Dublin: European Foundation for the Improvement of Living and Working Conditions, 89 p.

Walker, A. (1993). *Age and attitudes*. Eurobarometer. Brussels: Commission of the European Communities.

# Communication between fathers and adolescents in Dutch families

ELMA KWAAITAAL-ROOSEN, TILLY HOUTMANS & JAN GERRIS
KATHOLIEKE UNIVERSITEIT NIJMEGEN, THE NETHERLANDS

## INTRODUCTION

Although children in their adolescence begin to focus more on the world outside the family, the bond with parents remains important for most children (Brown, Mounts, Lamborn & Steinberg, 1993). The relationship between parent and child changes during adolescence from a relationship based on unilateral authority and regulation to a more equal relationship (Almeida & Galambos, 1993; Youniss & Smollar, 1985). For both parents and their children, this is a time of change and development.

In this study, the relationship between adolescents and their fathers is explored. There are many differences between fathers and mothers in the way they interact with their children. This continues to be the case during adolescence. The relation between fathers and adolescents will be compared with the relation between mothers and adolescents in order to focus on the role of fathers.

In the literature differences between the relations of fathers with their children and those of mothers with their children have been found. In their interaction with their sons and daughters, fathers emphasize competition, independence and achievement (Shulman & Klein, 1993) and they also challenge their children more cognitively than mothers do (Hauser et al., 1987). According to Shulman and Klein fathers have a different interaction style from mothers. Shulman and Klein use Gilligan's classification to indicate the differences between fathers and mothers. Men accentuate separation and differentiation, whereas women accentuate connectedness and closeness. Men are more disengaged, which does not mean that they are totally uninterested or uninvolved. Furthermore, fathers spend less time with their children than mothers do (Hosley & Montemayor, 1997; Larson, 1993; Montemayor & Brownlee, 1987; Montemayor, McKenry & Julian, 1993). Fathers and mothers have different ways of spending their time with their children. Fathers prefer to spend their time together in an active way with leisure activities and recreation, for example. Mothers also spend time on leisure activities, but, in addition, they talk more, do more household chores and homework with their children (Montemayor & Brownlee, 1987; Youniss and Smollar, 1985). Steinberg (1987) found that adolescents have fewer conflicts with their fathers than with their mothers, probably because fathers tend to value and support autonomous behavior more than mothers do. Compared to mothers, fathers express more positive emotions resulting from their own competence (Shulman & Klein, 1993). In summary, there is evidence for differences between fathers and mothers in parenting of adolescents. These differences point to the complementary roles of fathers and mothers in parenting (Collins & Russell, 1991).

If we consider the role of fathers and mothers during adolescence from a developmental perspective, it seems logical to look at the separation individuation process in which fathers play a major role. Since they focus more on separation and freedom, and less on involvement, fathers are a good example and partner for adolescents, who are trying to disengage themselves from their parents both emotionally and physically. Moreover, the fact that fathers spend less time with their sons and daughters can have a positive influence on the separation individuation process. Because of their way of interacting, which is more distant than that of mothers, fathers offer their adolescent sons and daughters more opportunities to make choices or decisions and to take responsibility in the areas of school, study, work and career. They also enable adolescents to achieve autonomy and to develop an identity of their own (Shulman & Klein, 1993). Because fathers express positive emotions related to their own competence, they have a positive influence on the development of self-esteem and self-confidence of their adolescent children (Shulman & Klein, 1993). Taking the separation-individuation perspective as a theoretical framework, we conclude that fathers can make a special contribution during adolescence.

In this study we will examine the relation between fathers and adolescents. Our main question concerns the quality of communication between fathers and their adolescent sons and daughters. First, we will investigate the communication style, since so far little attention has been paid to this topic. Second, we will examine the way in which adolescents experience the communication with their fathers. To highlight the contribution made by fathers, we will contrast the results of fathers and mothers.

## METHOD

### Sample
This study is part of a longitudinal research project about parenting in Dutch families. On the basis of municipal records, a nationwide sample of Dutch fam-

ilies was composed in 1990 to conduct a study on childrearing in Dutch families with at least one child between nine and fourteen years of age. In 1995, the families that had taken part in 1990 and had agreed to participate in the second wave were invited to participate again. Of the 627 families which had agreed in 1990 to participate in this second wave, 484 (77%) actually did participate in 1995. The family members (father, mother and target child) were interviewed about problems in the family. They were also asked to complete a battery of questionnaires on childrearing behaviors, personality characteristics, family characteristics, beliefs and values regarding childrearing, education, religion, and society. To answer our research questions, we will only use data based on the questionnaires.

Sex and age of adolescents will be used as the major background variables in this study. Of the 484 families which took part in our study, 231 had a son as target child (47.7%) and 253 a daughter (52.2%). 249 of the adolescents (51.4%) were aged between 13 and 18, while the other 235 (48.6%) were aged between 18 and 22. The fathers were on average 47 years old, while the mothers were 45 years old. Since we want to compare data of fathers to data of mothers, we selected the two parent families for our analyses.

## Measures

The first questionnaire used in this study is the Parent Adolescent Communication Scale (PACS) developed on the basis of Olson et al. (1983). The original PACS assesses two aspects of communication: the degree of openness in the communication (The Open Family Communication Scale) and the extent of the problems in the communication between parent and adolescent (The Problems in Family Communication Scale). The adolescents were asked to complete the questionnaire for their fathers and mothers separately. The parents also completed this questionnaire. For each item the respondents had to indicate on a seven point Likertscale how applicable the statement for them was. After factor analysis of the data of the original PACS two new factors emerged: open communication (five items, Cronbach's alpha for adolescents about mothers: .82, for adolescents about fathers: .82, for mothers: .82 and for fathers: .77) and conflictual communication (four items, Cronbach's alpha for adolescent about mothers: .65, for adolescents about fathers: .78, for mothers: .67 and for fathers: .75). An example of an item of open communication is: 'My daughter finds it easy to discuss problems with me'. 'My father has a tendency to say things to me that would be better left unsaid' is an example of an item of the conflictual communication scale.

The second questionnaire in this study assesses the feelings of the respondent evoked by communication and is based on the work of Youniss and Smollar (1985). For each item on the list the adolescents had to indicate on a seven point Likertscale how applicable the statement for them was. After factor analysis of the data, three factors emerged: negative feelings (eight items, example of an item: 'dishonest', Cronbach's alpha for feelings towards mothers: .79, and for feelings towards fathers: .83), feelings of trust (five items, example of an item: 'secure', Cronbach's alpha for feelings towards mothers: .72, and for feelings towards fathers: .76) and feelings of cautiousness (two items, example of an item: 'thoughtful', Cronbach's alpha for feelings towards mothers: .78, and for feelings towards fathers: .76).

## RESULTS

To test differences in the relation of adolescents with their fathers and with their mothers, a number of MANOVAs were conducted. Sex of parent was the within-subjects factor and adolescent sex and age were the between-subjects factors. With respect to age the group of adolescents was divided into two subgroups: those from 13 to 18 years of age and those from 18 up to and including 22 years of age. Our main interest is in differences between fathers and mothers, but we will also investigate effects of sex and age of adolescents. These latter effects will only be reported if they turn out to be significant.

### Communication style

To investigate the differences in communication style of adolescents with their fathers and mothers respectively, we conducted MANOVAs on the two subscales of our version of the PACS. Tables 1 and 3 report the mean scores on the two subscales of the PACS as indicated by fathers and mothers for the four groups of adolescents separately. In Tables 2 and 4 the mean scores are given as reported by the adolescents on the same scales.

The subscale open communication (parental version) yields the following results. There is a significant main effect for sex of the parent: ($F(1,334) = 37.26$; $p < 0.001$): mothers reported to communicate more openly with their children than fathers do. Furthermore, there is a significant interaction between sex of the parent and sex of the adolescent ($F(1,334) = 12.04$; $p < 0.005$): while mothers communicated more openly with their daughters than with their sons, fathers reported the same score for daughters and for sons. There is also a significant main effect of sex of the adolescent ($F(1,334) = 12.68$; $p < 0.001$): parents communicated with their daughters in a more open manner than with their sons. Moreover, we find a significant main effect of age of adolescents ($F(1,334) = 4.90$; $p < 0.05$): parents reported a more open communication style with the older adolescents.

Table 1. Mean scores (on a scale from 1 to 7) for open communication, as indicated by parents

|  | Boys younger than 18 | Girls younger than 18 | Boys 18 and older | Girls 18 and older |
|---|---|---|---|---|
| Open communication (father) | 4.44 | 4.51 | 4.50 | 4.71 |
| Open communication (mother) | 4.49 | 5.01 | 4.75 | 5.34 |

Subsequently, we take a look at the answers of the adolescents on the same sub-scale. There is a significant main effect for sex of parent ($F(1,378) = 46.12$; $p < 0.001$): adolescents communicated more openly with their mothers than with their fathers. Furthermore, there is a significant interaction between sex of the parent and sex of the adolescent ($F(1,378) = 5.14$; $p < 0.05$): the communication of daughters with their mothers was more open than with their fathers; the difference between fathers and mothers in openness of communication was much smaller for sons. There is also a significant main effect of age of adolescent ($F(1,378) = 5.36$; $p < 0.05$): older adolescents communicated more openly. The interaction between age and sex of adolescents is significant ($F(1,378) = 12.04$; $p < 0.005$): older girls communicated more openly than younger girls, but there was no difference in openness between the two age groups of boys.

Table 2. Mean scores (on a scale from 1 to 7) for open communication, as indicated by adolescents

|  | Boys younger than 18 | Girls younger than 18 | Boys 18 and older | Girls 18 and older |
|---|---|---|---|---|
| Open communication (father) | 4.31 | 3.89 | 4.05 | 4.51 |
| Open communication (mother) | 4.48 | 4.51 | 4.50 | 5.11 |

The following results are found for the conflictual communication subscale (parental version). There is neither a significant main effect of sex of parent nor a significant interaction between sex of parent and sex of adolescent. However, there is a significant main effect of sex of the adolescent ($F(1,332) = 6.13$; $p < 0.05$): parents reported more conflictual communication with their sons than with their daughters.

Table 3. Mean scores (on a scale from 1 to 7) for conflictual communication, as indicated by parents

|  | Boys younger than 18 | Girls younger than 18 | Boys 18 and older | Girls 18 and older |
|---|---|---|---|---|
| Conflictual communication (father) | 2.60 | 2.43 | 2.52 | 2.31 |
| Conflictual communication (mother) | 2.68 | 2.29 | 2.34 | 2.36 |

Finally, we will look at the answers of the adolescents on the same subscale. Again, there is no significant main effect for sex of the parent. But we do find a significant interaction between sex of the parent and age of the adolescent ($F(1,380) = 5.80$; $p < 0.05$): older adolescents reported less conflictual communication with their fathers than younger adolescents did, but there was no difference in the level of conflictual communication with mothers for the two age groups. In addition, there is a significant main effect of age of the adolescent ($F(1,380) = 11.17$; $p < 0.005$): younger adolescents reported more conflictual communication with their parents than older adolescents. There is also a significant interaction between age and sex of the adolescents ($F(1,380) = 4.20$; $p < 0.05$): older and younger boys indicated the same level of conflictual communication; however, younger girls indicated more conflictual communication with their parents than older girls did.

Table 4. Mean scores (on a scale from 1 to 7) for conflictual communication, as indicated by adolescents

|  | Boys younger than 18 | Girls younger than 18 | Boys 18 and older | Girls 18 and older |
|---|---|---|---|---|
| Conflictual communication (father) | 2.75 | 3.00 | 2.53 | 2.27 |
| Conflictual communication (mother) | 2.75 | 2.91 | 2.71 | 2.58 |

## Feelings evoked by communication

Our second research question concerns feelings of adolescents associated with communication. Table 5 presents the mean scores of the four groups of adolescents on the three subscales: negative feelings, feelings of trust, and feelings of cautiousness in their communication with fathers and mothers, respectively. For the negative feelings subscale, the sex of the parent has a significant effect ($F(1,414)$ = 4.64; $p < 0.05$): adolescents reported more negative feelings towards their fathers than towards their mothers. Furthermore, there is a significant main effect of age of the adolescent ($F(1,414)$ = 9.37; $p < 0.005$): younger adolescents experienced more negative feelings than older adolescents. There is also a significant interaction between sex and age of the adolescent ($F(1,414)$ = 4.90; $p < 0.05$): older and younger boys reported the same level of negative feelings; older girls reported fewer negative feelings than younger girls. For the feelings of trust, there is neither a significant main effect of sex of the parent nor a significant interaction between sex of the parent and age or sex of the adolescent. However, there is a significant main effect of sex of the adolescent ($F(1,430)$ = 4.16; $p < 0.05$): girls indicated more feelings of trust than boys. Concerning the feelings of cautiousness, there is neither a significant main effect of sex of the parent nor a significant interaction between sex of the parent and age or sex of the adolescent. However, there is a significant main effect of age of the adolescent ($F(1,419)$ = 8.43; $p < 0.005$): older adolescents reported fewer feelings of cautiousness than younger adolescents.

Table 5. Mean score (on a scale from 1 to 7) for feelings associated with communication (negative feelings, feelings of trust and feelings of cautiousness), as indicated by adolescents

|  | Boys younger than 18 | Girls younger than 18 | Boys 18 and older | Girls 18 and older |
|---|---|---|---|---|
| Negative feelings towards father | 2.56 | 2.74 | 2.53 | 2.38 |
| Negative feelings towards mother | 2.57 | 2.60 | 2.48 | 2.29 |
| Feelings of trust towards father | 5.21 | 5.25 | 5.33 | 5.55 |
| Feelings of trust towards mother | 5.22 | 5.42 | 5.32 | 5.58 |
| Feelings of cautiousness towards father | 3.01 | 3.27 | 2.78 | 2.62 |
| Feelings of cautiousness towards mother | 3.06 | 3.11 | 2.72 | 2.51 |

DISCUSSION

In this study, we found that the relation of adolescents with their fathers differs in a number of aspects from the relation they have with their mothers. Communication between fathers and adolescents was less open than communication between mothers and adolescents, both when adolescents and when parents reported on the communication. In addition, adolescents had higher scores on negative feelings associated with the communication with their fathers (such as 'withdrawn', 'not accepted', 'distant') than on negative feelings associated with their mothers.

On other aspects of communication there was no difference between mothers and fathers. There was no difference on conflictual communication between fathers and adolescents on the one hand and mothers and adolescents on the other hand, both when adolescents and when parents reported on the communication. In other words, fathers do not evoke more or fewer conflicts in the communication with their adolescent sons and daughters than mothers do. Moreover, there were no differences in scores on feelings of trust ('trusting', 'playful') and feelings of cautiousness ('careful what I say', 'thoughtful').

The mean scores of fathers on the five measures indicated that fathers are good parents. They had high scores on positive aspects and low scores on negative aspects of communication. But compared to the scores of mothers, their scores were slightly lower: the scores deviated no more than one point on a seven point scale. It should be pointed out that we looked at means for fathers and mothers rahter than at individual scores. Presumably, in our sample some fathers are really bad parents and others are excellent.

The fact that fathers scored somewhat less positively than mothers does not necessarily imply a negative impact on adolescent development. During adolescence sons and daughters are disengaging from their family and prepare themselves for their adult roles. This separation individuation process can be influenced positively by fathers, who are somewhat distant and less open towards their children. In this unobtrusive way, fathers can play a positive role in raising adolescents. Of course this does not imply that mothers are not able to do so.

One of the critical notes that can be raised about this study concerns the fact that social desirability may cause the quite positive mean scores of our respondents. These high mean scores indicate that the relations between fathers and mothers on the one hand and adolescents on the other hand have a positive nature. The social desirability explanation is contradicted by the fact that both parents and adolescents paint the same picture. In addition, the questionnaires were part of a large survey project, in which questions about ethnocentrism and delinquent behaviors were also asked. Scores on these questionnaires showed that they are not influenced by social desirability.

Another point of criticism is that only subjective experiences of adolescents and parents were collected. These subjective experiences were not verified in any other way. However, we think it is exactly these subjective experiences that are important for the functioning of the family.

Another point is whether the differences in the communication of adolescents with their fathers and with their mothers are seen as undesirable by the adolescents. Communication with father and mother may proceed exactly the way the adolescent expects and wants it to proceed. Adolescents might appreciate father and mother playing a different role in parenting. In a follow up study we plan to investigate these different roles more extensively.

With this study, the research on relations of fathers with their children at adolescence age has not been completed yet. In particular, we could change the viewpoint and focus on the developmental phase of the fathers. Research on men who are in a period of midlife stress (Montemayor, McKenry & Julian, 1993) has shown that the developmental phase of the father can play a major role in the quality of the relation with their adolescents. While their children are at the adolescent age, the fathers experience a transition period themselves: a period of midlife stress. During this transition period, many fathers evaluate their values, norms, and the goals they wanted to chase and did actually reach. After this period men often become less masculine (for example, less focused on competition and achievement and less involved in their role of bread winner). In addition, they develop more female characteristics (for example, being more involved in relations with friends and family). Montemayor, McKenry and Julian found that, as a result of these changes, their general life satisfaction increases after this period of life.

In follow up research, we will emphasize the role of characteristics of fathers in the father-adolescent relationship. In particular, we will relate age, level of depression, role restriction, all kinds of aspects of the job, and the scores on typically feminine and masculine characteristics to the relationship of fathers with their adolescent children.

Both in the media and in the social sciences, fathers have been receiving a lot of attention nowadays. This attention is rather prescriptive and sometimes even condemning. Therefore, it seems necessary for the image created of fathers to be nuanced by objective scientific research.

REFERENCES

Almeida, D.M. & N.L. Galambos (1993). Continuity and changes in father-adolescent relations. In: S. Shulman & W.A. Collins (Eds.). *Father-adolescent relationships. New directions for child development, 62*. San Fransisco: Jossey-Bass publishers, p. 19-40.

Brown, B.B., N. Mounts, S.D. Lamborn & L. Steinberg (1993). Parenting practices and peer group affiliation. *Child Development, 64*, 467-482.

Collins, W.A., & G. Russell (1991). Mother-child and father-child relationships in middle childhood and adolescence: a developmental analysis. *Developmental Review, 11*(2), 99-136.

Hauser, S.T., B.K. Book, J. Houlinanh, S. Powers, B. Weiss-Perry, D. Follansbee, A.M. Jacobson & G. Noam (1987). Sex differences within the family: Studies of adolescent and parent family interaction. *Journal of Youth and Adolescence, 16*, 199-213.

Hosley, C.A. & R. Montemayor (1997). Fathers and adolescents. In: M.E. Lamb (Ed.). *The role of the father in child development*. New York: John Wiley & Sons, p. 162-179.

Larson, R.W. (1993). Finding time for fatherhood: The emotional ecology of adolescent-father interactions. In: S. Shulman & W.A. Collins (Eds.). *Father-adolescent relationships. New directions for child development, 62*. San Fransisco: Jossey-Bass publishers, p. 7-18.

Montemayor, R. & J.R. Brownlee (1987). Fathers, mothers, and adolescents: Gender-based differences in parental roles during adolescence. *Journal of Youth and Adolescence, 16*, 281-291.

Montemayor, R., P.C. McKenry & T. Julian (1993). Men in midlife and the quality of father-adolescent communication. In: S. Shulman & W.A. Collins (Eds.). *Father-adolescent relationships. New directions for child development , 62*. San Fransisco: Jossey-Bass publishers, p. 59-72.

Olson, D.H., H.I. McCubbin, H.L. Barnes, A.S. Larsen, M.J. Muxen & M.A. Wilson (1983). *Families: What makes them work*. Beverly Hills: Sage Publications.

Shulman, S. & M.M. Klein (1993). Distinctive role of the father in adolescent separation-individuation. In: S. Shulman & W.A. Collins (Eds.). *Father-adolescent relationships. New directions for child development, 62*. San Fransisco: Jossey-Bass publishers, p. 41-58.

Steinberg, L. (1987). Impact of puberty on family relations: Effects of pubertal status and pubertal timing. *Developmental Psychology, 23*, 451-460.

Youniss, J. & S. Smollar (1985). *Adolescent relationships with mothers, fathers and friends*. Chicago: Chicago University Press.

# The perception of private life forms.
# An empirical survey of Louvain students[*]

KOEN MATTHIJS & ANN VAN DEN TROOST
KATHOLIEKE UNIVERSITEIT LEUVEN, BELGIUM

## INTRODUCTION

The vocabulary of late 20th-century family sciences uses terms that were barely known half a century ago. Some examples: the reconstituted family, new father, cohabitation contract, sandwich family and home-based business. This points to a changed and changing (experience of the) social reality, and is a thought-provoking challenge to subject the post-war family sociological theories – often centred around the nuclear family – to critical examination and to adapt them to recent trends with intellectual creativity and flexibility. J. Murdock's 'empirical' definition of the family anno 1949 – true to the spirit of that time – was in fact the description of the nuclear family (Murdock, 1949: 1). Today, he would find himself immediately accused of empirical blindness, ideological prejudice and scientific one-sidedness. In the middle of the 20th century, the ideal-typical family construct did more or less approximate reality. In a sense, model and type dovetailed together. The family was stable, the prelude and the finale were identical (or similar) for many, and the division of labour between men and women was clearly delineated and socially accepted. Half a century later, things are different. The traditional post-war standard family went into rapid quantitative and qualitative decline through the social emancipation of all manner of new life forms. Families are now more complex, more heterogeneous, and in constant flux and mutation. This creates not only knotty problems for the sociology of the family, but also fresh and interesting challenges: it is faced with the challenge of finding conceptual and theoretical accommodation for the new developments. The difficulties begin right from the outset: what may/should the term

---

[*] This study is the result of a survey carried out during the 1997-'98 academic year by students of the second 'licentiate' (second year of the second cycle) in sociology (K.U.Leuven) as part of a seminar assignment. Our thanks are due to all the students who took part in the survey and provided us with the views young persons have of the family.

'family' (not) be taken to mean, and are the distinguishing features of the nuclear family still valid in today's social and scientific discourse? The question is not easy. J. Trost (1990: 439) has shown that there is much ambivalence among family scientists in their views and classifications of the family, that there is considerable doubt about the road of theory to be followed and that even public opinion is gripped with scepticism. J. Bernardes (1985a) goes even further, asking the challenging and at the same time relevant question as to whether we really know what a family is and whether any such thing as a family exists at all. To ask the question is to voice critical doubt.

Our research is in line with this theme. We examine some ideas and attitudes of university students regarding the family. In concrete terms, we look into which life forms are considered to be families, and the degree to which this differs according to sex and the socio-economic and marital status of their parents. We thus attempt to reconstruct the concept of the family in a socially and culturally important reference group. A key question is whether, to what extent and in which groups the family is identified with the nuclear family or whether, on the contrary, greater latitude of interpretation is admitted. The content of the life forms under review differs according to the marital status and sexual disposition of the respondents, their parenthood, the fact whether they are living with someone or not, and the presence of third parties within the family. Before proceeding to present the research and its findings, we shall first briefly outline its context, i.e. contemporary currents in the family.

## CHANGES IN THE FAMILY CYCLE AND IN FAMILY ORGANIZATION

As stated earlier, the family in the middle of the 20th century – the period of the baby boom generation – was a model and a type in one: nearly everyone got married young, promptly had several children and followed an established life-path with little room for individual experiment. All family sociology and demography indicators point in the direction of what was later called the standard life course. Contours shifted during the mid-60s. First, there was a downturn in fertility swiftly followed by a succession of other social and cultural changes. It was not a matter of internal dynamics, but rather a social about-turn, sometimes referred to by the term 'second demographic transition'. The traditional interweaving of marriage, sexuality and procreation (according to some even love) was unpicked, a process that today sees a – tragic or encouraging? – outcome in the (discussion on all kinds of) fertility techniques. The number and relative percentage of extra-marital births also increased during the last two decades; cultural resistance to illegitimate birth was hollowed out from the inside and the discriminatory legal measures were gradually scrapped. At the same time, this was a blow for the classical nuclear family.

The intensity of marriage and remarriage has slackened off in almost all Western European countries since the early 70s while the likelihood of divorce continued to increase. The institute of marriage waned in quantitative and qualitative importance in favour of extra-marital cohabitation and living alone. Unmarried cohabitation in its present form is structurally and culturally new, it is encountered in all layers of the population and sometimes the run-up, but much more frequently an alternative to marriage. The conclusion of marriage is therefore no longer the obvious transition mechanism from the orientation family towards the procreation family. Starting a new relationship is less formal, the bond less permanent. But also the final outcome has changed. The divorce rate in Belgium during the 70s was 10% to 15%, now it is 30% to 35% which roughly means that one out of three marriages entered into will end in divorce. Historically, this is completely new. Many people eager to marry take that calculated risk with their eyes wide open. The divorce explosion is one of the most significant recent social changes. In only a short time it has generated plethora of individual and social consequences, inter alia in the parent-child relationship, the relationship between the ex-partners, the tension between biological and sociological parenthood and the problem area of new step relationships after remarriage or post-marital cohabitation. Some men and women have to look after children with whom they have no biological, let alone any social, bond. The children themselves are confronted unbidden with situations for which there are neither clear rules of behaviour nor social labels, and must adapt themselves, with varying degrees of success, to new expectations and to new and sometimes complex types of family.

In the 70s and the 80s women also became more involved in education and employment. To overstate the case somewhat: older men (often full-time workers) were being replaced on the shop floor by young women (often part-time workers). Some people maintain that the work culture increased even at the cost of the family culture. Be that as it may, many men and women now experience difficulties in harmonizing their professional and family responsibilities. This is one of the major post-modern challenges, both for government policy and for families. The increase in the number of families with two partners working outside the home has led to a shift in the distribution of income and wealth. Whether one partner or both partners work outside the home is a new factor in social inequality. Some of the single earners are elbowed into lower income groups while the double earners climb into the higher prosperity groups. In a certain sense double income has become the wealth norm which creates, unintentionally, new forms of social disadvantagement. Increased education and employment outside the home has given women more individual possibilities and more chances for self-fulfilment. But this also brought with it new forms of social pressure and discrimination. The balance of power between partners shifted in favour of the woman, with all manner of unexpected consequences. One example is the phenomenon of balancing: women working outside the home and earning more than their partner, curiously enough, do more at home than other women and more than their partner. Have they developed a new – socially induced – sense of guilt for which they try to compensate through overacting? (Hochschild & Machung, 1989: 221).

The last three decades of the 20th century have thus seen the family undergo considerable changes, both social and cultural, structural and functional, material and symbolic. These changes in the family more or less mesh in with other social developments (Beck, 1992: 85-150). The new configuration is described by terms such as informalization, privatization and individualization, three quite vague and ambiguous terms with, nonetheless, a common social background, i.e. the breaking up of the time-honoured, rigidly prestructured social foundation and the creation of a more individual autonomy. Individualization points to the erosion of the traditional social props and to more personal decision-making space and freedom of action. Whether people today marry or not, live together or not, have children or not, all these semi-private decisions contain – besides the ever-present social standardization – a greater portion of individual choice. Is this the start for the shift from a standard life and family biography to an individual-choice biography? Large groups in fact no longer follow the standard life course, and the gender roles and sexual identities are now less sharply delineated. This indicates the shift from the family of command to a family of negotiation, from formal family rules to informal individual consultation. Some would describe this as the adaptation of the private living environment to the demands of post-industrial and post-modern society, but others take these new-fashioned trends as a cause for concern and sustained attention. The social changes do in fact seem confused and chaotic. As stated earlier, the semi-institutionalized ways of life and the more or less generally accepted standard biography are being replaced by more multiple and multi-interpretable life courses with ample individual interpretation and experimentation. Sometimes even simultaneously within the same life forms. Many of them orbit around the unlinking of parenthood and partnership. That has had an appreciable impact in many respects on at least one dependent group, the children. But what this new social learning environment – which they have nothing to do with – will mean for them in the long term cannot be stated at present, for that learning situation is historically new, and we cannot simply fall back on experiences from the past.

THE RESEARCH

The foregoing shows clearly that the youth and young adults of today are living in a turbulent world. Certainly as regards the private living environment. The intention of our small-scale survey is to take stock of their views of the family and the characteristic features of the family. In so doing, our research continues the line taken by I. Levin and J. Trost (1992) and by D. Ford (1994), both during the early 90s. Levin and Trost's research group consisted of 948 20-59 year-olds from the province of Uppsala (Sweden). The aim was to explore how adults define the concept of family (generally and personally). A questionnaire listed 16 life forms, and the respondents had to say whether these life forms were families. Ford conducted a similar experiment with 462 university students in 1994 (Mid-East of the USA). The average age of her research population was 24.4 years, 65% were female, 80% had not had a previous marriage and 85% had no children.

We used the Levin-Trost questionnaire for the Louvain survey, but with the addition of five more life forms. First names were adapted to the Flemish context. The questionnaire was submitted to first-year students (Katholieke Universiteit Leuven, Belgium) in five faculties: psychology, paedagogics, physics, mathematics and information technology during a formal lecture in November 1997. This therefore concerns a select, limited group, not the K.U.Leuven student, nor the Flemish 17 to 18 year-old. Completing the questionnaire took approximately 30 minutes. 674 analysis units remained after removing nine cases from the survey for various reasons.[1] Four fifths of the respondents attended a humanities course, with respectively 339 (74%) and 194 (26%) of that number in psychology and paedagogics. One in five took an exact science course, with respectively 68 (48%), 51 (36%) and 22 (16%) in information technology, mathematics and physics. The average age was 18.2 years (standard deviation: .68), and 71% were female. The humanities courses included 81% girls and 19% boys, the exact sciences including respectively 33% and 67%.

Our research group belongs to the baby bust generation, their parents to the boom generation. This generation gap has major sociological consequences – different generations indeed speak a different social and cultural language. The parents belonged to the generation that subscribed to the social changes in the second half of the 20th century briefly discussed earlier. They, in their turn, grew up with parents who had married young shortly after the Second World War, promptly had several children and organized their (family) life according to a strict man/woman division of labour. In other words, the classical standard life course. Our respondents' parents overturned this particular applecart. As stated above, they wrote a different demographic and sociological history: their birth rate was low, their marriage and remarriage intensities were lower and their divorce figures higher than before. These parents were the authors of the contemporary family trends which prompt modern sociologists to ask critical questions about the prevailing notions of family. But that is everyday fare for the young respondents themselves – after all, they have never known any other way. They are the first generation to be confronted en masse with divorce, single-parent families, remarriage and complex family situations. Precisely this makes the study of their views on the family and the hallmarks of a family so interesting.

Table 1. Respondents according to sex and course of study

| Course of study | Population (P) | | Research group (R) | | R/P | Sex | |
|---|---|---|---|---|---|---|---|
| | N | % | N | % | % | Boys | Girls |
| Humanities | 814 | 80 | 533 | 79 | 65 | 101 | 432 |
| Exact Sciences | 210 | 20 | 141 | 21 | 67 | 95 | 46 |
| Total | 1014 | 100 | 674 | 100 | 66 | 196 | 478 |

The age of the parents ranges from 36 to 68 years. The average age of the (natural) fathers is 47.3 years and 45.3 years for the (natural) mothers. 86% of the natural parents are married, 11% divorced and 3% widowed. The great majority (87%) of respondents live together with their married or unmarried parents, a small percentage live with their mother only (with or without her new partner, if any), and a still smaller percentage live with their father only. The parents of those questioned have a relatively high social status: 46% of the students come from a family with middle-class status and 37% come from a family with a middle-high or a high socio-economic status. One quarter of the respondents described themselves as Catholic, and approximately the same number as Christian. There are remarkably high percentages of atheists and free-thinkers, with 17% and 14% respectively. One student in eight claimed no particular religious conviction.

Table 2. Respondents according to socio-demographic type

| Parents' marital status | N= 674 | Actual life situation | N= 671 |
|---|---|---|---|
| Married | 85.9 | With both parents | 86.9 |
| Divorced | 10.8 | With mother only | 6.3 |
| Widowed | 3.2 | With mother + new partner | 3.1 |
| | | With father only | 1.9 |
| | | With father + new partner | 0.9 |
| | | Other | 0.9 |

| Highest diploma, father | N= 616 | Highest diploma, mother | N= 621 |
|---|---|---|---|
| Primary education | 2.4 | Primary education | 2.7 |
| Lower secondary education | 6.3 | Lower secondary education | 3.9 |
| Higher secondary education | 27.9 | Higher secondary education | 29.3 |
| Higher education | 32.8 | Higher education | 43.6 |
| University education | 30.5 | University education | 15.0 |

| Socio-economic status | N= 666 | Political conviction* | N= 660 |
|---|---|---|---|
| Low | 3.6 | Don't know | 30.9 |
| Middle-low | 9.6 | AGALEV | 22.3 |
| Middle | 45.8 | None | 16.1 |
| Middle-high | 31.1 | VU | 9.1 |
| High | 5.7 | CVP | 7.1 |
| Outside labour market | 4.2 | VLD | 5.0 |
| | | SP | 4.7 |
| | | Other | 3.8 |
| | | Vlaams Blok | 1.1 |

| Religious conviction | N= 669 | Church attendance | N= 332 |
|---|---|---|---|
| Christian | 25.7 | (Almost) weekly | 17.7 |
| Catholic | 24.1 | About monthly | 14.2 |
| Atheist | 16.9 | Holidays/special events | 52.4 |
| Free-thinker | 13.8 | Once a year | 6.6 |
| None | 11.7 | Never | 9.0 |
| Don't know | 4.5 | | |
| Other | 3.4 | | |

\*    AGALEV: green party; VU: Flemish Nationalist party; CVP: Christian Democrats; VLD: Liberal party; SP: Socialist party; Vlaams Blok: Right-wing party.

FAMILY PERCEPTION: GENERAL

Table 3 shows the 21 life forms included in the research. They are classified according to the share of students that regard the life form in question as a family. The share that gave no answer is also stated, and is remarkably low. However complex and plural some of the life forms may be, most respondents were able

Table 3. Number of respondents considering the various life forms a family

| | 1997, Belgium Matthijs & Van den Troost | | | 1994, USA Ford | | 1992, Sweden Levin and Troost | |
|---|---|---|---|---|---|---|---|
| | % Yes | Rank | % N.A. | % Yes | Rank | % Yes | Rank |
| Ilse and Dirk are both thirty and married. They have a six year-old son. Are they a family? | 99 | 1 | 0 | 100 | 1 | 99 | 1 |
| Anja and Stijn are in their thirties, living together, unmarried. They have a six year-old daughter, Hedwig. Are these three a family? | 98 | 2 | 0 | 85 | 5 | 97 | 2 |
| Kristel has divorced and remarried a man without children. She has a six year-old son from her first marriage. Are these three a family? | 91 | 3 | 1 | * | * | * | * |
| Cecilia is divorced and has a 10 year old daughter, Karin, living with her. Are they a family? | 90 | 4 | 1 | 93 | 3 | 83 | 4 |
| Lena and Lisa are in their thirties, living together as partners. Lotte, Lisa's six year-old daughter, lives with them. Are these three a family? | 87 | 5a | 1 | 65 | 11 | 38 | 9 |
| Eva and Peter are married with a daughter, Naomi, who lives with them. They also have a son, Bart, who lives in another town. Are these four a family? | 87 | 5b | 1 | 95 | 2 | 84 | 3 |
| Jef and Maria are the grandparents of young Kim who lives with them. Kim's mother and father are divorced and live elsewhere. Are the grandparents and their grandchild a family? | 81 | 7 | 1 | * | * | * | * |
| Anna and Marcel are a middle-aged, childless married couple. Are they a family? | 80 | 8 | 0 | 84 | 6 | 75 | 5 |
| Fanny and Fred have a teenage son, Jan. Jan's friend Henk lives with them. Are these four persons a family? | 67 | 9 | 2 | 70 | 9 | 42 | 8 |
| Greta and Patrick are in their thirties and have lived together, unmarried, for three years. Are they a family? | 65 | 10a | 0 | 44 | 12 | 60 | 6 |
| Can a dead person still be thought of as a member of the family? | 65 | 10b | 3 | * | * | * | * |

| | 1997, Belgium Matthijs & Van den Troost | | | 1994, USA Ford | | 1992, Sweden Levin and Trost | |
|---|---|---|---|---|---|---|---|
| | % Yes | Rank | % N.A. | % Yes | Rank | % Yes | Rank |
| Jan, An and Jasper are brothers and sister, all aged around thirty. They live in the same house. Are they a family? | 61 | 12 | 2 | 92 | 4 | 50 | 7 |
| Karel and Kurt are both thirty and live together as partners. Neither of them has a child. Are they a family? | 60 | 13 | 3 | 39 | 13 | 30 | 12 |
| Annie lives with her friend. They have three dogs. Are these five a family? | 48 | 14 | 1 | * | * | * | * |
| Veerle and her husband are living under the same roof as Veerle's brother-in-law. Are they a family? | 39 | 15 | 1 | * | * | * | * |
| Kurt is divorced from Griet. They have a young daughter who now lives with Griet. Kurt lives in another part of town. Kurt sees his daughter at least every other weekend. Are daughter and father a family? | 37 | 16 | 3 | 68 | 10 | 34 | 10 |
| Wouter's parents are separated. Wouter lives with his father. His mother, Inge, lives in another part of town and sees her son every other weekend. Are Wouter and Inge a family? | 37 | 17 | 2 | 72 | 8 | 34 | 10 |
| Jaak and Mona are married and have a 10 year old daughter. Mona has a close friend with whom she can talk about anything and open her heart. Are these four a family? | 18 | 18 | 1 | 26 | 15 | 8 | 15 |
| Inge and Erik have been living together for some time and are now separated. They have a young son, Wouter, who now lives with his father, Erik. Are Inge, Erik and Wouter a family? | 15 | 19 | 1 | 37 | 14 | 13 | 14 |
| Maria and Jean are the grandparents of Daniel, but they live apart. Are these three persons a family? | 12 | 20 | 1 | 81 | 7 | 23 | 13 |
| Peter is divorced from his wife Kathy. They have a young son who went to live with Kathy after the divorce. Are Peter and his ex-wife a family? | 4 | 21 | 1 | 17 | 16 | 8 | 15 |

(*): not asked; N.A.: no answer

to assess them to be a family or not. It should be pointed out, however, that the answer category 'no answer' was not provided in the questionnaire.

A factor analysis was carried out in order to gain some idea of the underlying structure of these life forms, highly divergent with regard to content and outer form. There are six factors. The first factor (items 10a, 8, 13 and 14 - see Column 3: Table 3 rank) concerns cohabiting heterosexual or homosexual childless couples. The second factor (items 16, 17, 19, 21 and 4) includes those life forms affected by a divorce. The third factor (items 9, 15, 5a, 7 and 12) concerns the cohabitation of a couple with one third party or several third parties, and cohabiting non-couples. The fourth factor (items 18, 20 and 3) is difficult to interpret. The fifth factor (items 1 and 2) refers to a married or cohabiting couple with children. The two items of the sixth factor (life forms 10b and 5b) relate to non-cohabiters. In general terms, it has to do with the elements respondents bore in mind when judging the life forms: parenthood, living situation, sexual inclination and marital status.

Almost all respondents regarded a married couple with a child and an unmarried heterosexual couple with a child as a family. If a couple has a child and live together, the marital status makes no difference. Life forms of homosexual couples with and especially without children are less accepted as families. The six highest rated life forms (actual score: more than 85% Yes voters) have two elements in common: parenthood and cohabitation. The latter element is absent however in the sixth life form (married couple with two children, one having left home). Apparently, the parent-child relationship is more important than the marital status but, if there are no children involved, marital status emerges as a discriminating criterion.

There is a break after the first six life situations. The percentages drop substantially for life forms where there is no parent-child relationship and the only issue is cohabitation. But the marital status and sexual inclination of the couple also matter. Four out of five respondents regarded a married couple without children as a family, unmarried couples living together without children scoring two out of three. This dropped to 60% for childless homosexual couples. Many respondents therefore do not take cohabitation as a sufficient condition for speaking of a family. Only a minority of respondents described as family those life forms in which the parties concerned lived apart. But a parent-child relationship alone is also insufficient evidence of family. A particular form and a particular degree of cohabitation is necessary. One notable exception is that as many as two out of three of the respondents judged that a dead person can still be part of the family.

Two life forms of cohabitation were regarded as family by a minority only: a cohabiting couple with dogs, and a cohabiting couple staying with a brother-in-law. The same difficulty with 'outsiders' occurs for those life situations where there is a friend of the son living as a member of the household and a friend of the mother not living with the family. Whether an extended life form is regarded as a family thus depends on the social characteristics of the persons living in it.

As stated earlier, the life forms that most respondents took to be families share two elements: parenthood and cohabitation. In other words, the classical type of family. Other life forms were measured off and weighed up against this standard, but further considerations were brought into the equation, such as marital status and sexual inclination. A childless married couple was more often described as a family than was a childless couple living together or a homosexual couple. Life forms where the couple was not living (or no longer living) under the same roof were less often or rarely considered as being families. The difference between family and households – however difficult and delicate it may be – belongs to the regular linguistic tools. To exaggerate slightly, this means: a family is almost always a household, but by no means all households are families. But the opposite also applies: some life forms that cannot be sociologically described as households are quite often perceived as a family.

Life forms where the parties concerned do not share activities such as sleeping, eating and bringing up children are not readily accepted as families. These observations run broadly parallel with the Swedish and the American survey. Besides the similarities, however, there are also differences. The American survey shows much higher positive scores for cohabiting brothers and sisters, for grandparents not living with their grandchild, and for a father or a mother not living with his or her child. Three of the six life forms that were described as families by a minority in the Belgian and the Swedish research were described as family by at least 68% of the American students. Each time it concerned cases of non-cohabitation. Cohabitation is apparently a less stringent condition for acceptance as family in the USA. The sociological distance between 'family' and 'household' is different there.

FAMILY PERCEPTION ACCORDING TO SEX

Table 4 classifies the life forms according to the size of the difference in the share of Yes answers between men and women (see last column). It is clear that women have broader, more open or tolerant views of family than men: 16 of the 21 life situations were considered as family by more women than men. For the pure types, such as the classical nuclear family and slight variations thereon, there are hardly any differences. But women accept more deviation from the standard model; apparently they are less strongly influenced by the traditional family standards. Ford came to the same results in the USA.

Table 4. Number of respondents accepting the various life forms as family, according to sex

|  | Women | | Men | | Difference |
|---|---|---|---|---|---|
|  | % Yes | Rank | % Yes | Rank | % |
| Can a dead person still be thought of as a member of the family? | 73 | 9 | 47 | 13 | 26 |
| Eva and Peter are married with a daughter, Naomi, who lives with them. They also have a son, Bart, who lives in another town. Are these four a family? | 91 | 4 | 77 | 7 | 14 |
| Kristel has divorced and remarried a man without children. She has a six year-old son from her first marriage. Are these three a family? | 95 | 3 | 82 | 4 | 13 |
| Jef and Maria are the grandparents of young Kim who lives with them. Kim's mother and father are divorced and live elsewhere. Are the grandparents and their grandchild a family? | 84 | 7 | 72 | 8 | 12 |
| Lena and Lisa are in their thirties, living together as partners. Lotte, Lisa's six year-old daughter, lives with them. Are these three a family? | 88 | 6 | 82 | 4 | 6 |
| Annie lives with her friend. They have three dogs. Are these five a family? | 50 | 14 | 44 | 14 | 6 |
| Fanny and Fred have a teenage son, Jan. Jan's friend Henk lives with them. Are these four persons a family? | 69 | 10 | 64 | 9 | 5 |
| Anja and Stijn are in their thirties, living together, unmarried. They have a six year-old daughter, Hedwig. Are these three a family? | 100 | 1 | 95 | 2 | 5 |
| Karel and Kurt are both thirty and live together as partners. Neither of them has a child. Are they a family? | 61 | 12 | 57 | 12 | 4 |
| Greta and Patrick are in their thirties and have lived together, unmarried, for three years. Are they a family? | 67 | 11 | 63 | 10 | 4 |
| Kurt is divorced from Griet. They have a young daughter who now lives with Griet. Kurt lives in another part of town. Kurt sees his daughter at least every other weekend. Are daughter and father a family? | 39 | 15 | 35 | 16 | 4 |

| | Women | | Men | | Difference |
|---|---|---|---|---|---|
| | % Yes | Rank | % Yes | Rank | % |
| Wouter's parents are separated. Wouter lives with his father. His mother, Inge, lives in another part of town and sees her son every other weekend. Are Wouter and Inge a family? | 38 | 17 | 35 | 16 | 3 |
| Anna and Marcel are a middle-aged, childless married couple. Are they a family? | 81 | 8 | 79 | 6 | 2 |
| Jan, An and Jasper are brothers and sister, all aged around thirty. They live in the same house. Are they a family? | 61 | 12 | 59 | 11 | 2 |
| Veerle and her husband are living under the same roof as Veerle's brother-in-law. Are they a family? | 39 | 15 | 38 | 15 | 1 |
| Cecilia is divorced and has a 10 year old daughter, Karin, living with her. Are they a family? | 90 | 5 | 90 | 3 | 0 |
| Ilse and Dirk are both thirty and married. They have a six year-old son. Are they a family? | 99 | 2 | 99 | 1 | 0 |
| Peter is divorced from his wife Kathy. They have a young son who went to live with Kathy after the divorce. Are Peter and his ex-wife a family? | 4 | 21 | 6 | 21 | -2 |
| Maria and Jean are the grandparents of Daniel, but they live apart. Are these three persons a family? | 11 | 20 | 14 | 20 | -3 |
| Inge and Erik have been living together for some time and are now separated. They have a young son, Wouter, who now lives with his father, Erik. Are Inge, Erik and Wouter a family? | 14 | 18 | 20 | 19 | -6 |
| Jaak and Mona are married and have a 10 year old daughter. Mona has a close friend with whom she can talk about anything and open her heart. Are these four a family? | 13 | 19 | 29 | 18 | -16 |

The difference is remarkably large for the question as to whether a dead person can still be part of the family: 71% of the women but only 46% of the men answered Yes. Does this mean that women find the emotional bond between members of the family more important than men do? Does this mean, linea recta, that American culture – insofar as it exists – is more feminine for this aspect of social reality than European culture? The difference between a more emotional and a more de facto family perception is borne out by the observation that, at a certain moment, the number of Yes answers from men is greater than from women. These are precisely the four life forms with the lowest average scores (see also Table 3), which concern atypical and special life forms remote from the classical 'emotional' nuclear family.

FAMILY PERCEPTION ACCORDING TO SOCIO-ECONOMIC STATUS

Table 5 shows the distribution of the family perception according to socio-economic status.[2] Respondents with a low socio-economic status described slightly more life forms as a family; they are apparently more open to regarding de facto households as family. There is broad consensus among all groups to regard the classical life forms as families. However, especially where there is no mention of a parent-child relationship, the higher status groups are rather more restrictive. Slightly less than 90% of the low status groups described a childless married couple as a family, compared with only 76% of the high and 82% of the middle groups. The sexual disposition of a childless cohabiting couple made little difference in the high socio-economic groups: 58% called both a heterosexual and a homosexual couple a family, while this was 72% and 68% respectively in the low socio-economic groups. There is also a difference between the status groups with regard to the question as to whether a dead person can still be counted as a member of the family: 74% of the low group and 65% of the high and middle groups answered this question with Yes.

The low-status students thus have fewer difficulties calling various kinds of life forms a family, even where certain central elements of the nuclear family may not be present (for example, brothers and sisters living together). In the case of a divorced mother (father) not living with her (his) child, 43% (44%) of the low-status groups accepted this as a family against 41% of the high and 33% of the middle group. Apparently parenthood and cohabitation are less important in the lower socio-economic groups as descriptors of a family. That may be connected with the fact that these groups are more frequently confronted with all kinds of atypical life forms. But there is also a cultural factor: in certain high-status groups, the appearance of family must be kept up at all times – this

Table 5. Number of respondents accepting the various life forms as family, according to socio-economic status

| | High | | Middle | | Low | |
|---|---|---|---|---|---|---|
| | % Yes | Rank | % Yes | Rank | % Yes | Rank |
| Ilse and Dirk are both thirty and married. They have a six year-old son. Are they a family? | 100 | 1 | 99 | 1 | 100 | 1 |
| Anja and Stijn are in their thirties, living together, unmarried. They have a six year-old daughter, Hedwig. Are these three a family? | 97 | 2 | 98 | 2 | 100 | 1 |
| Cecilia is divorced and has a 10 year old daughter, Karin, living with her. Are they a family? | 93 | 3 | 88 | 4 | 90 | 4 |
| Kristel has divorced and remarried a man without children. She has a six year-old son from her first marriage. Are these three a family? | 90 | 4 | 92 | 3 | 88 | 6 |
| Lena and Lisa are in their thirties, living together as partners. Lotte, Lisa's six year-old daughter, lives with them. Are these three a family? | 88 | 5 | 85 | 6 | 89 | 5 |
| Eva and Peter are married with a daughter, Naomi, who lives with them. They also have a son, Bart, who lives in another town. Are these four a family? | 85 | 6 | 86 | 5 | 94 | 3 |
| Jef and Maria are the grandparents of young Kim who lives with them. Kim's mother and father are divorced and live elsewhere. Are the grandparents and their grandchild a family? | 79 | 7 | 80 | 8 | 87 | 8 |
| Anna and Marcel are a middle-aged, childless married couple. Are they a family? | 76 | 8 | 82 | 7 | 88 | 6 |
| Fanny and Fred have a teenage son, Jan. Jan's friend Henk lives with them. Are these four persons a family? | 67 | 9 | 67 | 10 | 69 | 11 |
| Can a dead person still be thought of as a member of the family? | 65 | 10 | 62 | 12 | 74 | 9 |
| Greta and Patrick are in their thirties and have lived together, unmarried, for three years. Are they a family? | 58 | 11 | 70 | 9 | 72 | 10 |
| Karel and Kurt are both thirty and live together as partners. Neither of them has a child. Are they a family? | 58 | 12 | 59 | 13 | 68 | 13 |

| | High | | Middle | | Low | |
|---|---|---|---|---|---|---|
| | % Yes | Rank | % Yes | Rank | % Yes | Rank |
| Jan, An and Jasper are brothers and sister, all aged around thirty. They live in the same house. Are they a family? | 54 | 13 | 63 | 11 | 69 | 11 |
| Annie lives with her friend. They have three dogs. Are these five a family? | 41 | 14 | 50 | 14 | 58 | 14 |
| Wouter's parents are separated. Wouter lives with his father. His mother, Inge, lives in another part of town and sees her son every other weekend. Are Wouter and Inge a family? | 41 | 15 | 33 | 16 | 43 | 16 |
| Kurt is divorced from Griet. They have a young daughter who now lives with Griet. Kurt lives in another part of town. Kurt sees his daughter at least every other weekend. Are daughter and father a family? | 41 | 16 | 33 | 16 | 44 | 15 |
| Veerle and her husband are living under the same roof as Veerle's brother-in-law. Are they a family? | 37 | 17 | 42 | 15 | 39 | 17 |
| Inge and Erik have been living together for some time and are now separated. They have a young son, Wouter, who now lives with his father, Erik. Are Inge, Erik and Wouter a family? | 17 | 18 | 13 | 19 | 15 | 19 |
| Jaak and Mona are married and have a 10 year old daughter. Mona has a close friend with whom she can talk about anything and open her heart. Are these four a family? | 17 | 19 | 19 | 18 | 20 | 18 |
| Maria and Jean are the grandparents of Daniel, but they live apart. Are these three persons a family? | 12 | 20 | 12 | 20 | 13 | 20 |
| Peter is divorced from his wife Kathy. They have a young son who went to live with Kathy after the divorce. Are Peter and his ex-wife a family? | 5 | 21 | 4 | 21 | 7 | 21 |

despite the fact that they have greater material possibilities and more cultural capital to abandon the well-trodden social paths. However: that is difficult via the atypical life forms, because they are held in low esteem and are associated with a low status. Probably the classical family model is strongly internalized among the higher classes, an attitude that has to be defended in the discourse. This is one of the reasons why deviating life forms are less conceptualized as families. Apparently, people have the moral attitudes they can buy.

FAMILY PERCEPTION ACCORDING TO MARITAL STATUS OF PARENTS
Respondents of separated or legally divorced parents apply a wider definition of family than others, but this trend is very faint (Table 6). Globally, the differences in family perception on the basis of the marital status of the parents are slight. Almost all life forms more readily judged by children of divorced couples to be families are life forms in which the members of the family live together, or homosexual couples (with or without children). It is noteworthy that children of divorced couples are more critical of divorced couples (see penultimate life form, Table 6). The actual experience of divorce apparently has far-reaching effects on the perception: the original couple is no longer regarded as a family by the children. The effect of the concrete experience is most probably felt differently by the children of widowed parents: more than the others, they tend to regard a deceased person as still being a member of the family.

CONCLUSION AND DISCUSSION
Our research permits only few definite conclusions. The sample is limited to a small, relatively homogeneous group, the members of which have approximately the same age, socio-economic status, lifestyle and areas of interest. This makes extrapolation to other students, to peer groups or to society at large difficult. Sociologically however, it is an interesting group: social new-comers delineating the future life forms and functioning as role model and reference group for others. This group distinguishes clearly between family and household, via a subtle weighing up of elements such as the parent-child relationship, living situation, sexual inclination and marital status. The effect of each of these factors differs according to the value of the next. A limited number of combinations leads to a number of specific life forms recognizable as families to almost everyone. Other combinations are judged more critically, varying according to the sex of the respondent and the marital and socio-economic status of the parents. Family perception thus varies according to social characteristics and is, in this sense, the subject of social opposition and political conflict.

Table 6. Number of respondents accepting the various life forms as family, according to marital status of parents

|  | Married | | Divorced | | Widowed | |
|---|---|---|---|---|---|---|
|  | % Yes | Rank | % Yes | Rank | % Yes | Rank |
| Ilse and Dirk are both thirty and married. They have a six year-old son. Are they a family? | 99 | 1 | 100 | 1 | 100 | 1 |
| Anja and Stijn are in their thirties, living together, unmarried. They have a six year-old daughter, Hedwig. Are these three a family? | 98 | 2 | 99 | 2 | 100 | 2 |
| Kristel has divorced and remarried a man without children. She has a six year-old son from her first marriage. Are these three a family? | 90 | 3 | 89 | 5 | 90 | 3 |
| Cecilia is divorced and has a 10 year old daughter, Karin, living with her. Are they a family? | 89 | 4 | 95 | 3 | 90 | 4 |
| Eva and Peter are married with a daughter, Naomi, who lives with them. They also have a son, Bart, who lives in another town. Are these four a family? | 87 | 5 | 81 | 6 | 82 | 5 |
| Lena and Lisa are in their thirties, living together as partners. Lotte, Lisa's six year-old daughter, lives with them. Are these three a family? | 85 | 6 | 93 | 4 | 90 | 6 |
| Jef and Maria are the grandparents of young Kim who lives with them. Kim's mother and father are divorced and live elsewhere. Are the grandparents and their grandchild a family? | 81 | 7 | 78 | 8 | 77 | 7 |
| Anna and Marcel are a middle-aged, childless married couple. Are they a family? | 80 | 8 | 79 | 7 | 77 | 8 |
| Fanny and Fred have a teenage son, Jan. Jan's friend Henk lives with them. Are these four persons a family? | 67 | 9 | 66 | 12 | 57 | 12 |
| Greta and Patrick are in their thirties and have lived together, unmarried, for three years. Are they a family? | 65 | 10 | 70 | 9 | 62 | 11 |
| Can a dead person still be thought of as a member of the family? | 64 | 11 | 59 | 14 | 67 | 9 |
| Jan, An and Jasper are brothers and sister, all aged around thirty. They live in the same house. Are they a family? | 59 | 12 | 67 | 10 | 55 | 14 |

| | Married | | Divorced | | Widowed | |
|---|---|---|---|---|---|---|
| | % Yes | Rank | % Yes | Rank | % Yes | Rank |
| Karel and Kurt are both thirty and live together as partners. Neither of them has a child. Are they a family? | 59 | 13 | 67 | 11 | 62 | 10 |
| Annie lives with her friend. They have three dogs. Are these five a family? | 46 | 14 | 60 | 13 | 57 | 13 |
| Veerle and her husband are living under the same roof as Veerle's brother-in-law. Are they a family? | 38 | 15 | 41 | 15 | 41 | 15 |
| Wouter's parents are separated. Wouter lives with his father. His mother, Inge, lives in another part of town and sees her son every other weekend. Are Wouter and Inge a family? | 37 | 16 | 38 | 16 | 14 | 14 |
| Kurt is divorced from Griet. They have a young daughter who now lives with Griet. Kurt lives in another part of town. Kurt sees his daughter at least every other weekend. Are daughter and father a family? | 37 | 17 | 36 | 17 | 27 | 17 |
| Jaak and Mona are married and have a 10 year old daughter. Mona has a close friend with whom she can talk about anything and open her heart. Are these four a family? | 16 | 18 | 22 | 18 | 33 | 16 |
| Inge and Erik have been living together for some time and are now separated. They have a young son, Wouter, who now lives with his father, Erik. Are Inge, Erik and Wouter a family? | 15 | 19 | 17 | 19 | 10 | 20 |
| Peter is divorced from his wife Kathy. They have a young son who went to live with Kathy after the divorce. Are Peter and his ex-wife a family? | 13 | 20 | 3 | 20 | 19 | 18 |
| Maria and Jean are the grandparents of Daniel, but they live apart. Are these three persons a family? | 5 | 21 | 1 | 21 | 5 | 21 |

To explain the various perceptions in sociological terms, it appeared to be useful to distinguish between an emotional or immaterial and a more de facto or material perception of family – which brings us to the difference between families and households. This is also a point of departure which helps to explain the differences between a more American and a more European family perception, and the differences between the various socio-economic groups.

Women have a more liberal view of the family than men. This may be regarded as a form of male conservatism in the private living environment. This is encountered in other fields, too. For example, relationships and marriages are more frequently terminated by women than by men. Apparently, men find themselves in a difficult position here. There are numerous demographic, socio-psychological and sociological explanations for this. One possible point of departure is the theory of asymmetrical sex ratio of M. Guttentag and P. Secord (1983). They suggest that all manner of quantitative and qualitative trends in marriage, family and role patterns are directly or indirectly influenced by the unequal numbers of men and women, which in turn is connected with the fact that more boys are born than girls. Imbalanced sex ratios have an effect on the dyadic or relational power of men and women. In the real-life situation, members of the minority sex have a competitive advantage in their private living environment, because they are less dependent on their partners; there are always escape routes if things go wrong. This makes them less bound up in existing relationships and better able to cross over to alternatives. The opposite applies for members of the majority sex. Their quantitative ascendancy places them at a relative disadvantage since they are unable to migrate from one relationship to the next 'just like that'. They try to avoid this by clinging conservatively to existing relationships. The hypothesis can be extrapolated linea recta to the perception of private life forms and, in this sense, offers an explanation of the broader and more open vision of women. It should be pointed out here that the differences in the numbers of men and women in the countries of Western Europe and North America are currently relatively small. This is therefore only a limited aspect of the explanation. The numerical ratio is furthermore dependent on all kinds of variables, such as birth and death. In this sense it is subject to change and can even take a complete turn. Differences in perception of the family between men and women are therefore subject to change in the course of time. That is sociologically highly plausible but unfortunately not possible to evaluate with the available data. This viewpoint is also at odds with a more (socio-)biological perspective. Men are not always certain of their fatherhood. Some authors say that men try to work off their innate jealousy in the social arena

(Hrdy, 1981). They will respect all rules, standards, laws and institutions that offer them more security. Hence their preference for a classical family in which individual experimentation is frowned upon and structurally hamstrung. What is the sociological weight of this attitude, and does it also offer an explanation for the differences in the family perception by young people?

The respondents certainly do not cling to a classical definition of the family. Different life forms whereby one or more elements of the nuclear family are missing are still regarded as families by the majority. In connection with D. Cheal's (1991: 125-132) diagnosis, this indicates a content expansion of the concept of the family in society. This looks to increase further in the future. Our survey indeed found on a number of occasions that the actual experience of alternative life forms leads to a greater readiness to consider 'deviant' or atypical life forms as families. The perception of the family will therefore become more liberal and open the more the social trends continue to evolve in this direction. This should incite family scientists to increased intellectual creativity and flexibility. The urgent plea of J. Bernardes (1988: 72-81) in favour of the new family studies is more than justified in this context. In the same sense, J. Scanzoni (1987: 404 ff.) insists that in view of their broad diffusion and social acceptance all kinds of new life forms can no longer be called 'alternative' – implying as it does a deviation from the nuclear family. The concept of the 'family' had its meaning in a clearly defined historical and cultural context, and still has to a certain extent. But family scientists are working on a new paradigm for the study of 'structured interpersonal bonds' and 'primary relations'. J. Trost's (1996: 397 ff.) remedy must likewise be situated within that conceptual dissatisfaction. He sees a solution in concepts such as partnerhood – or even more neutrally: cohabitation unit – and the parent-child unit. A family then becomes a social group consisting of at least one parent-child unit or at least one cohabitation unit. Other life forms may be socially and sociologically typified through inclusion of other and/or additional dyadic units. One major difficulty with the issue of conceptual (im)purity is that, at present, there is no clear idea about the processes of inclusion and exclusion. What are the necessary and/or the minimum conditions for considering this or that configuration as a family or as some other life form? And does this vary according to sex? New research is urgently needed to fill in this gap in our knowledge. That would at the same time help to discover the motivation of the perception of families, households and life forms. Earlier we stressed that certain life forms that elude sociological classification as households may still be perceived as families. The next step is to see what status the social actors assign to the various life forms. Is it only a difference – as our survey discusses – or does it imply also consequences in terms of assessment? What, if any, are the policy conclusions if an actual life form is not seen as a family by the majority of the population? To what extent must/can family scientists take this into account when developing their models and theories?

## NOTES

[1]   683 questionnaires were completed. Nine were not included in the analysis. One was incorrectly completed and eight respondents were older than 21 and/or married.

[2]   The socio-economic status of the family of origin is determined by reference to the educational attainment and the occupation of the members of the family. There was a choice between four categories. The concrete indexing of socio-economic status can be provided on request.

## REFERENCES

Beck, U. (1992). *Risk society, towards a new modernity*. London: Sage.

Bernardes, J. (1985a). Do we really know what the family is? In: P. Close & R. Collins. *Family and economy in modern society*. London: McMillan, p. 192-211.

Bernardes, J. (1985b). Family ideology: Identification and exploration. *Sociological Review*, *33*(2), 275-297.

Bernardes, J. (1988). Founding the new 'family studies'. *Sociological Review*, 57-86.

Bernardes, J. (1990). The family in question. *Social Studies Review*, *6*(1), 33-35.

Cheal, D. (1991). *Family and the state of theory*. New York: Harvester Wheatsheaf.

Dumon, W. (1997). The situation of families in Western Europe: A sociological perspective. In: Dreman, S. (Ed.) (1998). *The family on the threshold of the 21st century. Trends and implications*. New Jersey: Lawrence Erlbaum Associates, p. 181-200.

Ford, D. (1994). An exploration of perceptions of alternative family structures among university students. *Family Relations*, *43*(1), 68-73.

Guttentag, M., P. Secord (1983). *Too many women? The sex ratio question*. Beverly Hills: Sage.

Hrdy, S.B. (1981). *The woman that never evolved*. Boston: Harvard University Press.

Levin, I. & J. Trost (1992). Understanding the concept of family. *Family Relations*, *41*, 348-351.

Hochschild, A. & A. Machung (1989). *The second shift*. New York: Avon.

Murdock, J. (1949). *Social structure*. New York: McMillan Company.

Scanzoni, J. (1987). Families in the 1980s: Time to refocus our thinking. *Journal of Family Issues*, *8*(4), 394-421.

Settles, B. (1987). A perspective on tomorrow's families. In: M.B. Sussman & S.K. Steinmetz (Eds.). *Handbook of marriage and the family*. New York: Plenum Press, p. 157-180.

Sprey, J. (1991). Current theorizing on the family. In: A. Booth. *Contemporary families: Looking forward, looking back*. Minnesota: National Council on Family Relations, p. 12-27.

Trost, J. (1990). Do we mean the same by the concept of family? *Communication Research, 17*(4), 431-441.

Trost, J. (1992). *Family formation and reformation.* Revised version of a paper presented at the XXVIIth International CFR Seminar in Taiwan.

Trost, J. (1996). Family structure and relationships: The dyadic approach. *Journal of Comparative Family Studies, 27*(2), 395-408.

Future of the family

# Prioritising families in the future in the United Kingdom

JON BERNARDES
THE UNIVERSITY OF WOLVERHAMPTON, UNITED KINGDOM

## A PERSONAL NOTE

I am sure that there are many of us who share an admiration for Professor Wilfried Dumon and his tireless work in support of families at a Belgian National Level, a European Union International Level, and at a Global Level. What follows is, I believe, quite rare for an academic from the United Kingdom where the discipline of Family Studies hardly exists and there is no co-ordinated government concern to support families. Whilst I am sure that my friend Wilfried Dumon might eagerly dispute the finer points of my arguments, I very much hope that he will recognise his own influence in enabling this particular UK academic to develop arguments to better support families in the UK and elsewhere (Bernardes, 1997).

## INTRODUCTION

Most people in western industrialised societies consider family living as the most important aspect of their lives. In the first report of the Research Centre on Micro-Social Change, Scott and Perren (1994: 263) observe that 'Family events were by far regarded as the most important aspect of people's lives...' A report for the European Commission demonstrated that 96% of the population identify family living as the single most valued aspect of life across the European Union (Commission of the European Communities, 1993: 60).

The most serious problem for anyone wishing to study family lives is their own closeness to the topic. This is not a matter of bias but rather the strength of beliefs about family lives. For most of our lives, 'our family' is the most important thing of all. Most of us are born into families and spend, whether we choose or not, most of our childhood and teenage years within 'our family'. Even single people living alone can readily identify both immediate and more distant members of 'their family'. Thereafter, most of us set up some kinds of partnerships that may 'become a family' with the birth of children. We then begin another period within a family as a partner and parent perhaps divorcing, remarrying and becoming a new parent. Even when our children have left home, we may find ourselves again closely involved as grandparents in gift giving, family celebrations or child care. It is also within families that 'we first experience differences, divisions and hierarchies, which in "the family" are structured around gender and age' (Ribbens, 1994: 213).

In view of the centrality of family lives and the passion with which we believe family living to be important, it would be reasonable to expect the study of family living to be the most important academic discipline in schools, colleges and universities in the UK. This is simply not the case. Whilst Family Studies is common in the USA and exists in some European countries, there are no departments of Family Studies in the UK.

## THE IMAGE OF 'THE FAMILY'

Despite enormous real world variation and diversity, a common and popular image of 'the nuclear family' portrays a young, similar aged, white married heterosexual couple with a small number of healthy children living in an adequate home. There is a clear division of responsibilities in which the male is primarily the full-time breadwinner and the female primarily the caregiver and perhaps a part time or occasional income earner (Bernardes, 1997: 2-3).

There is something very strange about this image: it is quite simply unrealistic. Most simply put, this image of 'the family' omits the rich detail of everyday living and certainly ignores any possible 'negative' side of family living. It is equally clear that this simple model of 'the family' has not reflected the realities of peoples lives at any stage in recorded history. This model does not allow for divorce, single parenthood, family abuse, sickness or impairment, cultural and ethnic diversity, poverty, homelessness and very many other important variations. The model of 'the nuclear family' does not reflect my experiences as a son, a husband, a father. This model does not speak of the experiences of those I know and love: relatives, friends, wife, children.

## THE POWER OF 'THE FAMILY'

The idea of 'the nuclear family' is very powerful. This idea is attractive to opinion leaders because it asserts the correctness of clear gender divisions, parental responsibility for children and the privacy of 'the family'. Ordinary people resist giving up the idea of 'the family' because it is so simple and justifies so much behaviour. We do not need to worry about the justice of women doing all the child care and housework or the justice of male dominance in paid work and many positions of authority (Bernardes, 1990).

Everyday people have little choice but to accept the kinds of statements made in public and religious life. One of the key means by which ordinary everyday people continually receive the idea and image of 'the family' is through religion and associated morality. A wide range of religious tracts contain notions of 'the family', just as they contain notions of God and faith. This itself has important links to 'scientific' arguments about biology and universality. These views also coincide with conservative beliefs, especially ethnocentric views emphasising the superiority of white western societies. Even in the more secular western societies, religious beliefs remain as foundations of widely accepted social beliefs.

Generations of competent social scientists have accepted the existence of 'the family'. This is both a puzzle and an indicator of the enormous power and strength of beliefs about 'the family'. Considering debates about 'the family' involves considering central and fundamental issues about the nature of society. Not least are issues of sex and gender, paid work versus unpaid family work, the purpose of 'the family', and changes in family life associated with socio-historical events. These, and many more issues, are central to the way social science is undertaken in western societies. Despite a popular idea that social science is critical, even radical, social science is remarkably conservative in this area. This conservatism reflects popular ideas about 'the family' contained in biology, history and morality.

## THE DIFFICULTY OF THEORISING FAMILIES

As a scholar and teacher, I spend regular sessions each year explaining to students that 'the family' does not exist and all those things we think of as 'new problems' have existed for centuries or longer. Dual worker families are probably the norm throughout history and throughout the contemporary world. Single parent families have always been common in periods of industrial development. Polygamy as an ideal or reality has probably been far more common throughout human history than monogamy; polygamy is still a major form of partnering across the world. Abuse and violence between intimates are as old as any human mythology.

For far too long, lay people and social scientists themselves have allowed the idea that understanding society is easy to flourish. I have never accepted this. When you look at the differences and similarities between children, partners and parents, it is rather like watching millions of dice (so beloved of statisticians). Not only do the dice give untold numbers of different results but they are different sizes, colours, weights and have different systems of numbering.

We must recognise that modern societies are much more difficult to understand than any natural scientific topic. The objects of natural scientific enquiry do not much care what the scientists think, and only sometimes respond to what they might do. On the other hand, ordinary people are likely to select and seize upon popular accounts of what some family sociologists and others think and say about family living; for example, debates about divorce, single parenthood or children and television watching. This can most obviously seen in media images and in the pronouncements of moral and political leaders on divorce, violence, parenting and so on (Durham, 1991).

## THEORETICAL DIFFICULTIES: FAMILY IDEOLOGY

The main problem in theorising family life is that of family ideology. It is surprising in many ways that so-many sociologists have failed to recognise the depth and power of family ideology. The nature of the difficulty presented by family ideology can be seen in the way in which 'the family' is located in sociological theorising. Notions of 'the family' are embedded in accounts of the biological bases of sexual inequality, explanations of the process of industrial change involving the shift from 'extended' to 'nuclear family' types. Given this centrality, it is possible that critical re-evaluations of 'the family' have been largely unthinkable on the part of those whose careers are based in the validity of such theorising.

Levin (1990: 18) noted that 'If one has a closed and non-problematicised concept of family, certain types of interpretations of social reality are made ... The concepts we use decide what we see.' Family ideology supported by family sociology, has ensured that we have paid attention to white, middle class, two parent families. At the same time, family ideology ensures that some aspects of social existence are simply not seen or become invisible. For example, traditional family theorising has ignored the possibility of widespread abuse or unhappiness in 'the family'.

## MODERNIST THEORISING

The bulk of family theory is North American, especially from the United States itself. Family Sociology and Family Studies in the USA go back at least into the moralistic period of prohibition of the 1930s, through the anti-Communist moralism of the 1950s up to the present day.

Until recently, in the UK there were relatively few texts that drew upon family theory in any depth. The works of David Morgan (1975 and 1985) stand out as rare and thorough accounts of family theory in the UK although these use largely American source material. A Canadian, Cheal, identifies a post World War II 'convergence' towards the view that 'systematic' and 'scientific' work would eventually generate a single theory of 'the family'. Cheal locates a key problem in all this as the assumption that there is some 'universal core to family life, which can be given an objective definition as "the family"' (Cheal, 1991: 8).

Modernist Family Sociology has been deeply positivist. Positivism is the traditional, natural science based, approach in the social sciences that assumes the existence of facts, stability and order, which seeks to be objective and detached. Perhaps the easiest way to think of positivism is that it involves the assumption that everything is 'out there'. The world is external, objective, factual and requires technical expertise from us to capture, analyse, describe and explain it. Positivism in the area of family living usually places a heavy emphasis also upon rationality, the idea of a clearly structured 'system' and the idea of the 'purpose' or 'function' of behaviour and institutions within that system.

## POST MODERNIST THEORISING

The term post modern family life was developed by Stacey 'to signal the contested, ambivalent, and undecided character of contemporary gender and kinship arrangements' (Stacey 1990: 17). Post modernism is the area of theoretical work that has developed new tools and approaches that seek to understand family lives in new ways. Perhaps most easily thought of as looking at family lives 'in here' (in our heads). Cheal characterises post modernism as 'an approach that engages in sceptical reflection on the culture of modern society or, in other words, modernity and its dominant world view, namely modernism' (Cheal, 1991: 5). In exploring what might be involved in a sociology of post modern families, Cheal argues that 'Post modernist thought in sociology begins from contemporary experiences of pluralism, disorder and fragmentation, which were not predicted by the modern paradigm of universal reason' (Cheal, 1991: 9).

Modernist work asserts that 'the family' exists and, for example, that men are primarily breadwinners and that women are primarily nurturers. Whilst this is a clear value position, it is often not recognised as such because so many believe it to be 'true'.

A postmodernist approach to Family Studies does not assert what is 'true' but rather seeks evidence about what family life is actually like. In finding family lives to be enormously complex, Family Studies adopts the notion of family practices and pathways to encompass variation and diversity.

The future of families is certain: what remains to be seen is whether we will leave families alone to cope as best they can or decide to take a positive role and seek to put families first to enhance the quality of family lives, just as we have enhanced the quality of material living over recent decades.

## WHY PUT FAMILIES FIRST?

In developing his own argument for 'putting families first', Wicks commences from an essentially economic argument by observing that 'If things do not change Britain will spend billions of pounds on family breakdown by the year 2000' (Wicks, 1994: 18). Whilst there are clear economic grounds and those which may be linked to particular political positions, it is important to realise that there are also clear sociological reasons why we should Put Families First.

## IMPORTANCE OF FAMILY LIVES

The determination of human beings to create and maintain the secure intimacy of family living should be taken as a signal that this is the single most important feature of human social existence. As the recent Commission on Social Justice (1994: 311) reminded us, 'Families are the first social institutions children know and the means by which they are introduced to all the others.' The very centrality of family living to human social existence speaks very clearly of the need to do everything within our power to put families first.

It needs reiterating that the major part of the lives of the vast majority of citizens is oriented towards partnering and parenting. Whether we like it or not, these are major life preoccupations for virtually all citizens. Certainly there are those who, having spent one or two decades in families as children, may reject the idea of family living for the rest of their lives. Even for these people, it is not possible to avoid orientation towards belief systems, housing patterns, fashion and paid work systems that relate to family living.

In attempting to indicate what might be involved in developing a 'family perspective', Wicks (1991: 182) argues that 'The development of a "family perspective" within the policy making process is, perhaps, one step that all parties and groups concerned about the family might support.' One of the key vehicles of pursuing a family perspective in policy making, adopted from the United States and proposed by the Study Commission on the Family, is that of 'Family Impact Statements'. Such statements are seen as involving assessments of:

'1. The impact of the proposed policy on different family units, including one parent and dual worker families, for example.

2. The assumptions made about family life, including male and female roles.

3. The association between the new policy and existing related polices and the likely cumulative impacts of these measures.

4. The rights and responsibilities of families.
5. The intelligibility of the new policy - questions of access, complexity and so on.
6. The policy goals in relations to families and how these will be achieved, and procedures for monitoring and evaluation' (Wicks, 1991: 181-2).

Families are the key transmitters of cultural values and the main models of both acceptable and unacceptable behaviours. We should not leave families to engage in this work alone but support them in developing basic human values around: respect, tolerance, acceptance of diversity, equality, service, responsibility for others, truth, decency, honesty and co-operation.

Curiously, modernist family sociology often asserts that 'the family' is the most important thing of all yet supports a system that declines to interfere in 'the family' and often makes life unnecessarily difficult for those families that somehow fail to conform, such as disabled parents, unemployed parents or dual-career parents. This hardly seems to be a reasonable means of supporting 'the most important thing of all'. More to the point, such an approach often denies the responsibilities of sociologists and others. In asserting the moral correctness of 'the family', such sociologists have been happy to label millions of families as somehow being 'problems' in experiencing abuse, unhappiness, divorce, or single parenthood. In a similar vein, the Commission on Social Justice (1994: 313) argues that 'A strong community should support its families, rather than expect strong families to make up for the limitations of weak communities.'

POLICIES FOR FAMILIES RATHER THAN FAMILY POLICY
Many commentators have argued that the UK should develop a Family Policy. The simple point is that we need policies for families rather than a distinct 'Family Policy'. All policies need to be oriented to the varied and diverse nature of families.

The essence of successful family living is neither enforced dependency nor isolated individualism but a situation in which families and the state are interdependent. In this, we need to recognise that families are social and not natural and that it is the process of maintaining family living that matters rather than the formal structure or label. We need to also recognise that families distribute both material and non material goods and bads; policies for families will therefore need to address material and non material issues as being of equal priority.

We must recognise that the services performed by families vary significantly over time and should offer appropriate continual preparation, support and assistance to improve the quality of these. This may be directed towards enhancing the ability of people to help themselves as well as the ability of people to help each other. As Coote et al. (1990) argued, we need to work with the grain of change and not oppose change that is already going on. Similarly, we should encourage, educate and facilitate rather than coerce.

In the 1994 All Party Parliamentary Hearings on Parenting, one of the main conclusions revolved around the need to better co-ordinate policy and practice. This co-ordination was seen as required between central government departments as well as within local government and between central and local government. Perhaps one of the most important points was the argument for 'a single government department to be given the job of ensuring that the policies of other departments are favourable to families' (Soley, 1994: 6).

## WORK, PAID AND UNPAID

Modernist family sociology whilst valuing 'the family' also values individualism and materialism. Many men work extremely hard to provide a decent living for their families only to find themselves strangers in their own homes (Ferri & Smith, 1996). Parents are encouraged to exert authority, control and discipline over children on the basis of family love in a society that seems only to value wealth and material rewards. These things are unlikely to change overnight and indeed may be unchangeable. This should not, however, prevent us from exploring different approaches to understanding family living.

## PARENTING AND HOUSEWORK

Our paid workers produce remarkable goods and services. Our unpaid workers, especially mothers and housewives, produce similarly remarkable goods and services. In attempting to develop a new approach to understanding family lives, it is absolutely vital that we begin to pay equal attention and respect to paid and unpaid work.

In putting families first, clearly we should recognise the labour involved in child care and housework as proper work and it should be given no more or less priority than any other form of work. Whilst it is easier to think of domestic work such as cooking or laundry as somehow unimportant, Ribbens (1994: 59) makes the important point that much of this work should be seen as invisible production. Mothers also take on the stress and responsibility of caring, coping and doing a wide range of 'emotional work' that creates and sustains families. Equality of recognition and respect between paid work and motherhood and housework should be developed; most obvious would be the end to discrimination in eligibility for welfare benefits.

CARING IN FAMILIES

We can all care better for our elders, our partners, our children and ourselves and we have a duty to care better. We also have, however, a right to expect training, support and help in caring better. In contributing to a better society, we certainly can and do have obligations as individuals but society itself (through both state and influential organisations) has a prime obligation to facilitate that care. The 1994 All Party Parliamentary Hearings on Parenting identified three elements of the need to care for the carers:

'1. Support for carers must be improved, including increased provision of day care and respite care. Social Services should assess carers and their needs.

2. Friendly employment practices, which make provision for carers, should be encouraged.

3. The earnings limit for invalid care allowance should be increased' (Soley, 1994: 8).

Wise and Stead (1985: 9) observe that 'Current community care policies which assume the "natural" ability of families to provide care, seem to justify non-intervention by statutory services, except where families appear to be "inadequate". ... This argument is spurious, since the state has no hesitation in intervening in other areas, such as education.' The need for intervention is quite obvious in view of the extent and costs of domestic violence and marital breakdown. It is now time to construct a case to facilitate the best possible care within families.

We currently under-use a huge volume of potential caring from all kinds of people not 'connected' to families. Many single people, unemployed, disabled and elderly people might be willing to undertake caring if it was recognised and valued. Many families have needs around the care of children, elderly members, disabled members or the sick. Mobilising these resources, especially by developing systems of caring for carers, would allow us to both strengthen community and keep more people independent.

CHILD CARE

Many writers on women's issues have focused upon the provision of child caree. Whilst we need to be wary of child care becoming a 'dumping ground' whereby women become 'more equal to men', it is nonetheless true that good quality child care outside family homes may add considerably to the quality of family lives by both reducing stress on families and improving young people's long term life chances (Soley, 1994: 7). The Commission on Social Justice (1994: 320) asserted that 'Children are 100 per cent of the future.

Investment in their life-chances is the best social and economic investment we can make. Key reforms include: child care and nursery education for under-fives.'

The All Party Parliamentary Hearings on Parenting argued, as many before, for Nursery education for all children and, more specifically, 'More high quality, affordable child care must be provided. Both under-fives, after school and holiday care are needed and a wide range of providers should be encouraged' (Soley, 1994: 8). Child care provision should be much more than simply making available nurseries, play schools and crèches. The key is to develop flexible child care systems that are available when needed (even 24 hour availability), where needed (both larger units and small distributed units), and how they are needed (two or three short sessions a week through to full-time respite care when a parent or sibling is seriously ill). Such child care may give respite to parents, perhaps caring for new-born or young children, and introduce children to the wider social world; it may also lay a firm foundation for later educational achievement.

### CARE OF THE ELDERLY

The declining condition of the very elderly, especially the sick and frail, is a matter of concern throughout Europe. In the UK, frail dependent old people have been released from hospital into private nursing homes until the bulk of their 'savings' have been exhausted. To see the care of the elderly only as an issue of resources and who should 'pay the bills' is absurd. It seems clear that an emphasis upon putting families first should concentrate upon empowering families. Enabling families to care would not only improve the condition of many old people but it would also enhance their dignity and reduce tensions between the generations. Baldock (1993: 146) argues that there is a three cornered battle over who will care for the elderly and who will pay for it; the three parties being the state, the elderly and current or potential carers. Whilst seeing the care of the elderly in this way is popular, it is essentially flawed because it reduces human relationships and the status of elderly people to crude economics. Motenko and Greenberg (1995: 382) have argued that we should revise our perspective on later life 'A perspective of old age as a time of continued, positive growth and change is proposed. Dependence is not a marker of decline and deterioration, but a necessary development for positive growth and enhancement of later-life family reciprocity.' The elements of such care systems include training, preparation, financial resources, equipment, health care provision and respite care.

GENDER AND PAID WORK

Feminists have rightly identified gender inequality in paid work as one of the key forms of discrimination in modern societies. Brannen and Moss (1988: 168) conclude that: 'While other countries have slowly begun to try to connect the world of employment and the world of parenthood, Britain has ignored the matter, remaining wedded to an outdated view about parenthood and child care. The time for change is long overdue.'

This issue is especially relevant among feminists who have long argued against the sole homemaker role for women and for integration into the male world of work. Landau (1992: 47) argued that women's secondary place in the labour market is no solution to inequality but rather 'The solution is to follow strategies that promote equal responsibility between men and women for child-care and housework, rather than encouraging women to work only in the home or to make their double burden [of paid work and housework/child care] work.' The simplest and clearest solution here would be to insist that parents with pre-school children do exactly this, they put their families first. Women already do this in large numbers, it is time to encourage men to do so. On the one hand, fathers should be given parental leave on full wages or salary. On the other hand, mothers should be encouraged, if they wish, to maintain paid employment. In exploring the nature of working women and their families Lerner (1994: 96) suggests the need to put families first by concluding that 'A consensus needs to be achieved... Ultimately, what is needed is an approach that puts the families in the forefront and is responsive to the changes that confront them.'

Again, carers of children should be legally entitled to care for their children first before paid work. In this way, time for child care during sickness, flexible hours to facilitate school delivery and out of hours care should be mandatory and free from gender bias. The Commission on Social Justice (1994: 313) has argued that 'we need to empower women to share financial, as well as emotional and practical, responsibility for their children' and that 'we need to encourage and enable men to share the emotional and practical, as well as the financial, responsibilities of parenthood.'

WORKPLACE FAMILY POLICIES

Much paid employment conflicts with the needs of parents and children in the number of hours worked or the scheduling of those hours. A simple shift would be from employing individuals to employing members of families and developing legislation that seeks to protect and enhance those families. All employers should be encouraged by law to develop and deliver Family Policies within the workplace.

There are some examples of family friendly workplace policies in Europe, the USA and Australia such as paid paternity leave, flexitime for carers (of children, the sick, the disabled, and the elderly), and career break options (see Commission of the European Communities and the Belgian Ministry for Employment and Labour, 1992. As Pleck (1993) has noted, these tend to focus upon women and their familial roles; the shift to supporting families more widely demands that men be involved in the same way. The key change is to see employers moving away from merely running an enterprise to a wider recognition of the location and role of that enterprise in the local community and the family lives of workers, residents, clients and customers. Such a wider recognition can occur with the provision of child care, links with local family associations and/or child care agencies, and the provision of flexible work scheduling.

## WAGES AND BENEFITS

The obvious change would be in matching payments for labour, not only to effort, but to family responsibilities and moving towards accepting and supporting the 'full costs' of caring within families, understanding that this changes over time with family development. Costs vary by the age of dependants (new-born, school-age, elderly) and conditions (healthy, impaired, sick). Again, this can warrant positive discrimination, say in investing in the children of single parents to seek to avoid later heavy social costs of ill health, abuse or delinquency.

This could be achieved by moving towards a unified wage and benefit system oriented towards families. It remains the clearest indictment of the way we organise ourselves in modern western societies that children born to poor parents experience impoverished childhoods. This can be in no-one's best interests, certainly not those of poor parents and their children. We know, for example, that single parenthood is a key route into poverty for a large number of women and children in the UK. Whilst we should certainly seek to enable people to avoid single parenthood if they wish (by way of education, availability of support systems when family problems arise, etc.) we should also recognise the penalties paid by such families and consciously discriminate in their favour to avoid poverty.

What is proposed here is a simple and clear device by which society might say to individual families, we recognise the work you do for society, we recognise that this falls outside the usual paid work, and want to make sure that each parent receives sufficient income to properly care for all our children. This could most easily be achieved by way of a Negative Income Tax system geared towards family living.

## MEN AND WOMEN

Coote et al. (1990: 34-36) argued that families need strong, self-reliant women. Whilst an important point, this needs to be treated carefully; we really do not want a situation where women become as aggressive and exploitative as men. The last thing we need is to leave Patriarchy untouched and build instead a female version that is just as powerful and destructive of family relations. What we really need to do is to encourage women to be more self-reliant whilst also encouraging men to be less self-reliant. The All Party Parliamentary Hearings on Parenting concluded that, amongst other things, strengthening the role of fathers, especially by 'Helping men to be involved with their children is one way of providing a positive sense of identity' in the battle to reduce youthful crime (Soley, 1994: 8). We need adults who, above all else, put all families first: not just their own families but all families.

## GENDER INEQUALITY AND PARENTING

The single clearest inequality between the genders in contemporary societies relates to parenting. Most simply put, parenting is a primary activity for women and, at best, a secondary activity for men. The fact of childbirth does not mean that women are somehow best suited to shop for food, prepare meals, make beds, do the laundry, or any of the other hundreds of elements of contemporary child care and housework. The putting of families first can most obviously and clearly be achieved by confronting and dismantling the gendering of parent-hood. It is also vital to prepare all citizens for future parenting, with or without partners, and seek to do all we can to avoid people parenting in poverty or other stressful conditions. The simplest and clearest way of achieving this is to aim to facilitate 'male mothering'. It should be our aim to achieve the position where we can no longer assume that it will be the female who takes responsibility for child care.

## CONFLICT AND ABUSE

It is vital to grasp that individuals are not the simple products of nature or nurture but are complex beings, often decent and honest but also capable of being devious, deceptive and abusive. Indeed, we sometimes applaud these mixtures in folk tales and popular media. We know that families distribute the bads of conflict and abuse as well as the goods of warmth, love and material comfort.

149

We need to seek to understand and reduce the extent of family conflict and abuse as a matter of urgency. We may be able to reduce family abuse by making men more like women in breaking their work patterns for childrearing and placing them in situations of nurturance. Exposing more men to full-time childrearing may encourage 'female' virtues of co-operation and value placed upon non material goods and skills.

Also needed is a readiness to support families in periods of stress and conflict, many of which are predictable, such as unemployment or the birth of a first child. Family members need to be willing to accept and value such support intended, as it should be, to prevent pain and harm rather than as 'interference'. It is also clear that insofar as conflict and abuse arise out of material poverty, we should be ready to provide material support in both long and short periods of crisis.

## MARRIAGE AND DIVORCE

Despite rising divorce rates, the wish to create and sustain intimate partnerships is clearly a major life preoccupation for nearly all adults. In view of this, it is  shocking to see how little investment is made in preparing people for partnering and de-partnering.

Divorce represents huge human, social and economic costs. We know that divorce is linked to ill health, emotional disturbance, addictions and subsequent family poverty. Clearly we need to make the processes and outcomes of divorce far less damaging to all involved.

Family conciliation and reconciliation are obviously important. It also seems very clear that we should seek to prevent people arriving at the situation of wishing to divorce not by making the process more difficult or painful but by doing all we can to support marriage and partnerships. The quality of intimate relationships is easily as important as the quality of paid work relationships. It is in the wider interests of society to prepare people for stable, long term intimate partnerships.

## HUMAN SERVICES: PREVENTION

Modern western societies have generated a wide range of voluntary or state based service delivery systems and professions. It has long been known that many of these overlap, compete, even conflict with one another. Further to this is the well-known argument that prevention is far better than cure. Utting (1995: 54-71), working within the Joseph Rowntree Foundation's priority on 'Supporting Families, Preventing Breakdown' spends a considerable section of his text exploring the means of prevention. Utting explores a wide range of current activities. I suggested some time ago that this might lead to the linking, even unification, of services and systems under local democratic control (Bernardes, 1988).

FAMILY LIFE EDUCATION

One of the main conclusions of the All Party Parliamentary Hearings on Parenting in 1994 was the need to engage in funding 'Relationship Education', especially in schools, and noted that this required suitable training for teachers and outside educators as well as a renewed emphasis upon sex education (Soley, 1994: 6; Baker, 1996). Senior figures in the National Children's Bureau have long argued for a coherent policy for parent education. To some this might seem like an unaffordable luxury. In detailing an agenda for action, Pugh et al. (1994: 235) have developed a detailed suggestion for education for family life in schools, further education and the Youth Service as well as clear support and care for prospective parents before they conceive a child. The key to grasping the importance of such an agenda lies in realising that having ourselves all being children once is no guarantee that we will make competent parents. Indeed, in view of emerging evidence of child abuse by parents and other forms of behaviour regarded as 'poor parenting', it seems clear that we need to rebuild all human service provision towards facilitating better family living. Clearly the UK's National Curriculum should be fundamentally reoriented towards family living. In 1984, Pugh and De'Ath set out a very detailed case for Family Life Education on behalf of the National Children's Bureau. Education needs to be about preparing individuals to be decent citizens, have decent relationships and partnerships. Family abuse, intimidation and discrimination all need to be tackled, not as 'additional items' but by reorienting the curriculum.

At the moment, much formal education seems to be about paid work and individual citizenship. We need to add unpaid work and family life. Also needed, as Utting (1995: 57) notes, is continuing education, not just for 'career changes' but much more importantly for family life changes (such as childbirth or the parenting of adolescent children) which involve all family members.

This education does not need to be paternalistic, formal or authoritarian. All schools have at hand a huge reservoir of expertise in the parents of their pupils. Moreover, there are very large commercial interests which profit from family consumption. Together, surely current parents and industry could better prepare all pupils for family living.

HEALTH

Interestingly, the World Health Organisation (1986: 16) developed a clear argument for prevention in a conference held in 1984 that concluded, among other things, that 'Much greater emphasis should be placed on primary and secondary prevention. This should include work in schools on the roles and responsibilities of marriage and parenthood, work with mothers who have young children, high risk families and people in mid life crises.' The report drew upon the increasingly clear evidence that partnering, parenting and the stresses of family living have lasting impacts upon the health of family members. We also know that most family carers act as primary health workers and have an important role in health education and prevention.

At the simplest possible level it is vital to recognise that a great deal remains to be done about health in the western nations. Whilst preventive work is an obvious, though often neglected step (Townsend, 1988: 1-27), another vital development is family oriented health provision. There is much American work that identifies the importance of families in health and the importance of health in family life (Doherty & Campbell, 1988). In developing family education and preparation for partnering and parenting, there is a clear opportunity to prepare people for improved health.

SOCIAL WORK

The anti-discriminatory ethos of contemporary social work in the UK does not match beliefs about traditional family values and casework dealing with both 'family problems' and 'problem families'. Whilst it is plain that we should act to help those in trouble, the logic of social work seems fundamentally flawed. As the 1994 All Party Parliamentary Hearings on Parenting made clear, priority needs to be given to preventative work with families. Whilst priority was given to supporting voluntary sector organisations in this respect (Soley, 1994: 7), the first priority of statutory social work should be the support of all ordinary families to avoid, prevent or lessen the chances of 'problems' emerging. This requires a total and complete reorientation of social work practice. Current practice maintains the status quo of beliefs about traditional families and, as we see all too often, fails to even adequately deal with emerging problems, such as child sexual abuse.

Utting (1995: 59-61) developed a clear argument for the role of a wide range of voluntary organisations, such as Relate and Home-Start in what he terms 'secondary prevention'. One of the major problems facing such organisations is that of adequate funding which, in turn, relates to the extent to which multi-agency co-operation can be developed. It seems clear that a much more general priority of putting families first would begin to address both parts of this problem.

## LAW AND CRIME

Simply put, all criminals have families that may both be part of the basis of criminal behaviour and significantly affected by the criminal justice system. Similarly, the victims of crime are members of families and their families can suffer just as much at the hands of criminals as do individual victims.

In the 1993 report, 'Crime and the Family', Utting (1993: 27) discussed an extensive 'family based delinquency prevention programme'. Included in this scheme were family planning and preparation by family life education in schools, ante-natal and post-natal care, and a national mass media campaign on parent education. To support this, parental skills training, good quality child care and pre-school education must all be made available.

Utting (1995: 66) argues that 'No discussion of the scope for prevention would be complete without considering the ability of the law and the legal system to inhibit or exacerbate the more adverse consequences of family breakdown.' The way in which legislation and the legal system operates partly reflects and often partly influences community values about family life (such as marriage and divorce). It is within this context that many debates about the extent and nature of variation and diversity within families occurs (for example, debates about single parents or lesbian mothers). The law needs to recognise the rights of families in legal practice.

## FAMILY ASSOCIATIONS

Perhaps the most important point remaining to be made relates to the potential role of Family Associations in taking a major role in putting families first. Family Associations across much of Europe set out to address the needs of families as families (Bernardes, 1995a; 1995b). In many European countries, these associations play an important, at times even central, role in national policy debates about family life and related matters. The Union of Large and Young Families in the Flemish Community of Belgium covers the majority of the population and plays a major role in debates around child care, care of the elderly and welfare benefits for families (Bernardes, 1997: 64-68 and Bernardes & Keddie, 1998 forthcoming).

Work in the UK (Bernardes, 1995a; 1995b) has revealed that there are very many more associations relating to family life than might have been expected.

The majority of these are small, relatively recently formed (especially in the 1980s which seems to have been a boom time in founding such associations), and have very specific service aims relating to the needs of particular types of families and/or particular types of family needs. Research in the UK has not revealed any significant membership organisations on the model common in partner nations, exemplified by the Union of Large and Young Families in Belgium.

Family associations are uniquely placed, even if somewhat under-developed in the UK. In many ways Family Associations are the foremost experts on what families need and how those needs may be met. Such associations are already meeting a wide variety of perceived urgent needs of many kinds. There is an enormous amount of good practice and novel initiatives that meet needs in imaginative and efficient ways. Family Associations, if expanded to include a model of membership more like the European model, would be very well placed to play a crucial role in determining how to put families first. Family Associations, working on the basis of existing good practices, could survey what families feel would be valuable and determine how those perceived needs could be met.

## FAMILY LIVES IN THE FUTURE

In working in the United Kingdom, I long ago became accustomed to being regarded as faintly odd, studying 'family life' is usually seen as rather dull, boring and even uninteresting. 'Family living' is regarded as 'already understood' and as peripheral to 'real issues' in politics, business and industry, and social science. It has always seemed clear to me that the major shift to achieve is that of prioritising families in both popular and academic agendas.

Western societies have developed and become modern, and perhaps postmodern, over the last few hundred years. Nowadays, many other societies are changing beyond all recognition within decades or less, skipping from pre-modern to postmodern conditions. These terms reflect primarily material and political culture. What is missing is any parallel development of social structures. Societies do not 'evolve' in some 'natural' way. We have seen clearly enough that conflict, abuse, international war and genocide are as common in the 20th century as ever. We have not allowed technology to 'evolve' in some 'natural' way but have taken an active role in development, so we should take an active role in social development.

It is now time to recognise that ours are not the best possible societies, although they may not be among the worst either. We have simply failed to employ critical intellectual endeavour in those areas of life we think of as intensely 'private', that is 'family lives'. It is time to change this. In the pursuit of such a change, my job as a scientist and academic is to generate the best possible 'new understandings' I can.

It is my belief that a new discipline requires a new and radical vision, no matter how inadequate and unimaginative that may be judged in years to come, At the same time, there is stark evidence that past responses to 'family problems' and 'problem families' have all been inadequate.

The most obvious thing to change is the general belief in 'the family' for a sensitivity to the existence of many different kinds of family practices and pathways. Many contemporary issues in families (abuse, divorce, single parenthood), and about families (inequality, racism, etc.), arise as a direct result of individualism and materialism. We value healthy productive workers at the expense of their families. If children grow up knowing possessions and wealth are more important than families, then crimes to obtain wealth and power are hardly surprising.

Clearly families will keep on evolving, changing and rebuilding themselves whilst participants go on loving, hating and despising one another, sometimes all at the same time. Continual change in families is certain, it is for this reason that we must focus upon the varied and diverse family practices and pathways currently pursued. It is time to abandon faith in 'the family' and begin working instead towards improving some practices and pathways whilst discouraging others. It is obvious to me, for example, that we should seek to discourage conflict and abuse by encouraging preparation for partnering and parenting. This can be achieved by insisting, at every possible opportunity, that government, business and society are committed to take action towards putting families first (Bernardes, 1997).

REFERENCES

Baker, N. (1996). *Building a relational society: New priorities for public policy.* London: Arena.

Baldock, J. (1993). Old age. In: R. Dallos & E. McLaughlin. *Social problems and the family.* London: Sage, p. 123-153.

Bernardes, J. (1988). Founding the NEW 'family studies'. *Sociological Review, 36*(1), 57-86.

Bernardes, J. (1990). The family in question. *Social Studies Review, 6*(1), 33-35.

Bernardes, J. (1995a). Family associations in the UK: A national research. In: International Centre for Family Studies. *Family associations in Europe.* Milan: International Centre for Family Studies.

Bernardes, J. (1995b). *Family organisations and associations in the United Kingdom: A directory.* London: Family Policy Studies Centre.

Bernardes, J. (1997). *Family studies: An introduction.* London: Routledge.

Bernardes, J & D. Keddie (1998 forthcoming). *Family associations in the United Kingdom and Europe: A Belgian exemplar.* Submitted to the *Journal of European Social Policy.*

Brannen, J. & P. Moss (1988). *New mothers at work: Employment and childcare.* London: Unwin.

Cheal, D. (1991). *Family and the state of theory.* Hemel Hempstead: Harvester-Wheatsheaf.

Commission of the European Communities and the Belgian Ministry for Employment and Labour (1992). *Europe '93 - Business and the family: What strategies to bring them together.* Brussels: Commission of the European Communities.

Commission of the European Communities (1993). *Eurobarometer 39.0. The Europeans and the family: Results of an opinion survey.* Brussels: Commission of the European Communities.

Commission on Social Justice (1994). *Social justice: Strategies for social renewal.* London: Vintage.

Coote, A. et al. (1990). *The family way: A new approach to policy-making.* London: Institute of Public Policy Research.

Doherty, W.J. & T.L. Campbell (1988). *Families and health.* Beverly Hills, USA: Sage.

Durham, M. (1991). *Sex and politics: The family and morality in the Thatcher years.* Basingstoke: Macmillan.

Equal Opportunities Commission (1991a). *The key to real choice: An action plan for child care: A discussion paper.* Manchester: Equal Opportunities Commission.

Equal Opportunities Commission (1991b). *The key to real choice: An action plan for child care: Summary and recommendations.* Manchester: Equal Opportunities Commission.

Ferri, E & K. Smith (1996). *Parenting in the 1990s,* London: Family Policy Study Centre.

Landau, R. (1992). On making 'choices'. *Feminist Issues, 12*(2), 47-72.

Lerner, J.V. (1994). *Working women and their families.* London: Sage.

Levin, I. (1990). *How to define family. Family reports, No 17.* Uppsala, Sweden: University of Uppsala.

Morgan, D.H.J. (1975). *Social theory and the family.* London: Routledge and Kegan Paul.

Morgan, D.H.J. (1985). *The family, politics and social theory.* London: Routledge and Kegan Paul.

Motenko, A.K. & S. Greenberg (1995). Reframing dependence in old age: A positive transition for families. *Social Work, 40*(3), 382-390.

Pleck, J.H. (1993). Are 'family supportive' employer policies relevant to men. In: J. C. Hood (Ed.). *Men, work and family,* London: Sage, p. 217-237.

Pugh, G. & E. De'Ath (1984). *The needs of parents. Practice and policy in parent education.* Basingstoke: Macmillan.

Pugh, G. et al. (1994). *Confident parents, confident children: Policy and practice in parent education.* London: National Children's Bureau.

Ribbens, J. (1994). *Mothers and their children: A feminist sociology of childrearing.* London: Sage.

Scott, J. & K. Perren (1994). The family album: Reflections on personal and family life. In: N. Buck et al., *Changing households*. University of Essex: ESRC Centre on Micro-Social Change, p. 263-290.

Soley, C. (Chair) (1994). *Report of the All Party Parliamentary Group on Parenting and the International Year of the Family*. London: Exploring Parenthood.

Stacey, J. (1990). *Brave new families: Stories of domestic upheaval in late twentieth century America*. New York: Basic.

Townsend, P. et al. (1988). *Inequalities in health: The Black Report, the health divide*. Harmondsworth: Penguin.

Utting, D. (1995). *Family and parenthood: Supporting families, preventing breakdown*. York: Joseph Rowntree Foundation.

Utting, D. et al. (1993). *Crime and the family: Improving child-rearing and preventing delinquency*. London: Family Policy Studies Centre.

Wicks, M. (1991). Family matters and public policy. In: M. Loney et al., *The State or the Market*. London: Sage, p. 169-183.

Wise, V. & B. Stead (1985). *Change or choice: Community care and women as carers*. London: Greater London Council.

World Health Organisation (1986). *Children and family breakdown*. Copenhagen: World Health Organisation.

# The future of the family: A sociobiological approach

ROBERT CLIQUET
CENTRUM VOOR BEVOLKINGS- EN GEZINSSTUDIËN, BELGIUM
DRAGANA AVRAMOV
POPULATION AND SOCIAL POLICY CONSULTANTS, BELGIUM

## INTRODUCTION

The recent changes in the family and especially their demographic effects have raised, in several scientific disciplines, considerable concern about the future of the family and society (e.g. Cooper, 1986; Kaufmann, 1991). Doom-mongering about the dying occident, the end of the family and as consequence the disappearance of society (e.g. John Paul, 1994) arise here and there.

The cultural variation in family types induced many family sociologists to conclude that the family is by no means a natural phenomenon, the existence of which can be explained by biological facts, but that it is a social construction which finds its basis in cultural factors (e.g. Ditch et al., 1995; Zonabend, 1996).

The social-constructivist conception of the family, as much as the doom-mongering on the future of the family, are examples of a short-term, proximal-causal, non-evolutionary approach to the family. They largely build on the predominantly ideological way of thinking (e.g. Eid & Vaskovics, 1982). By contrast, a long-term, evolutionary and ultimate-causal approach shows that the fundamental 'raison d'être' of the human family is of a biological-evolutionary nature and that the family may still have a long future ahead.

In this contribution we approach the debate about the future of the family from the viewpoint of sociobiology – the discipline which studies the biological-evolutionary bases of social behaviour. In the last few decades a number of fundamentally new insights were developed in this discipline (cf. Hamilton, 1964; Maynard Smith, 1964; Trivers, 1971; 1972; 1974; Williams, 1966). They have proved to be of such importance that some are currently speaking of the 'second Darwinian revolution' (Horgan, 1995) which brings new understanding of social relations between individuals, between groups and particularly between genders, parents and offspring. They threw light on behaviour such as altruism, reciprocity, nepotism, sexually differentiated reproductive strategies, inter-individual and inter-group competition.

In human sociobiology the evolutionary approach of social behaviour has considerably grown in importance (e.g. Alexander, 1979a; Barkow et al., 1992; Betzig, 1997; Chagnon & Irons, 1979). This, *inter alia*, applies to the social structures known under the name of 'family' (e.g. Filsinger, 1988; Van den Berghe, 1979).

In this contribution it will be argued that: 1) families originated as mechanisms of sociobiological adaptation to individual biological needs specific for the human species; 2) families will continue to be tested in the future against their biologically adaptive value by means of Darwinian selection; 3) Darwinian selection influences gene frequencies as well as cultural values underlying family formation.

## THE ORIGIN OF THE FAMILY

Questions on the future of human features, either of a biological or a cultural nature, have in sociobiology always been approached from the analysis of the origin of these features. Sociobiology has built a solid theoretical frame of reference – namely the theory of evolution and adaptability as its testing criterion – to describe and evaluate the existence and function of these features. The underlying premise is: within a particular ecological context, biological as well as cultural features can have a neutral, positive or negative effect on the survival and/or reproduction of individuals. Neutral features can spread or disappear by chance, positive features will be retained and negative features will be eliminated by means of Darwinian selection. Consequently, the presence of biological or cultural features in a population are either due to chance phenomena in the case of harmless (i.e. neutral) characteristics or to positive selection in the case of those features which have an adaptive advantage.

Using adaptability as the testing criterion we will argue that the origin of the family is in essence associated with the increasing need of help of the human child in the process of hominisation. Infant's prolonged dependence necessitated a rise in parental investment, by the male gender as well, and this in turn required a more enduring partnership and an increasing control of sexual behaviour.

The transition to man occurred, four to five million years ago, as some anthropoid apes changed locomotion as an adaptation to the altering ecological conditions east of the Great Rift Valley in Africa. The environmental conversion from the tropical forest to a mixed woodland – savannah forced arboreal anthropoids to adapt to life on the ground. The advent of bipedalism had several adaptive advantages as it served to free the hands and resulted in the increasing use of tools and tool-making. This effected a shift of the selection pressure to the production of a better brain control mechanism, i.e. led to a gradual increase of the big brain hemispheres (e.g. Tobias, 1975). The encephalisation was in its turn accompanied by a number of ontogenetic and reproductive changes which were mainly characterised by the longer maturation and the increasing need of help of the hominid infant. The successive types of hominidae have adapted to these developments and have even facilitated the evolution by, *inter alia*, the invention of 'the family' – a social structure which provided the after-birth womb (Gough, 1971; Lampert, 1997, Mellen, 1981; Van den Berghe, 1979): 'The human family is, very simply, the solution our hominid ancestor evolved over three to five million years to raise brainy, slow maturing, neotenic, highly dependent, and therefore, very costly (in terms of parental investment) babies.' (van den Berghe, 1988: 43).

The longer maturation and the increasing need of help of the hominid infant basically required two sociobiological adaptations: an increasing parental investment and a more enduring partnership of parents. The development of the first ensured the biologically needed intensification and prolongation of care and socialisation. The second developed as a reinforcing mechanism which made greater paternal care and protection of mother and child(ren) feasible. Parental investment and enduring partnership originated and persisted throughout the hominisation process as the two basic family functions. All other family functions could either be deduced from these basic functions or be linked to them. The specific form and the relative importance of other family functions has been largely dependent upon the ecological, economic and cultural living conditions in which families function.

## Increasing parental investment

The brain expansion during hominisation resulted in an increasing immaturity of a new-born and a longer postnatal maturation for two reasons: 1) the brain expansion was not accompanied by a proportional lengthening of pregnancy; 2) the evolution of the hominid brain was coupled with a gradually continued transition from an instinctive to a conscious control of behaviour.

The first had as consequence that the hominid infant was born increasingly helpless and required a more and more intensive and longer postnatal care; the second that ever more complex and lengthy learning and socialisation processes were required (Leutenegger, 1982; Portmann, 1944).

The hominidae are monoparous – they normally give birth to only one infant at a time. On average, more than one child must be born in order to ensure generation replacement. Under conditions of high infant and child mortality which prevailed during the hunters and gatherers cultural phase – one out of two to two out of three live-born children died before reaching puberty (Acsádi & Nemeskéri, 1970) – in order to avoid the danger of extinction, fertility had to stand at between five to eight children. It may be argued that the invention of the family contributed largely to keeping infant and child mortality below extinction level and made the continued evolution of the early *hominidae* to the current *Homo sapiens* possible.

Research on child development in contemporary culture has shown that infants and children have a need for an enduring, affectionate relation with a small number of adults and that the fulfilment of this need is a requirement for normal physical, intellectual and emotional development. If such a relation is lacking there is a risk that the child will be impaired in development. Depending on the age at which the emotional deprivation arises, on its duration and intensity, phenomena such as higher mortality, stunted growth, higher morbidity, emotional disorders, lower cognitive performances and socialisation difficulties may be perceived (e.g. Bowlby, 1951; Montagu, 1957).

All available phylogenetic and ontogenetic evidence points in the direction of the conclusion that the basic function of the family during human evolution has been protection, care and education of children. The maturation pattern in humans is characterised by lengthy growth and development which starts with conception and following birth continues in successive phases of growth totalling 15 years. In the advance industrial culture the passage to adulthood may take as long as 20 to 25 years.

The human specific maturation pattern ultimately explains the universality of the family. Parental investment and enduring partnership between parents as two basic family functions have been partly biologically selected for and are therefore codetermined by biological factors.

## The emergence of an enduring partnership

In many animal species, including the primates, there is a negative co-relation between the sex difference in parental investment in offspring and partnership endurance (Chagnon & Irons, 1979; Trivers, 1972). Sexual difference in parental investment leads to sexually different reproductive strategies. The sex which invests a lot in each individual descendant will produce fewer offspring than the sex that invests a little. The parent investing much in offspring will have a more quality-oriented attitude, or, will aim at having fitted out each descendant as well as possible (Daly & Wilson, 1978). The reproductive success of the less investing sex can, by contrast, be enhanced by producing as many descendants as possible, i.e. by developing a quantitative strategy.

With regard to couple formation this means that the less investing sex – the male sex – will try to obtain and impregnate as many partners as possible. This leads to short-term relationships and intra-sex competition. However, the more investing sex – the female sex – will be characterised by a more selective choice of partner(s). After all, a higher investment involves a higher risk; it is therefore in the interest of this sex to choose the partner(s) who is/are expected to offer the greatest chances of survival for the descendants.

The intra-sex competition among the males, on the one hand, the more meticulous choice of the females, on the other, leads to an enhancement of sexual dimorphism for some secondary sex features which can be regarded as proxies for the reproductive success of the descendants. This double sexual selection leads to marked sex differences in the morphological, physiological and psychological field. The less investing sex – in the case of a selection through a physical trial of strength – becomes stronger and taller and therefore abler for competition and aggression. Everything points out that a very marked sex dimorphism still existed among the first hominids (e.g. McHenry, 1996). It is deduced from this that they were still polygynous.

In the process of hominisation, together with the increase in parental investment and partnership endurance, a regression of sexual dimorphism occurred. In the male it was especially characterised by a reduction in the robustness of the bodily structure and the related behavioural features with regard to competition and aggression. Consequently the human male has come to show a closer resemblance to the female gender. In the human evolution, the decrease in sexual dimorphism implies that the male underwent a 'feminisation process' (e.g. Cliquet, 1984).

In the hominisation process the female also underwent extremely radical changes. Whereas the male evolution was especially associated with a reduction in robustness, i.e. with secondary sexual features, the changes in the female related above all to primary sexual features: ovulation, breast development, orgasm and menopause. Several of these changes are connected to the shift from a cyclical to a non-cyclical readiness of the female for sexual intercourse – a nearly unique human phenomenon. The human female is characterised by a hidden ovulation. Moreover, the human female has the aptitude to be sexually active during the whole menstrual cycle, thus also beyond the short period around the ovulation. Not only the absence of a visible ovulation and the non-cyclical sexual activity of the female, but other specifically human sex features as well, like the permanent presence of large breasts and the achievement of orgasms, point to the continuous sexual potency or force of attraction of the female.

The human maturation pattern is not only responsible for the selection of the above gender characteristics but also for the development of the human-specific neuro-hormonal constitution which enabled the development of enduring, affectional partner relationships (Lampert, 1997; Mellen, 1981). The origin of love between heterosexual adults, as well as the family itself, go back to the early hominidae. Love constituted the psychological foundation of the social bond which was of fundamental importance to the survival of the vulnerable human infant. There is ample evidence that romantic love is a virtually universal human phenomenon. Jankowiac & Fischer (1992) undertook a world wide investigation into the existence of romantic love in humans and examined 166 cultures. They found evidence of romantic love in human populations in 88 percent of examined cases.

The view that human love is also a phylogenetically developed feature selected in function of the children's long-term need for help and growth, might seem less obvious than the relation between affection and ontogenetic development itself. After all, in many cultures protection, survival and economic motives in arranged marriages seem to be more important than affectional needs. The existence of the biological aptitude for love does not imply that it will manifest itself automatically and universally. Although the sexual and neurological specificities of man facilitate the development of enduring and affectional relationships, these features are not fully genetically programmed. Moreover they can be in competition with other impulses or needs, or their development can be repressed under certain circumstances. They can depend on the extent of sustained compatibility between the partners. Allowance must also be made for the individual variation in the genetic and ontogenetic determinants which develop enduring affectional feelings. Given the incomplete genetic programming of the urge towards affection and the competition with other factors, this aptitude needs to be culturally and socially supported. Consequently, a quite considerable variation in the occurrence and the extent of the development of enduring love relationships, both inside and between populations, may be expected.

Survival needs have traditionally reinforced the economic motives for establishing and maintaining enduring relationships. They may have predominated over affectional needs. Roussel (1989) argues that the idea of happiness became the dominant basis of western marriage and family life only from the 18th century onward. Emotional needs of individuals could win more space and even predominate as criteria for the formation of couples once economic circumstances enabled the satisfaction of the vital individual and group survival needs. It may be said that the basis and the binding texture of family life during the modernisation process underwent a shift from survival to love (Farrell, 1993; Sternberg & Barnes, 1988). However, it would be a mistake to think that romantic love as basis for marriage is a western social construction (Buss, 1994; Jankoviak & Fischer, 1992). The western family pattern, in which reciprocal affection of the partners gained importance, is not merely a cultural variant as some authors assert. It builds on fundamental changes in gender relations associated with the economic independence, greater self-reliance and self-respect of women. Modern technology and culture favour the development of the biological potencies of women (as well as men) in fulfilling their emotional needs also with respect to partnership.

Pursuit of happiness and romantic love as basis of family life resulted in an increasing variety of family forms. Indeed, in western societies in which societal and parental control over partner choice is disappearing or weakening cross sectional data document, more particularly in recent decades, an increasing variation in living arrangements. Longitudinal surveys show that in a life course perspective there has been an increase in the frequency of transitions between different forms of partnership and families (Avramov, 1992). Research also confirms that the majority of people do not opt for unrestrained promiscuity or celibacy but overwhelmingly build enduring relationships (Corijn, 1995; Laumann et al. 1994). The major part of those who cease to cohabit or divorce start very quickly a new enduring partnership or look for a more satisfying or successful enduring relationship (Fisher, 1992).

THE FUTURE OF THE FAMILY

The multiplication of family forms in recent years, rather than the analysis of fundamental family functions in an evolutionary perspective, constitute the basis for the majority of hypotheses regarding the future. In recent literature (e.g. Cornish, 1979; Duvold, 1995; Roussel, 1989) we find that mainstream 'visions of the future' fall in one of the three scenarios: 1) the disappearance of the family; 2) the restoration of the traditional family; 3) the persistence or further increase of family variation.

We will first identify the hypotheses underlying each of these scenarios and comment on the interpretation of the data used for each of these assumptions.

Then we will discuss each scenario from a sociobiological view, i.e. from the perspective of the evolutionarily adaptation of the family to the specific human needs.

## The disappearance of the family

The recent trends of various demographic indicators of family life, may at first sight, seem to confirm that the family is about to vanish: nuptiality and fertility are decreasing, divorce rates are increasing. But, do we not need a more comprehensive causal analysis? Should signs of change inevitably be identified with the symptoms of a fatal disease? Should we not look at changes in a broader time perspective?

While it may be argued that the strong decline in nuptiality rates is indicative of a loss of appeal of a certain type of legally regulated partnership, they do not necessarily foreshadow the disappearance of the family. Lower propensity to conclude matrimony or postponement of formal marriage are (more than) compensated for by other types of partnership such as non-marital cohabitation and LAT-relationships. Evidence from a variety of sources shows that most people establish an enduring relationship and eventually marry. Moreover, investigations have shown that cohabiting couples strongly resemble married couples in many ways (e.g. Brown & Booth, 1996). The need for an enduring partnership combined with some other sexually or reproductively related personality features (e.g. jealousy, nepotism) implies that communes as types of partnership disappeared in modern culture as quickly as they arose (Behnam, 1990).

An increase in divorces may be interpreted as the retrogression of a certain model of family. It may be argued that the present level of divorce reflects rather the difference in gender expectations with respect to partnership that the rejection of the enduring relationship. More particularly many men seem to be unable to adapt to an emancipated partner. However, research also shows that most divorced people want to and do establish new, enduring relationships.

The fertility decline has been fairly spectacular. But, recent fertility surveys in many countries (e.g. Cliquet & Callens, 1993) as well as demographic registration data (e.g. Gadeyne et al., 1998) point to a nearing stabilisation of fertility, although at a low level. Fertility surveys also show that the vast majority of the married and unmarried couples want to have children. In fact, they affirm that they want more children than they currently have or expect to have.

A nuance analysis of demographic data reveals the shallowness of 'the death of the family' scenario based on a quick reading of statistics. But, even stronger arguments against the disappearance scenario are found in the human biogram.

After all, humans have been selected – for reproductive ends – to form enduring, not necessarily lifelong, sexual bonds. Indeed, there is ample evidence that in modern culture, where a wider range of relational options has become available, the vast majority of the population continue to want to develop enduring relationships in which romantic love is seen as a buttress (Laumann et al., 1994; Sternberg & Barnes, 1988). The same holds for bearing and rearing children. In large majority parents want to have children and want to raise their children themselves (Cliquet & Callens, 1993; Spiro, 1958).

Moreover, sociobiology offers another argument against the disappearance thesis. This argument is concerned with the effect of Darwinian selection, i.e. of the differential reproduction of carriers of various genes or ideas. The potency of this evolutionary mechanism is generally underestimated, either because knowledge about evolution is still insufficiently disseminated or because it meets with ideological opposition. Another reason may be that the selection mechanism only shows results in the long-term and long-term perspective is not in vogue.

Sociobiology shows that not only genes but also ideas are under the pressure of Darwinian selection. Indeed, ideas may be regarded as the genes of cultural development (e.g. Dawkins, 1976; Lumsden & Wilson, 1981). From an evolutionary point of view, culture can be considered as an exosomatic system that facilitates adaptation. Consequently, adaptation-promoting cultural innovations will have a positive effect on reproductive fitness. However, not all cultural innovations promote fitness. Just as for the genes themselves, there are favourable, neutral and unfavourable cultural variants. A substantial difference between genes and ideas is that ideas can both vertically and horizontally be passed on, whereas genes, as yet, are only vertically inherited – i.e. passed from parents to children (Alexander, 1979b).

Let us examine in the light of evolutionary mechanisms the below-replacement fertility. As long as there are groups in society, even minority groups, who maintain or achieve above-replacement fertility, the survival of the family and the long-term continuity of society will be ensured. The under-reproducing sections of the population will be selected out through Darwinian selection. Together with the disappearance of the genes of this group – assuming that genes affect their physical or emotional personality features leading to under-reproduction – their values and norms, which induced low fertility, will disappear or become marginal. Initially some serious social problems associated with excessive ageing of the population and regional depopulation may be expected to arise. But, in the long run families with a replacement fertility will gradually predominate again.

Selection processes as a result of differential reproduction can be perceived. Some authors argue that the end of the demographic transition will be characterised by a uniform, very low fertility. But this hypothesis may not prove to be valid over a longer time span. Indeed, already today we find a number of modern three- and four-child families. These large families are neither a result of failed contraception nor do they function according to values and norms of the agrarian era and asymmetrical gender relations.

To summarise. The emancipatory opportunities associated with technological and cultural modernisation are reshaping human relations. Modern humans may be facing an inconsistency between growing opportunities and raising individual aspirations, on the one hand, and present-day societal structures not yet well adapted to the new environment, on the other hand. From a broad evolutionary and historical perspective, modernisation is in fact a revolutionary innovation, totally different from the Environment of Evolutionary Adaptedness (EEA) (Symons, 1979) in which the human emerged and evolved. It is a cultural mutation, i.e. a sudden change requiring adaptation in many respects, either by genetic or by cultural means.

The diagnosis about multiplication of forms and increased frequency of transitions between different family forms provides no justification for the 'vanishing of the family' scenario. From a sociobiological point of view as well as on the basis of available empirical data on relational and reproductive behavioural changes in modern culture 'the death of the family' scenario is most improbable. Care of child(ren) and enduring (not necessarily life-long) relationship persist as two basic family functions in modern culture.

## Back to the traditional family?

What should be understood by 'traditional family'? Is it the traditional biological family as it existed under conditions of high mortality and high fertility which produced high frequencies of one-parent families and step-families as a result of death of a spouse? Is it the traditional economic family with the father as the sole breadwinner and the mother as homemaker? Or is it simply the traditional ideological family in which sexuality, nuptiality and reproduction are expected to be inseparable? Is it the model of a family which excludes contraception, premarital sex, unmarried cohabitation and which starts with heterosexual matrimony and produces (many?) children in a lifelong monogamy.

We can be brief concerning the biological traditional family. It is difficult to imagine that anybody would want to re-introduce a generalised high mortality, implying the necessity of a compensating high fertility. The traditional economic family model, however, with its clear-cut gender-segregated role and task division, is not yet completely out of the air. Not only some ideologically conservative pressure groups continue to advocate this model, but many a would-be patriarch is filled with nostalgia for the times gone by. However, aspirations of younger generations of women show that this model can be dismissed. All recent surveys show that the overwhelming majority of young women want to join the labour force, to earn money or to develop a career (e.g. Van Dongen et al., 1995). Career and family aspirations rule-out asymmetrical partner roles.

What are the chances of the revival of the traditional ideological family? A social counter-move can never be excluded completely, as may be evidenced by the appearance of new religious movements (e.g. Bromley et al., 1981). However, these movements manifestly affect only a minority, as yet at least. A generalised return to the ideological family, however, must be regarded as unlikely because the biological, economic and cultural basis for such a return is simply no longer available. Modern science which provides efficient means for individual control of fertility has made the socially controlled abstinence redundant as a fertility check. Mortality and fertility control and new insights on man and society have eroded the functional basis of traditional ideologies.

All this does not mean that some of the current development tendencies of family formation might not lead to a partial countermove. A sustained very low fertility by generalising the one-child family would produce unfavourable social effects in the long run, e.g. as regards intergenerational continuity and intergenerational transfers. Therefore it is quite possible that subsequent generations will draw lessons from the reproductive behaviour of former generations and increase their fertility spontaneously. It is even more likely that the state will try to prevent a sustained very low fertility and will implement a wide range of family supporting measures (Roussel, 1991). But, the two- or three-child family obviously does not imply a return to the traditional family.

## Modern family variation

The family demography of modern society shows an increasing variation in household types and more complex family life courses in recent decades. Family and household variation is, however, not a completely new phenomenon. In pre-Victorian societies, some family and households types – e.g. celibacy, monoparental families, reconstituted families – were as common if not more common than today, but the causes of their prevalence – mortality levels, economic constraints, ideological choices – were different from the current ones (Laslett, 1965). What is also different, is the ideological attitude towards family variation.

With modernisation we clearly evolved from a uniform ideal towards the tolerant acceptance of a pluriform variation which is the outcome of individual choice.

The social security networks and the abundant recreational opportunities offered by modern culture, as well as the ideologies of equality and liberty of pluralist democracy promote individualisation. These circumstances combined with the existing variability in personality features and, more particularly, the still existing, although strongly reduced differences in sexual and reproductive strategies of both genders (Batten, 1994) give reason to expect that the recently increased diversity of family and household types, more specifically in the matter of partnership, will be largely maintained or will even continue to increase (Hoffmann-Nowotny, 1987; Höpflinger, 1990; Roussel, 1989).

## Partnership

By reason of the bio-psychical specificity of the human need pattern it may be argued that most people will continue to strive after enduring relationships, even though they will not necessarily or always be of a lifelong nature. Moreover, surveys have corroborated that most people want to develop enduring relationships and, even, want to marry (e.g. Corijn, 1995; Kiernan & Wicks, 1990). All this leads us to expect that both the individual biographies and the family cycles may become even more complex and differentiated that they are today.

Since the external pressures – e.g. familial, religious or general social influences – and also the internal pressures – e.g. economic dependence, a large family – have weakened, if not phased out the maintenance of a 'legalised' partnership, intimate relationships become more and more dependent on individual personality features and decisions. In addition, the demands made upon intimate relationships become greater and greater. It follows that families become much more vulnerable and may, to no inconsiderable extent, end in separation or divorce. The result may be a further increase in the frequency of one-parent families. Some authors (e.g. Rivera, 1994) even predict that the one-parent family headed by the mother will become the future family pattern or, at least, one of the most occurring family types. This would mean that the pre-hominid mother-child bond would become again the basic unit of society. It is legitimate, however, to question whether we are not confusing one-parent households with one-parent families. Co-residence is not necessarily a good enough indicator of the functional roles of parents. Joint or shared custody may becoming more prevalent. Modern working conditions are leaving more time to working fathers to enjoy their role of carers. Men may not wish to abdicate as fathers when they cease to function as husbands.

The rising separation and divorce rates do not necessarily have to result for long in one-parent or single-person families. Most of the divorced people, with or without children, build up a new relationship or even remarry. Now that divorce is becoming a quite frequent phenomenon, we may expect values and standards relating to divorce and parenthood of divorced or separated persons to change as well. We may expect that divorced or separated people will adopt a more appropriate attitude towards relationships between former family members (partner and children). We may expect society to develop more effective means to prevent that children are used as bargaining counters. However, considerable efforts will be needed here to neutralise or balance innate drives such as dominance, possessiveness, jealousy and nepotism, which are deeply embedded in the human biogram.

It is to be expected that the frequency of one-parent families, at least as transitional family stage in the life course, will increase or remain high. Given the facts that today most one-parent families are headed by women, that women's social position is still relatively weaker than that of men and that women, more than men, have to cope with the existing incompatibilities between gainful employment and family life, and especially child care (Avramov, 1993; Van den Bergh & Van Dongen, 1998), we may expect that in the near future this type of family will remain a vulnerable social group.

The combination of the drive to develop enduring relationships and the increasing vulnerability of relationships, resulting in divorce, may lead to the maintenance, or even, a rise in the frequency of reconstituted families by way of marriage or cohabitation.

Biology and culture are leading to the re-emergence or re-enforcement of serial monogamy. An important innovation in this respect is the considerable increase in life expectancy in modern culture which allows or forces partners to have a continuous partnership of more than half a century. The long life expectancy is a novelty to which the human species is perhaps not well adapted, especially now the traditional biological, cultural and economic constraints leading to family bonding, have loosened up. Serial monogamy may be a better adapted system, although it is probably also not free from particular constraints, such as the relations between stepparents and stepchildren in the presence of surviving biological parents, and the gender differences in reproductive clocks and ageing patterns.

Unmarried cohabitation, especially as a premarital phase, may continue to increase. In some more advanced countries cohabitation is already a generalised stage in the life course. Nevertheless, we may expect that, in the end, most people will continue to marry for a variety or a combination of reasons such as the emotional need for an enduring affectional relationship, certainty of fathering for the male, guaranteed paternal investment for the female, legal advantages, social status, pressure of the family, social advantages, ideological grounds and the magic effect of rituals. Furthermore, the removal of the traditional impediments to divorce may decrease the growing reluctance to marry or the current trends of delaying marriage.

Several aspects of modernisation, mainly the increased career opportunities for women and the increased geographical mobility, also offer the possibility or, as the case may be, necessitate developing a LAT-relationship ('living-apart-together'). Little is still known about this type of family. It presumably concerns a very heterogeneous category which is opted for because of a variety of factors and circumstances (personality type, employment conditions and location, mobility requirements, family phase, financial position, etc.). Given the economic and psychological burden which, in many cases, weighs on this type of partnership, we may suppose that LAT-relationships will remain a minority or constitute a transitional stage in a person's life course.

It may be expected that some people will, at least during some stages in their life course, opt for free and variable relationships. Recent surveys showed that this category of people, especially consisting of young males, is rising (Corijn, 1995; Laumann et al., 1994). Given the multiplicity and diversity of human needs and drives, it is not surprising that, in the absence of stringent life or welfare threatening environmental pressures, a larger variation in behavioural choices manifests itself. It is also not surprising that this is more striking for the human male, given his still relatively lower parental investment and less tight reproductive clock.

Homosexual relationships as they become less stigmatised may be expected to increase or, at least, become more visible to the general public. As more evidence is corroborated that homosexuality is largely determined by biological factors (e.g. Hamer et al., 1993) we may expect that the social acceptance of homosexual households and families may increase. Moreover, in our modern multi-million people societies such relationships do not constitute a threat to the reproductive continuity of society. Both evolutionary insights and sexological surveys reveal that homosexual relations are extremely rare.

Celibacy is a phenomenon that in circumstances of pre-modern culture was not uncommon for various economic, biological and ideological reasons. Several features of modern culture, such as the higher standard of living, the improved state of health, the ideology of equality and secularisation, cause this phenomenon to regress. Nevertheless, celibacy may be expected to persist, not only because a number of people will not succeed in being singled out for appropriate partnership, but also through the fact that some regard celibacy as their conscious choice. In this connection, it may be observed that surveys found that the latter group clearly constitutes a minority (Corijn, 1995). Here again, modern living circumstances with their life and welfare protective systems at the societal level, are less compelling towards developing survival and protection strategies at the family or household level.

All forms of forced partnership or sexual exploitation, such as enforced or arranged marriages, paedophilia, incest, rape, constrained prostitution, may be expected to regress, not because their biological basis would have disappeared, but because circumstances of modern culture promote the existence of emancipatory ideologies, more particularly as regards the child and the woman. Forced partnership or sexual abuse are incompatible with modern cultural values.

## Parenthood

Fertility surveys (e.g. Cliquet, 1985; 1996) repeatedly and amply show that we may expect that most people will continue to want children, but – given the current social, economic and cultural circumstances – in restricted number, not more than one or two. Owing to the unavoidable occurrence of wanted and unwanted childlessness and one-child families, this will lead to a perpetuation of below-replacement fertility. Up to the moment that population categories with an above-replacement fertility predominate on account of differential reproduction.

Because of the social security systems and the individual's wider range of available emancipatory opportunities in the sphere of employment and recreation, the one-child family and even childlessness may in certain economic or cultural circumstances increase considerably. In Germany, 25% of the younger female cohorts and 33% of male cohorts are expected to remain childless (Dorbritz & Schwarz, 1996). However, it need be stressed that new forms of childlessness may be rather the effect of the postponement strategy, as a consequence of current role incompatibilities, than the conscious finite choice not to have children (Avramov, 1992). The still persistent partial incompatibility between family duties and employment, especially for women (Van Dongen, 1993; Van Dongen et al. 1995; Avramov, 1995) constitute one of the well-known bottlenecks.

The introduction of social security and other social protection systems and processes which in modern culture ensure survival and well-being largely independent of family circumstances, have complemented and even replaced the individual parental investment in the own offspring. They have also changed the way intergenerational transfer of resources and to a lesser degree services operates between adult children and aged parents. All this has lead in the last few decades to an erosion of parts of the functional basis of family. In the 1990s we have seen an increase in intentional lone motherhood (Miller, 1992) and a decrease in the interest and investment on behalf of fathers in the off-spring from the former relationship(s) (Roussel, 1991). Institutional solidarity which has replaced direct family transfers is part of the modernisation process which has made substantial changes in family relations and family structures possible.

Despite the weakening, or even the disappearance of several traditional social and economic functions of the family, it seems ineluctable that, on account of the human biogram, such variants will remain a minority phenomenon and that families will (have to) continue to fulfil their fundamental role in the production and primary socialisation of offspring and related functions, more particularly in the field of development and enduring intimate partner relationships. Both genders have in the process of hominisation been selected, maybe to a somewhat different extent, on the basis of emotions which promote enduring relationships as well as care for own offspring. Moreover, being successful in modern culture requires, despite the existence of social structures, a high individual parental investment in offspring, an effort which most parents want to continue. Nepotism is a particularly strong driving force (Alexander, 1979a). Consequently, it may be expected that the major part of the population will continue to consider the family as the most important unit for physical care and emotional security, for both children and adults. Experiments to entrust other institutions with family duties relating to primary socialisation of children or to have other than enduring partner relationships failed miserably because of either their poor results (Prigent, 1955), their high economic cost, or their emotional dissatisfaction (Bowlby, 1951; Montagu, 1957).

WHAT ABOUT A MORE REMOTE FUTURE?
The 'future-of-the-family' scenario's in the recent sociological literature (e.g. Cornish, 1979; Duvold, 1995; Roussel, 1989) all look at the family in a relatively short time perspective. A sociobiological or evolutionary approach, however, always envisages a longer time perspective. So, one may raise the question how the recent changes in relational and reproductive behaviour might evolve in a more remote future?

The evolutionary approach allows to explain the past on the basis of insights in the evolutionary mechanism and the reconstruction of the Environment of Evolutionary Adaptedness (EEA). We can apply these insights to the knowledge we have about our present novel environment, but it is much more difficult, on the basis of our present level of knowledge, to foresee what the future evolutionary environment will be and consequently to give a long-term evolutionary forecast.

What can be said is that, if the present cultural progress continues, the future environment and future life will increasingly be shaped and steered by human intervention. It can also be supposed that this will be directed towards the furthering of quality of life, even at the expense of quantitative goals which were so important in the past (Cliquet, 1996-1997).

Promoting quality of life, however, can be pursued in different directions. For instance, it can uni-directionally concentrate on individual need satisfaction, promoting individualism, if not solipsism to the utmost, or pay also attention to social relations, at the meso- as well as at the macro-level. The future of the human, and of its most basic sociobiological institution – the family – will in other words also depend upon the future value system that will be chosen and the developmental goals we will set for ourselves.

As far as family life is concerned, and more particularly its two basic functions – care of long maturing offspring and enduring adult partnership – we shouldn't foster unrealistic illusions. Unless we succeed in changing fundamentally the human genome in those respects, it will not be so easy to liberate ourselves from our evolutionary past. On the contrary, it might be that some of the past trends in human evolution – e.g. the increasing maturation time and the need for enduring and profound affection – may even be re-enforced. Last but not least, it might be that we do not want to eliminate such deeply embedded emotional needs, result of millions of years of evolution.

SUMMARY AND CONCLUSIONS
In this contribution we started from sociobiology to probe the origin and fundamental functions of the family. We argued that the family originated from specific biological needs which arose in the Environment of Evolutionary Adaptedness (EEA) and that even today, in the novel environment of modern culture, it owes its '*raison d'être*' to biological needs without which it probably would have disappeared completely.

The human family resulted from the increasing need for help of the child in the process of hominisation. The family is a social institution of which the essential function is of an adaptive-biological nature, i.e. it contributes to what in current sociobiological jargon is called the 'maximisation of inclusive fitness' of its members. Parental investment and enduring partnership constitute the two basic functions of the family. All other family functions can be derived from or linked with these two basic functions. The concrete form and relative importance of these other functions are largely dependent upon the ecological and economic living conditions in which families function and upon related cultural values and norms.

Several possible scenario's of the future are tested against the human biogram and considered within the context of a further developing modernisation. It may be expected that modern culture will continue to foster a variety of family forms. However, as regards partner relationship, it is argued that, on the basis of the bio-psychical specificity of the human need pattern, most people will continue to aim at enduring relationships, even though those will not necessarily or always be of a lifelong nature, resulting in a further increase in serial monogamy. As far as parenthood is concerned, it is to be expected that families will continue to fulfil their fundamental role in the production and primary socialisation of offspring and that they will remain the most substantial unit for physical care and emotional security, for both children and adults. With respect to fertility, we may expect that most people will continue to want children, but in restricted number, not more than one or two. Owing to the ineluctable occurrence of wanted and unwanted childlessness and one-child families, this will, in the current socio-economic and cultural circumstances, lead to some perpetuation of below-replacement fertility. The underreproducing sections of the population, however, will gradually be eliminated by means of Darwinian selection and, together with them, their genes as well as their values, leading to low fertility, will disappear or at least be reduced.

As far as concerns the more remote future, it is expected that this will increasingly be shaped and steered by human intervention, directed towards the furthering of quality of life. In such a perspective, it might not be so easy to abandon evolutionarily based family functions, required for fulfilling deeply embedded emotional needs, unless we would succeed in changing fundamentally the human genome in those respects. On the contrary, it might be that some of the past trends in human evolution, such as the increasing maturation time and the need for enduring and profound affection, may even be re-enforced.

REFERENCES

Acsádi, G & J. Nemeskéri (1970). *History of human life span and mortality*. Budapest: Akadémiai Kiadó.

Alexander, R.D. (1979a). *Darwinism and human affairs*. London: Pitman.

Alexander, R.D. (1979b). Evolution and culture. In: N.A. Chagnon & W. Irons (Eds.). *Evolutionary biology and human social behaviour*. North Scituate, Mass.: Duxbury Press, p. 59-78

Avramov, D. (1992). *Pojedinac, porodica i stanovnistvo u raskoraku* (Individual, family and population in mismatch, published in Serbo-croat language with the executive summary in English). Beograd: Naucna knjiga.

Avramov, D. (1993). Child care, school time schedules, and professional activity of parents. In: A. Blum, J.-L. Rallu (Eds.). *European population, demographic dynamics*. Paris: INED-John Libbey.

Avramov, D. (1995). *Welfare and solidarity*. Results from the Population Policy Acceptance (PPA) Survey about the Respondents Expectations from the State. Proceedings of the International Colloquium Attitudes on Population in Europe. Brussel: CBGS-Documenten, Centrum voor Bevolkings- en Gezinsstudiën.

Barkow, J., L. Cosmides & J. Tooby (1992). *The adapted mind*. New York: Oxford University Press.

Batten, M. (1994). *Sexual strategies. How females choose their mates*. New York: G.P. Putnam's Sons.

Behnam, D. (1990). An international inquiry into the future of the family: A UNESCO project. *International Social Science Journal, 42*, 4 (126), 547-552.

Betzig, L.L. (Ed.) (1997). *Human nature. A critical reader*. New York & Oxford: Oxford University Press.

Bowlby, J. (1951). *Maternal care and mental health*. WHO Monograph Series no 2. Geneva: World Health Organization, p. 46-47.

Bromley, D.G., A.D. Shupe & D.L. Oliver (1981). Perfect families: Visions of the future in a new religious movement. *Marriage and Family Review, 4*(3-4), 119-129.

Brown, S.L. & A. Booth (1996). Cohabitation versus marriage: A comparison of relationship quality. *Journal of Marriage and the Family, 58*, 668-678.

Buss, D.M. (1994). *The evolution of desire*. New York: Basic Books.

Chagnon, N.A. & W. Irons (Eds.) (1979). *Evolutionary biology and human social behavior. An anthropological perspective*. North Scituate, Mass.: Duxbury Press.

Cliquet, R.L. (1984). The relevance of sociobiological theory for emancipatory feminism. *Journal of Human Evolution, 13*, 117-127.

Cliquet, R.L. (1985). Predictive and political significance of the C.B.G.S. fertility surveys. In: J. Schmid & K. Schwarz (Eds.). *Politische und prognostische Tragweite von Forschungen zum generativen Verhalten*. Berlin: Deutsche Gesellschaft für Bevölkerungswissenschaften, p. 63-110.

Cliquet, R.L. (1996). *Below replacement fertility and gender politics*. European Sociobiology Society/IPSA/APLS Meetings, Alfred, 22-27 July 1996. CBGS-Documenten, 1996/7.

Cliquet, R.L. (1996-1997). The demographic future of the human species: From quantity to quality? In: F. Deven & H. Van den Brekel (Eds). *Population and family in the Low Countries.* NIDI/CBGS Publications, Vol. 33. Brussels/The Hague, p. 15-42.

Cliquet, R.L. & M. Callens (Eds.) (1993). *Gezinsvorming in Vlaanderen: hoe en wanneer? Resultaten van de Enquête Gezinsontwikkeling 1991 (NEGO V).* CBGS-Monografie, 1993/1. Brussel: Centrum voor Bevolkings- en Gezinsstudiën.

Cooper, D. (1986). *The death of the family.* Harmondsworth: Penguin.

Corijn, M. (1995). *De overgang naar volwassenheid in Vlaanderen. Resultaten van het NEGO V-onderzoek.* CBGS-Monografie 1995/1. Brussel: Centrum voor Bevolkings- en Gezinsstudiën.

Cornish, E. (1979). The future of the family: Intimacy in an age of loneliness. *Futurist,* 13, 45-58.

Daly, M. & M. Wilson (1978). *Sex, evolution, and behaviour. Adaptation for reproduction.* North Scituate, Mass.: Duxbury Press.

Dawkins, R. (1976). *The selfish gene.* Oxford: Oxford University Press.

Ditch, J., H. Barnes, J. Bradshaw, J. Commaille & T. Eardley (1995). *European observatory on national family policies. A synthesis of national family policies 1994.* York: University of York.

Dorbritz J., K. Schwarz (1996). Kinderlosigkeit in Deutschland – ein Massenphänomen? Analysen zu Erscheinungsformen und Ursachen. *Zeitschrift für Bevölkerungswissenschaft,* 231-261.

Duvold, E.M. (1995). The Norwegian family: Scenario's for 2020. Future consequences at the micro level of present-day family patterns. In: C. Lundh (Ed.). *Demography, economy and welfare.* Lund: Lund University Press, p. 28-44.

Eid, V. & L. Vaskovics (1982). *Wandel der Familie – Zukunft der Familie.* Mainz: Matthias-Grünewald-Verlag.

Farrell, W. (1993). *The myth of male power: Why men are the disposable sex.* New York: Simon & Schuster.

Filsinger, E.E. (1988). *Biosocial perspectives on the family.* Newbury Park: Sage.

Fisher, H.E. (1992). *Anatomy of love. The natural history of monogamy, adultery, and divorce.* New York: W.W. Norton and Company.

Gadeyne, S., E. Lodewijckx & R. Schoenmaeckers (1998). *De vruchtbaarheid in België. Analyse van de volkstellinggegevens 1991* (in press).

Gough, K. (1971). The origin of the family. *Journal of Marriage and Family, 33*(4), 760-771.

Hamer, D.H., S. Hu, V.L. Magnuson, N. Hu & A.M.L. Pattatucci (1993). A linkage between DNA markers on the X chromosome and male sexual orientation. *Science,* 261, 321-327.

Hamilton, W.D. (1964). The genetical evolution of social behaviour, I & II. *Journal of Theoretical Biology,* 7, 1-52.

Hoffmann-Nowotny, H.J. (1987). The future of the family. In: *European Population Conference 1987,* Plenaries. Helsinki: Central Statistical Office of Finland, p. 113-200.

Höpflinger, F. (1990). *The future of household and family structures in Europe.* Seminar on present demographic trends and lifestyles in Europe. Strasbourg: Council of Europe.

Horgan, J. (1995). The new social darwinists. *Scientific American, 273*(4), 150-157.

Jankowiak, W.R. & E.F. Fischer (1992). A cross-cultural perspective on romantic love. *Ethnology, 31*(2), 149-155.

John Paul II (1994). *To Mrs. Nafis Sadik, Secretary general of the 1994 International Conference on Population and Development and executive director of the United Nations Population Fund.* The Vatican: 18 March.

Kaufmann, F.X. (1991). *Zukunft der Familie. Stabilität, Stabilitätrisiken und Wandel der familialen Lebensformen sowie ihre gesellschaftlichen und politischen Bedingungen.* München: C.H. Beck.

Kiernan, K. & M. Wicks (1990). *Family change and future policy.* London: Family Policy Studies Centre.

Lampert, A. (1997). *The evolution of love.* Westport, Connecticut & London: Praeger.

Laslett, P. (1965). *The world we have lost further explored.* London: Methuen.

Laumann, E.O., J.H. Gagnon, R.T. Michael & S. Michaels (1994). *The social organization of sexuality. Sexual practices in the United States.* Chicago & London: The University of Chicago Press.

Leutenegger, W. (1982). Encephalization and obstetrics in primates with particular reference to human evolution. In: E. Armstrong & D. Falk (Eds.). *Primate brain evolution.* New York: Plenum, p. 85-95.

Lumsden, C.J. & E.O. Wilson (1981). *Genes, mind, and culture. The coevolutionary process.* Cambridge: Harvard University Press.

Maynard Smith, J. (1964). Group selection and kin selection. *Nature,* 201, 1145-1146.

McHenry, H.M. (1996). Sexual dimorphism in fossil hominids and its socioecological implications. In: J. Steele & S. Shennan (Eds.). *The archeaology of human ancestry. Power, sex and tradition.* London & New York: Routledge, p. 91-109.

Mellen, S.L.W. (1981). *The evolution of love.* Oxford & San Francisco: W.H. Freeman.

Miller, N. (1992). *Single parents by choice. A growing trend in family life.* New York: Plenum Press.

Montagu, A. (1957). *The direction of human development. Biological and social bases.* London: Watts.

Portmann, A. (1944). *Biologische Fragmente zu einer Lehre vom Menschen.* Basel.

Prigent, R. (1955). *Renouveau des idées sur la famille.* Institut national d'études démographiques. Travaux et documents. Cahier n° 18. Paris: Presses Universitaires de France.

Rivera, M. (1994). Single-parent families: The family model of the future? *RS, Cuadernos de Realidades Sociales,* 43-44, 27-43.

Roussel, L. (1989). *La famille incertaine.* Paris: Jacob.

Roussel, L. (1991). Les 'futuribles' de la famille. *Futuribles,* 153, 3-21.

Spiro, M.E. (1958). *Children of the Kibbutz.* Cambridge: Harvard University Press.

Sternberg, R.J. & M.J. Barnes (Eds.) (1988). *The psychology of love.* New Haven & London: Yale Universty Press.

Symons, D. (1979). *The evolution of human sexuality.* Oxford: Oxford University Press.

Tobias, P.V. (1975). Brain evolution in the hominidea. In: R.H. Tuttle (Ed.). *Primate functional morphology and evolution.* The Hague: Mouton, p. 353-392.

Trivers, R.L. (1971). The evolution of reciprocal altruism. *Quarterly Review of Biology,* *46*(1), 35-57.

Trivers, R.L. (1972). Parental investment and sexual selection. In: B. Campbell (Ed.). *Sexual selection and the descent of man.* Chicago: Aldine, p. 136-179.

Trivers, R.L. (1974). Parent-offspring conflict. *American. Ecologist, 14*(1), 249-264.

Van den Bergh, B. & W. Van Dongen (1998). Eenoudergezinnen. CBGS Documenten. Brussel: Centrum voor Bevolkings- en Gezinsstudiën.

Van den Berghe, P.L. (1979). *Human family systems.* New York: Elsevier.

Van den Berghe, P.L. (1988). The family and the biological base of human sociality. In: E.E. Filsinger (Ed.). *Biosocial perspectives on the family.* Newbury Park: Sage, p. 39-60.

Van Dongen, W. (1993). *Nieuwe krijtlijnen voor gezin, markt en maatschappij. Een geïntegreerde benadering.* Leuven-Apeldoorn: Garant.

Van Dongen, W., D. Malfait & K. Pauwels (1995). *De dagelijkse puzzel 'gezin en arbeid'. Feiten, wensen en problemen inzake de combinatie van beroeps- en gezinsarbeid in Vlaanderen.* CBGS Monografie 2. Brussel: Centrum voor Bevolkings- en Gezinsstudiën.

Williams, G.C. (1966). *Adaptation and natural selection.* Princeton: Princeton University Press.

Zonabend, F. (1996). An anthropological perspective on kinship and the family. In: A. Burguière, C. Klapisch-Zuber, M. Segalen & F. Zonabend (Eds.). *A history of the family. Volume One. Distant worlds, ancient worlds.* Cambridge: Polity Press, p. 8-70.

# Postmodern societies – Postmodern families?*

Kurt Lüscher
Universität Konstanz, Germany

## Introduction

Speaking of 'postmodern societies' entails what may be called (with reference to Karl Mannheim's formula) making a 'diagnosis of our times'. The term almost inevitably provokes objections to a certain arrogance inherent in its construction. For critics, the word modern means contemporary; thus speaking of postmodernity seems to involve a contradiction. Critics also ask how we could possibly judge the present historically? These objections imply meta-theoretical and methodological considerations which are being debated in connection with philosophical notions of 'postmodernism'.

In this contribution I will basically concentrate on the connection between 'postmodernism' as a perspective used to analyze contemporary societies and its fruitfulness for the study of contemporary families.[1] In the first part I will attempt, to outline a few theoretical and empirical implications of the concept of 'postmodernity' – as opposed to modernity. In the second part I will present a few thoughts on how the conception that we live in a postmodern society is supported by the observations we make in family research. In this connection I shall refer to the following thesis: Changes in public societal structures and private life styles, thus also the family, and changes in our knowledge and our notions of them mutually influence and intensify one another; in this way the development of the family contributes in a specific manner to social developments.[2] This thesis mirrors ideas connected with the concept of 'famiglia autopoetica' (Donati, 1989a).

## Postmodern societies

### Postmodernity – toward a sociological definition

The word postmodern evokes associations with 'postindustrial'. This is a label which enjoys wide acceptance among sociologists because it refers to the domi-

---

* I would like to thank James Brice for his help in linguistic and stylistic matters.

nance of certain modes of production that – as evidence suggests – are being increasingly superseded. 'Postmodern' seems comparatively more general, and in this sense, more ambitious. It displays a certain polysemy which provokes interpretation. Overall, it refers especially to culture as a dominant sphere of social change.

This observation is confirmed by the origins of the concept. Although we can find scattered references to the term in the thirties, forties, and fifties (in the work of Arnold Toynbee), a genuine debate on postmodernism began in the sixties in American historiography, literary criticism and the field of 'American Studies'. From there, it spread to architectural criticism and the discourse on art and music (see Koehler, 1977 for an outline of the history of the term).

Thus, it is an empirical fact that there is an ongoing discussion of cultural manifestations for which the label postmodern is used. If we agree that works of art can be seen as symbolic manifestations of major societal concerns, a basic connection can be assumed between artistic, literary and architectural 'interpretations' and sociological interpretations of current themes concerning human sociability.

I shall argue that this is even more the case for postmodernism than for other periods of art, because the attempt to judge this art in epocal terms is occurring extremely close to its point of creation. In other words, production and evaluative commentary take place simultaneously. This also means that we have to pay attention both to works and their interpretation. There seems to be a special unity between production and its general labeling. This in itself is – meta-theoretically speaking – characteristic of the postmodern, namely the awareness that like works of art, 'texts' in general are not inherently meaningful, for they acquire meaning only through context-dependent interpretation. This is of course also true for the texts created, collected and analyzed by sociologists, both in their qualitative and their quantitative versions, for case studies as well as for tables.

## Examples of postmodernity

What is postmodern literature, architecture, art and music? One could say, and here I follow Gitlin: 'It is Michael Graves's Portland Building and Philip Johnson's AT&T, ... it is photorealism, ... Rauschenberg's silkscreens, Warhol's multiple-image paintings and Brillo boxes, ... William Burroughs, Italo Calvino, ... Donald Barthelme, ... the Kronos Quartet, ... Laurie Anderson, ... the Centre Pompidou, the Hyatt Regency, ... it is Michel Foucault, Jacques Derrida, Jacques Lacan, Jean Baudrillard ...' (Gitlin, 1989a: 100). – These artistic manifestations are closely interwoven with everyday behaviors and experiences like 'brocilage fashion … news commentary cluing us in to the image-making and "positioning" strategies of candidates: it is remote-control-equipped viewers 'zapping' around the television dial' (ibid.).

From a similar account by Boyne and Rattansi (1990: 9-11), the following references are of special relevance to my argumentation: 'There is, in the first place, an attempt to dissolve the boundaries between "high" and "mass" culture, to find new languages which synthesize and reconstitute new forms out of and beyond the old divisions … Warhol's Pop Art, with its recycling of popular images, and the combination of features from "jazz" and "classical" music in Cage and Glass furnish some well-known instances. There is also a concern to merge "art" and "life", again reminiscent of an earlier avant-garde, which is evident in "happenings" and other art forms. An eclectic mixing of codes and styles, as in architecture, which uses motifs from Egyptian, classical and modernist styles – James Stirling's Neue Staatsgalerie in Stuttgart is often cited … The exploration of ethnic minority and feminist perspectives is a significant element of postmodernism …. The term postmodernism, then, has some purchase on a set of aesthetic and cultural projects. But it is often extended to include poststructuralist work in literary theory, philosophy and history (Derrida, Foucault, Lyotard), Rorty's form of pragmatist philosophy, post-positivist philosophy of science (Kuhn, Feyerabend), the textual movement in cultural anthropology (Clifford, Marcus), and so on. However, this is arguably an over-extension of the term.'

What do works of 'postmodern art' have in common? Let me first give a few shared qualities on a preliminary level of generalization:

– Most works use a plurality of stylistic and aesthetic means. Their structural logic cannot be easily detected. Works of visual art look like collages or like patchwork, with elements of different sizes, shapes and colors. Often there is a strong concern for surface. The formal perfection (and the expenditure it requires) may contrast sharply with the banalities of content.

– There is a free use of materials and a mix of media. For example, compare a performance by the Julliard String Quartet with one by the Kronos Quartet. Julliard plays on a neutral stage with uniform lighting; the four musicians wear dark suits. The Kronos members appear on stage in stylized costumes; there are subtle differences in their clothing, just enough to attract attention. During the performance, the lighting changes in color and intensity. Chamber music thus becomes a multi-media spectacle.

– All sorts of quotations are frequent in works of postmodern art and architecture. 'To quote' can be called a stylistic means. A seemingly vast combinatorial or synthetic freedom creates the impression that 'everything goes'. Juxtapositions appear in rich profusion. In this way, the familiar is used in an unfamiliar way. As a consequence, the context of artistic expression has no clear boundaries. This is also true in regard to the contents. Different genres as well as different media are interwoven. Temporal references mix. Playing with chance and contingency is frequent.

Some of us may object with references to works created earlier in this century, especially in the teens and twenties. What about the literature of Joyce, of Doeblin, of Pirandello, of the Dadaist movement or the music of Charles Ives? Looking or sounding like artistic patchwork quilts, they cross over the boundaries of genres. Mixing styles, they delight in provoking without being too serious. One may consider three tentative answers:

- First, one may argue that these artists engaged in a program to create a new aesthetic canon for a language of meanings with an internal logic of its own. In short, they were working within the project of modernity (to use Habermas' term). Postmodern artists no longer seem to follow this ideal. They just do what they like to call art. They do it here and now. They experiment, but without an obvious purpose, not even engaging in the search for purpose.
- Second, works of postmodern art are produced (and I mean produced) mostly within a context of abundance, a context of wealth. I am not thinking only of financial resources, although they may be important. Even more relevant is the abundance of materials and techniques. And there is, most importantly, the abundance of media. Postmodern art may be seen as play within contemporary media ecologies.
- Third, large segments of the population, so to speak the masses, are exposed to postmodern cultural works and manifestations. Not only do artists use different media, they work in societal situations which allow them to refer to and draw upon the general public's familiarity with these media, with postmodern television patchworking, the perfection of the trivial, playing with chance and the fragmentation of information. This again marks a difference from the movements and the developments of the early decades of our century.

## Theories of postmodernity and their relevance for social theory and sociology

Increasing numbers of scholars are trying to interpret the postmodern within a sociological framework. One group tries to locate it in an ideal-historical spectrum. Thus Gitlin argues: 'The premodernist work aspires to a unity of vision.

It cherishes continuity speaking with a single narrative voice or addressing a single visual center. It honors sequence and causality in time and space. – The modernist work still aspires to unity, but this unity ... has been constructed ... – In the postmodernist sensibility, the search for unity has apparently been abandoned altogether. Instead we have textuality, a cultivation of surfaces endlessly referring to, ricocheting from, reverberating onto surfaces ... The work interrupts itself. ... Anything can be juxtaposed to anything else. Everything takes place in the present, 'here', that is nowhere in particular.' (Gitlin, 1989a: 101-102).

In this context Gitlin also relates the postmodernist spirit to the culture of multinational capitalism, where 'authentic use of value has been overcome by the universality of exchange value'. Politically, 'postmodernism plays in and with surfaces'. Referring to intergenerational relations, he locates postmodernism as 'an outlook for ... Yuppies – urban professional products of the late baby-boom born in the late fifties and early sixties' ... Among other things 'they cannot remember a time before television, suburbs, shopping malls'. Finally, he sees postmodernism as specifically, although not exclusively, American. He refers to juxtaposition, which is – in his words – 'one of the things we do best.'

A somewhat similar historical view is offered by Boyne and Rattansi (1990). They distinguish two sides of modernity which perhaps could be encapsulated in two pairs of key concepts: enlightenment and oppression, emancipation and alienation. Modernism, in Boynes and Rattansis' view, represents a critical approach to modernity, an interest in its dark sides, which are to be uncovered and brought to consciousness.

Donati (1989b: 167) interprets the transitions from an epistemological view: the passage from the pre-modern to the modern happens if the reality of such things and of phenomena is no longer taken for granted, but becomes problematized. This leads to an interest in modes of experience and of cognition. But modernity still presupposes the existence of 'subjects'. Postmodern thinking arises out of radical doubts about this convention.

A second category of interpretation elaborates on specific features of postmodernity. Thus, Welsch (1987) emphasizes what he calls radical plurality. The term radical is meant in its true sense: as reaching to the roots of and including all spheres of experience and of expression. In this sense, for Welsch, pluralism is fundamentally related to democracy. Welsch also states that each form of knowledge, each life project and each pattern of action stands on its own. It can claim legitimacy by itself. Consequently, we must speak of truths, of justices and of humanities in the plural.[3]

Also, postmodern culture, as Welsch interprets it, is radically anti-authoritarian and anti-monopolistic. Finally, for Welsch, the coincidence of postmodern phenomena in literature, architecture, the arts and in society generally can be seen as evidence that the term refers to a cultural and social reality.

My own approach (Lüscher, 1988; 1993) to interpreting the major implications of postmodernity is based – as mentioned in my opening remarks – on a pragmatistic perspective. To repeat: its main proposition is to understand postmodernism in literature, architecture and art as a symbolic expression of dominant features of social life in contemporary western societies. Furthermore, I consider it as useful to account for the different discourses in which the concept is used (Lüscher, 1997). Postmodernism is primarily analyzed in terms of the way it draws upon everyday experience. It displays the contradictions, ambiguities and ambivalences which ultimately lead to what, from a pragmatistic perspective, may be called the problematization of personal identity. This may be true for the comprehension of personal identity as such, e.g. the notion of self, as well as for its enactment and acquisition.

The pluralism of our time not only displays a high level of differentiation: it extends across all spheres and levels of social life, its private as well as its public domains, the economy as well as the arts. This omnipresence is highly correlated with the mutual interpenetration and mutual interdependence of domains and of systems of knowledge. To put it simply: there is a notion and a feeling that everything seems to depend upon everything else; that, in our daily actions, we are dependent upon and bound to large numbers of other people. We may not know them; but we can include them in our thinking on the social world. The media often suggest that we may have access to them. Reference-groups become numerous, and in specific ways partially abstract, partially personalized. Thus, life in the contemporary world is life under conditions of overwhelming multi-perspectivity.

One may use the concept of perspectives in two different ways. First, one may define it – in a way approximating that of everyday usage – as the organization of perception and related experiences. Multi-perspectivity, then, refers to the awareness of different points of view. It bears the probability of juxtapositions and of contradictions. Again, art may be a successful way to bring them to our attention. I recall, as a single example, the picture series of one of the Belgian predecessors of postmodern art, René Magritte, entitled 'This is not a pipe.'

Within a sociological theory of action, we may use a second definition of the concept of perspectives. It draws upon the ideas of G.H. Mead, and more generally speaking, on pragmatistic orientations. Here, a perspective is defined as the objective expression of an interpretation of the interrelationships between a person and the world in which he lives. Perspectives contain an element of reflection, and this makes them constituents of personal identities (Lüscher, 1990). If one accepts the pragmatistic notion of perspectives, one can also accept the idea that most people are living under conditions of continuous exposure to choices and to claims of how to best define personal identity. This entails a high probability of ambiguities and ambivalence.

To summarize: To talk of 'postmodern society' implies, first, an attempt to make a 'diagnosis of our times'. It could be summarized in the simplifying thesis: postmodernity entails, in relationship to society, the notion that the accomplishments of the modern world, also including the emancipation of the individual, are being radically problematized today. This means that it is not only asked (as by the critics of modernism), whether these developments have been realized, but whether they are at all realizable or – a variant – if it is meaningful (in view of the results of development) to want to realize them. Thus, radical pluralism, multiperspectivity and the problematization of identities may be considered key concepts for a characterization of postmodernity within a pragmatistic approach to sociological analysis.

In regard to sociological work, it is a matter of doing justice to multi-perspectivism. This requires reconstructing objective social contents and social developments from the perspectives of as many participants as possible. The sociological perspective represents an attempt to do justice to the multiplicity of perspectives, which are now considered appropriate. Thus postmodernist sociology rejects the claim that scientific knowledge is superior to other forms of knowledge, at least *a priori*.[4]

'POSTMODERN FAMILIES'

Not only the characterization of contemporary societies as postmodern, with its implied objective content, but also the implications of such a characterization represent, in my opinion, an exciting challenge for family sociology - and conversely the latter may be suitable for judging the scope and importance of the postmodern perspective. In the following section I would like to illustrate this on the basis of a few topics in family sociology.

*Interpreting recent changes in families*

Over the last three decades, most western societies have witnessed – to varying degrees – a decline in the number of children in families, larger proportions of couples or of women who decide to remain childless, a historically rising number of divorces, remarriages, and redivorces. There are also women who want to have a child without living with their child's father; there are lesbian and gay couples with children who claim to be families.

As a result, we can observe a plurality of family forms. But family historians tell us that this is nothing really new. However, historically novel is the widespread knowledge of the diversity of family forms in connection with the claim to tolerate this diversity and to recognize the new forms as families. A brief but apt empirical illustration is the variety of designations for families which today are suggested in public and in sociological literature. To offer just a few examples from recent publications in the German and English literature: commuter marriage, living-apart-together, serial marriage, successive marriage and family, multiple parenthood, fragmented parenthood, patchwork family, matrix family, hybrid family.

Here we are doubtlessly moving within a 'postmodern' topical area. The consciousness and problematization of plurality are an expression of multi-perspectivalism. To refer again to the general thesis presented at the beginning: what has changed over the last 30 years is not the forms of family life alone, but the conceptions that large segments of the population have of family life. They are not all compatible with each other. Consequently, we are witnessing a public discourse over the meaning of the concept of family. Some arguments refer overtly to the definition of family, others do so covertly; the latter is the case in connection with mothers' participation in the work force or in debates on abortion, the so called 'politics of motherhood'. There are obvious contradictions. For instance, representatives of the state refer to the family as a haven for emotional support and mutual personal acceptance. But forms of living together based solely on emotional ties without formalized relationships are denied the status of being families.

## Defining 'family' [5]

In this situation it is increasingly difficult, and particularly so in sociological work, to define the concept of family. In our research we attempt to deal with this problem by explicitly referring in the definition of the family to the tensions between behavior and legitimation and by distinguishing among various levels of comprehending the family. The following definition results from this:

– The concept of family (as a social category) refers, in contemporary western society, to life styles constituted primarily through the structuring of intergenerational relationships between parents and children and between parents themselves which are as such (as groups or relations sui generis) societally recognized (legitimized).[6]

- In a narrower sense a family is a relationship between parents and children, as well as between parents themselves. In a broader sense, a family includes (certain) relatives.
- We speak of family types, if individual features or constellations of features (qualities, modes of behavior) are regarded as characteristic for the structure and development of families.
- We refer to an individual family when we think of features (qualities, modes of behavior) which are viewed by members of a family or by outsiders as the expression of personal experiences or of a personal understanding of the family.
- The concept family policy designates public activities, measures and institutions whose aim is to recognize, to influence and to modify family behaviors and patterns. This implies the legitimization of the private life forms which ought to be accepted as families. In other words: family policy not only presupposes a notion of family, but is also a means to stimulate change and/or to reject or deligitimize certain social definitions of the family.

## Plurality, identity and pragmatic attitudes toward institutions

As for our thoughts about plurality, I tend to the following understanding. On closer examination it is apparent that various distinct dimensions can be employed to characterize family types. Specific dimensions refer to marriage or to the consequences of divorce, others to the household and still others to the process of beginning a family. If one holds the dimensions constant, it appears that there are in fact hardly any new family forms. There have always been stepfamilies, some created after widowhood, some after separation and divorce. There has always been 'single parenthood'.

Thus, in regard to partnership relationships, for example marriage, parenthood and household, we can say that the spectrum of possibilities is basically the same today as in earlier historical periods (with which meaningful comparisons can be made). However, the quantitative distribution has changed, at least in the course of the last few decades. Previously dominant forms have declined, and certain other forms have increased in importance. On the whole, the spectrum is more evenly occupied. This also means that there has been a decline in the importance of forms which, viewed from a quantitative perspective, were previously regarded as normal. From a qualitative perspective this is related to a weakening or retrenchment of older conceptions of normality.

This concepts of plurality and of pluralization were worked out for example in a study of the different patterns in the temporal interrelationships between conception, birth of the first child and marriage, (or the rejection of marriage), in Switzerland and Baden-Württemberg (Lüscher/Engstler, 1991; Engstler et al., 1992). To interpret these sequences we draw on the following considerations and pose the following thesis: the weakening or retrenchment of concepts of normalcy means that the societal significance of institutions, namely of marriage, has declined. For women or couples this has led to increasing options. They can deal with institutions more pragmatically. They can weigh the question of whether it is individually, thus subjectively, worthwhile to marry. They can thus decide on a more personal basis. To be sure: they also must decide on a more personal basis. Thus plurality and general knowledge are related to individualism and lead to a pragmatic 'use' of institutions.

More generally speaking, pluralism and options for individual choice not only concern the products we buy and the services we use, but also, within the family, affect existential decisions for the individual life course. To have or not to have children, the timing of birth, marriage, divorce, remarriage: these and many other choices are, at present, options of which large segments of the population are aware, even if they are not always available to them. The options suggest a freedom of choice, which has grown as traditions, customs, the experience and authority of parents have lost much of their binding power. In turn, and because of the weakness or even the absence of these constraints, choices must be made. They are – so to speak – imposed upon individuals from without (see also: Stacey, 1990, 1998).

Now to be sure one can justifiably object that there are many population segments which do not live in abundance and which accordingly do not have the opportunity to choose among a variety of options. Naturally we should consider that most members of these population segments are consumers of modern mass media, especially of television. In the picture of reality which they are exposed to on TV, there is a thoroughgoing plurality, a permanent 'juxtaposition', a weakening of conceptions of normalcy. To the degree that media influence people's day-to-day thinking and feeling, they certainly participate in the experience of 'postmodernity'. This also applies with particular weight to topics like love, partnership, family and kin. These have a privileged place in media programs and people's awareness, including – not insignificantly – those of children and older people.

There is one further point to be elaborated: for large segments of the population this should be seen within the broad context of everyday living situations. The plurality of options in and across all spheres of life, and the knowledge of them multiplies the perspectives individuals may have on their interrelationships to the world in which they live. To define one's own identity in acting out decisions which are inevitable, even imposed, becomes a permanent preoccupation of large segments of the population in contemporary society. As life-spheres interpenetrate and boundaries become blurred, the constitution of personal identity becomes more difficult. For some it is a major preoccupation, although many people may be unaware of it, at least not continuously. What has been seen as a major concern of modern thinking becomes problematic.

CONCLUSIONS

Indeed – how do people react to these features of the postmodern situation? One reaction may be seen in a high sensitivity to risk and chance. Another reaction concerns the rising awareness of ambiguities and ambivalences in intergenerational relations (Lüscher & Pillemer, 1998). It is a reflection of aleatory aspects of social structures. In daily behavior, it seems to be related to certain kinds of irrationalism. The permanent claim to construct personal identity may furthermore be seen in connection with tendencies toward radical forms of subjectivism. It may also favor the submission to totalitarian (or even fascist) forms of personal identity. Both of these tendencies can be observed in the analysis of works related to postmodernism. To raise the public awareness of these possibilities is certainly an important task of the sociological analysis of contemporary societies. It is in this sense, too, that the notion of 'postmodern society' may be a useful sensitizing concept.

In relation to the family and the tasks of a sociology of the family a number of exciting challenges arise. I would like to present them in the form of questions: Can an understanding of the 'family', i.e., of the tasks to be achieved in and by the family be attained which is not simply 'restorative', but pluralistic, individualistic and solidary? What would a so-oriented 'family policy' be like?

Relative to the criteria for such a family policy, I would like to formulate the following five points:
– Family policy should basically recognize the services performed in and by the family.
– Family policy should offer help for self-help in cases of special burdens.
– Family policy requires reliable data on the actually experienced family forms.
– Family policy requires a plurality of bearers.
– Family policy should promote the family as an institution in which all members are able to realize their right to the free development of their personalities.[7]

Understandably with these considerations I have by no means completely demarcated the broad field of relationships between society and family under postmodern conditions. Especially to be considered is the role of the state in the development of family policies, and more recently, the relevance of the process of European unification will play. The theses presented should – if the method-ological premises of postmodernism are taken seriously – be considered from the perspectives of women and children. And obviously much of what I have pre-sented ought to be differentiated on the basis of exact observations. That we can pose many such questions, taking into account the contemporary societal situa-tion and the latest scientific developments, clearly shows that family sociology has become an important part of general sociology.

## NOTES

1   This presentation continues my many discussions with Wilfried Dumon on this topic. I also rely on my presentations made within the Erasmus and Socrates pro-grams.

2   This thesis is based on propositions which have their roots in a pragmatistic (not pragmatic!) approach to sociological theorizing and research. In brief, it states that any knowledge of social reality is bound to language (which in turn can be conceived as the most general social institution or the base of human sociality). Consequently, in doing sociology, we have to take into account the conditions, processes and inter-ests under which (scholarly) statements on social reality become possible and are made. Thus while social reality is not simply 'constructed' (as the propositions of a 'naive' constructivism state), our awareness of it is always bound to conceptions and methods of observation which have historical roots and are interrelated with human sociality. Doing research means to focus on specific topics, consequently, making exchanges between one field of knowledge and another is an important strategy. It underlies the argumentation in this paper, insofar as it is an attempt to connect the notion of 'postmodern' developed in art criticism with a sociological analysis of the family.

3   For an excellent recent assessment of the connections between pluralism and post-modernism in the perspective of sociology see Thompson (1996).

4   To be added is that – as was mentioned initially – sociology is to a very considerable degree obligated to the project of modernism; it is, in fact, practically a child of modernism. The works of the classic sociologists – Comte, Durkheim, Weber – express this unambiguously. With them as well, where they made critical comments on modernization, this was done with a, shall we say, constructive intention, namely with the intention to expose false developments and, as a whole, with the intention of rationally contributing to the program of modernism. Possibly this is also true of Marx. If contemporary societies are then analyzed as postmodern and thereby – more or less explicitly – it is established that radical doubt is forthcoming as to the modernist program, indeed may even be appropriate, then this is not without con-sequence for its theoretical and methodological program. In this connection, Agger

(1991) sees a close interpenetration between critical theory, poststructuralism and postmodernism.

⁵ The task to 'define' what is meant by 'family' in the context of contemporary (western) societies is a major concern of Wilfried Dumon. See for instance the elaborated treatment of the topic in Dumon (1993). This text also testifies to Wilfried Dumon's long-term commitment to creating a bridge between the worlds of international organizations and academia.

⁶ This definition includes the notion or the belief (in Peirce's understanding of this concept) that the family 'is' a reality (or a 'relation') sui generis. However, this idea, which has a long history, must be confirmed, and this confirmation occurs, sociologically speaking, through processes and struggles over the 'legitimization' of specific forms as 'family'. The proposed 'definition', oriented towards research, points to the necessity, for social scientists, to look for the explicit and implicit processes of this acknowledgement or legitimization, and, especially, to the struggles over them. This can be done by looking at how certain forms are debated in public, or how they are integrated into (or excluded from) family policy.

⁷ This criterion should be seen in the context of a historical view of the family and of the changing role of women. Let us agree that families need a certain amount of solidarity in order to fulfill their task. Historically speaking, and especially in the reality and – even more – the idealization of the 'bourgeois family', creating this solidarity was overwhelmingly the duty of the wife and mother. Given the practical and political advances of women's emancipation (which certainly cannot and should not be reversed), and family policy should promote conditions which favor – in this sense – more equity between the sexes.

REFERENCES

Agger, B. (1991). Critical theory, poststructuralism, postmodernism. *Annual Review of Sociology*, 17, 105-31.

Boyne, R., & A. Rattansi (Ed.) (1990). *Postmodernism and society*. London: Macmillan.

Donati, P. (1989a). L'emergere della famiglia 'auto-poietica'. In: P. Donati (a cura di). *Primo rapporto sulla famiglia in Italia*. Cinisello Balsamo; Edizioni Paolini, p. 5-69.

Donati, P. (1989b). La categoria della relazione sociale nella sociologia moderna e postmoderna. In: C. Mongardini & N.L. Maniscalco (a cura di), *Moderno e postmoderno Romana*. Roma: Bulzoni, p. 165-199.

Dumon, W. (1993). *The situation of the family in Western Europe. United Nations consultant paper*. Malta Conference.

Engstler, H., T. Schwarz, I. Cornelius & K. Lüscher (1992). Formen der Familiengründung in Baden-Württemberg. Eine Analyse der Geburtenstatistik 1970 bis 1989. In: *Materialien und Berichte der Familienwissenschaftlichen Forschungsstelle im Statistischen Landesamt Baden-Württemberg*, Heft 24.

Gitlin, T. (1989a). Postmodernism: Roots and politics. *Dissent*, 100-108.

Gitlin, T. (1989b). Phony gardens with real toads in them. *Tikkun*, 4, 68-70.

Koehler, M. (1977). Postmodernismus: Ein begriffsgeschichtlicher Überblick. *Amerikastudien*, 8-18.

Lüscher, K. (1988). Familie und Familienpolitik im Übergang zur Postmoderne. In: K. Lüscher, F. Schultheis & M. Wehrspaun (Hrsg.). *Die 'Postmoderne' Familie. Familiale Strategien und Familienpolitik in einer Übergangszeit*. Konstänzer Beiträge zur sozialwissenschaftlichen Forschung. Band 3. Konstanz, Universitätsverlag, p. 15-36.

Lüscher, K. (1990). The social reality of perspectives. On G.H. Mead's potential relevance for the analysis of contemporary societies. *Symbolic Interaction, 13*(1), 1-18.

Lüscher, K. (1993). Generationenbeziehungen - Neue Zugänge zu einem alten Thema. In: K. Lüscher & F. Schultheis (Eds.). *Generationenbeziehungen in 'postmodernen' Gesellschaften*. Konstanz: Universitätsverlag, p. 17-47.

Lüscher, K. (1997). Postmoderne Herausforderungen an die Soziologie. In: S. Hradil (Hrg.). *Differenz und Integration*. 28. Kongress der DGS, Dresden. Frankfurt/New York: Campus Verlag, p. 94-117.

Lüscher, K. & H. Engstler (1991). *Formen der Familiengründung in der Schweiz*. Bern: Bundesamt für Statistik.

Lüscher, K. & K. Pillemer (1998). Intergenerational ambivalence: A new approach to the study of parent-child relations in later life. *Journal of Marriage and the Family, 60*, 413-425.

Lüscher, K., F. Schultheis & M. Wehrspaun (Eds.) (1988). *Die 'postmoderne Familie'*. Konstanz: Universitätsverlag.

Thompson, K. (1996). Social pluralism and post-modernity. In: S. Hall et al. (Eds.). *Modernity*. Cambridge, Mass.: Blackwell, p. 564-594.

Stacey, J. (1990). *Brave new families*. New York: Basic Books.

Stacey, J. (1998). *In the name of the family. Rethinking family values in postmodern age*. Boston: Beacon Press.

Welsch, W. (1987). *Unsere postmoderne Moderne*. Weinheim: VCH, Acta Humaniora.

# Are we moving towards a single family model in Europe?

Louis Roussel

Institut National d'Etudes Démographiques, France

There was a time when everyone thought there was only one family model in the world - his own. The world of 'barbarians' lay beyond the limits of the city or ethnic group and included all those who did not really belong to the human race.

This unitary concept was succeeded by one equally cut and dried – namely, that there were as many family models as societies. Today there are hundreds, and there have certainly been thousands through the course of history. This dispersion was replaced by a progressive paradigm: the multiplicity was gradually being corrected by a general movement towards a single, ideal model – our own – which formed part of the industrial civilisation which was finally to absorb all cultures. At least, this is what T. Parsons believed he could establish with regard to Europe and North America.

This remains subject to debate, but demographic data is available today to support ethnological, economic, historical and philosophical arguments – the recent evolution of family behaviour, measured by statistical indicators, shows a growing together of models, and the upheavals of the last thirty years really are consistent with a great convergence movement.

The question appears to require no more than simple statistical analysis. In actual fact, however, it is much more complex and some brief, methodological observations are necessary before we even attempt to answer it.

PRELIMINARY OBSERVATIONS

Firstly, because of my own personal area of expertise, but also because these countries enjoy a specific kind of social history, we will leave to one side those countries that used to be called Eastern Europe. We will only deal with the countries of Western Europe here.

It should also be noted that the answer to the question may differ depending on the temporal perspective from which we approach it. We can certainly limit ourselves to the period since the Second World War, although we must also allude briefly to the situation before the war. Only this information can give us an indication of the direction of changes observed in the post war years. In brief, 1930s Europe offered clear analogies with relation to family structures, and particularly the Christian model, which for more than a thousand years, gradually brought about this relative homogeneity. Important shifts could clearly be seen between predominantly Catholic and predominantly Protestant countries. It can also be seen that the general trend towards a fall in the birth rate was more pronounced in some countries than in others. And it can also be observed that divorce had not been legalised in some countries, but where it was, it remained a rare occurrence. In short, there was relative cohesion in Europe, as all its cultures were rooted in Christianity.

It should also be noted beforehand that international convergence does not exclude some diversity within each country. To speak of a gradual coming together of countries is not the same as to affirm that each one displays internal homogeneity. The diversity of socio-cultural situations is continuing and, as is generally recognised, becoming more pronounced. This therefore inevitably leads to variations in concepts of the family within the same country. These divisions may be the same from one country to the next. Here the differences between one group and another are very clear, as in the United States, where this is the case among white Protestants, but also among Hispanics and blacks. But this is a different problem, which requires an in-depth study of its own.

In Europe, we can generally distinguish between three groups in each country – those who are referred to as 'excluded', characterised by a certain degree of lawlessness in terms of family behaviour; the fundamentalists in favour of a return to the 1950s family (back to basics) and finally, the vast majority, who are more or less in favour of recent changes. The percentage of these sectors of the population varies from country to country, but the first two are minority groups everywhere. The real question is, how do we know whether these national populations with their internal diversity will draw closer to one another?

Another grey area as far in defining the title of this article is what exactly is meant by 'growing together'. It can be imagined that some countries have high but falling figures for a given characteristic, while others with a low coefficient might be experiencing a rise in that area. It should be said from the offset that this type of growing together has not been observed. What is happening, however, is a growing together of the differences between countries which are all evolving in the same direction.

Finally we need to explain what we mean by the term 'model' here. We are not referring here to purely morphological structures, but to more radical characteristics which touch upon the very purpose of a union. We will not go into typologies in any detail here, but will simply refer to the excellent account given by Déchaux (1997). We will satisfy ourselves by confirming a common trend found in these qualitative typologies – namely, that between 1950 and 1990, marriage, whether legal or not, has undergone a transformation in terms of both its purpose and the way it is regulated. It involves, in one way or another, finding one's identity in the relationship with one's spouse and children, which implies a clear separation between the public field and the private domain. The public domain consists of all the constraints necessary to live together in society. The private domain is the only place to find authenticity. This is a fundamental change. It brings with it a division of life into two domains, which are not very strongly related – social life and intimacy. Marriage is longer defined by external standards; it is a union whose objectives and resources are regulated by a singular contract which can be both modified and reversed. The real question here is, how do we know whether all the countries of Europe are in fact moving towards this type of union, whose very meaning has changed?

THE IMPOSSIBLE DEMONSTRATION
There seems to be one easy way of resolving the problem, whose results may appear conclusive. Do we not already have demographic indices for all the countries of Europe? Do they not demonstrate characteristic behaviours of the demographic model being followed? Do they not, therefore, demonstrate behavioural clusters, themselves defined by qualitative regulators?

*The current situation*
From these indices, Europe appears to be even more differentiated today than before the last war. We have clearly seen, after the population explosion in the 50s, a general fall in the birth rate, which showed a clear convergence, but in some paces the divorce rate is high, while in others it is rare or very rare; in some places cohabitation before marriage is the norm, in others, it is still the exception; in one place the majority of women work full or part-time, in others, the model of the woman at home is holding firm. By looking at two key situations – divorce and children outside marriage – we can distinguish statistically between three models in Western Europe – in one, more than 50% of marriages end in divorce and 60 to 70% of first births take place outside of marriage; conversely, in the other models, these two behaviour patterns account for less than 10% of the population, whereas in the last model, the indices are in between the two, but closer to the former group of countries.

If we now look at the geographical map, it can be seen that these models correspond to continuous zones, the first in Northern Europe, the intermediate model in the centre, and the last one in the Mediterranean countries. Ireland is the sole exception, but it will be seen that this is a significant exception – whilst being geographically close to England, it is culturally close to Italy. Clearly this is no coincidence. And obviously this situation requires an explanation.

## Recent developments

At the beginning of the 60s, the Scandinavian countries, especially Sweden, occupied a position that appeared exotic at the time – types of behaviour were widely accepted there which were still scandalous in the rest of Europe – premarital cohabitation, children outside marriage and a relaxed view of medical contraception.

It was between 1960 and 1980 that the situation changed in the central zone. The break occurred in around 1965, and affected all demographic behaviour almost simultaneously. All the countries, to varying degrees, drew closer to the northern countries, which for their part, continued to evolve in the same direction, but more slowly. The Mediterranean countries remained relatively stable. The main gap was no longer between the North and the rest of Europe, but between the Centre and the South.

Since 1980, the North and the Centre have continued to draw closer together, but more slowly. What is new is that the South, in turn, has started moving. It is still closer to the central indices, but the wave of change is reaching it now, with considerable effects on the birth rate, but with a much more modest effect on the other phenomena. In terms of this great shift, the current diversity can be interpreted as a temporary stage in an evolution, where the calendar could be is defined as taking place early in the North and late in the South, but which should ultimately lead to a relatively homogenous situation in both North and South.

To what can we attribute this disparity, or more specifically, the demographic revolution that took place around 1965 in the central European zone, in this hypothesis? It would seem we must point to the simultaneous emergence of two series of changes. Firstly, this was undoubtedly the result of the sudden and unforeseen breakdown of what was legitimising both the regulators and constraints of marriage, including marriage in its modern form – no doubt religion – and in a broader sense most normative values. More specifically, the privacy of life disqualified the outside authorities and gave rise to a kind of sovereignty of the couple and privatisation of the family. Secondly, a series of social changes and scientific developments meant that everyday life could be controlled to a far larger extent, bringing about a gradual emancipation from the constraints still in force. This double revolution, namely the cultural emptiness and increasing control through machines, accounts for the real change in the environment of the 1960s – women's struggle resulted in the equality of the sexes in principle, revolts by young people served as evidence that the former peace that had existed between the generations had been broken, and that the rules imposed by adults had become more or less obsolete.

It almost goes without saying that the discrediting of religion has played a considerable role in this revolution. The geographical exception of Ireland shows that the progress of new family models from North to South is simply a *de facto* expression of dechristianisation, though we should, along with Y. Lambert (1995), recognise the ambiguity of the word 'religion', which can mean both a normative framework which organises life on the basis of a 'nominal Christianity used as a reference point without any significant personal implications'. The greatest change has undoubtedly been this shift from the first type of Christianity to the second.

## Two findings

We can quickly see two factors that confirm the reality of this evolution from North to South. First of all, the article by Bozon and Kontula (1997) on sexual initiation. Amongst other things, they point out the later incidence of initial sexual relations in the South than in the North, as well as a greater age gap with regard to gender. In short, the South is behind the rest of Europe.

More controversial, with regard to the hypothesis on the convergence of these developments, is the comparison of family policies in Europe. W. Dumon has made a key contribution in this area. There is nothing more delicate than to analyse and synthesise a wide range of legal situations which are at least subject to cyclical variation. We know that family policy is within the field of subsidiarity in the European Union, with each Member State looking after its own. The laws promulgated by the State are intended to ease current problems, in short, to reduce the intolerable gap between morals and the law. This does not regulate morality, but rather expresses it. What we are clearly witnessing here is the development of more precocious and radical changes in legislation from the North to the South. The report from the Observatoire sur l'Evolution de la Politique Familiale Nationale in 1996 points in the same direction and confirms this notion of gradual convergence.

## *The significance of these findings*

If we take the above trends further, it seems to be difficult to reject the idea that these indices will at least draw closer, as the facts are already revealing, even if they do not ultimately converge. There are two objections to this thesis, however, which prevent us from supporting it without more information. There is no scientific proof, first of all, that analogous statistical data does not conceal qualitatively different types of behaviour. Divorce rates may be similar, but within matrimonial systems which give them a different meaning – so that there is little to gain from comparing the figures.

Furthermore, a current convergence is not guaranteed to continue in the same, or even in a similar, way in future. Before we say, for example, that the evolution will continue in the same direction in the Mediterranean countries, it is necessary to demonstrate why this should be the case. The fact that a movement has started does not prove that it will continue in the same direction. We should therefore exercise caution, and not assume that an initial approximation will result in a final convergence. We must therefore avoid the naïve illusion that everything necessarily always moves in the same direction.

The notion that family models will ultimately converge, at least in industrial countries, is a persistent one. Durkheim extended the field of gradual identification to all cultures. But the demographic arguments have not supplied – and cannot supply – real demonstrations. They only observe some degree of approximation in Europe – they cannot predict what will happen tomorrow.

Caution is required, particularly since some authors give serious reasons why we should not fall for the charms of statistical series. This was the thinking behind the two surveys organised by the Foundation for the Study of Value Systems in Europe (1981 and 1990), with questions relating to family models. These were taken over two separate periods. Galland and Lemel (1995) analysed and compared the results of these two surveys. It was hoped, despite the rather short passage of time between the two studies, that they would reveal a clear growing together of viewpoints. Those who were counting on such a result were disappointed. The authors do demonstrate, however, that the studies do not show differences increasing, but rather a stability between differences, and a general movement in the same direction in all Member States. The gap between the two studies appears to be sufficient, especially in a period of rapid change, to reveal the expected growing together if it had been taking place.

Hence there is an inertia, more visible in opinions than in behaviour, which maintains the fundamental traits separating the models of marriage, while they all simply shift in the same direction, even in a Europe inspired by Christianity for so long, and which has now reached a fairly uniform economic level. Here we recall the position taken up by E. Todd (1998), who labelled this stubborn diversity to a form of anthropological determinism, and more specifically to the basic dichotomy between nuclear family systems and the 'extended family' system. In the former, the basic unit, which is therefore the essential goal of the model, is the individual; in the latter it is the cohesion of the family group. There is a homology between the family structure and the social organisation and, first and foremost, between family structure and economic organisation. Finally, the key to the essential differences between countries is found in the family models which have evolved according to different forms, whilst essentially travelling in the same direction with regard to basic orientations. We therefore progress, in a very logical and intellectually attractive manner, towards a single explanation for all the differences. We see here that the dominant paradigm in the works of E. Todd is that of the very pronounced inertia of basic anthropological characteristics. Are contemporary families still defined as much by these trends as by the subsequent changes?

Without seeking to enter into a general debate at this point, I would simply like to demonstrate through two examples, deliberately taken from the recent past of family models, that these are still fragile and unstable, and that they are based on identifiable factors. N. Elias (1991) refers in *The Society of Individuals* to Indian tribes in North America whose whole culture, including family norms, was based on warrior values – these had to disappear or become integrated when the Europeans arrived, i.e. they had to pass from a stage where the individual tribe defined the social habit of the individual to an organisation where the American state played this role. Equally, both in Africa as in North America, 'the basic scheme', writes Elias, 'is always the same. The dynamic of non-programmed social evolution which forces the tribes to unite within the framework of the larger integrative unit of a State is almost inevitable (p. 277).'

Closer to home, we have surely seen the disappearance of equally marked interregional differences in France which were still very much alive a century or two ago? These characterised very different family models. Etchelécou, for example, speaks of the evolution of the family high in the valleys of the Western Pyrenées and he emphasises how this model and its gradual erosion was caused by the physical environment and cultural pressure from the dominant neighbouring country, France.

Can we draw a general principle from these examples and conclude that unification will take place between European countries, just as integration took place among the Indian tribes or the French provinces, and that the net result of this tomorrow in the countries of Europe will be the same as what has already taken place yesterday among the tribes or the regions? There is clearly insufficient evidence from the arguments presented here to support such an assumption – in fact, we have demonstrated neither the inevitability of a final convergence nor its impossibility – the State is perhaps a more stable authority than the tribe or the region. But by arguing from simple evidence we are perhaps not taking the correct approach.

TOWARDS A MORE CAREFUL DEFINITION OF THE PROBLEM
The evidence gained, even over several decades, cannot tell us anything about how these movements are likely to act in the future, since they may cease or go into reverse. At the level of observed evidence there are always surprises. It is therefore necessary to adjust the level to find at least probabilities, and to ask what factors lie behind the current movements and whether they guarantee inertia, or not. This is the only way of deciding whether the movements currently taking place will tail off or are likely to continue.

First of all we can say that demographic changes are based on cultural factors and instrumental factors, as well as on collective representations such as controls and restraints. In other words, a dominant system of representations, expectations and constraints exists, and this is favoured or hindered by resources which are more or less appropriate for this purpose. The resulting complex, which we will call 'civilisation', determines the demographic behaviour of the majority.

This is not, however, a simple co-existence of independent factors. Cultural factors give rise to resources, where possible, and these intensify the expectations. A dialectic comes into being here between one and the other, so that there is never such a thing as purely cultural or purely natural. It is what A. Garapon (1988) has already termed 'the non-stop, ever-recurring interaction between our values and our tools... negotiations which create absurdity within a culture.' We desire more what we cannot do, but what we cannot do limits our desires and imposes patience. Look at the situation in Europe today with regard to family models. We shall limit ourselves to the dominant model in its common forms.

We have already outlined this model above. It reserves the necessary norms to maintain the existence of society for public life. You must not kill, steal, or drive through a red light. All this is prescribed by law. When it comes to private life, on the other hand, all that is required is the agreement of your partner. Marriage in the broad sense has endured, because it is governed only by a free contract between two persons who commit themselves in a way that is reversible. Equality between the sexes is the necessary basis for this model. This union has no legitimacy without this reciprocal consent to equality: neither has a model received from a foreign authority, whether God or the State; it is the adoption of a collective plan, either spontaneous or the result of negotiations which are not clearly defined. The woman is no longer just a precious and dependent object – she now has an equal weight in the debate, she contributes an equal share to the decision-making process and she is responsible for the man's identity as the man is for hers.

It is widely agreed that both of them, during this long interaction, are looking for their own happiness and the flourishing of their own identity. Is this sufficient reason to term this model 'individualism'? Why not, but as long as we point out the ambiguity of the term, which has rarely been mentioned until now. However, we will come across this distinction more and more.

It is that which separates individualism in the moral sense and egoism in the most basic sense and on the other hand, the principle that the individual conscience is the only foundation on which to build legitimacy – this touches upon individual knowledge with its objectives and competence. Secondly, we take Kant's line, according to which the individual conscience imposes a universalist understanding of human relations. One author has recently emphasised this distinction. Ch. Taylor (1992) writes in *Le malaise et la modernité* that 'authenticity is clearly self-referential – such and such should be my orientation. But that is not to say that at another level, the content must also be self-referential – that would mean that my objectives should express or satisfy my desires and my aspirations as opposed to something else beyond them.'

The word 'individualism', on its own, is not satisfactory. If we are moving towards a certain unity in the field of family models, a unity which is demanded by our general value system, is this towards an egotistical and permissive form of individualism or towards a universalist individualism which we direct ourselves? It is a difficult question. What we can see, however, is that the 'sovereignty' of the couple is often used to satisfy our personal expectations and desires. We have the feeling that each person is thinking of himself and his own pleasure first, and that within the family itself, the solidarities between partners or between generations sometimes give way to these personal objectives which are too important. The absence of long-term relationships between a large proportion of divorced or separated fathers and their children is a disturbing indicator of this here. The European model is actually tending towards matrilinearity.

Faced with such a pessimistic view, Inglehart brings in the results of his successive opinion surveys. They seem to establish the gradual dominance of what he terms post-materialist values, such as liberty, aesthetic pleasures and solidarity. We have entered a period where these are given priority, both the family domain as well as within the others. This is a certain degree of altruism which paradoxically takes it towards individualism. The general rise in the level of education, an indisputable phenomenon, is said to explain this evolution.

Several observations can be made in opposition to this optimistic interpretation. First of all, the power – and this mainly applies to the USA – of the group of 'conservatives', whose objectives are located within the family domain. They are certainly not individualists, of the former or latter variety, but we should not underestimate their influence on opinion. However, it is true that their 'universalist' opinions place them among individualists. It is normal today to be for the rights of the child, for total equality between the sexes, for freedom of the press and against any form of totalitarianism. Confirmation of these principles goes a long way towards satisfying our consciences. But in reality the dominant fact is indifference, non-commitment. The significance of Inglehart's arguments therefore appears to us to be limited. It is his optimism that has made this author successful, rather than his rigour.

In the absence of clear cultural norms, recognised principles or accepted constraints, behaviour tends to conform to our personal aspirations. Through the weakening of culture, nature – further aided by acquired cultural characteristics – defines its own objectives. Naturally, these are individual and immediate. But the mass individualism which is seen today seems to declare family models which, temporarily at least, are inspired by this concept of individualism.

Should we conclude that this glut of 'universal' normative cultures, whether conservative or individualist is on the verge of disappearing altogether? Where we are tempted to believe this, we would do well to recall the results of the referendum recently held in Portugal on abortion. With a high abstention rate and a low turnout among voters, the legalisation of abortion was still rejected. The family model which is diffusing is therefore still encountering considerable ideological resistance. This resistance will fade to the extent to which religion continues to lose its power of normalisation in private life.

But will there not also be more tangible obstacles? Does not the generalisation of a phenomenon like juvenile cohabitation presume a sufficiently developed national housing supply, and does not marital instability impose additional burdens? More to the point, in a period of economic crisis and insecure employment, is not cohesion a more pressing objective than greater permissiveness in individual behaviour? Will the current economic crisis effectively curb the evolution of models of marriage and restore the importance of solidarity to these models?

This is unlikely. There is no evidence to show that economic difficulties necessarily result in a tightening of the lines of solidarity. It is possible that a greater degree of cohesion may appear to be the best solution when the difficulties reach a certain level, while an 'each man for himself' philosophy prevails when the situation is not so severe. In short, it would be too optimistic to expect a return to values – which have already been largely surrendered – simply because of a prolonged crisis.

This opinion is based on two clear observations. Firstly, stereotyped media water the seeds of opinion, by a process of continuous immersion, churning out the same images and cultivating the same desires in all countries. Thanks to the very effective 'no-man's lands' which were still in existence in Africa not long ago, it was still possible for people to live side by side, ignoring the differences which separated them. Today, everyone knows everyone else, in a manner of speaking – we watch the same programmes on television. Advertising leads us to desire the same things. Our towns are similar, just like our desires. Secondly, increasingly strong economic pressures standardise our behaviour in the direction desired by those in power. At the same time our specifically national characteristics are eroded by the power of information and money – after all they are always the same...

We can see, from the evolution which is taking place, that not everything is moving in the same direction, but to make even a very brief assessment, it seems to us that in the short term at least, the lines of convergence will move even closer – at the moment they are pushing us in the direction of a mainly permissive form of individualism. In our view the response of Elias seems the most pertinent – he summarises it in a single word: retardation. We are in a phase where cultural inertia is the main source of differentiation – this factor is still particularly influential in the Mediterranean countries and takes its strength from a still 'confessing' Catholicism, to use Lambert's term.

With reference to the assimilation of tribes and their integration into the nation, Elias (1991: 279) suggests a necessary delay of three generations. But he adds 'it will perhaps take more than three generations for the transitional problems to settle down.' During this period of transition, instrumental factors will probably play a decisive role.

Finally, we should not understand 'convergence' as a development towards a strict single model – it is, with all the associated consequences, the shift from a model of marriage defined by an external body based on a unique contract whose stipulations depend only on the parties. There will clearly be variations between countries in Europe. These, however, can be reduced to elements of cultural nostalgia. For a time at least, they will be strong expressions of local identities. In actual fact, they promote the move towards a new model, by giving the illusion that nothing has been lost, neither normality nor specificity. But these residual differences are no longer offering real models of actual behaviour.

## CONCLUSION

The national specificity of family models is not an independent problem. The real question is that asked by A. Cazes: 'Is there such a thing as an axiological Europe?' If the answer is yes, and we do indeed share a common system of basic values, it is likely that in time this global convergence will affect the specific area of family models. For cultural and instrumental reasons, it seems to us possible to answer to the first question concerning the general system in the affirmative; and we are forced also to answer the second question, about family models, in the same way. Aside from the specific arguments, this has been the main factor determining our choice.

This answer does, however, require that we simultaneously admit another hypothesis. Certainly there is such a thing as cultural inertia, and family models are one expression of this. But can we explain everything by this persistent ethnological difference? Should we not rather refer to a constant interaction between neighbouring cultures, between culture and nature, family models and environments, the desire for specificity and the pull of more attractive models? We have clearly settled for the latter option here. This is why, and I repeat, we have thrown our weight behind the 'retardation' theory. We should perhaps add that the probable drawing together does not signify that this result is the best one.

Finally, and to expand this comment, a problem will emerge in time, but perhaps sooner than anticipated, which will raise all the questions and responses presented here – is the model towards which we seem to be converging a viable one? It seemed at first, say around 1990, that the distribution of the new model would not entail many malign consequences – for example, people were living freely together as in marriage. The number of children born outside of wedlock had increased, but the difference between legitimate and illegitimate children had ceased to be relevant. What may have appeared to be a revolution at first now seemed, to put it simply, to be simply a reorganisation. After all, surely in the majority of cases people ended up getting married, thus regularising the children's situation? The problems which have arisen recently, the depth of which we still find it hard to measure, are taking place among the children more than between the spouses. We see that this peaceful world is suddenly becoming agitated, we see more public disorder, we see that all authority is challenged, we see lethal weapons being used more and more. This phenomenon is undoubtedly more severe in some sensitive areas on the edge of large cities, but no area can escape it now – large city or small provincial town, or even in the countryside. No area escapes and no social environment escapes, even while there are still substantial differences between them. We see that the authority of the adult generation over children is challenged, and more specifically, we see that 'transmission' is coming under threat and that the generations involved in this violence are getting younger all the time. In Europe, we see that violence has entered the world of the child. What will we do, as adults, if children become uncontrollable?

REFERENCES

Bozon, M. & O. Kontula (1997). Initiation sexuelle et genre: comparaison des évolutions de douze pays européens. *Population*, (6).

Déchaux, J.-H. (1997). *Le souvenir des morts*. Paris: PUF.

Elias, N. (1991). *La société des individus*. Paris: Fayard.

Galand, O. & Y. Lemel (1995). La permanence des différences. *Futuribles*, (7-8).

Garapon, A. (1998). La biologie et la volonté, une fausse opposition. *Esprit*, (mai), 186 et sq.

Lambert, Y. (1998). Vers une ère post-chrétienne. *Futuribles*, (7-8).

Taylor, Ch. (1992). *Le malaise de la modernité*. Paris: Cerf.

Todd, E. (1998). *L'illusion économique*. Paris: Gallimard.

# LAT relationships now and in the future[*]

JAN TROST
UPPSALA UNIVERSITET, SWEDEN

## FROM MARRIAGE TO COHABITATION

At the end of the 1960s and the beginning of the 1970s the marriage rates in most of the western world started decreasing, in some countries very rapidly, as in Sweden and Denmark, in some other countries slower as in, for example, Belgium. At the same time cohabitation started to increase (cf. Trost 1979). Traditionally, i.e. before 1970, four elements were closely connected: a) the marriage ceremony; b) moving in together; c) having sexual intercourse together; d) having the first child about a year later.

By this is meant that these four elements were not only connected but they normatively stuck together. With some exemptions, the marriage ceremony and the moving in together occurred truly at the same time, meaning the same day. This seems to have been true for all western societies and independent of official ceremony. To start having sex together after the marriage ceremony was also normatively prescribed. In some countries more than in others, premarital sex was prohibited for all, but especially for women. In some countries more than others, the norm against premarital sex together was only an ideal norm and not a behavioral norm. Sweden is a good example of this: the ideal norm prescribed chastity before marriage but in practice almost all couples had sex before they married. One indicator of this is that around 1960 one third (Befolkningsförändringar, 1968) of all brides were pregnant at time of wedding (97% of the weddings were with a religious ceremony).

The fourth element had also a connection to the other in a double way. Preferably and normatively children should not be born by not married mothers. At the same time the norms said that a child should come soon after the wedding, i.e. within a year or so.

When cohabitation came and became a social institution these four elements lost their normative power – in some countries that power was important, in

---

[*] The study upon which this reporting is based is supported by the Swedish Council or Social Research, 97-0165:1C, Magn Bergwalls Foundation, and SKOP.

others mere cosmetics. The four elements are no longer connected to each other. When cohabitation has become a social institution of the sort we find in, for example, the Scandinavian countries, there is no connection between the four elements.

In some countries, for example Belgium, there is still a connection between having a child and being married. All or most of the couples there seem to start their relationship with some sort of courtship which ends in a cohabiting relationship. When the couple has decided that it is time for a child they marry and might have the planned child some time later. So seems not to be the case in Sweden except for some relatively few couples. This can be seen by the fact that in Sweden more than half of all children born and about two thirds of all first born children, are born by a not married mother. In 1996 46% of all children were born by a married mother, it is estimated that another 38% were born by a mother cohabiting with the father of the child and that the rest, about 16% were born by a mother not living with the father at time of birth of the child. It should be noted, however, that the number of cohabiting couples is a very low so called conservative estimate, only the number of married mothers is truly correct (Befolkningsstatistik, 1997). As a contrast, in Belgium only about one out of seven of all children born are born by a not married mother.

## DEFINING LAT RELATIONSHIP

The definition of a LAT relationship is a couple, where the two do not share the same household, each of them lives in his or her own household, in which other persons might also live, they define themselves as a couple and they perceive that their close surrounding also does so. The two can be a married couple or a not married couple. The couple can be an opposite gender couple, which is most common, or a same gender couple.

Leridon and Villeneuve-Gokalp (1989) are the first I have found to calculate the numbers of LAT relationships. They do not define the relationships as clearly as here and they mean simply that if a person at the time of the interview said that he or she was living in a couple relationship that person was treated as living in a LAT relationship. This means that their estimates probably are overestimates, especially among the non-married population. Younger couples can be assumed to be steady going couples and not in a LAT relationship, at least some of them. Schneider (1996) in his German study defines what he calls *Partnerschaften mit getrennten Haushalten* as LAT relationships that have lasted for at least one year and it seems that his definition is very close to Leridon's and Villeneuve-Gokalp's.

Here I must return to the issue of impact upon our thinking from the arrival of cohabitation as a social institution. Within the traditional system persons were involved in a courtship process during which a couple might eventually be formed: a steady going couple. As discussed above they were supposed not to have sex together and they were certainly supposed not to show any indications to that effect. For example, 'respectable' hotels would typically require that a couple had to be married in order to share a hotel room. This system has changed totally. This means that couples who under the traditional system were to be classified as a steady going couple nowadays might be classified as either a steady going couple or a couple living in a LAT relationship. The difference between these two forms is that the latter would have been living together had they not lived separately. This sounds as self evident, but the alternative for the steady going couple is not to be a couple at all.

Our LAT relationships in the western world could be compared to the 'friending' system in the Caribbean as described by Rodman (1971). He shows that at least among the lower classes there are three kinds of relationships associated to coupling. Typically a man and a woman met and realized there were some erotic feelings between them, then they would fairly soon start a 'friending' relationship which meant that they remained in their households separately and they would see each other and have sex. Children from the 'friending' relationship were taken care of by the mother and oftentimes also by the father in sort of a joint physical custody existing in the villages. If the 'friending' did not break up the next step would be 'living', which simply was what we call cohabitation. If that relationship did not break up the next step would be marriage.

Well, is then 'friending' the same as LAT relationships? My answer is: no. But let us take a look at my arguments. The two phenomena have some similarities of which one is that they are a couple as perceived by themselves. Another similarity is that they live in separate households. The more important differences are according to my opinion that quite a few of these 'friending' relationships are looked upon as temporary in the meaning that they are not supposed to result in a 'living' or in a marriage. Another important difference is that within the social system the goal is to marry. Thus cohabitation or 'living' was in the Caribbean a temporary arrangement before one would marry, which was the societal as well as the individual goal. Why then not marry? Because of poverty; they could not afford to marry and therefore they did not. Some few did but most relationships were broken either by separation or death of one of them before they had 'time' to marry.

For most of the couples living in LAT relationships marriage is not at all a goal. For some to move together is a goal, but not for all. And there is no societal goal that these couples should move together or marry.

Society in form of the legal system does not at all care about LAT relationships, not yet. Society does not even notice the phenomenon. There are somewhat more one-person households than if LAT relationships did not exist, there are more traveling especially for those living far from each other, just to mention some effects of frequent LAT relationships.

## HOW COMMON ARE LAT RELATIONSHIPS?

According to the estimates of Leridon and Villeneuve-Gokalp (1989) they found in a study from 1985 in France about 2 to 3% of the married couples were living as a couple but separately. They seem all to be in the age range of 21-44 years and how many, if any, of these couples who were in the process of finally divorce is not clear. I would also guess that some of these couples are not LAT relationships but commuting marriages. Among unmarried couples between 7 and 8% were in my terminology living in LAT relationships, but again how many would reasonably to be classified as steady going couples is unclear. Even here some could be commuting cohabiting couples but how many is unknown.

Schneider (1996) in his study where more than 10,000 persons aged 18 to 61 were interviewed in 1994 he found that 9% of the respondents were living in LAT relationships and only 8% were non-maritally cohabiting. However, a big majority are 'young adults who are under education, mainly studying, or they are in their early period of gainful employment' (Schneider, 1996: 96, my translation). Thus quite a few of the LAT relationships in Germany are what traditionally would have been labeled as steady going couples.

In a quantitative study in Norway a questionnaire was sent to a the population of persons divorced in 1992 and 1995, data were collected in 1996. About 8% of the respondents were living in a LAT relationship. Even if these figures do not say much since one cannot know what they stand for, they at least give some credibility to the Swedish data presented below.

In August of 1993 data were collected in an omnibus study among Swedes aged 18-74 and with a conservative estimate we can conclude that about 2% of the population in those ages were living in LAT relationships. The sample size (based upon slightly more than 1,000 interviews) is too small for an analysis of the 2%. Somewhat more than four years later we repeated the questions in two omnibuses in January and February, 1998. This time it is clear that out of all individuals interviewed more than 4% are living in LAT relationships. Since the sample is statistically quite representative (and more than 2.000 persons were interviewed) for the Swedish population aged 18-74 years we can with fairly good safety conclude that somewhat more than 4% of the population of those ages are living in LAT relationships, which means at least 250,000 persons.

If one would compare with the data from France more than ten years ago, using the same method of calculation, one would find that at about 1% of the married couples are in LAT relationships. How many of the cohabiting relationships that have 'ended' in a LAT relationship we do not know. We cannot with our Swedish data calculate how many of the unmarried or non-marital couples are living in a LAT relationship, but out of all not-married persons (including all persons who are not married) about 7 to 8% are living in a LAT relationship.

Who are those living in a LAT relationship? Our quantitative data show that among the youngest age group (18-29) 8% are living in a LAT relationship. In higher ages only between 3 and 4% are. Members of LAT relationships are slightly overrepresented among better educated, which is quite reasonable with the age structure; younger persons are as an average better educated than older. They also seem to be slightly over represented among people living in the larger cities. About one out of six say that they live with one or both parents. Again this can be an effect of age, but we also know that some of those in LAT relationships are taking care of elderly parents and therefore they do not want to move in together with the partner. Otherwise those living in LAT relationships seem to be just 'regular' people.

Since our data come from some few questions in omnibuses we cannot do more comparisons between couples living together (married or not married) and LAT couples. Neither can we do many comparisons between single individuals and the two kinds of couples living together. Our data are as Leridon's and Villeneuve-Gokalp's and Schneider's: they are collected via simple questions in surveys and we cannot be sure that all classified as LAT couples really are so. But, the Swedish term *särbo* is very well known and understood by almost all Swedes.

## FROM MARRIAGE AND COHABITATION TO LAT

About ten years ago we could notice that some couples were formed who were not living together but saw themselves as couples and not as steady going couples but something else. The most visible ones at that time were either couples where one or both were divorced (or separated from a cohabiting relationship) and elderly couples where both were widowed. An important difference between these couples and the traditional going steady couple was (and is) that they openly visited each other and stayed over night. Without the changes of the four elements and the arrival of non-marital cohabitation as a social institution I mean that LAT relationships would not have come as that social institution which it is in the process of being.

In the beginning and the middle of the 1960s Swedish society came into a turmoil. I will here mention some of the relevant issues making this turmoil, most were not typical for Sweden but common almost all over the western world.

- Not only came the neo-marxist movement as in many other western countries but also many other forces came.
- In 1964 the contraceptive pill became permitted and in 1967 the intra uterine device (IUD) was permitted. These two contraceptive means changed the contraception from a coitus related one to one that is not at all coitus related.
- The Swedish Government as well as the industry suddenly 'realized' that there was a great latent and hidden work force in all the housewives. During the 1950s and the 1960s Sweden had a labor shortage and she 'imported' skilled and semi-skilled workers from Finland, Poland, Yugoslavia and other countries. Now attempts were made to recruit housewives and train them for jobs in the labor market.
- The women's liberation movement woke up at about the same time. It soon turned over into a set of strong feminist movements acting together with or alongside the more, as it at that time was called, sex-role and equity forces or movements.
- TV came fairly late to Sweden but when it came the market exploded and TVs were soon in almost all homes. This had as one of the effects that the Vietnam war came into the living rooms of the Swedes and made quite a few anti-America which in its turn meant discussions and demonstrations.
- The flower power movement came and it advocated for communal living of various sorts, some of a group marriage kind and others with an emotional background such as if several couples with children live together, if one of the parents dies or leaves, the effect upon his or her children would not be so severe since many other adults in any case would take care of the children and remain significant others.
- The ideology of the neo-marxists had in effect the same message but with a different background: theirs built upon the idea that the capitalists gained from the nuclear family model – all households need a refrigerator, a freezer, a vacuum cleaner, to mention some few examples, and therefore the capitalists are in favor of small and many households. With communal living the capitalists would not gain so much.

At about the same time the marriage rates started decreasing; in Sweden the decrease started in 1966 and it intensified very rapidly. The communal living came to some extent but it disappeared rapidly. But the marriage rates went on decreasing and the decrease was to the effect that within a ten year period the rate was half of what it was in 1965. At the same time non-marital cohabitation came and soon, within an approximate ten year period, became a social institution alongside marriage.

I do not mean to say that the turmoil indicated above would have *caused* the decrease in marriage rates and the enormous increase in non-marital cohabitation. But all these changes during the 1960s fit together like a *system* of occurrences. With this is meant that we can understand one change as a part of an entire system of changes – one did not cause any other but they all occurred more or less simultaneously as parts in a system does. All parts of this system went in the same direction: toward what some would say to be toward a normless society. I would not be ready to draw such a conclusion.

The conclusion is that what happened was that some of the traditional norms changed in structure towards a liberalization of society. What does liberalization mean? Here it means that old traditional norms which had existed only because of tradition were changed allowing more individual freedom. In the past they forced people either to follow the norms or to act with a double standard – pretending to behave according to the norms. During this period of change more and more couples openly lived together, which previously was not to think about. The norms easily have a 'cultural lag'. But, in the middle of the 1960s the old norms connecting the four mentioned elements were eventually changed and cohabitation came, which means that in these respects people could (and can) live together without being married.

One can, as Rodman (1971) does, say that a husband-wife relationship exists when the two are 'married' according to society's or the community's criterion of marriage. The approval of the society was usually in the form of a set of rituals but the approval could also be tacit and thus some marriages were established through open rituals and other without these rituals. When saying so one uses the term marriage as a sociologist or anthropologist would and not as a legalist might do. Thus after cohabitation had come as a social institution alongside official marriage we can say that we have two sorts of marriages: those we call marriages, established through a religious or civil ritual, and those we call cohabitation, which are (when a social institution) established without a ritual but tacitly.

According to my analysis the fact that cohabitation came as another social institution alongside marriage made it possible for LAT relationships to arrive.

Had the norms connecting the four elements remained there could be no LAT relationships since the norms would have been too much violated by such 'immoral' behavior. Since the norms have changed there is no 'immorality' of the same sort. And LAT has become or is in the process of becoming a social institution alongside marriage and cohabitation – at least in some countries. When LAT relationships are a social institution there are three sorts of 'marriages': what we regularly call marriage, what we call cohabitation, and what we call LAT relationships. And the two latter are established without any societal rituals but they are societally recognized. Those cohabiting are not united by an official ritual but some of the LAT relationships are, most are not.

One of our informants in our qualitative studies describes her situation like this: She is living in a university town studying and her partner is living in a town about 500 km away. They are in a LAT relationship, according to her, because of her studying there and he has a job in the other town. When they will be in the same town, or if they were living in the same town, they would cohabit and thus not be in a LAT relationship. Before cohabitation became a social institution couples like these would have looked upon themselves as a going steady couple or a couple engaged to be married and their social surrounding, their significant others, would have defined them the same way (now the status of the couple is that of a LAT relationship).

Thus, without the change toward cohabitation as a social institution alongside marriage as a social institution, LAT would still not have been visible. And LAT relationships would not have been as common as they are. With the relatively high divorce and separation rates we have in many western countries LAT relationships are common and also visible, especially when cohabitation is a social institution. Historically, LAT relationships have occurred but certainly not as commonly as now and they have been almost invisible. The higher the divorce and separation rates are, the higher is the likelihood not only for remarriages and recohabitations but also for LAT relationships to be formed. When dealing with the formation of a recohabiting relationship clear is that there is a household change, either one moves in to the other or they both move from separate households to a common household. In most cases of remarriage, traditionally, the same happens but some few remain in separate households.

Some couples who have lived together in a marriage or in a cohabiting relationship, separate from a common household to two separate households but they do not separate their relationship; they just form a LAT relationship out of a living together relationship.

## WHAT ABOUT THE FUTURE?

The mortality rate is an important factor, the lower the mortality rate the higher is the likelihood not only for a person to survive longer but also, for example, to be divorced, separated or widowed and thus also the likelihood, *ceteris paribus*, for the person to start a LAT relationship as well as any other new relationship. With a high mortality rate the need for divorces or separations is not as prevalent as with a low mortality rate. With a high mortality rate many of the happy as well as the unhappy marriages are dissolved by death. A good indicator of this can be seen in the demand for a new divorce law in, for example, Sweden. The mortality rate decreased a lot during the 19th century and the divorce law was very restrictive. At the beginning of the 20th century demands came for a reformation of the divorce law and from 1916 in Sweden both fault and no-fault grounds for a divorce were available. And the divorce rate went on increasing.

The labor market has changed to a higher degree of specialization and the educational system has followed the same tendencies. This means that more persons have less chances to switch jobs and to move to a site somewhere else than where there is a relevant and attractive job for them. This is the case for both men and women and the tradition of women to follow their husbands' to the place where he has a job, has decreased in importance and thus also in numbers. The relatively short history of housewives is almost over in many countries and in some clearly just a historical phenomenon. In order to really understand the new structure of relationships such as LAT relationships, one has to look into the processes toward equality and equity between women and men.

Previously, the informal social norms prescribed that the two in a couple should live in the same household, to have the same domesticity, which was a sign of being a couple and a married couple. In cases where the two could not live together, taken for granted was that the living arrangements were only temporary. With the high divorce rate, women's gainful employment and the equity process, society and its norms have changed somewhat. Tendencies toward equity in this field have had consequences for intimacy and couple relationships (cf. Giddens, 1994). Through LAT relationships the couple is given the possibility not to choose between, for example, the responsibility to care for an elderly parent, one's children and one's new partner. The pressure on a common dwelling has decreased and society has opened up for several both-and solutions. Or as Lewis and Meredith (1989) correctly remark, some adult children live together with a parent out of care for the parent but also since they like to spend time with the parent. This is connected to what Finch (1989) calls cumulative responsibilities, responsibility for the parent and responsibility for oneself.

With the frequency of travel for vacation or for job related issues lots of people meet others living in other places. Some of these meetings result in couples falling in love. Many of these relationships will last and if one or both cannot or does not want to move they might form a long distance LAT relationship. Travel for leisure or for work will probably increase and not decrease even if the technology for IT communication will develop further. On the contrary, many more couples than now might be formed over IT communication and eventually form LAT relationships. Thus we will probably see an important increase in LAT relationships whether they are married or not.

It is often said that LAT relationships can occur only among those who are financially well off. Our studies show that one can find LAT relationships among all sorts of people. Of course, a good financial situation simplifies and makes it easier to maintain two households and certainly it simplifies long distance LAT relationships with easing the costs for telephone and travel (a good financial situation also simplifies for those living in the same household). One household is cheaper to maintain than two are. We would not argue against such a statement. But, in many, probably most, cases of LAT relationships the two already have one household each. Thus they are both used to their own household and they are used to the costs.

From a financially rational perspective most reasonable for many or most of the LAT relationships, who live close or in the same community, would be to move in together. Financial rationality is, however, not the same as social rationality. Furthermore, to move together requires several decisions to be made, for example, where to live, what furniture to share, what books to bring, etc. All the decisions also have to be implemented in activities. Decision making and the implementations in combination make a long process when or if once started and therefore some LATs are dissolved through death of one of the two or by a separation of the relationship before they have moved together.

In our western countries lots of people have a stable financial situation even if it is on a low level. In many of the countries there are social subsidies supporting persons who live single or who have minor children living with them (child allowance, child support, housing subsidies, are just some examples). Even if they do not have good salaries their financial situation might not be bad. Most important could be the habit of taking care of the home and when meeting a new significant other realistically the two do not have to live together if other aspects talk against a move. The financial aspects are not the sole ones.

There are many reasons to predict LAT relationships to be more common in the near future. The labor market will probably not return to the relatively simple structure it had some few decades ago; specialization will likely be even more common than now. People will probably not decrease their travel for vacation and job related issues even if IT will be more important than previously. In fact, IT might become more common as a way for people to meet new partners.

Same gender couples might come out of the closets even more and form cohabiting as well as LAT relationships more visibly and more frequently. An example of this is that in countries where laws are almost the same for same gender couples who have registered their relationship as for married couples one can see announcements in newspapers about same gender couples who have registered.

Divorce and separation rates will probably not decrease and thus lots of people will meet new partners. LAT relationships might be a solution to a difficult marriage or cohabitation. The mortality rate will probably decrease in most countries making people live longer and be more healthy and thus more prone to find new partners. More married and cohabiting couples will probably try to save their relationships by separating and thus to form LAT relationships out of shaky marriages or cohabitation.

The three 'marriages' mentioned can be said not only to be social institutions but they are also in a way parallel to each other and they 'recruit' couples from each other. There are three ways out of a cohabiting relationship: separation is one possibility, another is that one of the two in the couple dies, and the third possibility is that they marry and turn the relationship into a traditional marriage. Similarly there are three ways out of a LAT relationship: one is that they separate in the meaning of dissolving the relationship, another is that one of them dies, and the third possibility is that they move in together and start living in a common dwelling. For the traditional marriage where the two are legally married with a social ritual of some sort and where they are living together there are also three ways out: one of them is a divorce, another one is that one of them dies, and the third possibility is that they separate their dwellings and turn the relationship over into a LAT relationship.

With historically very low mortality rates, with historically very high divorce and separation rates, with frequent traveling, with frequent IT communication, with high specialization of the labor market, with historically fairly high degree of equity between the genders, with liberal societies the propensity for movements between the three 'marriages' as well as in and out of them will remain frequent and probably in the near future be even more frequently occurring. From this follows reasonably that there will be many more LAT relationships than now in most western societies.

REFERENCES

Befolkningsförändringar (1968). *Befolkningsförändringar* (Population changes). Stockholm: Statistiska Centralbyrån.

Befolkningsstatistik (1997). *Befolkningsstatistik 1996* (Population statistics). Stockholm: Statistiska Centralbyrån.

Finch, J. (1989). *Family obligations and social change.* Cambridge: Polity Press.

Giddens, A. (1994). *Intimitetens forandring* (Intimacy in change). København: Hans Reitzels forlag.

Leridon, H. & C. Villeneuve-Gokalp (1989). The new couples. Number, characteristics and attitudes. *Population,* English selection, 44, 203-235.

Lewis, J. & B. Meredith (1989). *Daughters who care.* London: Routledge.

Rodman, H. (1971). Lower-class families. The culture of poverty in Negro Trinidad. New York: Oxford University Press.

Schneider, N.F. (1966). Partnerschaften mit getrennten Haushalten in den neuen und alten Bundesländern. In: W. Bien (Ed.). *Familie an der Schwelle zum neuen Jahrtausend.* Opladen: Leske + Budrich, 88-97.

Trost, J. (1979). *Unmarried cohabitation.* Västerås: International Library.

Family Policy

# Changing families, changing social security

BEA CANTILLON
UNIVERSITEIT ANTWERPEN, BELGIUM

The increase in the participation of women on the labour market and the desta-bilization of the family have profoundly affected the adequacy of social security. Fragmented family lives increase the risks of slipping through the family centred social security while, because of the generalization of two-earner families, in many cases the sole labour income – and, *a fortiori* the sole wage labour centred social security income – have become insufficient to cover the minimum family needs. At the same time, the changes in values are eroding the legitimacy of the family-adjusted system, not in the least through the emerging of new forms of discrimi-nation between insured men and women and between paid and unpaid work.

Thus social and demographic changes and their consequences on the struc-ture of needs, as well as on the cost, effectiveness and legitimacy of social secu-rity, do give rise to a complex problem, namely: how to optimise social protec-tion mechanism in responses, on the one hand, to the problems of the increased social burden resulting from the ageing of the population and individualisation and, on the other hand, to the problems of poverty and inequality that are aris-ing due to social and demographic developments. The problem is compounded by the need to take into account the fundamental principles of non-discrimina-tion, prevention, strengthening self-sufficiency and preventing social protection from having a perverse impact on the social and demographic behaviour of indi-viduals and families. The present paper asks whether, and how individualization of social security can solve these problems. The first part of this paper docu-ments the consequences of socio-demographic developments on the cost, ade-quacy and legitimacy of social security. The second part investigates the main objectives of future policy. The third part contains some practical recommenda-tions for future policy.

The present analysis is based on the Belgian social security system, which is characterized by a moderate earnings relation in contributions and benefits. However, the diagnosis on the relationship between social security and the basic institutions of the family work applies probably to most social security systems in the rich industrialized countries.

## THE DIAGNOSIS: SOCIAL SECURITY AND THE BASIC INSTITUTIONS OF FAMILY AND WORK

The socio-demographic context in which social security was conceived was marked, first, by one-earner families – if not as a rule then still as the norm and the ideal to be striven for – and, second, by stable family structures that were threatened only by the death of one of the members. The socio-demographic developments have now thoroughly changed this situation, and here lies an important cause for the inadequacy and legitimacy crisis of social security.

### Inadequacy

In the socio-economic and demographic context in which the foundations of the social security were laid down, one may assume that the occurrence of one of the risk-events covered by social security almost automatically gave rise to a need situation while inversely a good deal of the needs flowed from such events.

Because unemployment, sickness, old age, or death of the breadwinner often led to the loss of the only labour income of the family, these risk-events were a good indication of need. Inversely, need situations arose primarily by the loss of the income from the generally full-time job of the breadwinner by unemployment, sickness, old age, or death. Thus a universal protection system was structured in which risk was the basis for benefits and in which the stigmatizing means test could be avoided. This system offered, in the given socio-demographic context, the advantage of the virtual coincidence of 'contributional equity' and 'distributional equity'.

The socio-demographic developments have now changed this situation fundamentally: first, because the occurrence of a social risk-event no longer leads automatically to a need situation; second, because new needs have arisen that are not covered by the traditionally risk-events traditionally insured by social security.

A new relationship between needs, risk, and risk coverage

The strong increase in the number of two-earner households, of solo men and women, and of single-parent families has polarized categories for which the occurrence of a social-risk event leads to a severe – and generally too severe – drop in income and categories that can themselves absorb to a certain extent the loss of income because of the presence of another income in the household.

Replacement incomes are very inadequate for households that have to live exclusively from them, but for two-income families, the protection system is adequate to a much larger degree. The occurrence of a social-risk event has thus very divergent consequences in terms of needs for the different groups of bene-ficiaries. This leads to tensions within the social security system between the principle of solidarity and the principle of insurance. Because a risk-event is no longer a good indicator of needs, it has indeed become very difficult to satisfy at the same time and in one and the same universal system the double objective of 'guaranteed minimum income in function of needs' and 'income maintenance in function of risks and contribution payment'. In the present socio-demo-graphic context, in other words, the question arises of whether and how distri-butional equity can be reconciled with contributional equity.

New social risks
The socio-demographic changes gave rise to new needs that are not or only par-tially and fragmentarily covered by social security. Here it is important to note that only 40% of the households that are below the poverty line are beneficiar-ies whose replacement incomes are too low. A large majority (60%) of the households with an income less than the poverty line are households that live from inadequate income from labour (mainly one-income households and sin-gle-parents).

This ratio indicates that the inadequacy of social security is associated not only with social security benefits that are too low but also with insufficient pro-tection of unpaid work, too little compensation for the costs of children, and the almost complete absence of any protection in the event of divorce. Within social security, the necessity of double incomes, the indirect costs of children (and, more generally, of unpaid work), and marital instability thus create prob-lems concerning the link between social protection, work and family.

The risk of unpaid work
The risk of unpaid work has changed in nature. Previously, this risk-event occurred only when the income of the main breadwinner disappeared because of death, and it was satisfactorily taken care of by the system of survival pensions.[1] The high degree of subsistence insecurity among one-income families and one-parent families (also when working) shows that the risk relating to unpaid work also occurs now in the presence of labour or replacement income of the bread-winner.

The cause lies in the necessary nature of double incomes and the enduring incompatibility of two full-time jobs and the care for the children. By the changed consumption patterns (particularly the shift from consumption of self produced goods to the consumption of market goods which can only be acquired by cash incomes) and by the generalization of women in paid work, the double income has increasingly become the reference income. The limits of need have been shifted and double incomes have become the new standard of well-being. Today one notes that, with one modal labour income, let alone one replacement income, the poverty level can hardly be attained. The Belgian data indicate in this regard that the average wage level of unskilled workers is 14% less than the minimum for a household with one child and 20% less than the minimum for families with two children. Consequently the income of almost one fourth of one-earner families with the head of household in paid work is not enough to make ends meet.

This situation has led to a problem of security of subsistence for single-income households, especially where there are dependent children. For more than 30% of these households, the single income is not enough to make ends meet. Considering only those households that live on social security, the proportion is more than 58%.

On the assumption that the women's income were to disappear, the number of double income households not attaining the poverty level would, other things being equal, rise from 5%, as it stands today, to 47% in the hypothetical distribution.

"Very few men's wages are insufficient to cover at least two adults and one child" (Beveridge, 1942). What was the case in Beveridge's time is thus no longer so today. Here we touch on a problem which is generally not taken into account, either in studying the factors determining 'new' poverty, or in studies of the adequacy of social security.

The indirect cost of children

In the two-earner era, the idea that child benefits would provide the working population with the means necessary to bring their family income up to the poverty level has been overtaken. The child benefits cannot compensate for the inadequacy of one income and they thus no longer succeed in guaranteeing a minimum income to many single-income families with children. Indeed, the persisting incompatibility of two jobs and the care for two, three or more children, particularly in lower social strata, makes the well-being of families with children no longer solely a function of the direct costs of children but also and primarily of their indirect costs.[2] These costs, which have arisen through the generalization of two-income families, are not corrected by the child-benefit system. This system is thus today inadequate to assure child-poor and child-rich families the same level of well-being and an equal degree of security of subsistence. Young families with three or more children have on average a lower living standard than small families in the same age group: in spite of current family policy (which is relatively generous in Belgium) and in spite of the positive correlation between the father's income and the number of children, the standard of living of large young families is on average some 10% lower than that of small families in the same age group.

Divorce
In Belgium, as in all other industrialised countries, and whatever the criteria used, the empirical evidence indicates a much higher poverty risk among divorced one-parent families than in other types of household, including those of elderly persons. Moreover, one-parent families are more likely to stay in poverty than the average poor households.

The high poverty risk faced by single divorced mothers is the combined result of several factors: the need to 'make ends meet' with only one income, socio-economic weaknesses related to the fact of being a woman (educational level, amount of time spent in paid work and low wages), and the inadequacy of the private and social protection mechanism (low social security benefits and maintenance payments). Their insecurity of subsistence is thus related to the fact that the sharp increase in women's labour market participation has not been matched by a proportionate increase in their actual rate of employment and in the level of their earnings, and to the poor social protection for the risk arising from divorce.

The very limited coverage of the combined risk 'unpaid work – divorce' is the consequence of the economic and family linkage in the system of social protection. Because of the economic link (both the right to benefits and their amount depend on the financial contributions to the scheme), people who have not completed a full working career or have been working part time can claim only reduced entitlements and benefits, while those who have not been on the labour market have no direct social security entitlements at all. In both cases, those affected are mainly women. No doubt the family linkage of the benefits is even more important. This basic principle of social security finds its concrete expression in the system of derived entitlements (old-age pensions, family allowances and health care). As the effectiveness of such a system depends on the stability of family bonds, fragmented family patterns increase the risks that people will slip between the meshes of the net that protects them. Here one should mention the difficulties, which are mainly administrative ones, met with by single-parent families in obtaining their entitlements under the family allowances schemes.

*Unemployment and improper use of unemployment benefits*

The flow of women onto the labour market resulted in the growth and the feminization of the labour force, in sharply increased unemployment rates, and in the *de facto* change of the concept of 'full employment' (previously: one worker per household, now two workers per household).[3]

In spite of decreased fertility rates, which have already led to a drop in the number of persons of working age, the expected increase in women's participation rates will in the near future be responsible for a further growth in the labour force, assuming that men's participation rate does not change. Consequently, unemployment rates will remain high and feminisation of the labour force will grow.

For social security, this raises not only a cost problem but also a problem of adapting to the needs of the new type of worker who, more than his predecessor, the man earning the households income, has to combine paid work with unpaid work (care of children, sick or elderly parents). At the present time, neither the labour market nor social security is sufficiently adapted to deal with this new type of worker.

In fact full protection in social security schemes presumes a full career and full-time work. This not only creates problems of insecurity of subsistence for families which decide to have several children and a temporary interruption of the individual's working life (the problem of making ends meet on a single income) but also leads to abusive, but necessary, utilisation of unemployment benefits.

According to data of the Centre for Social Policy, there is a positive correlation between unemployment of married women and the number of children, even after controlling statistically variables such as age, level of education, occupation and sector of activity.[4] The idea that two-income households are more often and for longer periods subject to unemployment because of being less available for work is thus confirmed by empirical data (Cantillon, 1990).

But these data also show that unemployment benefits received by married women with children are a necessary complement to the household income for a large number of them. For more than 16% of these households, the single labour income plus the unemployment benefit is not enough to make ends meet. On the assumption that the women's unemployment benefit were to disappear, the number of double-income households with unemployed wife not attaining the poverty level would, other things being equal, rise to more than 52%.

The abusive but necessary utilisation of unemployment benefits in Belgium therefore reflects the negative effect of the failure to adjust working conditions and social security to the specific problems of combining two full-time jobs with child care requirements, especially for women with a low level of education and in the lower social groups.

## Discriminations

As a consequence of socio-demographic developments and the related changes in values, social security has given rise to new forms of discrimination, while older forms of discrimination are becoming more visible. This evolution is so important that discussion on social security policy is increasingly dominated by the question of the extent to which and how such direct and indirect discrimination should be combated. The most important types of discrimination are that between men and women covered by social security on the one hand and that between paid and unpaid work on the other.

In the recent past almost all the forms of direct discrimination against women in social security have been removed. The problems are now primarily situated around the application and the interpretation of the principle of indirect discrimination (see Article 4 of Directive no. 79 (7) EEC of the Council of 19 December 1978). In general terms, what is understood here is the discrimination that arises because an apparently neutral procedure turns out to affect in practice predominantly persons of a particular sex. With regard to Belgian law, the discussion on the application of this legal principle concentrates primarily on the question of whether the 'family adjustments' of the earning related benefits should or should not be removed from the unemployment, sickness, disability, and retirement schemes because statistically women are predominantly disadvantaged.[5]

With regard to the unequal treatment of paid and unpaid work, there are two lines of argument. Some contend that working married women pay contributions 'for nothing' because derived entitlements cannot or can only partially be combined with individual rights. Therefore, the derived entitlements emerge as a discriminatory and anti-emancipatory system, "coming from those households that contribute twice to those who contribute only once" (Université des Femmes, 1987). The problem arises in particular with family allowances, where women's work has entirely changed the relationship between benefits and contributions and has brought to light the distortions in the nature of the two sides of the balance sheet – benefits and contributions. "One thus sees a redistribution from working to non-working women, irrespective of the incomes of their spouses and the size of the family ... By their contributions, women contribute to financing family policy, without receiving any counterpart" (Ekert, 1985; see also Coutière, 1983; Hatchuel, 1985).

Others call attention to the discrimination against the socially and economically important unpaid labour. The consideration here applies that in the wage labour centred social security unpaid work is only very rarely covered by specific benefits and individual social security rights.

## Calculating behaviour

Because choices regarding marriage, cohabitation, divorce, and remarriage are no longer ruled by the same values as in the past, it is generally accepted that (potential) beneficiaries make, more than previously, use of the opportunities offered by the complex social security provisions, sometimes even adjusting their demographic behaviour to the institutional environment. Because social security is not (nor can be, even with the strategy of basic income) neutral with respect to the family situation chosen, this leads to a self-reinforcing mechanism whereby social protection itself could act as a factor affecting socio-demographic behaviour (Sullerot, 1984; Murray, 1984).

On the existence, scope, and nature of calculated behavioural forms the empirical data is however not univocal. This is not surprising. Decisions regarding the organization of family life are influenced by a multiplicity of social, cultural, and psychological factors. The financial aspect (including the social protection) is only one of them. An empirical separation of the direct influence of social security on behaviour, therefore, is therefore very difficult to achieve. Nevertheless, the question regarding the influence of social security benefits on marriage, divorce or remarriage is of great political significance. Indeed, regulations that discriminate against marriage and for divorce impair the legitimacy of the system and thus must be avoided as far as possible.

THE OBJECTIVES OF FUTURE POLICY

Three policy problems emerge with this diagnosis. First, how and in what degree can, within the universal context of the social security system, selectivity be built in so that need and risk coverage can converge (the tension between solidarity and insurance). Second, how can the protection be adapted to the new family context (relationship between social security, individual, and family). Third, how must the new risk-event of unpaid work be defined and with what resources can it be covered by social security (principle and interpretation of the requirement of willingness to work).

These questions are difficult to answer: "not all good things are compatible, still less all the ideas of mankind, in the realm of social security as in other areas of human life" (Titmuss, 1970). Nevertheless, in what follows we will attempt to link concrete policy recommendations to our empirical analysis. We start from the following principles.

## The relationship between insurance and solidarity

The objective of social security is twofold: guaranteeing a minimum income by virtue of the principle of solidarity (protection against poverty) and income maintenance by insurance (graduated benefits related to previous income when at work).

Both objectives are necessarily complementary. The unavoidably low level of minimum protection compels its supplementing with higher, wage-related benefits. Inversely, insurance is also a necessary basis for solidarity. Thanks to the insurance social security can rest on a large commitment which is necessary to be able to offer acceptable minimum security to high risk and/or low income groups, that is, those with little capacity to contribute. In this sense, the minimum protection of the system does not exclude the insurance character: income maintenance is, on the contrary, a necessary condition for achieving an acceptable level of minimum protection. Moreover, the inequalities of income related schemes backed by compulsion must be motivated also by egalitarian considerations, because by state insurance systems the possibility of income maintenance is made available to *all* workers (and not only to white collar workers and 'good risks' as on the private market).

Nevertheless, the future social security policy will have to be inspired more by solidarity than by insurance. This is necessary because of the immense welfare expenditure (which will automatically increase in the future because of ageing and other institutional and socio-demographic factors) and because of the inadequate protection against want with large numbers still living 'in poverty'.

## The relationship between work and social security

A majority (60%) of the households with an income less than the poverty line are living on the labour income of one earner. This ratio indicates that poverty (and the inadequacy of social security) is related not only with benefits that are too low in the event of unemployment, sickness, and old age but also with the inadequacy of the sole labour income for many one-income families. This is one of the main reasons why the vast social security outlay (the annual social security expenditure corresponds to one fifth of gross national product and 78% of all households is in receipt of a cash benefit of some kind at any one time) does not seem sufficient.

Two approaches are possible to this diagnosis. Either one maintains that the problem of one-income families is situated on the labour market and therefore can be resolved by an active employment policy (generating more two-income families by more labour and better adaptation of the labour market to family life). Or one argues that the high degree of insecurity of subsistence of one-income families with children arises because the social security no longer adequately covers the social risks linked to unpaid work, the care for children and divorce. The derived rights to benefits (regarding survivor pensions, child benefits, and health care) would no longer provide adequate protection and should be supplemented by direct, individual coverage of the risks associated with the performance of unpaid work (care).

Because of the complexity of the social problems, the diversification of preferences and values, the interrelatedness of the distinct state and private welfare provisions, and the necessary cost containment in social security, neither of these remedies of themselves are sufficient: integrated action in several sectors of social policy is necessary.

In the context of a prevention policy, not in the least to keep calls from being made upon social security benefits, an active employment policy must be urged, a policy that gives particular attention to the weaker categories: less educated, women, and immigrants.

However, without minimizing the importance of and the need for such an employment policy, there are reasons to doubt the results from this one option: first, because of the persistently very high unemployment rates; second, because the strong increase of the labour market participation of women has thoroughly changed the content of the notion of 'full employment' and therefore the post-war consensus according to which social security and full employment were complementary.

Because of this change and the importance of more than one income for security of subsistence, the link between paid work, unpaid work and social security is up for revision, and the question of the content of the concept of work, and the requirement of willingness to work cannot be avoided.

A radical strategy would be to strive for some kind of basic income. It is not possible to discuss here the many arguments that have been put forward against basic income (work incentives, level of benefits, costs, injustice linked to over-simplification of social protection, given the complexity of social problems). What is central here is that basic income – a version of postmodern tolerance – rejects the possibility and the responsibility to influence and to approve the use of time, in paid employment or in time not spent in paid employment for socially usefull purposes. In our view the question of how 'socially usefull work' must be delimited for social security coverage and thus constitute a legitimate reason to receive social benefits (only care for children under three years of age? also care for sick, disabled or elderly persons? employment interruptions for training purposes?) cannot and may not be avoided and must, publicly be discussed.

In the past, by widening the concept of work, social security has substantially supported the policy of 'redistribution of the scarce available work'. Today, we have to evaluate, quantitatively and qualitatively, the results of these policies and consider adjustments. Most important is the dramatic change of the distribution of work between age categories since 1960. The decrease of labour participation at young (longer school careers) and old (early retirement) ages, together with the generalisation of two-earnership, have made the active life span very short and concentrated in the family formation phase (see Table 1).

Table 1. Activity-rates by age and sexe (1970, 1980, 1990, 2000)

|  |  | 1970 | 1980 | 1990 | 2000 |
|---|---|---|---|---|---|
| Men |  |  |  |  |  |
|  | 14 – 19 | 35.6 | 24.3 | / | / |
|  | 20 – 24 | 83.3 | 79.6 | 68.7 | 60.5 |
|  | 25 – 29 | 96.0 | 95.8 | 93.0 | 90.0 |
|  | 30 – 34 | 97.3 | 97.3 | 97.0 | 97.0 |
|  | 35 – 39 | 96.7 | 96.3 | 96.8 | 96.8 |
|  | 40 – 44 | 94.8 | 94.5 | 95.2 | 95.2 |
|  | 45 – 49 | 92.2 | 91.3 | 90.0 | 90.0 |
|  | 50 – 54 | 89.2 | 86.3 | 83.8 | 82.0 |
|  | 55 – 59 | 82.3 | 70.2 | 51.7 | 43.0 |
|  | 60 – 64 | 63.7 | 33.1 | 18.3 | 11.0 |
|  | 65 + | 6.8 | 3.9 | 2.5 | 2.0 |
| Women |  |  |  |  |  |
|  | 14 – 19 | 29.5 | 19.2 | / | / |
|  | 20 – 24 | 60.9 | 72.7 | 69.5 | 75.0 |
|  | 25 – 29 | 49.6 | 74.3 | 86.5 | 88.0 |
|  | 30 – 34 | 39.3 | 62.0 | 80.2 | 88.0 |
|  | 35 – 39 | 35.2 | 54.6 | 68.0 | 78.0 |
|  | 40 – 44 | 33.3 | 46.7 | 59.6 | 74.0 |
|  | 45 – 49 | 30.7 | 38.4 | 46.2 | 55.0 |
|  | 50 – 54 | 27.6 | 29.9 | 33.0 | 36.5 |
|  | 55 – 59 | 20.3 | 17.3 | 16.5 | 15.7 |
|  | 60 – 64 | 7.6 | 5.9 | 5.5 | 4.5 |
|  | 65 + | 2.2 | 1.6 | 0.6 | 0.5 |

Source: NIS

## *The relationship between individual, family, and social security*

In spite of the individualization in the social reality, the security of subsistence of individuals remains determined to a very large extend by the structure and the composition of the household to which they belong: by the incomes of others within the household unit, by the costs of income-dependent members, by the advantages of common housekeeping, by the benefits of domestic production. If the social security system is effectively intended to offer a minimum income guarantee as well as income maintenance to individuals and households, then these factors have to be taken into account. Given the high number of social security recipients and the costs involved, it is indeed very difficult to achieve more adequacy with universalistic policies. We therefore must try to target within universalism, one of the possibilities is precisely family adjustment of benefits.

The social security system has to monitor the striving for an equal distribution of income and welfare between men and women. However, emancipation is, for the social security system, not an objective of the first order. If the principle of minimum income guarantee imposes this, and insofar as no direct discrimination is built into the system, family adjustments of the benefits are thus possible. Moreover, it should be considered that, given the persistent gender related socio-economic inequalities and division of paid and unpaid work, a complete individualization of social security benefits can do nothing other than work to the disadvantage of women.

SOME PRACTICAL RECOMMENDATIONS FOR FUTURE POLICY

Complex problems cannot be solved by social security alone in its strict sense. In particular, in relation to covering the cost of care for children, disabled and elderly, the idea of developing a policy for community services and facilities, assistance at home and family adapted working conditions is essential since it responds to the various needs that are directly related to the security of existence. It makes it possible to assist families to reconcile the requirements of paid work and family responsibilities, thereby guaranteeing income from work. The challenge is to find a just balance between the various social measures for the members of the family that provide the care, who are mainly women. In any event, there has to be better co-ordination between social security measures, tax reliefs and the system of community facilities and services.

As social security in its strict sense is concerned, arguing that the described discrepancies can be completely eliminated if the system were fully individualized overlooks:

– first, the great inadequacy of the social benefits for families that have to live exclusively from them, particularly if there are dependent children;
– second, the very high level of unemployment because of which it is illusory to think that the problem of one-earner families will be resolved in the short or even the middle term only through the implementation of an employment policy;
– third, the enduring inequalities between men and women whereby complete individualization can only work to the disadvantage of women.

To the question of the need for individualization or family adjustments of social benefits, therefore, the answer must be nuanced. The following principles can serve as guidelines.

### Family adjusted benefits

Recognition of the polarisation we have noted, between, on the one hand, households for whom social risk involves a too substantial loss of income and, on the other hand, households which can themselves to some extent compensate for the loss of an income through another income, leads us to ask how, within the universal framework of social security, one could increase the selectivity so as to achieve more convergence between the concepts of need and risk coverage.

Given the very high degree of inadequacy of the replacement incomes for families who have to live exclusively from them, there must be positive discrimination for one-income families not only to be able to guarantee a minimum income for these families but also to be able to assure them income maintenance at a sufficiently high level. Family adjustments remain, after the introduction of separate taxation, the only possible way – while maintaining the universal nature of social secuirty – for taking account of the fact that, for different groups of beneficiaries, the occurrence of a social-risk-event has widely divergent effects in terms of needs.

However, the possibility of achieving a more adequate distribution of the resources by means of family adjustments is limited for three reasons.

First, because positive and negative discrimination assumes that the target groups are sufficiently homogeneous. The ever larger, and thus ever more heterogeneous, group of two-income families appears incapable of fulfilling this condition. This makes it difficult to cut the benefits by simple reference to the presence or not of other family incomes, thus without taking account of the real income level.

Second, because of the 3rd EC Directive, which forbids all forms of direct and indirect discrimination against women. The European Court of Justice has recently (May 1991) rejected the complaint submitted by the *Comité de Liasons des Femmes* against the Belgian State regarding the family adjustments in unemployment, sickness, and disability insurance. The grounds were that indirect discrimination is permitted insofar as this is necessary to assure a minimum income. Although the insight has thus rightly emerged in the course of the years that 'equal treatment' can hardly have first priority on the list of social security objectives, this important judgement means, a contrario, that benefits for dependents and for loss of the sole income are only possible in the minimum part of the protection but not in the supra-minimum (see the previous Teulings judgement).[6]

Third, it must also be considered that even a strong positive discrimination of one-income families cannot fundamentally resolve the problem of the high degree of insecurity of subsistence and the pronounced inadequacy of the benefits for these groups. Indeed, the essential core of the problem is outside the social security system: the necessity of two incomes. Even a high increase of the replacement incomes for one-income families can do nothing in the face of this structural problem. For such an increase can only be small (because of the relationship to minimum wages), while the inadequacy of lower wages remains, of course, unresolved. Therefore solutions have to be sought outside the framework of the risks traditionally covered by social security whereby the risk of unpaid work (care) is secured not only by derived rights but also by direct benefits.

Given these restrictions, one must strive for the necessary adjustments of the social protection in function of family circumstances, preferably achieved by a) the granting of individual benefits for unpaid caring work and b) by maximum coverage of the costs of children.

Although under these modalities, equal benefits may apply for a very large group of beneficiaries, a certain degree of adjustment of the amounts still is necessary. First, because of the scale advantages from joint housekeeping and, second, because of the fact that not all one-income situations can be covered by special benefits given the available resources.

To keep the level of the replacement incomes from being either higher than necessary for couples with two incomes or too low for one-income families and especially people living alone, the amounts of the benefits must be differentiated in function of the presence or absence of dependents and/or of other family income.

In the application of this adjustment scheme, account has to be taken of the actual criterion of dependency and the joint housekeeping. Because one proceeds from a basic rate for 'couples with two incomes' to which supplements can be granted under certain conditions, the problem of proof is no longer insurmountable. Whoever claims supplementary allowances has to supply the proof.

## *Individualisation of social security entitlements*
Marital instability and the participation of women in the labour force raise problems as to the adequacy and legitimacy of derived rights to benefits through the contributions of others. Indeed, fragmented family careers increase the chance of slipping through the meshes of the family-linked social security net, while working women pay contributions 'for nothing' because derived entitlements cannot or can only partially be cumulated with individual entitlements.

In the light of these problems cost-covering benefits (child benefits and health care) have to be individualized and universalized.

The idea of individualisation of derived entitlements to old age pensions should be considered with more caution.

If one wants to provide a universal income maintenance, then there is no other solution than maintaining the system of derived entitlements. Indeed, the standard of living of individuals is not only a function of individual incomes from labour but also of the family unit of which they are or were a part. Here it must also be considered that, because of the enduring wage differentials between men and women (partially because women generally take more family responsibilities), a complete individualization of pension entitlements can only work to the disadvantage of women (and, more generally, of all those who, during a particular period of their life are more concerned with unpaid work than with paid work).

In the light of the problems linked to family break down and to cope with the increasing number of two-earner families (i.e. double contribution payment and living standard determined by the incomes of both man and women) and also with the desire of many women to have their own independent income, the modalities of the derived entitlements should however be adjusted in the sense of individual derived entitlements, for example, by the system of 'credit splitting'. In analogy with the old age pensions for divorced women, individual entitlements could be assigned the size of which are determined by the entitlements that were built up jointly by the partners during the period of marriage/cohabitation.

## *A broader concept of work*
The adaptation of social protection to social and demographic changes should be guided, first, by the idea that the increase in the number of two-income

households has given rise to a new type of worker who, more than his or her predecessor, is faced with the problems resulting from the combination of paid and unpaid work; and second that the striving for 'full employment' in the sense that each individual would have a complete career during the entire active working age is neither feasible nor desirable. The generalization of the two-earner family thus supposes an employment policy that is oriented to a) a better tuning of work and family circumstances and b) a redistribution of the available work over the active life span of individuals with due regard for the possibilities and needs proper to each family and life phase.

Social security should act in support of this policy by taking account of family circumstances to a higher and different degree. What is central here is that the risk of unpaid work has changed substantially. Formely this risk occured only when the income of the breadwinner disappeared on death. The high level of insecurity of subsistence of solo income households shows that the risk relating to unpaid work now arises also where there is a 'breadwinner' wage or replacement income.

The logical consequence of these observations is that the new risk of unpaid work must be financially covered within the social security system. Not only should periods during which individuals decide to reduce or temporarily cease their work on account of family or parental responsibilities be taken into account in calculating pension entitlements, but social security should also provide direct benefits enabling persons to interrupt their work temporarily. This coverage should be conceived as a horizontal redistribution between those who are at a stage in their family life during which they can combine two full-time jobs and those who are at a stage during which the double income is necessary but difficult to reconcile with unpaid work. Provided that such coverage is combined with public arrangements in the field of child care and improved re-employment possibilities, compensation of the risk relating to unpaid work would make it possible to solve the problems arising from the inadequacy of social security for both single and two-parent families which have only one income, without violating the principles of action programmes for equal opportunities for women.

CONCLUSION

Arguing that the discrepancies in social security can be completely eliminated if the system were fully individualized overlooks:
- first, the great inadequacy of the social benefits for families that have to live exclusively from them, particularly if there are dependent children;

– second, the very high level of unemployment because of which it is illusory to think that the problem of one-earner families will be resolved in the short or even the middle term only through the implementation of an employment policy;

– third, the enduring inequalities between men and women whereby complete individualization can only work to the disadvantage of women.

To the question of the need for individualization or family adjustments of social benefits, therefore, the answer must be nuanced. The following principles can serve as guidelines:

1) The necessary adjustment of the social protection in function of family circumstances must occur preferably by:
    – the granting of individual benefits for unpaid work;
    – maximum coverage of the costs of children.

2) Although under these modalities equal benefits can be applicable for a very large group of beneficiaries, a certain degree of adjustment of the amounts (depending on the presence or not of household expenses and/or of other family incomes) will still be necessary.

3) Cost-covering benefits (child benefits and health care) have to be individualized and universalized.

4) If one also wishes to work out 'in solidarity' the protection above the minimum (income maintenance) then there is no other way than to stick to the system of derived benefits regarding survivor pensions. The modalities of these entitlements, however, should be reviewed in the sense of 'individual derived entitlements', for example, by the system of credit splitting (granting individual entitlements for which the amount is determined by the contributions that were built up jointly by the partners).

## NOTES

[1] In Belgium the spouse of a deceased, insured employee or self-employed person is entitled to widow(er)'s pension of the level of 80% of the retirement pension of the deceased insured person, subject to the condition that the widow(er) is over 45 years of age or has a dependent child, or is incapable to work.

[2] Our figures show that among mothers of three or more children it is almost exclusively those with a high educational level who are in paid work. Among low-skilled women, the participation rate drops from 61% when they have only one young child to 13% when they have three or more. Among women with higher education, the participation rate remains much higher: 88% when they have only one young child and 79% when they have three or more.

[3] From 1976 to 1985, the total Belgian working population increased by 172,000 units. There were three underlying mechanisms involved:

1) Demographic factors that provided temporarily for a more rapid increase in the working population than in the total population. Young people entered in larger numbers on the labor market because of the baby boom of the 1960s. Over against this was a small amount of departure from the labor market. The employees who retired on pension between 1975 and 1985 were born in the 'lean' birth years of the First World War.

2) Among men, these demographic factors were neutralized by the reduced degree of activity. The male working population consequently declined by 87,000 units.

3) Among women, the demographic factors were reinforced by the increasing degree of participation: both mechanisms provided for an increase of the female working population by 259,000 units.

The growth of the population at the active age and the increased degrees of activity among women account for 95% of the increase of the enemployment figures (1976-1985).

[4] In Belgium unemployment benefits are not limited in time.

[5] Family adjustment modalities in Belgian social security:

(a) unemployment

The level of unemployment benefit is expressed as a percentage of the (ceiled) wages previously earned: i.e. 25% plus:

— an allowance of 5% for loss of income, payable to the single unemployed person and to the unemployed person who cohabitates with his dependent (i.e. without labour or social security income) spouse and children.

— an adjustment allowance of 20% during the first year of unemployment;

— and extra allowance in respect of dependent family member, egual to 20% after the first year of unemployment, subject to the condition that the beneficiary is the head of household.

(b) incapacity for work

During the first period of one year benefit normally consists of 60% of the wage. From the second year on head of households (with dependents) obtain 65%. Otherwise, this percentage is 45 or 40% of the previously conveyed wages (depending upon whether or not the lost income was the sole income).

(c) old age pensions

The retirement pension of employees amounts to 75% or 60% of the average wage over the period between twenty years of age and the attainment of pensionable age, depending upon wether the insured person is married head of household (with dependent wife).

[6] In this judgement, too, the European Court of Justice ruled that 'objective reasons' constituted acceptable excusation grounds for an existing form of discrimination. Teuling had received a Dutch sickness benefit that was not increased because her husband's income was too high. On this, the Court ruled that Article 4 of Directive No. 79 (7) EEC of the Council of 19 December 1978 has to be interpreted in such a way that a system of entitlements for labor disability where the level of the benefit is partially determined by the marital status and the income from or in connection with the labor of the spouse, is in harmony with this regulation when this system has the objective of guaranteeing an adequate subsistence level by means of an increase

of the social security benefits to beneficiaries with a spouse or dependent children by offering compensation for the higher expenses relative to those of people who live alone (for a further discussion, see Sjerps, 1988).

## REFERENCES

Beckerman, W. (1979). *Poverty and the impact of income maintenance programmes.* Geneva.

Berghman, J. (1986). *De onzichtbare sociale zekerheid.* Deventer: Kluwer.

Berghman, J. (1991). Defining social security. In: D. Pieters (Ed.). *Social security in Europe.* Brussel: Bruylandt.

Bergmann, B., J. Devine, P. Gordon, D. Reedy, L. Save & C. Wide (1980). The effects of wives' labour force participation on inequality in the distribution of family income. *Journal of Human Resources,* (3), 452-455.

Beveridge, W. (1942). *Social insurance and allied services.* London: Her Majesty's Stationery Office.

Blau, D. (1984). Family earnings and wage inequality early in the life cycle. *Review of Economics and Statistics,* (66), 200-207.

Cantillon, B. (1989). *Socio-demografische veranderingen, inkomensverdeling en sociale ze-kerheid, 1976-1985. (*doctoral thesis). Antwerpen.

Cantillon, B. (1990). *Nieuwe behoeften naar zekerheid. Vrouw, gezin en inkomensverdeling.* Leuven/Amersfoort: ACCO.

Cantillon, B. (1991). Socio-demographic changes and social security. *International Review of Social Security,* (4), 399-426.

CERC (1986). *Constats de l'évolution récente des revenus en France.* Paris.

Coutière, A. (1983). Arguments sur l'impôt sur le revenu: des mesures de portée inégale. *Economie et Statistique,* 21-35.

Decoster, A. et al. (1982). *Arbeidsmarktinformatie en arbeidsbemiddeling in Vlaanderen.* Leuven: HIVA.

Deleeck, H. (1989). The adequacy of the social security system in Belgium, 1976-1985. *Journal of Social Policy,* (18), 91-117.

Deleeck, H. & K. Van den Bosch (1990). The measurement of poverty in a comparative context: empirical evidence and methodological evaluation of four poverty lines in seven EC-countries. In: R. Teekens & B.M.S. Van Praag (Eds.). *Analysing poverty in the European Community.* Luxembourg: Eurostat News Special edition (1), p. 153-186.

Deleeck, H. et al. (1991). Indicateurs sociaux de la sécurité sociale 1985-1988. *Revue Belge de Sécurité Sociale,* (10-11-12), 711-761.

Deleeck, H. et. al. (1992). *Poverty and the adequacy of social security in the EC.. A comparative analysis.* Avebury: Aldershot.

Ekert, D. (1985). Les effets redistributifs du système des prestations familiales sur le cycle de vie. In: D. Kessler, A. Masson (Eds.). *Cycles de vie et générations.* Paris: Economica, p. 261-272.

Engel, B. (1985). Stetige und diskrete private Transfers: Zur Bedeutung von Erbschaften und privaten Unterhaltszahlungen für die Einkommens- und Vermögensver-teilung. In: R. Hauser & B. Engel (Hrsg.). *Soziale Sicherung und Einkom-mensverteilung.* Frankfurt-am-Main: Campus Verlag, p. 239-253.

Gronau, R. (1982). Inequality of family income: Do wives' earnings matter. In: Y. Ben-Porath (Ed.). *Income distribution and the family. Population and Development Review, 8*, 119.

Harris, R. & J. Hedderson (1981). Effects of wives' income on family income inequality. *Sociological Methods and Research*, 211-232.

Hatchuel, G. (1985). *Transfert sociaux et redistribution*. Paris: CREDOC.

International Social Security Association (1992). *Social security and changing family structures*. Studies and Research n°29, Geneva: ISSA.

Lehrer, E. & M. Nerlove (1981). The impact of female work on family income distribution: Black-White differentials. *Review of Income and Wealth*, 423-432.

Murray, C. (1984). *Losing ground: American social policy*. New-York: Basic Books.

O'Higgins, M. (1984). *Inequality, redistribution and recession: The British experience*. Rockefeller Foundation's Bellagio Conference Center (mimeo).

Parker, H. (1989.) *Instead of the dole*. London: Routledge.

Rainwater, L. (1984). Mother's contribution to the family money income in Europe and the US. *Journal of Family History* (4), 198-211.

Rainwater, L., M. Rein & J. Schwartz (1986). *Income packaging in the welfare state*. Oxford: Clarendon Press.

Rein, M. & R. Freeman (1988). *The Dutch choice. A plea for social policy complementary to work*. 's Gravenhage: HRWB.

Royal Commission on the Distribution of Income and Wealth (1977). *Lower incomes*. Report n°6, London: HMSO.

Sjerps, C.M. (1988). Dames en heren, en dan nu: gelijke behandeling! *Sociaal Maandblad Arbeid*, 305-324.

Sullerot, E. (1984). *Pour le meilleur et sans le pire*. Paris: Fayard.

Therborn, G. & J. Roebroek (1986). The irreversible welfare state. Its recent maturation. Its encounter with the economic crisis. Its future prospects. In: W. Albeda (Ed.). *The future of the welfare state*. Maastricht: Presses Universitaires Européennes, p. 63-86.

Titmuss, R. (1970). Equity, adequacy and innovation in social security. *International Social Security Review*. Geneva: ISSA, (2), p. 259-268

Whiteford, P. (1985). *A family's needs: Equivalence scales, poverty and social security*. Research Paper n°27, Melbourne: DSS.

Wilson, T. & D. Wilson (1991). *The state and social welfare*. London/New York: Longman.

Winegarden, C. (1987). Women's labour force participation and the distribution of household incomes: Evidence from cross-national data. *Economica*, (214), 223-236.

# The new citizenship of the family

Pierpaolo Donati
Università degli Studi di Bologna, Italy

## THE PROBLEM: RETHINKING THE SOCIAL ROLE OF THE FAMILY

The UN International Year of the Family held in 1994 has provided the opportunity for a vast, worldwide debate that has enormously emphasized the central role of the family in society and social policies. At the European Union level, we have witnessed a renewed debate on the meaning, future and social functions of the family in a search for a more precise and effective policy to protect, support and promote the family as such. Central to this debate has been the contribution provided by the work done in his academic career by Wilfried Dumon (Aldous & Dumon, 1980; Dumon & Nuelant, 1994; Dumon, 1994).

National and regional governments and the European Union itself are trying to acknowledge – in facts, not just words – the central role of the family qua talis for the purposes of their development model. Many social actors certainly show good intentions, but uncertainties and ambivalences still prevail, and the concept of family policy remains as dense with misunderstandings as ever (Hantrais & Letablier, 1996; Commaille & de Singly, 1997; Ditch et al., 1998).

As Wilfried Dumon did many years ago, we wonder today: why? The explanation I would like to put forth here is as simple as it is rich with implications. It says that, in a world projected towards globalization and post-modernity, emphasizing the family implies acquiring a new way of considering the family and its presence in society. Concretely, it implies developing a new concept of 'family citizenship', with all of the theoretical and practical baggage this concept brings along with it.

The experts know that a sharp divide is emerging internationally in how the family is considered throughout the world: while non-western countries tend to increasingly emphasize the family as the basic cell of society (by stressing its nuclear form even when they share a culture which legitimizes other forms), western countries on the contrary emphasize the crisis of the family (i.e. its nuclear form), and thus tend to consider it as simply one of the many forms of living arrangements (Goldthorpe, 1987; Cherlin, 1988; Glendon, 1989; Bernardes, 1997; Gillis, 1996).

Many explain this divide by saying that it occurs because non-western countries are still 'modernizing', and thus 'behind', while the west has by now surpassed modernity and thus no longer has a need for the family (i.e. the nuclear monogamous form) as a basis for its development. The validity of such an evolutionary philosophy still remains to be proven. For the moment, it only justifies the fact that this is how the West legitimizes exporting lifestyle models to the rest of the world that no longer refer to the nuclear family as a basic model for social organization.

In this paper, I start from the idea that these trends should be discussed. It is then a matter of seeing whether the nuclear family continues to be a social good, even in our so-called advanced or late-modern societies, and if so whether it is an 'optional' or 'non-optional' good.

My thesis is that the concept of family citizenship is a valid guiding idea for all countries, worldwide, notwithstanding the variety of legal and socio-cultural orders which define the family in a different way. But in particular, this idea may encounter new meanings and operative applications in those countries whose modernization process makes it necessary to prepare responses that can counter the shattering of social fabric, widespread anonymity, mass individualism, solitude, and in general all of the individual and collective pathologies that originate in the failure to acknowledge the social value of the family.

Since the most radical challenge to families falls within the later contexts, which are those in the area ranging from North American to Europe, I will concentrate my topic on these countries, especially those of the European Union.

## RELEVANCY OR IRRELEVANCY (DIFFERENCE OR INDIFFERENCE) OF THE FAMILY TO THE CIVILIZATION PROCESS?

Postwar western society has been characterized by two basic trends regarding the family: a) It has assumed the family as something already there, always there, to perform its tasks. In other words, it has implicitly taken the existence of the family for granted, and in a certain way its 'strength' as well, as though the dissolution of the institutional aspects of the family had only positive and not problematic consequences. Priority in social protection has been given not to the family in ordinary life, but to disorganized and dissolving forms of the family; and – in any case – privileges have been accorded to the needs of individuals in order to free them from the obligations inherent in families ties. By this way, it has become apparent that the welfare state relies upon the commons (like the families), but it cannot regenerate them. b) It has attempted to resolve the problems of the family through social policies that make only indirect reference to the family. It was assumed that by giving work, home, and services to people in cash and in kind we could also solve the problems of the family. In agreement with the above attitude, the family has always remained in the background of the welfare state as an implicit reference. It was assumed that the diffusion of public (government) intervention would all fall not on single issues, but on family life as such, and with only positive consequences.

In short, the family qua talis has been treated 'residually' (more or less, depending on the national context). We must not be fooled by the fact that governments have granted the population an increasing number of welfare benefits. Even where welfare policies have been very 'generous' from the standpoint of an economic commitment to the population and with full or nearly full coverage of certain risks, even here interventions have been aimed at individuals and 'groups of individuals', without the family being foreseen as an operator (mediator) of their inter-subjective and structural relations. While there has been a considerable effort to protect the rights and needs of individuals, there has certainly been a much weaker (and often non-existent) effort to protect family relations as a good in itself.

The reasons why these trends have dominated until now are undoubtedly complex. But here I wish to emphasize the fact that these cultural attitudes, and the relative societal government directions, have been possible due to the convergence of two strong lines:
- the line of those who thought that the family should not be regulated by the government (for the majority of western – and in particular European – legal systems, the family is a private sphere into which the state should enter as little as possible, although the opposite often occurs),
- the line of those who thought that the family should change with society's progress, and that its deinstitutionalization represented, all told, a way toward emancipation from a more backward state of humanity, and in any case a positive and generally desirable transformation against the need to guarantee greater social rights for individuals as such.

With quite different but convergent motivations and plans, both laissez-faire (pro-deregulation) and welfare supporters have considered the family to be a 'private', 'traditional', 'surviving' social form, a 'primordial' element in social organization that would change within the broader changes of society, in a way that is positive in the end for both people and social life.

All these lines of thought never wondered what social consequences would be caused by the alienation of the family. On the contrary, they have proffered unconditionally positive judgement on the fact that political society – in the form of the welfare state – prevailed over the 'particularism' of family relations.[1] In their opinion, any negative consequences to society due to family transformations could be perfectly managed within the political framework of welfare institutions.

But that has not been the case. The family, treated residually, has become an increasingly problematic reality, with heavily negative effects on the entire social framework:

- the publicizing of family relationships (and part of its functions) has increased the privatization of the latter, and the privatization of the family (in the sense of reducing it purely to the sphere of emotions and private interests) has led to depoliticizing society as a whole as well, in the sense that individuals now regulate their own opinions, attitudes and interest in every realm of life, without taking the common good into any account;
- the detachment from a solid ideal of the family (in the sense of a sphere having essential, irreplaceable social functions) has led to a widespread dehumanization of social, interpersonal and generalized relationships;
- in the end, we must note that so-called civil society no longer has any idea – much less a plan – of civility; civil society reveals itself to be uncivil, according to the ideologies of modernity.

The overall result has been – and still is – a deep and at times dramatic disorientation of the so-called life-worlds, with a considerable drop in civility. This may be observed in the lack of motivations and orientations to pursue further significant goals in the process of human civilization.

Among the empirical indicators of this drop we can point out:

- social-demographic trends: low birth rate (an increasing part of Europe has fallen below the zero growth rate), rapid and increasing aging of the population, decrease in marriage rates, increase in births outside of marriage, increase in one-parent families, increase in the number of singles;
- social problems: children's difficulties in socializing, youthful maladjustment, communication pathologies in couples, isolation of the elderly (in private housing, but also in protected residential structure), child abuse;
- psychological and cultural reflexes: diffusion of new mental and psychosomatic pathologies, increased suicide rate (especially among youths, even children, and the elderly), drug use and widespread drug addiction, boredom and the lack of a sense of the meaning of life, weak production of motivations for active, participatory social activity.

All of these phenomena denounce a profound crisis in the European model of civility. At the heart of this crisis is the implosion of the family. Implosion here does not mean that the family's social functions have disappeared, as they indeed continue to persist and even increase; it alludes instead to a 'shriveling', a sort of lack of vitality, a loss of meaning of the 'family symbolic complex', as that which binds the genders and generations in a shared life project that goes beyond a single generation ceases to exist.

We must acknowledge that the symbolic complex of the family has been deeply torn and weakened. And this means something very specific: the family has lost its public and social relevance. Its irrelevance to community life has increased.

At the center of the current disorientation as to what is a family, what 'makes a family', there is an impoverishment of the people's abilities to relate, first of all symbolically. They are only able to represent what they are interacting with at a given moment ('the attractor'). And this is done more through commercials and images than through words and conversation. One is sensitive only to what one sees, touches, that stimulates one's senses – and often not even that. Grown up in a climate of ethical indifference to the family, the new generations of youth are prey to emotionalism, irrationality, and hedonism. For the young people facing our times, the 'other' realities – hidden, latent, long-term, that go beyond visible confines or which do not immediately come to light – such as family relations and what they mean in terms of identity and existential meaning for people, remain unspoken, unimaginable, unexpressed, and in the end unthinkable.

No wonder, then, that the very idea of family has become so vague and uncertain. It tends to be assimilated with any form of cohabitation under the same roof. But that is not the case. The family cannot become an undifferentiated relationship that cancels out the confines between the sexes and the generations, or even reverses them (such as when the woman takes on the role of the man or vice-versa; or when the adult acts like a child or, vice-versa, children need to grow up ahead of time) (Roussel, 1989; 1991). When this occurs, the primary identity of people is missing and society becomes mired in quicksand. The symbolic complex of the family is the first point of support, the primary glue of society. This is proven by the fact that family counts even when far away, because it is present as a symbolic reality that determines the psychological experiences and existential meaning for people.

The truth is that the family is not a place, a space, a house, even though it takes form in these images and requires a spatial reference, a 'home'. Nor is it simply 'being together'. The family is the symbolic and structural relationship that binds people together in a lifelong project that intersects a horizontal dimension (the couple) and a vertical dimension (relationships with descendents/ascendants). Thus the family consists of and requires a bind between the sexes as a couple and/or a generative relationship. Family exists if and only if we have a group of people that are linked together by one or both of these types of binds: (i) reciprocity between the genders in the couple, legally formulated as a contract, and/or (ii) reciprocity within the parent-child relationship.

A social policy that refers purely to the 'de facto family' would have to be ineffective and destined to fail.[2] I do not mean by this that we should introduce forms of discrimination among the various types of families. Instead, I mean to state that any social policy achieves effective results if and only if it supports those who take on the obligations of reciprocity, rather than make social protection indifferent to people's behavior (Mead, 1986). If social policy is indifferent to the assumption of obligations as members of a couple and/or as parents, in the end it penalizes the relationships of social solidarity. The crisis of the European welfare state is indeed the consequence of the fact that, within its political arrangements), it has become increasingly irrelevant in terms of social protection whether or not one assumes family obligations (Donati, 1998a).

The legal definition of the family is necessary in order for the welfare state to operate; otherwise it runs into serious trouble. If the family were any form of cohabitation, how could we calculate the contributions and access rights for welfare services based on the relationships of solidarity that must be faced as husband/wife or as father/mother of children? If the definition of family did not require specific relationships as couples and parents, how could we avoid perverse effects in using the benefits related to these roles? For example, one partner could enjoy benefits without any obligation of solidarity towards the other partner. Those who attempt to make the so-called 'free unions' (hetero- and homosexual) equal to the family need not to look for such a solution. One can maintain that this equalization is not necessary, since we can acknowledge the human rights of the individuals that live in different types of relationships without thereby abandoning the idea that the full reciprocity between members of a couple and between parents and children is a specific common good that should be protected and promoted as such in a peculiar way.

In my view, without denying that people enjoy their inalienable individual and subjective rights in civil, political, social and cultural terms, family rights as such should be defined and promoted today. Legally, the family exists if and only if there is a contract of reciprocal responsibility within the male-female couple or a parent-child relationship (and, more generally, an ascendant/descendant relationship, such as between grandparent and grandchild). It should be noted that even those states that acknowledge the so-called 'living together arrangements' never make families based on marriage fully equivalent to those that are not. There is indeed a tendency by legislation to attribute natural parents the same duties as legal parents, thereby demonstrating that the existence or lack of marriage is irrelevant in terms of the obligations that natural parents have towards their children.

Conjugal and parental relationships are certainly not easy to impose and carry forth. We are often not even able to see and define them. We are in any case ambivalent towards them, since we experience them as binds that limit us, while we then use them as resources. We generally see and confront them only from one side. For example, we see the costs of marriage and children, but not what they give us. We see the restrictions that family relationships force on us, but not the resources they offer and the opportunities they open up to us.

Certainly it is difficult to manage family relationships. But what I want to emphasize is the fact that European society in the last fifty years or so has done very little to build a culture (and social policy) that helps people to manage family relations in a synergic manner, and intergenerational relationships in particular. The negative consequences and reflections of this lack of development are increasingly evident.

Today's society has reached the point where the family is increasingly a form of life 'indifferent' to the public sphere, meaning that social institutions make no differentiation as to what family a person lives in. It sees no connection between lifestyle and internal family organization on the one hand, and social, non-family problems on the other, except when pathologies and outcasts appear.

Experts are well aware that the impoverishment and weakening of the symbolic complex of the family is the first cause of societal collapse. This collapse is normally long and painful, and does not take place over a few years, but leads to a deterioration that continues for several decades and at times for centuries.

We are faced with such a turning point in history. We must rethink our model of civilization. Civilization must find a new meaning of family, or it will be lost.

But how is this possible? The dilemma is truly among the most crucial and difficult to solve. We are still struggling between residual and institutionalizing orientations toward the family: on the one hand, family is an assumption or in any case left to the mercy of events, on the other it is thought that it may and must be somehow controlled and directed.

The tendency to make residual social policies toward the family still persists because, in some ways, it is impossible to do otherwise. Even when one does not intentionally wish to follow this path, in practice it is difficult to see how to address the family since one would need to refer to a specific, normative model of family relationships (based on marriage). But this model appears difficult to practice. Thus one takes refuge in the comment, 'we take note that this is how people live'.

The only alternative to mere residual pragmatism appears to be a new public commitment by individual nations for institutional welfare policies that attempt to meet the broadest possible spectrum of needs of the population, by addressing individuals and large categories (defined according to professional occupation, such as the self-employed, or by gender, or by age: children, young people, the elderly, etc.). But even this road has become (or is becoming) unsustainable, not only because it involves increasing economic costs, but also because it does not reduce social problems – and often multiplies them or shifts them elsewhere. In many cases it produces the very weakness or dissolution of the family that lies at the origin of the problems being fought (Opielka, 1997).

So what can be done? Herein lies the drama of today's social policies towards the family, forced to be residual even when they want to be institutional, and in any case nearly always with limited – if not perverse – effects.

To escape from this stalled position, we must view the situation from another perspective and ask new questions. We must get out of this dilemma that obliges us to choose between residual and institutional policies.

## THE DIRECTIONS OF SOCIAL POLICY AS DIFFERENT CONCEPTIONS OF THE FAMILY/SOCIETY RELATIONSHIP

The following have been characteristics of the dominant family social policies from the 1950s to the 1990s in Europe: a) There has been a substantial tendency to publicize the family's functions, in particular by transferring them to the welfare state. In other words, vis-à-vis the increasing social weakness of families, most countries have decided to meet the family's needs simply by offering newer and more widespread public provisions and services for daily life needs, from full-time schools to leisure services, by this way enlarging the eligibility for social rights and collective facilities on an individual basis. b) At the same time, widespread and profound privatization of family values has been encouraged, in the sense that the politically organized community has given up on selecting the common values to follow, and has made it increasingly irrelevant what type of cohabitation unit one lives in. c) Policies for the family have been undertaken mainly in an indirect way, since provisions have privileged generic social needs, from the house to employment, from income to services, without taking into account the structure and specific needs of the family nucleus, or with little regard for them (absence of selectivity aimed to favor the most disadvantaged nuclei, overloaded with tasks and socially weak, as nuclei and not as individuals). d) Implicit policy choices have been made toward the family, as the relationships were never addressed but merely the individuals as such and/or generic social categories (defined in terms of gender and age, like children, women, elderly people, etc.).

What have these tendencies produced? We can generally say that they have not been to the advantage of the family. a) The publicizing of family functions has led to an increasing difficulty for generations to recognize each other (as generating and generated) and to elaborate rules of social exchange between them. In addition, the diffusion and growth of government services today show signs of difficulty not only and not so much from an economic standpoint, but for their inadequacy to meet user (citizens') needs in terms of family needs, especially the life cycle of the family. b) The privatization of family values has produced lifestyles that depend excessively on mass consumption and are characterized by high risk, which in many ways reverberate on the family, producing problems that add to its crisis. c) Indirect policies have often ignored the family rather than support it, and in any case we must admit that the criteria of these policies (including the idea of equal opportunity between the genders) do not have immediately positive reflections on the family sic et simpliciter. d) Implicit policies have increased the rights – or, vice-versa, the obligations – of some at the expense of others. They have taken for granted that intervention on an individual (or age category) would be beneficial to family solidarity and a significant shared life-world; but this does not happen automatically. A relational perspective has been missing.

The need therefore arises to change tracks. In what directions? Generally speaking, I would say the following (see table 1): a) Publicized functions must be replaced with a clearly understood principle of subsidiarity according to which the broader social formations must not take the place of smaller ones, but support their independence by providing the rules and means necessary for them to perform their specific tasks on their own. More generally, the state must not absorb the functions of intermediate social formations, but help them – including through additional forms of association (such as family-based associations, for the family) – to manage the services that concern them (consider family counselors, nursery schools, care for children and the elderly, home services, etc.). b) The privatization of socio-cultural values must be replaced with processes of inter-subjective 'relational emphasis' of what are the 'valuable goods' in life. This is a path of dialogue that encourages human contact, the care relationship. In the family, rights are not individualistic in nature, but relational. Indeed, what happens in the family, especially how the family is socially designed and constructed, cannot be indifferent to the community. Every vital community develops a culture of whether or not such relationships are 'civil'. c) Indirect policies must leave room for policies directly aimed at the family nucleus as such; they must speak the language of 'family care work', 'home for the family', 'services for the family', 'family income', and aim in this direction for ad hoc operative measures. d) Implicit policies must be replaced with explicit policies for family relations as such, within the framework of inter-generational exchanges. When working with a generation, they must consider what the effects will be on other generations: the state may benefit or detriment a generation based not only on those measures taken directly for it, but also through the effects of measures taken for another generation. Positively speaking, a new 'social pact' is required between generations, both within the family and in the collective sphere (employment, the distribution and redistribution of resources, and especially citizenship relationships).

Table 1. Dominant trends thus far and new directions for family social policies

| Dominant trends from 1950 to 1990: | Need to revise towards: |
|---|---|
| a) Publicizing family functions | a) Implementation of the principle of subsidiarity between government and family |
| b) Privatization of family values | b) Processes to highlight the family as a relational good |
| c) Indirect policies (centered around the generic needs of daily life: such as housing, employment, food, health, education, etc. | c) Direct policies (centered arount the family nucleus as such: i.e., the tax liability of the family, services for the entire nucleus, etc. |
| d) Implicit policies (centered around individuals, for individual needs differentiated along the individual life cycle) | d) Explicit policies (centered around relations between genders and between generations for the mediating functions they perform) |
| = family as residual | =family as subject |

In short: the change must be made from social policies based on the residual nature of the family to social policies centered around the social subjectivity of the family.

THE FAMILY IS A SOCIAL SUBJECT REQUIRING A CITIZENSHIP OF ITS OWN
The family is a relational good shared by all. What happens in the family is not
without its consequences for everyone else living in a territorial community. The
problems of the family are also problems of the entire surrounding community.
The relationships between the genders and the generations forge the character of
a society, civil or uncivil.

Only those societies that hold these truths firm, and thus make sure to have
a strong and well-defined symbolic family code, are capable of confronting the
challenges and surviving. If the prohibition to reverse the sexes and generations
in the family fall by the wayside, the family falls into dissolution and drags the
entire society down with it.

It is the quality of the symbolic family code, elaborated in dealing with the
challenges inside and outside the family, that decides the quality of life, on one
hand, and, the psychological and social pathologies on the other hand, always
with consequences in every other sphere of life (economic, political, etc.).

All of this may be stated in another way: the family is a 'social subject'.

It is in a very precise way. That is, the family is an originative social formation that has its own autonomy in its internal relationships. People form couples
and generate children by autonomous choice. Autonomy, however, does not
mean absolute independence, because every healthy, vital society must place
requirements for social legitimacy on these relationships. In other words, it must
always be seen whether or not these relationships conform to human rights. It
cannot be otherwise, because the family is a specific type of shared good, which
I call 'relational common good'.[3] It is so for both those who belong to it and
those who enter relations with it.

The family is not a private life form that can give itself just any norms. The
family, as I have mentioned elsewhere, has an auto-poietic nature that is ambivalent in itself, since the family generates itself, but cannot do so if it is not in constant connection and regulation with the outside, with the surrounding society
(the norms that regulate the internal and external boundaries of the family can
never be purely private) (Donati, 1998b).

Now there is a brand-new and positive way in which the family becomes a
social subject in the above sense, more than ever. This is the empirical fact of the
new social mediations that it concretely puts into practice. These are mediations
between genders, between generations, between the private sphere of its internal
relations and the sphere of the surrounding community. As a matter of fact, in
the couple one partner mediates his/her own social world to the other. One generation transfers (or fails to transfer) something to the other, even unintention-

ally. The problem of the generational debt remains always, even when refused. In addition, we must observe that one participates or does not participate in civic and social life, and in many different ways, depending on the type of family one has.

The family counts more and more, and not less and less, in mediating relations between each of its individual members and the world outside the family: this is true for children, but even for adults and the elderly, though obviously in different ways.

These mediations are invisible relationships that society can keep hidden (fail to acknowledge and support) or render explicit (acknowledge and reward). Until recently, these mediations were handed down and shared, fully implicit and taken for granted. The social changes in recent decades have made them more invisible and problematic. Today they must be made more explicit and have their own voice. This voice is the citizenship of the family. Family citizenship means that the family as such must enjoy its own set of rights-obligations, as a reality of solidarity and not simply as the sum of the rights-obligations of its individual members.

Now more than before, if society wants to not only protect the family legally but also concretely promote it and support it in its social functions, political systems must give more importance to all of those associative forms that families create to organize shared actions, both to promote rights and manage services, for its own good and for the community at large. Thus, by extension, political systems must also acknowledge a new set of citizenship rights-obligations for family associations within a new configuration that I call 'societal', because citizenship here is an expression not of the state as an entity above, but of the pluralism of social autonomies within civil society (Donati, 1993; 1995).

What does 'family citizenship' mean, and what kind of social policy change does it imply?

When I first coined the expression 'family citizenship' and supported it at the European Union, I did not think it would receive all the attention it did (Donati, 1992). But, as happens in these instances, it is not enough to coin an expression with strong theoretical and practical connotations and provide data and arguments to support it in order for it to be adopted and applied. Misunderstandings and instrumental or misshapen reinterpretations are always lurking. Thus, today, we must say more to make the concept and its implications more explicit.

To clarify: the concept of family citizenship does not mean, as many have interpreted it, asking for additional aid for the needs of people's daily life –

women, children and the elderly in particular. Nor does it mean asking for special attention to single-income families and those with several children, which are penalized compared to others. Basically, it does not mean asking for more protection for the type of families that statistically fall or risk falling into the area of poverty. The expression means a lot more, and a lot else.

First of all, it means recognizing the social value of the family for the functions of solidarity and social reciprocity that it performs. The family does not ask for a 'reward', but asks instead to be treated with social justice for the functions it must carry out as an ordinary agency in everyday life. Indeed, the current mechanisms of welfare distribution and redistribution (in many aspects) penalize rather than acknowledge what it does, or could or should do. Here is where the concept of family citizenship begins to have its first and most correct meaning. How can we expect more solidarity among people and more care for infants if both of these behaviors are made more difficult and less convenient than the more selfish and individualistic behaviors of those who do not take on any family obligations? And how will it be possible to achieve solidarity among the citizenry if the government itself makes family solidarity indifferent, when it should be the first guarantor?

Within a broader perspective, the concept implies a radical change that puts an end to the concept of the welfare state as it has been constructed so far. This is no small turning point. The welfare state has been built on the idea that a government is more socially oriented to the extent to which it includes a growing number of individuals – classified by social category – within the State's guarantees. The concept of family citizenship overturns this view, in at least two ways. First, because it asks for citizenship not only for individuals (as such or as members of social classes or categories), but also for an intermediate social formation – the family – with everything this involves (this concretizes the passage from 'state citizenship' to 'societal citizenship'). Secondly, because it sees the social state as a system of decisions and intervention serving the autonomy of the family, and not vice-versa, where the welfare state has until now worked in an assistance mode, to relieve individuals of their family responsibilities (this concretizes the principle of subsidiarity).

Obviously, to acknowledge the principle of family citizenship means changing a few support structures of the entire organization of society. This is certainly no small thing.

Generally speaking, to grant citizenship means recognizing the relevancy of a subject, be it individual or collective (i.e. consisting of certain relationships, such as the family), for the public dimension of social life, within a complex of rights and obligations between the associates. In the case of the family, it means recognizing that the family-subject has relevancy for the public dimension of human life.

We cannot create a social policy (in the much larger sense than public policy) without a definition of the family, since it is essential to know whom one is referring to when deciding on concrete measures of intervention (as policy-makers and administrators are well aware). And definitions are not all equal, since each definition leads to different effects. If one adopts a vague definition of the family, as some proposed bills do, or if one defines it simply as people who live together, there are two negative effects: first, there is no policy to support those who spontaneously take responsibility within the couple or towards the children; second, since responsibilities are ignored or merely imposed by law, the welfare state goes bankrupt morally and financially. International experiences prove this, and that is why in no state is the family yet defined in the vague terms that some would prefer today.

Family citizenship is therefore bound to the reliability of certain functions or tasks that may be ensured by the existence of a certain reciprocal relationship within the couple and/or between parents and children.

It is important to emphasize the difference between the old and new forms of family citizenship. Many of the criticisms made to the idea of family citizenship are centered around two points: that it would privilege a certain model of family, and that such a social policy would bring with it a preceptive type of social order. I can confirm that neither is true.

In order to understand the historical discontinuities I am referring to, we can recollect that, generally speaking, the relations between families and governments have followed three typical patterns or stages. a) In the first half of the twentieth century, European welfare states used to address families and children mainly in terms of social control: families were granted economic, legal and material provisions in exchange for men's control over women and children. Family rights embodied individual rights so that people (in particular children) suffered from bonds which were too compelling. Children's rights were greatly restricted: they were almost completely subsumed under the family coverage. In case of family failure, total institutions were delegated to pick up the children. b) Since the second world war, European welfare states have, in a sense, reversed the pattern: they have acknowledged an increasing number of social rights and provisions for individuals and social categories (in particular women, handicapped people, old people, and children), but have left the family apart. The rights of the family as a social group and institution have been undermined in many respects. In a certain sense, the family has lost its citizenship. The overall outcome has been the decline of fertility and the creation of a social environment unfavourable to the reception of the newly born (be it a direct or an indirect effect). c) Nowadays the fifteen countries of the EU are entering a stage (or pattern) which is very different from the previous ones under many aspects.

On the one hand, the new trends contradict the pre-war pattern in so far as the family cannot be considered and handled as a social control agency which acts on behalf of the State: the family has acquired an increasing autonomy ('autopoiesis') and is oriented towards managing its generational problems even more privately.

On the other hand, the new trends must differ from the post-war pattern in so far as it becomes clear that the multiplication of individual rights is only a partial solution: we have to find new means to deal with the uneasiness and the disfunctionality in family relationships, particularly the breaking down of the social web, which deteriorates the relationships between generations. If we want to have a social environment which is more sensitive to children's needs, then we must give proper consideration to the repercussions that the lack of social support for families has on children. Families should become valid interlocutors of societal institutions and governments, at every level (regional, national, and European).

In the perspective of the development of citizenship rights, the new issues revolve around the need for a better compatibility between individual and family rights: both kinds of entitlements must be secured, and the pursuit of this target should be done in such a way as to foster relations of social solidarity and equity between generations.

This is our topic. From the point of view of the development of families and children rights the last decade has been one of lost opportunities. But, at the same time, it has been fruitful, since a new awareness has arisen and grown up precisely in respect to the need of introducing the generational issue into the welfare state.

The new family citizenship is essentially different from the old form. In patriarchal society, the family was recognized and supported with specific benefits to the extent to which the family head accepted the delegation of functions from the state for the social control of women and children. The new family citizenship, on the contrary, consists of access to certain rights, which are positive and relational rights granted to the family nucleus as such, in addition to and without reducing individual rights. The rights of family citizenship refer to the functions of the family as a social relationship of mediation. The family has a few more rights than individuals, its own rights as a relationship – or rather, as a social mediation relationship. This implements the dictates of national and international declarations that recognize the rights of the family as such, and not simply the rights of the individuals within the family.

We must carefully consider the idea that the family is a shared good to be promoted ex novo. This cannot and must not mean reduced efforts for women and children, and for all of the weaker members of the family and society. Individual rights may not be questioned. Instead, social policies must aim to resolve the problems of individuals and various social categories (children, the elderly, women) within a relational view of the rights-obligations of each and all, taking into account that these rights-obligations have a relational structure (are exercised in relationships) and live within/by a relational context.

In Europe as in America, it is by now clear that the modern arrangement of society based on favoring the individual-state axis has reached its limit. Many nations, parliaments and governments have realized this in recent years. If we continued in the direction of the past we could only produce deep breakdowns. We must instead take the best of the consequences of the past and place them within a new philosophy of society that sees the family – as well as other social formations known as 'intermediate' – the protection and ferment of an authentic process of civilization.

The concept of family citizenship helps to redefine the field of social policies, as it pushes to make new distinctions. a) Family policy differs from other, similar types of policy. It is not a demographic policy (to increase the birth rate). It is not a policy against poverty (which requires other measures). It is not simply a policy for social or other services. Family policy is the set of measures that make families better able and more independent in managing family relationships. Certainly, this also means supporting fertility according to the couple's desires. But this target is a different matter. The same holds true for the consideration accorded to the family dimension in many kinds of measures proposed to fight poverty. These measures are merely forms of income and resource redistribution based on the objective of increasing equality in the amount of income individuals can spend (and this is why calculations are based on the number of people who live together): but what does this goal have to do with family policy? Only very little, and only indirectly. Finally, welfare service policies are not family policies if they operate only on individuals or individual problems. In order to be real family welfare measures, they must operate on family mediations (for example, in the new services that help maintain parental relationships when the marriage relationship has broken up). Today, this is the case in only a few instances. b) Political systems must review the welfare state, from the taxation system to social security, so that families are recognized for their solidarity functions rather than penalized for them. The family must be made a fiscal subject and a subject of social security and pensions. More generally, one must discuss in terms of a family friendly school for children, a home for the family, a minimum family income, and so on. c) At the local level, all of this may be translated into a 'package' of measures centered around the family (which I cannot describe in detail here due to space limitations) that emphasize the care of people within the family and organizes external social services based on this objective. The entire system of local taxation and tariffs, especially for community services, should be regulated according to 'family equity indexes'. This is not a question of providing 'assistance' to families, but of redefining social equality by making the family an active, not passive, social subject. d) Political and social systems must review all social policies from a generational standpoint, in light of the following criterion: whether they increase or decrease reciprocity between ascending/descending generations. e) Family policy strictly depends on the fact that families have a voice, their own social, cultural and political representation. This means promoting family associations in all forms, at the local, regional, national and supranational levels. And then create federations and/or confederations of these family-based associations.[4] It is important that these associations and their federation or coordinating bodies not be considered equivalent to old associative forms, all of which in some way depend on other institutions. Thus they should be promoted both by universal facilitation measures, especially tax advantages, as well as by granting them autonomous consulting and representative powers through special consulting committees permanently established with central and local governments.

European society needs to completely rethink its model of development not only in terms of science or technology, models of production, consumption and communication, forms of transportation and so on, but especially concerning the very foundation of its society, as a civil society. The rest somehow follows as a consequence.

When we talk about the foundations of civil society we are talking about family. And the arrangement of local communities must be rethought beginning from the family, since local communities are 'networks of families', or 'networks of relationships between families'. After all, this has been the great lesson we have received as a legacy from Wilfried Dumon's scientific and cultural work.

NOTES

1   Particularism of the family here means its characterization as a closed community (Gemeinschaft), as it is usually defined in sociological theory: see J. Finch (1989).
2   A 'de facto family' is a set of people who simply state that they live under the same roof, regardless of the social and legal relationships among them.
3   On the concept of 'relational good' see P. Donati (1993 ch. 2).
4   A specific reflection has just begun in this regard: see P. Donati (1997).

REFERENCES

Aldous, J. & W. Dumon (Eds.) (1980). *The politics and programs of family policy. United States and European perspectives.* Notre Dame/Leuven: University of Notre Dame Press/Leuven University Press.
Bernardes, J. (1997). *Family studies. An introduction.* London: Routledge.
Cherlin, A. (Ed.) (1988). *American family and public policy.* Washington D.C.: The Urban Institute Press.
Commaille, J. & F. de Singly (sous la direction de) (1997*). La question familiale en Europe.* Paris: L'Harmattan.
Ditch, J. et al. (Eds.) (1998). *Developments in national family policies in 1996.* University of York: European Observatory on National family Policies.
Donati, P. (1992). The development of European policies for the protection of families and children: Problems and prospects. In: *Commission of the European Communities, child, family, and society.* Brussels, p. 103-130.
Donati, P. (1993). *La cittadinanza societaria.* Roma-Bari: Laterza.
Donati, P. (1995). Identity and solidarity in the complex of citizenship: The relational approach. *Innovation. The European Journal of Social Sciences, 8*(2), 155-174.
Donati, P. (1997). Family associations in Europe: A general outlook and typology, associations. *Journal for Social and Legal Theory, 1*(2), 235-255.
Donati, P. (1998a). Freedom vs. control in post-modern society: A relational approach. *The Annals of the International Institute of Sociology,* New Series, *9*(7).
Donati, P. (1998b). *Manuale di sociologia della famiglia.* Roma-Bari: Laterza.
Dumon, W. (Ed.) (1994). *Changing family policies in the member states of the European Union.* Brussels: Commission of the European Communities (DG V).
Dumon, W. & T. Nuelant (Eds.) (1994). National family policies in the member states of the European Union in 1992 and 1993. Leuven/Brussels: European Observatory on National Family Policies.
Finch, J. (1989). *Family obligations and social change.* Oxford: Basil Blackwell.
Gillis, J. (1996). *A world of their own making: Myth, ritual and the quest for family values.* New York: Basic Books.
Glendon, M.A. (1989). *The transformation of family law: States, love, and family in the United States and Western Europe.* Chicago: University of Chicago Press.
Goldthorpe, J.E. (1987). *Family life in western societies.* Cambridge: Cambridge University Press.
Hantrais, L. & M.T. Letablier (1996). *Families and family policies in Europe.* London/New York: Longman.

Mead, L. (1986). *Beyond entitlement. The social obligations of citizenship*. New York: The Free Press.

Opielka, M. (1997). Does the welfare state destroy the family? In: P. Koslowski & A. Follesdal (Eds.). *Restructuring the welfare state. Theory and reform of social policy*. Berlin-New York: Springer, p. 238-274.

Roussel, L. (1989). *La famille incertaine*. Paris: Editions Odile Jacob.

Roussel, L. (1991). *Les 'futuribles' de la famille*. Futuribles, 153, 3-22.

# Putting families in family policy and programs: Local, regional, national and international options[*]

BARBARA H. SETTLES
UNIVERSITY OF DELAWARE, USA

## INTRODUCTION

Families are a point of political controversy and a topic of concern especially in times of rapid social change. Family as an institution is often cast as the building block of society or given the credit or blame for social problems. Government, religion, education and other organizations have policies and programs that either address families directly or by omission and/or support of other social units affecting families' options and opportunities. Current political, demographic, and social changes have challenged family policies and programs. In the emerging Eastern European countries questions about how these new nations will continue or digress from previous family practice, policy, and law are being examined (Cseh-Szombathy & Somlai, 1996; Wejnert, 1996; Zvinkliene, 1996). In the European Union, the effects of differing family laws and regulations are being tracked and monitored, however, the EU is not deemed to have a direct role in family policy (Dumon, 1991; Ditch, Barnes, Bradshaw & Kilkey, 1996). Information and analysis of how other social and economic policies impact families are the key aspects of the European Union's approach to family policy in the 90's (Teirlinck, 1994).

In Europe decentralization of family policy is observed not only in federalized countries, but in some single government states (Dumon, 1994). In North America the devolvement of responsibility for the few national social, health, and welfare programs to state or provincial administration has created a major shift in family policy (Edin & Lein, 1996; Mirabelli, 1996). Across Latin

[*] Some of the concepts in this paper were first presented in Issues for Family Sociologists at Families and Rapid Social Change: Committee on Family Research 29th Seminar in Lithuania and in Changing Social Values, and some from A Concept Paper prepared at the request of the American Home Economics Association, Denver, Colorado, June 1992, revised in January 1995.

America, the Caribbean and North America, the private/public balance has moved to an increasing load on the private milieu and families (Keiren, 1998). Following the various international initiatives of the United Nations and the globalization of economic institutions, many countries have had a process of reexamining their legal codes and programs for families. The 1992 UN definition of violence against women and the local working groups organized in countries for 1994 International Year of the Family brought attention to domestic violence and child abuse and resulted in changing legal definitions and enforcement (Mogwe, 1994). The United Nations Conferences on the Decade for Women and pressures from other NGO's and governments influenced the World Bank to broaden its programs to be more inclusive in gender issues in lending (Murphy, 1995). Smaller economic development projects with women's groups benefited from the awareness created by the UN decade work (Yudelman, 1987).

Changes in family policies are built on assumptions about families and what are normal or ideal for their structures, functions and processes. Some of these assumptions are not based on current living arrangements, but rather on beliefs about families in the past. Hareven (1996) notes that there was no golden age of family relationships in western society. By characterizing the adaptations to change families and households have made as the cause of societal problems, bureaucracies are protected from dealing with social conflict and problems. Stacey (1996) suggests that the gap between the families we have and those families we esteem, create a genuine ambivalence felt about contemporary family and social change. If we do not face the political shortfall in accuracy and understanding of personal lives and family ties our programs and policies will fail to provide conditions to make the 'modern or any other kind of family viable, let alone dignified and secure' (Stacey, 1996: 11).

Systematic review of policy and programs presents a challenge. There are national themes and structures for supporting and regulating family life, but in many places the interface with policy for families is highly local. Whatever examples one might have of family policy or programs in the United States would need to be first limited to each of the fifty states and then further delimited by the local municipality or county for implementation or augmentation of the policy or program. 'Judicial discretion is increasingly important' (Liss, 1987: 790). Legal interpretation and bench practice vary not only at the local level, but also by the district appellate court. Locality shapes and reshapes outcomes because the appellate courts have been deferential to states. Disputes among jurisdictions are common and under family law not being a resident of the jurisdiction can be a liability. To speak of national family policy is to note trends and similarities in local implementation. The lack of a national effort to track family policy and programs has proven to be a barrier to policy analysis. Improving statistics and records at the state and local level and getting some of these data into the hands of decision-makers was a project of a private foundation that encouraged and funded reports (Kids' Count, 1997).

Even in small Latin American countries like Costa Rica and Panama that have had family, education and health policy leadership at the national level there is increasingly an emphasis on local and regional devolvement of authority and responsibility. It has been typical in Latin America for family initiatives to be generated from the First Lady's office and especially common to link private and international support in this way. Some of these programs are seeking to be more relevant at a local level by developing community based advisory and administrative groups (CONAFAME, 1996).

The relationship between sacred and secular institutions in shaping and administering family policy and programs varies widely. Israel has given regulation and implementation of marital law and immigration qualifications to religious institutions, while handling family support programs nationally and comprehensively (Katz & Peres, 1995). Most of the countries with Islamic majorities either leave the regulation of families to religious groups or include such religious law in the government codes. Many Catholic and single Protestant church dominated countries support a national church, but they may have policies supporting a much broader interpretation of family forms and normative structure suggested by doctrine. In the United States there is a formal separation of church and state, but various coalitions of religious groups and activists are able to shape public policy on narrow issues affecting families (Liss, 1987). Anti-abortion conservative groups have blocked public funds for family planning both in the United States and internationally. Activists have limited local availability of abortion through protest without having a direct place in government (Carton, 1995; Smolowe, 1995). Secular and sacred views of family policy are being negotiated both at the local and international levels.

Finding principles for understanding family policy and programs in an international perspective remains extremely difficult and must be couched in tentative terms. However, it is important to pursue this problem and begin to seek a theoretical framework. To illustrate an approach to developing an analysis of policy four areas of social change are suggested. They have policy implications for families and illustrate the process of family policy identification and analysis. These issues are by no means exhaustive of the responsibility to examine implications of social change for family policy and programs, but they are issues that meet the following criteria for action: a) each has a long-term trend underlying the change; b) each has a growing, solid research-documented body of knowledge as means and ends; c) each is currently receiving attention from policy makers world wide; d) each makes a real difference in quality of life and the future; e) each is of interest to family experts and program developers.

For this analysis four specific issues are used to analyze how policies and programs have differential impacts on families' quality of life: a) expansion of personhood; b) definition of family and household; c) social order and violence; d) the social contract with earth.

## THE EXPANSION OF PERSONHOOD

Personhood in this context means that an individual is thought to have capacity for choice, responsibility, contribution to the society. Racial, gender, ethnic, and religious barriers to participation have begun to drop away. Affirmative action, open educational opportunities, and a commitment to a level playing field are essential to keep these changes moving toward an expansion of personal efficacy. The United Nations Declaration of Human Rights and the Convention on the Rights of the Child provide a basis for defining personhood to include everyone.

The expansion of personhood has a long and distinguished heritage. All the promises that promote a broad inclusion of persons to rights within the society have not been accomplished, but the shared vision of equality, opportunity, and personal choice is well accepted and understood. Indicators of the expansion of personhood are found both in legal structures and informal practice. Voting rights illustrate the gradual expansion of personhood. In the United States, after the American revolution, white male citizens who owned property could vote. Slowly suffrage was extended to other white men based on long term residency. The Civil War brought black men theoretically into the electorate, but women's suffrage and votes for native Americans and lowering the voting age to eighteen were not achieved until the twentieth century.

The implementation of civil rights legislation and participation in elections have solidified these opportunities and produced electoral mobilization infrastructures (Andrews, 1997). The order and sequence of this expansion have been different in other countries. 'Between 1890 and 1994 women in 96% of all the nation-states acquired the right to vote and seek public office' (Ramirez, Soysal & Shanahan, 1997: 735). In their analysis they found a role for national independence as a window of opportunity, but see the dissemination of a more inclusive world model political citizenship as the critical change. Many impediments still remain in the implementation of universal suffrage and political participation.

The control of ones own person, income, and property rights reflect whether persons are respected both within families and in the larger social context. Siqwana-Ndulo (1998) examined the grave practical and theoretical difficulties faced by in the new South Africa in weighing rights to land redistribution to the dispossessed as it applies to women in traditional households and communities. Although there is a governmental policy paper committing to gender equity, the use of tribal elders and traditional decision making processes has effectively left women with little access to land. Access to income and property are problems in developed areas as well. Many scholars believe those who are in poverty are facing barriers that are becoming more difficult to overcome (Wilson, 1991). The entrenched and possibly intractable urban underclass has become the target of reform (Cheal, 1996).

Poverty is persistently associated with gender, although in industrialized countries demographic differences in employment, parenthood and marital status may be seen to accentuate or dampen the extent of the association (Casper, McLanahan & Garfinkel, 1994). The meaning of wives' and husbands' work is constructed in dual earners families differently. Negotiating the boundaries of gender and employment, they ascribe different values to the each other's work in terms of breadwinning and their own acceptance of their activities. Although being in paid employment is a necessary condition to be a breadwinner is not sufficient be considered one (Potuchek, 1997: 4). Discounting of women's earnings as not essential to the family means that women's work does not produce the same social entitlements usually associated with men's earnings (Feree & Hall, 1996). There is ambivalence in both the formal and informal commitments to gender equity.

Expansion of personhood suggests that everyone deserves to function as well as they can without undue interference. Legal rights for the handicapped have expanded and created opportunities. In addition a shift in public and professional opinion has occurred. Now it is thought that even severely handicapped children and adults can and should be cared for at home or in a sheltered independence. This expectation has many ramifications for the family especially mothers (Marcenko & Meyers, 1991). One person's freedom may be another's limitation.

Youth and children are still marginal, but increasingly their rights as persons are recognized in transitions as divorce and educational choices are being sought (McIntyre, 1995). In Europe there is a growing trend to allow more participation in adoption and name change (Ditch et al., 1996). Protection of youth, the aged and the infirm when they are not qualified to exercise judgment has become a highly controversial status and process. Privacy and protection against overstepping by kinship and friendship networks are issues that haunt every decision point.

Genov (1997: 416) questions the individual's ability to cope with the new choices challenges and suggests that: 'Individuals in the advanced part of the world are over-exposed to permanent stress'. In situations of rapid social change he believes that the expectation of expansion of the pool of choices may actually be felt as reduced options and deprivation. Empowerment objectives in all aspects of familial choice require an examination of choices and decision-making theory more closely and to make sure the reality matches the hope (Settles, Liprie & Hanks, 1988). For family policy to be effective, it must be cognizant of the delicate balance between protecting vulnerable persons as individuals and in families. The use of family as advocates, care givers, and social supports to their members without understanding inherent conflict of interest and power is particularly problematic.

DEFINITION OF FAMILY AND HOUSEHOLD

A major controversy in this century has been the conflict over how family and household could or should be defined. This issue is not just an interesting theoretical and conceptual problem but one that has major consequences for the quality of life, the social acceptance, and the availability of services and access which people have to important economic and social goods. Many census organizations and the World Bank have used household as a marker for family and do not make any separate estimates for families. Many statements made about families are based on unadjusted household figures. Rossi (1989) suggests that households are used preferentially to kinship status because of the difficulty in developing clear definitions. Policies and programs are shaped by the decisions made in recognizing or refusing to include some groups, households and configurations in the legal codes, implementation and program offerings. Definition is a part of many problem-solving processes at several levels in the society: a) personal; b) institutional; c) professional.

At the personal level the question resolves itself into those persons whom an individual perceives of as family and those whom he or she treats as if they were family and an examination of whether these perceptions and expectations are shared by the others. Levin and Trost (1992) provide a model for research and teaching based on individual family definitions. Therapists, researchers, and family life educators are interested in these personal definitions because they relate to the individual's functioning and reveal the needs for education and treatment. However, in the larger society these idiosyncratic and individualistic definitions may not be useful to analyzing and targeting programs for families. Individualistic perceptions of family and household arrangements may lack symmetry. Depending on the stage of life, the likelihood that several households will be involved in one family network is quite high. For example, remarried and reconstituted families also share complex definitions of family ties versus households. The entrances and exits of children to parents' homes may be repeated over and over again (Ganong, Coleman & Fine, 1994).

At the institutional level, the individual is usually the client or member. There may be an expectation that the person's family will serve as a supportive group. At the institutional level the personal definitions of family may conflict. Institutions may lag behind the society in recognizing diversity in family structure as normal and may promote certain family definitions. Recognition of diverse families requires a political process. In San Francisco city government, the decision to expand health insurance coverage to the household and therefore to expand how family coverage is defined has allowed alternative family forms including homosexual unions to benefit from these programs (Scanzoni & Marsiglio, 1991).

For the professional family service provider, the misuse of familial definitions or assumptions about family forms may lead to inadequate or inappropriate service (Gubrium & Holstein, 1990). An appreciation of the opportunities and constraints is fundamental to professional standards. Defining the family is often a boundary matter, who's in – who's out. Eligibility for insurance, programs, tax breaks, services are determined by such bureaucratic definitions. Dependency and care are usually a matter of legal as well as normative expectation. Even if a conventional definition is not used some problems for nontraditional families may occur.

Minow (1998) points out that a functional instead of a legal definition of who is family may be also be used by government to punish people or deny them benefits that they might otherwise be eligible to receive. Incentives for certain family forms and households may be built into codes, benefits, and contracts. The single family neighborhood, supported by a Housing and Zoning Code, is an example of enshrining family preference into opportunity structures and economic incentives. When communities exclude child care and elder care facilities from proximity to family neighborhoods, dual male-female work and family roles are undercut. The current US public housing eviction policy used to enforce drug prohibitions may overreach when the grandmother is defined as a member of the family for purposes of eviction. She may have little ability to prevent the use of drugs by younger relatives or ability to prevent them from being in her home (Minow, 1998). Not all policies are in legal codes or regulations. The all-adult retirement community may use contracts in the sales agreement, or by policies of the condominium board to exclude all younger people including grandchildren from all but brief visits. To a newly retired couple seeking a pleasant living situation free of noisy parties, their extended family may seem unimportant. Much later when a grandchild needs an alternative living arrangement, the couple realizes that their home is not theirs to offer that child.

Incentives for gifts and savings or limitations of withdrawals from retirement differentially reward some family forms. Now that a greater portion of working couples is earning similar wages in the United States, tax codes that were viewed as fair to families are seen as penalizing married couples (Congressional Budget Office, 1997). The historic understanding of ADC (Aid for Dependent Children), as with other New Deal programs, was that jobs were to be secured and protected for male heads of household and that others like the aged, the blind and the mothers with dependent children were to be pensioned off (Cauthen & Amenta, 1996). Again, the growing prevalence of dual earner families undercut this concept. The research finding that two-parent families can better support family children than the mother-headed family has not led to calls for better wages for men or pay equity for women, but rather resulted in reforms in ADC to pressure welfare mothers to marry and/or be employed.

Much of family policy stems from other political and economic processes. In the United States policy debate has featured at least three views of family, work, and gender programs: a separate spheres package with women in the home and men in paid employment; an equal opportunity package both men and women, but does not address division of labor; and a work-family accommodation package with recognition of family needs (Burstein, Bricher & Einwohner, 1995). While legislation has moved in the direction of accommodation, each view is still in the public debate. Even when policies are in place to give men and women equal access to family leave and benefits the informal cultural imperatives may limit how much men and women actually use the programs (Haas & Hwang, 1995). Even though there is a long tradition of family support has been in place, economic strains and needs in the European Union have resulted in a harsher climate for family policy and individual families and less attention to balancing work and family tensions (Ditch, Barnes & Bradshaw, 1995).

SOCIAL ORDER AND VIOLENCE

The concern for safety and risk in everyday life has given much political advantage to supporting law and order. More specifically in the United States vigorous prosecution and rigid sentencing, a return to capital punishment has become the standard political position for both major parties. Whether or not, there is indeed more crime or risk, the public has been encouraged to become uneasy and angry. Personal and family risk and safety have many dimensions in the society. Acceptable risks are defined by the current theory of action and ones' sense of efficacy and temporal horizon is engaged. To illustrate this phenomenon four areas of breaches of social order will be examined for potential linkages: a) violence within families; b) civility in daily life; c) organized criminality and the underground economy; d) global peacemaking, peacekeeping and family experience with war and terror.

Human beings have a high toleration for everyday violence and mayhem and a highly developed interest in the excitement and entertainment of violence. If you, yourself are in a position of safe viewing, you may tolerate real or fictional violence. In some respects we do not remember the past in terms of violence and risk any better than we do the perception of family and community in past times. Garrison Keillor (1982), the radio pundit, has entertained using ideas about small-town America in the remembered past. He suggests that we tend to remember our own childhood as secure because our parents and their friends went to great lengths to present that picture of the world. It may be more difficult for adults to create this childhood world of stability and safety today because it is a post-nuclear, post-industrial world that seems threatening to adults and is brought into our homes by a constant media barrage. Adults at all times had war, hunger, pestilence, and poverty close at hand, and violence was at close quarters. There have been changes in the social values about violence and expressed power in relationships. Not only are forms of violence being reexamined, but also there is questioning of whether toleration for violence is natural and immutable.

Prevention and intervention to alleviate violence within families have become a major thrust in family programs and policy. Several processes that changed the public understanding of domestic violence occurred in the second half of the twentieth century. In child abuse, the contemporary transition occurred with two factors. First, there was the publication in a respected medical journal of C. Henry Kempe and colleagues research that linked records of children taken to various emergency rooms in Colorado to a concept of the battered child syndrome (Johnson, 1997). Second there was a series of meetings drawing governmental and professional associations and NGO's such as the

American Humane Association under the leadership of Vincent de Francis. Together they built awareness and created model state legislation to protect and mandate professionals report symptoms of child abuse to authorities. Fifty states and territories adopted legislation within the next five years. Subsequently there was a great revolution in making professionals responsible and educating them for reporting symptoms of physical child abuse to authorities. However clear definitions of abuse and neglect are still significant problems.

Connecting atypical child abuse to the everyday aspects of parenting in terms of addressing physical punishment of children has not met with a similar positive consensus against corporal punishment. Sweden pioneered the legal limitation of spanking. Instead of following this policy quickly many states and countries are still debating. Religious and privacy barriers were used to avoid taking a stand against spanking and hitting children as part of parent child interaction. In a current article in the *Journal of Marriage and the Family*, parental and contextual variables are analyzed related to the use of spanking and it is suggested that intervention may need to be as complex as the patterns are (Day, Peterson & McCracken, 1998). Straus (1994) has examined a wide variety of data sets and analyses and has attempted to bring this knowledge to both the social and medical professions and the public. His most recent work highlights the improved cognitive functioning of children who receive discipline other than spanking (Straus & Paschall, 1998). Although spanking has been found to be associated with less skilled parenting and studies show no benefit to children or parents from use of physical punishment, the issue is not settled.

Many social defenses exist that prevent identifying violence within couple and spousal relations as a larger social issue in terms of power. The women's movement, the battered wives' shelter organizations, the leadership of NGOs and the United Nations have had diverse impacts in different parts of the world in creating awareness and action. Police have changed their standard procedures for dealing with domestic violence and rape cases, moving these problems up in terms of priorities for action and improving training. One of the major debates has been over whether aggressive use of arrest on the part of police and encouragement of the recipient partner to bring charges is helpful or potentially dangerous for the victim (Morris, 1994). Therapists and counselors are being asked to provide intervention services to those who are perpetrators well as support to those who are victims (Eisikovits, Edleson, Guttmann & Sela-Amit, 1991). Clinical and research response has sometimes accepted perpetrator explanations or diminution of the violence and battering as excuses for it or seen vulnerable recipients as attracting violent reactions (Eisikovits et al., 1991; Ptacek, 1998). Recognition and intervention have been necessary to limit domestic violence. Primary prevention of abuse and promotion of family life education for problem solving and non-violent strategies in couple relationships, child and elder care has had some success and is being tried more widely. Lloyd (1991) notes that the confusion among concepts of romance, violence and love in courtship allows couples to overlook, to forgive, to ignore the violent, or to exploitive behavior and may begin a continuing pattern. Cross cultural investigations and comparative work in family violence has met with many problems in understanding the context and definitions of violence and the consequences to respondents for participating in studies and programs (Fontes, 1998). Some concepts may not be interpreted similarly across cultures and sub-cultures. However, it is faulty reasoning to accept that physical punishment of anyone is an essential part of the culture.

Civility in daily life and standards for public living space are in question in many places and especially in urban centers. Commuter frustrations in transit to and from home have led to real fear in traffic jams of violent incidents. Drive-by shootings and casual violence terrorize some neighborhoods on a regular basis. Suicide, depression, and violent outbursts are documented in the press and media to the extent that many people report worrying about danger. The popularity of personal protection training and workshops reflects concern. Being trained to handle assault and rape is not a satisfying way to feel safer.

In many communities an increasing number of homeless are on the streets. Homelessness has a new face including many family groups that have entered homeless shelters because of a crisis event and may or may not be able to be transitioned back into housing as family groups (Anderson & Koblinsky, 1995). It has been estimated that many US cities have a shortfall of temporary housing of over 30% yearly (Anderson & Koblinsky, 1995). Policies that divide families or exclude older boys from shelters with their mothers need to be reexamined (Lindsey, 1998).

Homelessness affects everyone, not just those who are left without a real place to live. Public spaces are no longer leisure or work places when they become camps for the dislocated. Learning to ignore or avoid eye contact may help in getting by each day, but the quality of life for everyone is impaired (Axelson & Dail, 1988). Finding a policy response to homelessness that is humane is a challenge. Public safety initiatives and proactive community building are needed to create a civil environment and ally fears that limit people's freedom and options (The President's Council on Sustainable Development, no date). 'The idea that violence in America could be viewed as a public health problem has been slow to catch on...' (Taubes, 1992: 213).

Organized criminality, the underground economy, and illegal drug trade represent a vast complex network. Societies must reach a consensus on whether real change is wanted. The concentration of poverty and joblessness in inner-city ghettos creates a community of marginality. Violent persons in the drug scene have a powerful impact on communities (Wilson, 1996). When one looks at opportunities for poor urban youth, the contrast between cash returns in drug distribution and hamburger sales seems impossible to bridge. Of course the drug marketplace is not limited to impoverished areas. Even on the most prestigious campuses and corporations, the drug-based underground economy breaks into daily life. Because the nature of this trade is so insidious and world-wide, no real strategy to combat has been mounted to stem the destruction of social institutions by this fastest growing sector of the economy.

The splintering of ethnic, language, and religious groups in every part of the world suggest that we may have exchanged nuclear terror for everyday civil war and isolated acts of terror (Talbott, 1992). There is a sense that we may be returning to a tribal form of organization. The nation state is not a protector for individuals and families against such ethnic and racial groups and to be without an identity in the clan or party is to be vulnerable (O'Sullivan & Wilson, 1988). Fragmentation of societies and regions along ethnic and religious identities suggests that multi-culturalism might entail disasters on a grand scale (Genov, 1997).

If one can contemplate a world in which a constant war footing is not the basis of the whole economy, one could anticipate real paradigm shift; in which violence can be tamed into social order and values based on mutual benefit and concern replaces confrontation and destruction. Cole & Rueter (1993) have detailed the overlap of families and the larger societies in promoting a more peaceful everyday life and conflict resolution through other than violent means. The linkage of violence from the familial to community to civil and international conflicts suggests a source for change. Cannon (1996) explores these connections and sees family life education as a critical component in nurturing a more peaceful society. Both the promotion of positive approaches to problems and conflicts, and the prevention and elimination of violent and exploitive experiences in daily life and child rearing are vital to such a major change.

## THE SOCIAL CONTRACT WITH THE EARTH

United Nations conferences and programs on the environment have made a clear statement of changing social and economic values. People want to estimate risk and take actions that are more cognizant of long-term consequences and less dependent on the short term profits statements. The mechanisms and programs to accomplish these are not yet firmly understood or developed but the commitment to development is becoming more universal. Cole & Reuter (1993) note that respect for the fragile balance of ecosystems is necessary for survival of the planet Earth and all its inhabitants. Peace is dependent upon a balance of ecosystems that mutually reinforce and sustain each other.

In *The Hitchhiker's Guide to the Galaxy*, Douglas Adams (1974) suggested that the world might be conceived of as one huge computer system. The concept of world systems is well established in examining the larger impact of trends on the global scene. Contemplating and estimating the consequences of individual human action as it adds up and interacts within the system is not easily accomplished. Simplistic computer simulations often mislead when projecting the future from current actions. One decade we worry about a new ice age; the next, global warming. For example, both fertility and famine have played out quite differently than it was anticipated as recently as the 60s and 70s. At that time both population control and food supplies were seen as requiring some forceful intervention. As it has developed, the surprising robust finding is that giving women some opportunity in terms of economic access to work and income, education, and access to reliable contraception is usually sufficient to reduce fertility to level of stability (Fox, 1993). Only in a few places has government led fertility regulation been important, e.g., China (Sun, 1993). In Europe, concerns about a below replacement birthrate and an aging population distribution have been voiced (Dumon, 1998). Understanding the systemic relationships among limited resources, increased population density and demands, social conflict and violence are an important challenge to the field (Homer-Dixon, Boutwell & Rathjens, 1993). The microlevel decisions in families that involve fertility, mobility, and obtaining and using resources are summed in the total picture the macroprocesses of society (Huber, 1990).

Food resources have been expanded and now famine appears only when governments or armies use food supplies as a weapon of war. While malnutrition remains a problem, it is one that can be answered within available resources. What is needed is the commitment to action. Brown & Pollitt (1996) report on a study in Guatemala that showed intellectual gains for a modest nutritional intervention with children and suggest that such programs are well within our national and international resources. In the United States, the Supplemental Food Program for Women, Infants, and Children (WIC) has been shown to increase cognitive performance of children and to provide many other health benefits and yet full funding of this program has had difficulty in being achieved

(Ku, Cohen, & Pindus, 1994). Quality of life can be improved if it is seen as an appropriate investment.

To develop a reliable basis to identify changing social policies requires an examination of the debates about national images of values. The current political climate has created more heat than light. It is troubling to analyze the relationship between home and country. In the decade of debate surrounding immigration reform in the United States, fundamental problems about what makes a great and noble country have surfaced. Xenophobic reactions to new immigrant groups such as illegal Hispanics and over solicitous beliefs about the success of certain groups such as Asian students as a successful adaptation is still quite typical of over generalization about immigration and changing social values (Caplan, Choy & Whitmore, 1992; Settles, Hanks, III & Sussman, 1993).

In the areas of toxicity and waste, the old American busines paradigm was to dilute, dilute and further dilute the poisons and assume that the problem was solved. Now, understanding the systematic impact of priority in finding a better paradigm. Derkson and Gartrell (1993: 434) suggest that 'while most individuals express concern with the state of the natural environment, this concern translate into pro-environmental behavior only in certain situations.' They found in studying recycling that access to a structured, institutionally based program that made recycling easy and convenient was the most important determinant of behavior. Continued leadership in relating to families is required to help them take the steps needed for a safe environment. However, it is not enough to look to the smallest units; we must reexamine how we relate to corporate and government organizations and they are accountable for long-term consequences.

Globalization as a conception 'involves the compression of the entire world on one hand and a consciousness of the whole world, on the other' (Robertson & Khondker, 1998: 29). The sense that the world is a single place is an important change of perspective, that includes the clashes, conflicts and tensions in the process of change and the recognition that the preservation of local differences may itself be a global trend.

## CONCLUSION

These four issues: the expansion of personhood, the definition of family and household, social order and violence, and the social contract with earth are systematically linked to each other and to basic survival. Interdependency is a reality and the acknowledgment of its impact on further changing values requires our best scholarly and humanistic efforts. 'Family policy no longer belongs to the exclusive realm and authority of governmental power' (Dumon, 1998: 299).

Not only are negotiations among other actors in the economic area such as unions and employers, but also family organizations are asking to be involved in decision making at the European level. The distinction between public and private spheres in relation to family policy is related to the social context of various policy debates (Ditch, Bradshaw & Eardley, 1994). Families can affect the way institutions handle the social contracts that affect them if they are willing to invest in collective action or legal remedies. For example, Mothers Against Drunk Drivers resulted in the creation of Students Against Drunk Driving, which has reshaped secondary schools' responsibility toward this aspect of student life. The National Foster Parents Association is effectively redirecting evaluation of foster parents in the child welfare system. Other groups such as the American Association of Retired People have lobbied for programs sensitive to a changing understanding of the elderly and their potential. Internationally, Amnesty International has kept attention focused on repressive governments and human rights problems everywhere.

The provision of services and programs to families needs to be improved. At present, coordinating services and benefits is thought to be a panacea for a variety of social, health, and welfare services. Certainly many families who have multiple problems need comprehensive coordinated and intensive assistance and a system of narrowly defined programs, may frustrate and fail to serve needs efficiently (Voydanoff, 1995). Successful integration needs to be flexible and responsive led to a client centered and preventive orientation. Adding gatekeepers and monitors is often suggested as a cost-saving, quality-enhancing step. Stevens (1993) suggests that this approach oversimplifies the problems and is ill-advised.

The only dependable coordinator of care or evaluator of program impact today is the family itself. Institutions have limited capacity for long term monitoring. With staff turnovers, program changes, record-keeping fiascoes, eligibility requirements, and other institutional and organizational problems, the outcome for individuals and families in coordination is certain to be a disappointment unless they are proactive (Settles, in press). Ombudsmen and grievance systems have made some institutions more responsive, i.e., hospitals, universities and unionized workplaces. Legal action in the courts and through regulatory agencies remain a possibility but usually result in changes so late that the outcome does not help because the individual and family cannot out-wait bureaucracy and must move on developmentally (Settles, 1976).

At the societal level we have not been careful in our social accounting to closely examine who bears the costs for social decisions made at the broad societal level. For example, in the US, the reasonable investments we have made in our elderly have not been matched by attention to children's needs and we have not really assessed those long-term costs of this policy (Aldous & Dumon, 1990; Fuchs & Reklis, 1992). Targeted income transfer programs have dramatically changed the risks of being poor for the elderly, but not for children in Canada and the United States (Cheal, 1996). Currently, individuals and families underwrite corporation profits by absorbing the costs of disinvestment in their communities.

Family scholars have retreated to a scientific paradigm of objectivity, description, and distance from addressing social values. Sometimes unexamined assumptions have been promoted without proper examination. The need to be more careful and reflective in our choices of evidence for differing purposes is critical to advancing the profession and our applications (Lieberson, 1992). Professionals who are charged with certain knowledge and skill have had to face the dilemmas in dealing with lay persons over values-laden issues. A concept of 'best practice' has been put forward as a standard by which professional conduct could be measured. You cannot have 'best' practice until your profession has sufficient understanding of means and ends that the process can be specified to reach the product. Educators and social service providers are now liable for malpractice only because their fields have advanced to define best practice (Settles, Liprie & Hanks, 1988).

Family policy that is responsive to the multiplicity of actors, the interdependencies of families, and the context of local, regional, national and international family action is more complex, and more important than previously thought. Comparative study of policies, policy formation and implementation, and outcomes is needed to inform the process and the policy makers.

## REFERENCES

Adams, D. (1974). *The Hitchhiker's Guide to the Galaxy*. NY: Pocket Guide.

Aldous, J. & W. Dumon (1990). Family policy in the 80's: Controversy and concerns. *Journal of Marriage and the Family, 52*(4), 1136-1151.

Anderson, E.A. & S.A. Koblinsky (1995). Homeless policy: The need to speak to families. *Family Relations, 44*(1), 13-18.

Andrews, K.T. (1997). The impacts of social movements on the political process: The civil rights movement and black electoral politics in Mississippi. *American Sociological Review, 62*(5), 800-819.

Axelson, L.J. & P.W. Dail (1988). The changing character of homelessness in the United States. *Family Relations, 37*(4), 463-469.

Brown, J.L. & E. Pollitt (1996). Malnutrition, poverty, and intellectual development. *Scientific American, 274*(2), 38-43.

Burstein, P., R.M. Bricher & R.I. Einwohner (1995). Policy alternatives and political change: Work, family, and gender on the Congressional agenda, 1945-1990. *American Sociological Review, 60*(1), 67-83.

Cannon, N.H. (1996). *Roots of violence, seeds of peace: In people, families, and society.* San Diego, CA: Mclearoy Publishing.

Caplan, N., M.H. Choy & J.K. Whitmore (1992). Indochinese refugee family and academic achievement. *Scientific American, 266*(2), 36-45.

Carton, B. (1995). The dollars and cents of the abortion business. *The Wall Street Journal,* p. B1.

Casper, L.M., S.S. McLanahan & I. Garfinkel. (1994). The gender-poverty gap: What can we learn from other countries? *American Sociological Review, 59*(4), 594-605.

Cauthen, N.K. & E. Amenta (1996). Not for widows only: Institutional politics and the formative years of Aid to Dependent Children. *American Sociological Review, 61*(3) 427-448.

Cheal, D. (1996). *New poverty: Families in postmodern society.* Westport, CN: Greenwood Press.

Cole, C.L. & M.A. Rueter (1993). The family-peace connection: Implications for constructing the reality of the future. In B.H. Settles, R.S. Hanks & M.B. Sussman (Eds.). *American families and the future: Analyses of possible destinies.* Binghamton, NY: The Haworth Press, p. 263-278.

CONAFAME (1996). *Consejo Nacional de la Familia y de Menor, Primer Aniversario.* Available from CONAFAME, Box 2441, zone 3. Panama, Rep. de Panama.

Congressional Budget Office (1997). *For better or worse: Marriage and the federal income tax.* Washington, DC: The Congress of the United States.

Cseh-Szombathy, L. & P. Somlai (1996). Family research in Hungary. In M.B. Sussman & R.S. Hanks (Eds.). *Intercultural variation in family research and theory: Implication for cross-national studies.* Binghamton, NY: Haworth Press, p. 181-201.

Day, R.D., G.W. Peterson & C. McCracken (1998). Predicting spanking of younger and older children by mothers and fathers. *Journal of Marriage and the Family, 60*(1), 79-94.

Derkson, L. & J. Gartrell (1993). The social context of recycling. *American Sociological Review, 58*(3), 434-442.

Ditch, J., H. Barnes & J. Bradshaw (1995). *Developments in family policies in 1995.* Keighley, England: European Commission, Fretwell Print and Design.

Ditch, J., H. Barnes, J. Bradshaw & M. Kilkey (1996). *A synthesis of national family policies 1996.* Keighley, England: European Commission, Fretwell Print and Design.

Ditch, J., J. Bradshaw & T. Eardley (1994). *Developments in family policies in 1994.* Keighley, England: European Commission, Fretwell Print and Design.

Dumon, W.A. (1991). *Families and policies: Evolution and trend in 1989-1990.* Brussels, Belgium: European Observatory on National Family Policies, Commission of the European Communities.

Dumon, W.A. (1994). The European observatory on national family policies. In M. Teirlinck (administrator), *Social Europe 1/94: The European Union and the family.*

Luxembourg: Office for Official Publications of the European Communities, p. 38-41.

Dumon, W.A. (1998). Recent trends and new prospects for European family policy. In S.C. Ziehl (Ed.). *Multi-cultural diversity and families.* Grahamstown, South Africa: Rhodes University, p. 276-304.

Edin, K. & L. Lein (1996). Work, welfare and single mother's economic survival strategies. *American Sociological Review, 61*(2), 253-266.

Eisikovits, Z.C., J.L. Edleson, E. Guttmann & M. Sela-Amit (1991). Cognitive styles and socialized attitudes of men who batter: Where should we intervene? *Family Relations, 40*(1), 72-77.

Feree, M.M. & E.J. Hall (1996). Rethinking stratification from a feminist perspective: Gender, race, and class in mainstream textbooks. *American Sociological Review, 61*(6), 929-950.

Fontes, L.A. (1998). Ethics in family violence research: Cross-cultural issues. *Family Relations, 47*(1), 53-61.

Fox, G. (1993). A child is born: Contraception, fertility, and child rearing. In K. Altergott (Ed.). *One world, many families.* Minneapolis, MN: National Council on Family Relations, p. 27-31.

Fuchs, V.R. & D.M. Reklis (1992). America's children: Economic perspectives and policy options. *Science, 255,* 41-46.

Ganong, L., M. Coleman & M.A. Fine (1994). Remarriage and stepfamilies. In R.D. Day, K.R. Gilbert, B.H. Settles & W.R. Burr (Eds.). *Research and theory in family science.* Pacific Grove, CA: Brooks/Cole Publishing Co, p. 287-303.

Genov, N.B. (1997). Four global trends: Rise and limitations. *International Sociology, 12*(4), 209-428.

Gubrium, J.F. & J.A. Holstein (1990). *What is family?* Mountain View, CA: Mayfield.

Haas, L. & P. Hwang (1995). Company culture and men's usage of family leave in Sweden. *Family Relations, 44*(1), 28-36.

Hareven, T.K. (1996). Introduction: Aging and generational relations over the life course. In T.K. Hareven (Ed.). *Aging and generational relations over the life course.* Berlin: Walter de Gruyter, p. 1-12.

Homer-Dixon, T.F., J.H. Boutwell & G.W. Rathjens (1993). Environmental change and violent conflict. *Scientific American, 268*(2), 38-45.

Huber, J. (1990). Macro-microlinks in gender stratification. *American Sociological Review, 55*(1), 1-10.

Johnson, J.M. (1997). The changing concept of child abuse and its impact on family life. In M. Hutter (Ed.). *The family experience: A reader in cultural diversity.* Needham Heights, MA: Allyn & Bacon, p. 404-416.

Katz, R. & Y. Peres (1995). Marital crisis and therapy in their social context. *Contemporary Family Therapy, 17*(4), 395-412.

Keillor, G. (1982). Hog Slaughter: News from Lake Wobegon. *Prairie Home Companion Archives* (Cassette Recording, PHC 911, 1983). Minnesota Public Radio: Saint Paul.

Keiren, D.K. (1998). Building family well being in a new political context: Families and policies in Canada, the US, Latin America and the Caribbean. In N.B. Leidenfrost (Ed.). *An exchange between the Caribbean, South, Central and North America.*

Proceedings of the Americas Region Conference International Federation of Home Economics, July 11-12, 1998, Mayaguez, Puerto Rica, p. 62-69.

*Kids Count Data Book: State Profiles of Child Well-being* (1997). Baltimore, MD: Annie E. Casey Foundation.

Ku, L., B. Cohen & N. Pindus (1994). *Full funding for WIC: A policy review.* Washington, DC: The Urban Institute.

Levin, I. & J. Trost (1992). Understanding the concept of family. *Family Relations, 41*(3), 348-351.

Lieberson, S. (1992). Einstein, Renoir, and Greeley: Some thoughts about evidence in sociology. *American Sociological Review, 57*(1), 1-15.

Lindsey, E.W. (1998). The impact of homelessness and shelter life on family relationships. *Family Relations, 47*(3), 245-252.

Liss, L. (1987). Families and the law. In M.B. Sussman & S.K. Steinmetz (Eds.). *Handbook of Marriage and the Family.* New York: Plenum, p. 767-793.

Lloyd, S.A. (1991). The dark side of courtship: Violence and sexual exploitation. *Family Relations, 40*(1), 14-20.

Marcenko, M.O. & J.C. Meyers (1991). Mothers of children with developmental disabilities: Who shares the burden? *Family Relations, 40*(2), 186-190.

McIntyre, L.J. (1995). Law and the family in historical perspective: Issues and antecedents. In L.J. McIntyre & M.B. Sussman (Eds.). *Families and law.* New York: Haworth Press, p. 5-30.

Minow, M. (1998). Redefining families: Who's in and who's out. In K.V. Hansen & A.I. Garey (Eds.). *Families in the US: Kinship and domestic politics.* Philadelphia: Temple University Press, p. 7-20.

Mirabelli, A. (1996). *Approaching family policy in North America.* (International Seminar on Family Policy and Plans of Action, December 3, 1996). Ottawa, Canada: The Vanier Institute of the Family.

Mogwe, A. (1994). Patriarchy and the law: The marginalization of women. In S. Jagwanth, P. Schwikkard & B. Grant (Eds.). *Women and the law.* Pretoria: HSRC Publishers, p. 3-14.

Morris, A. (1994). International reform initiatives regarding violence against women: Successes and pitfalls. In S. Jagwanth, P. Schwikkard & B. Grant (Eds.). *Women and the law.* Pretoria: HSRC Publishers, p. 351-380.

Murphy, J.L. (1995). *Gender issues in World Bank lending.* Washington, DC: The World Bank.

O'Sullivan, S.K. & W.J. Wilson (1988). Race and ethnicity. In N.J. Smelser (Ed.). *Handbook of sociology.* Newbury, CA: Sage, p. 223-243.

Potuchek, J.L. (1997). Who supports the family? Gender and breadwinning in dual-earner marriages. Stanford, CA: Stanford University Press.

Ptacek, J. (1998). Why do men batter their wives? In K.V. Hansen & A.I. Garey (Eds.). *Families in the US: Kinship and domestic politics.* Philadelphia: Temple University Press, p. 7-20.

Ramirez, F.O., Y. Soysal & S. Shanahan (1997). The changing logic of political citizenship: Cross-national acquisition of women's suffrage rights, 1890-1990. *American Sociological Review, 62*(5), 735-745.

Robertson, R. & H.H. Khondker (1998). Discourses of globalization: Preliminary consideration. *International Sociology, 13*(1), 25-40.

Rossi, P.H. (1989). On sociological data. In N.J. Smelser (Ed). *Handbook of sociology.* Newbury Park, CA: Sage Publications, p. 131-154.

Scanzoni, J. & W. Marsiglio (1991). Wider families as primary relationships. *Marriage and Family Review, 17*(1/2), 117-133.

Settles, B.H. (1976). *The interface of family and society in sex role changes.* Paper Presented at The Theory and Methodology Workshop, National Council on Family Relations, NY.

Settles, B.H. (in press). The future of families. In S.K. Steinmetz, G. Peterson & M.B. Sussman (Eds.). *Handbook of marriage and the family* (2nd ed.). NY: Plenum.

Settles, B.H., D. Hanks III & M.B. Sussman (Eds.) (1993). Families on the move. *Marriage and Family Review, 19*(1-4). NY: Haworth Press.

Settles, B.H., M.L. Liprie & R.S. Hanks (1988). Ethics under ignorance: The role of family members on decision making teams in medical and educational settings. Paper Presented at a Symposia at the Ohio State University, Columbus, OH.

Siqwana-Ndulo, N. (1998). Is true equality in accessing land possible in the context of rural African family in south Africa? In S.C. Ziehl (Ed.). *Multicultural diversity and families.* Grahamstown, South Africa: Rhodes University, p. 38-55.

Smolowe, J. (1995). Fear in the land. *Time, 145*(2), 34-36.

Stacey, J. (1996). *In the name of the family: Rethinking family values in the postmodern age.* Boston: Beacon Press.

Stevens, C.M. (1993). Health care cost containment: Implications of global budgets. *Science, 259*(1), 16-17, 105.

Straus, M.A. (1994). Should the use of corporal punishment by parents be considered child abuse? In M.A. Mason & E. Gambrill (Eds.). *Debating children's lives: Current controversies on children and adolescents.* Thousand Oaks, CA: Sage Publications, p. 196-203.

Straus, M.A. & M.J. Paschall (1998). *Corporal punishment by mothers and the intelligence of children: A longitudinal study.* Paper presented at The 14th World Congress of Sociology, Montreal, Canada.

Sun, L.H. (1993). A great leap backward. Third world, second class: The burden of womanhood. *Washington Post reprint*: Washington, DC.

Talbott, S. (1992). Dealing with anti countries. *Time, 141*(24), 35.

Taubes, G. (1992). Violence epidemiologists test the hazards of gun ownership. *Science, 258,* 213-215.

Teirlinck, M. (1994). *Social Europe 1/94: The European Union and the family.* Luxembourg: Office for Official Publications of the European Communities.

The President's Council on Sustainable Development, draft document (no date). sustainable Communities: Task Force Report.

Voydanoff, P. (1995). A family perspective on services integration. *Family Relations, 44*(1), 63-68.

Wejnert, B. (1996). Family studies and politics: the case of Polish sociology. In M.B. Sussman & R.S. Hanks (Eds.). *Intercultural variation in family research and theory: Implication for cross-national studies.* Binghamton, NY: Haworth Press, p. 233-257.

Wilson, W. J. (1991). Studying inner-city social dislocations: The challenge of public policy agenda research. *American Sociological Review, 56*(1), 1-14.

Wilson, W.J. (1996). *When work disappears: The new world of the urban poor.* NY: Vintage Books.

Yudelman, S.W. (1987). *Hopeful openings: A study of five woman's development organizations in Latin America and the Caribbean.* West Hartford, CN: Kumarian Press.

Zvinkliene, A. (1996). The state of family studies in Lithuania. In M.B. Sussman & R.S. Hanks (Eds.). *Intercultural variation in family research and theory: Implication for cross-national studies.* Binghamton, NY: Haworth Press, p. 203-232.

# Bibliography Wilfried Dumon

1958   *Het begrip middenstand: proeve van een sociologische benadering.* Leuven: K.U.Leuven, School voor politieke en sociale wetenschappen, 188 p.

   *Opinie van bepaalde bevolkingsgroepen uit de gemeente Maldegem over inhoud en omvang van het begrip middenstand.* Leuven: K.U.Leuven, Licentiaatsverhandeling, 195 p.

1959   with M. Evers, J. Malherbe & F. Van Mechelen. *Problèmes du logement: une étude sociologique. Vol. 1: Enquête sur le niveau du loyer.* Leuven: K.U.Leuven, Centre d'études sociales. 75 p.

   with M. Evers, J. Malherbe & F. Van Mechelen. *Problèmes du logement: une étude sociologique. Vol. 2: Enquête sur la construction récente et son occupation.* Leuven: K.U.Leuven, Centre d'études sociales, 83 p.

   with M. Evers & F. Van Mechelen. *Journal 'La cité': approche sociologique de la stratification sociale de ses lecteurs et de leur sphère d'intérêt.* Leuven: K.U.Leuven, Centre d'études sociales, 69 p.

   with M. Evers & F. Van Mechelen. *Huisvestingsproblemen: een sociologische studie. Vol. 1: Onderzoek naar het niveau van de huur.* Leuven: K.U.Leuven, Centrum voor sociale studies. 85 p.

1960   Middenstand en platteland. *V.E.V.-Berichten, 32*(51), 2583-2593.

1963   *De middenstand als sociologische categorie: een explorerend onderzoek naar het middenstandsbegrip.* Leuven: Nauwelaerts, 254 p.

   De middenstand tegenover arbeid en vrije tijd. *Politica, 13*(1), 30-47.

1964   with U. Claeys, E. Goedleven & F. Van Mechelen. *Vrijetijdsbesteding in Vlaanderen: een sociologisch onderzoek bij de actieve Nederlandstalige bevolking van België.* Antwerpen: Ontwikkeling, 148 p.

   with G. D'Olieslager, J. Van den Bosch & F. Van Mechelen. *Het Davidsfonds: sociologische doorlichting van een kulturele vereniging.* Leuven: K.U.Leuven, Centrum voor Sociologisch Onderzoek, 235 p.

with F. Van Mechelen & L. Delanghe. *De sociale problematiek bij de bejaarde zelfstandigen: een explorerend onderzoek.* Leuven: K.U.Leuven, Centrum voor Sociologisch Onderzoek, 249 p.

1965 *Het Algemeen Nederlands Verbond (ANV): een sociologische verkenning.* Leuven: K.U.Leuven, Sociologisch Onderzoeksinstituut, Studiegroep voor cultuurbevordering, 53 p.

with F. Van Mechelen, E. Goedleven & N. Morlion. *Zalen bestemd voor kulturele doeleinden: overheidsinitiatieven in Nederland, Frankrijk, Engeland en Duitsland.* Leuven: K.U.Leuven, Instituut van economisch, sociaal en politiek onderzoek IESP, 144 p.

with F. Van Mechelen, E. Goedleven & N. Morlion. *Zalen bestemd voor kulturele doeleinden: overheidsinitiatieven in Nederland, Frankrijk, Engeland en Duitsland.* Leuven: Acco, 154 p.

& G. D'Olieslager. *Status, recruitment and training of cultural worker in Belgium.* Leuven: Centre for Sociological Research. 52 p.

1966 *Politieke en sociale wetenschappen in het secundair onderwijs: aantekeningen bij de colleges over 'bijzondere methodenleer der politieke en sociale wetenschappen'.* Leuven: Acco, 71 p.

1967 The problem of sampling and instrument construction in a study of the entrepreneurial family in Belgium and the United States: Some methodological problems of minor importance. *Journal of Marriage and the Family, 29*(2), 368-372.

Chronique: Sociologie de la famille. *Justice dans le monde, IX(2),* 218-230.

1968 with M. De Keyser & G. Keuppens-De Vel. *Jonge gezinnen: empirisch onderzoek naar de gezinssituatie van echtparen gehuwd met leeftijdsdispensatie (1965).* 2 vol., 223 p. + 244 p.

with H. Boogaerts & D. Coens. *De buitenshuisarbeid van de gehuwde vrouw met gezinslasten.* Leuven: K.U.Leuven, Centrum voor Sociologisch Onderzoek. 5 volumes. 161 p. + 221 p. + 250 p. + 229 p. + 80 p.

Welvaart en kultuur, een sociologische visie. *Volksopvoeding, 17*(4), 249-255.

1969  *Sociale woningbouw als huisvesting ten behoeve van jonge gezinnen: een onderzoek betreffende een nieuwe woonwijk te Herent.* Leuven: K.U.Leuven, 127 p.

*Dating behaviour. Een onderzoek naar opvattingen en gedragingen van studenten in de sociale wetenschappen aan de K.U.Leuven.* Leuven: K.U.Leuven.

*Methoden en inwijding in onderzoeken van gezinssociologie en van bevolkingssociologie.* Leuven: K.U.Leuven, Sociologisch Onderzoeksinstituut.

Demokratisering in de levensnabije sfeer, In: B.J. De Clercq, W. Dumon, W. Dewachter & B. Alfrink (red.). *Gezag en Demokratie.* Leuven: Davidsfonds, p. 23-34.

with B.J. De Clercq, W. Dewachter & B. Alfrink. *Gezag en demokratie.* Leuven: Davidsfonds, 163 p.

with J. Fontaine, L. Cammaer-Rimanque, A. Mattheeuws, A. Pals-Ghoos, L. Andries & R. Vandenabeele. *De ouder-kind relatie.* Brussel: Reinaert, 95 p. Wegwijzers voor het gezin 1.

& G. Keupens-Devel. Analyse van de procedure inzake leeftijdsdispensatie bij het huwelijk. *Bevolking en Gezin*, 18, 11-16.

Geboorteregeling, sociologisch bekeken. *Gezinsplanning.* Zele: Derde centrale ontmoetingsdag voor jonge gezinnen, 26 januari 1969, 15-19.

Overheid en kultureel beleid. *Kongresverslag Davidsfonds.* Leuven: Davidsfonds, 22-27.

*Early and enforced marriages: a study on a marginal group of young families in Belgium.* Rennes: 2nd International Seminar of the International Scientific Commission on the Family, 10-13 april 1969.

Wordt gezag nog aanvaard in het gezin? *Gezag, een hedendaags probleem.* Mechelen: Verslag van het 20ᵉ congres, november 1969, 11-16.

La position de l'enfant dans une société en transformation, *Organisation mondiale pour l'éducation préscolaire.* Bruxelles: Palais des Congrès, 26 novembre 1969, 21-24.

1970  *Modern systems theory and the family: a confrontation.* Leuven: K.U.Leuven, Sociologisch Onderzoeksinstituut, 21 p. Laudatio presented at the ceremonies conferring the degree of Doctor Honoris Causa to R. Hill.

De positie van het kind in een veranderende maatschappij. *Persoon en Gemeenschap, 23*(3), 134-138.

Wordt gezag nog aanvaard in het gezin? *Santé mentale/Geestesgezondheid,* (1), 11-16.

De leer van de Kerk inzake geboorteregeling: analyse van een ideologie, Liber Amicorum Prof. Mag. C. Van Gestel, *Politica, 20*(3-4), Leuven: 102-112.

Early and enforced marriages: A study on a marginal group of young families in Belgium, *Images and counter-images of young families.* Transactions of the 2nd international seminar of the International Scientific Commission on the Family ICOFA, Louvain, 148-154.

*The school and the family: some considerations on democratisation*; Paper voorbereid ten behoeve van de commissievergadering van de Commission of Education van de International Union of Family Organisations, London, June 4-5, 1970.

*Nieuwe Gezinsvormen* - Utrecht: Gezinssociologische studiedag van het SISWO, 11 december 1970.

1971 *Onderzoek naar de behoeften inzake home-care voor bejaarden in het arrondisement Leuven.* Leuven: K.U.Leuven, Centrum voor Sociologisch Onderzoek. 3 volumes.

De immigratiepolitiek in België: een sociaal pobleem. *Kontakten '72, 2*(1), 95-96.

La politique d'immigration en Belgique: un problème social. *Contacts '72, 2*(1), 89-90.

Functies van de vrije tijd. Een sociologische analyse. *Volksopvoeding, 20*(7-8), 241-246.

Opvattingen over of ideaalvoorstellingen van het gezin. *Kultuurleven, 38*(10), 938-943.

1972 Echtscheiding: een sociologische visie. In: *Mislukt huwelijk en echtscheiding. Vragen rond het mislukte huwelijk.* Leuven: Universitaire Pers Leuven: p. 25-36. Sociologische Verkenningen 2.

*Dating behaviour. Some findings resulting from an investigation on dating behaviour of students at the K.U.Leuven.* Leuven: 14th International Colloquium on Sexology, May 1972.

Opvattingen en voorstellingen over het gezin. In: M. Hinderyckx & A. Van Meervenne. *Gezin contra gezin.* Antwerpen/Utrecht: De Nederlandsche Boekhandel, 160 p.

Echtscheiding: een sociologische visie. *Sint-Lucas Tijdschrift,* (3), 12-20.

Bedenkingen van een (gezins)socioloog: het cognitieve en het evaluatieve moment in een leerproces. *Tijdschrift voor catechese, 2(1),* 38-39.

*Working mothers. An empirical research in a Belgian factory.* Moscow: 12th International Family Seminar, April 1972.

*Living conditions and everyday necessities of the aged.* Kiev (USSR): 9th International Congress of Gerontology, 2-7 July 1972.

1973   & M. Nesari-Slingerland. *Politique familiale: une bibliographie sélectionnée et annotée (1948-1972). Family Policy: a selected and annotated bibliography (1948-1972).* Leuven: K.U.Leuven, Sociologisch Onderzoeksinstituut, 163 p. Rapport 1973/4.

Vrouwenarbeid, bevoogding of emancipatie? *De Nieuwe Maand, 16*(9), 590-596.

*De rechtbedelende functie van het gezin: Inleidende bemerkingen bij de basistekst.* Leuven: Colloquium onderzoeksafdeling Moraaltheologie, 28-30 maart 1973.

& R.M. D'Hertefelt, e.a. *Document 2: Telling.* Leuven: Paper bij het hoor- en werkcollege van de afdeling Gezins- en Bevolkingssociologie, academiejaar 1972-1973.

De kwetsbaarheid van het gezin in de hedendaagse samenleving. In: W. Dumon, P. Nijs & N. de Jonghe (red.). *Verslagboek Colloquium Gezinsconsultatie, 14 oktober 1973.* Antwerpen: Federatie Vormingswerk voor het Gezin, p. 11-21.

with P. Nijs, L. Rouffa, O. Steeno. *Donor insemination: A preliminary social and psychological report.* Leuven: 2ième Congrès International de Sexologie, 31 mai 1973.

& R.M. D'Hertefelt-Bruynooghe. *Construction of the life cycle of the family: some remarks on the availibility of information.* Paris: 13th Seminar on Family Research, September 1973.

L'évolution et la participation des familles dans le monde actuel. In: *Les objectifs de la participation des familles dans une société en transformation.* Actes de la Conférence Internationale de la Famille, Liège, 3-7 septembre 1973. Paris: Union Internationale des Organismes Familiaux.

with P. Nijs & N. de Jonghe (red.). *Verslagboek Colloquium Gezins-consultatie, 14 oktober 1973.* Antwerpen: Federatie Vormingswerk voor het Gezin, 63 p.

*Het hedendaags gezin.* Brugge: Congres Katholieke Vereniging voor Geesteshygiëne 'Voor of tegen het gezin?', 27 oktober 1973.

*Vaderschap, van positie naar rol.* Brasschaat: Studiedag van de Gezins-school 'Vaders, vandaag en morgen', 11 november 1973.

1974  Het gezin als instituut en als systeem. *Praktische Theologie, 1*(3), 168-177.

La famille, la socialisation et l'éducation permanente. *Sauvegarde de l'enfance, 29*(3-4), 144-148.

Het hedendaags gezin. *Geestesgezondheid,* (1), 8-12, (speciaal nummer).

Educational adaptation of permanent migrants. *International Migration, 12*(3), 270-300.

Gezin en bevolking 1974: een sociologische benadering. *Gezin en Bevolking 1974,* 1-14.

*Gezin en bevolking 1974: een sociologische benadering.* Brussel: Colloquium van de Bond voor Grote en Jonge Gezinnen, 19 januari 1974.

*Adaptation culturelle des migrants.* Genève: Comité Intergouvernemental pour les Migrations Européennes, Séminaire sur 'L'adaptation et l'intégration des immigrants permanents', 29-31 mai 1974.

*Educational adaptation of permanent migrants.* Geneva: Intergovernmental Committee for European Migration, Seminar on 'Adaptation and Integration of Permanent Immigrants', 29-31 May 1974.

*La adaptación de los migrantes permanentes desde el punto de vista de la educación.* Ginebra: Comite Intergobernamental para las Migraciones Europeas, Seminario sobre 'Adaptación y Integración de los Inmigrantes Permanentes', 29-31 de Mayo 1974.

*Gezin en voedingsbudget.* Kortrijk: Tentoonstelling Interfreez vzw, 21 september 1974.

1975 *Vlaamse beweging. Elementen voor een beleid.* Leuven: K.U.Leuven, Sociologisch Onderzoeksinstituut, 28 p.

with Y. Nuyens, e.a. (éds.). *Le problème de la population: une interpellation aux hommes de notre temps.* Paris: Le Centurion. 198 p.

with M. Lembrechts, T. Jacobs, M. Matthys, M. Masui, M. Slingerland & R.M. Bruynooghe. *Vrouw en gezin. Relevantie van enkele gezinssociologische onderzoeken voor de vrouwenproblematiek.* Leuven: K.U.Leuven, Sociologisch Onderzoeksinstituut, 146 p. Sociologische Studies en Documenten 5.

with G. Bottu & M. Slingerland. *Alleenwonen, een poging tot verklaring vanuit kerngezin en gezinsfasen: onderzoek op basis van de volkstellingen 1961 en 1970.* Leuven: K.U.Leuven, Departement Sociologie. Hoor- en werkcollege Gezins- en Bevolkingssociologie, 23 p.

with M. Daems & M. Slingerland. *De eenpersoonshuishouding in België en Frankrijk.* Leuven: K.U.Leuven, Departement Sociologie. Hoor- en werkcollege Gezins- en Bevolkingssociologie, 23 p.

with H. Piqueur & M. Slingerland. *De Belgische gezinshoofden naar burgerlijke staat, leeftijd, geslacht en huishoudomvang: evolutie van 1930 tot 1970 aan de hand van de volkstellingen.* Leuven: K.U.Leuven, Departement Sociologie. Hoor- en werkcollege Gezins- en Bevolkingssociologie, 14 p.

Sociologische doorlichting. In: P. Van Moeseke & K. Tavernier (red.). *Het huis staat in brand. Colloquium over bevolking en vervuiling.* Antwerpen/Amsterdam: Standaard Wetenschappelijke Uitgeverij, p. 117-129.

De arbeid van de gehuwde vrouw met gezinslasten. Terugblik op een empirisch onderzoek. In: W. Dumon, M. Lembrechts, T. Jacobs, M.

Matthys, M. Masui, M. Slingerland & R.M. Bruynooghe. *Vrouw en gezin. Relevantie van enkele gezinssociologische onderzoeken voor de vrouwenproblematiek.* Leuven: K.U.Leuven, Sociologisch Onderzoeksinstituut, 1-21. Sociologische Studies en Documenten 5.

& M. Lembrechts. Het belang van de voeding in het gezinsbudget. *De Gids op Maatschappelijk Gebied, 66(12)*, 823-829.

*La migration des familles et le regroupement familial.* Genève: CIME, 2ième Séminaire sur 'L'adaptation et l'intégration des immigrants permanents'. Communication n° 1, 19-21 november 1975.

*Family migration and family reunion.* Geneva: ICEM, Second Seminar on 'Adaptation and Integration of Permanent Immigrants'. Paper n° 1, 19-21 November 1975.

*Migración de familias y reagrupación familiar.* Ginebra: CIME, Segundo Seminario sobre 'Adaptación y Integración de los Inmigrantes Permanentes'. Documento n° 1, 19-21 de Noviembre 1975.

1976 with M. Matthijs & C. De Paepe (1976). *Divorce in Western Europe: annotated bibliography / Le divorce en Europe occidentale: bibliographie annotée.* Leuven: K.U.Leuven, Sociologisch Onderzoeksinstituut, 335 p.

Migración de familias y reagrupación familiar. In: *Sociologia de la relaciones internationales. Tomo 2* Mexico: Asociación Internacional de Sociologia, 5-48.

Family migration and family reunion. *International Migration, 14*(1-2), 53-83.

Migratie van gezinnen en gezinshereniging. *Mozaïek, 8*(27-28), 42-53.

Uit werken met z'n twee. *Ondernemen, 32*(11), 481-483.

*Divorce and status of women.* Voorburg: Second European Population Seminar on 'The Demographic Aspects of the Changing Status of Women in Europe', 13-17 december 1976.

1977 *Het gezin in Vlaanderen.* Leuven: Davidsfonds, 93 p. Horizonreeks nr. 36. - 1977/2.

*Système d'observation permanente des migrations - Belgique 1976.* Paris: OCDE/SOPEMI, 38 p.

with H.M. Slingerland & C. Deneffe-Marcelis. *Gezinssociologische Documentatie - Jaarboek.* Leuven: Acco, 244 p., nr. 1.

& R.M. D'Hertefelt-Bruynooghe. Construction of the life cycle of the family. Some remarks on the availibility of information. In: Cuisenier, J. (ed.). *The family life cycle in European societies.* Den Haag: Mouton, 175-186.

Bevolkingspolitiek en gezinspolitiek. In: *Ethische vragen voor onze tijd. Hulde aan Mgr. Heylen.* Antwerpen: De Nederlandsche Boekhandel, 333-339.

Divorce in Europe: Belgium. In: P. Chester (ed.). *Divorce in Europe.* Leiden: Martinus Nijhoff, 125-146.

Menopauze: een sociologische benadering. *Leuvense Cahiers voor Seksuologie,* (1), 100-110.

Bevolkingspolitiek en gezinspolitiek. Verwarring in de definities en verwarring in de beoordeling. *Volwaardig gezinsbeleid in Vlaanderen,* 6(3), 16-21.

The activity of voluntary agencies and national associations in helping immigrants to overcome initial problems. *International Migration, 15*(2/3), 113-126.

*Bibliografische gegevens inzake gezinssociologie - Referaten 1975.* Leuven: K.U.Leuven, Sociologisch Onderzoeksinstituut, 201 p.

*The activity of voluntary agencies and national associations in helping immigrants to overcome initial problems.* Geveva: ICEM, Third Seminar on 'Adaptation and Integration of permanent Immigrants', 9-12 May 1977, Paper n° 1.

*L'activité des agences bénévoles et des associations nationales en vue d'aider les immigrants à resoudre leurs problèmes initiaux.* Genève: CIME, Troisième Séminaire sur 'L'adaptation et l'intégration des immigrants permanents', 9-12 mai 1977, Communication n° 1.

*La actividad de las organizaciones voluntarias y las asociaciones nacionales encaminada a ayudar a los inmigrantes a superar los problemas iniciales.*

Ginebra: CIME, Tercer Seminario sobre 'Adaptación y Integración de los Inmigrantes Permanentes', 9-12 de Mayo 1977, Documento n° 1.

1978   *Système d'observation permanente des migrations - Belgique 1977.* Paris: OCDE/SOPEMI, 32 p.

De problematiek van de buitenlandse werknemers in West-Europa, met speciale aandacht voor de gezinsproblematiek. In: C.D. Mak (red.). *De vrouw in het gezin van de buitenlandse werknemer.* Verslag van een colloquium gehouden onder de auspiciën van de Nationale Unesco Commissie te Helvoirt van 9-11 december 1976. Den Haag: Nationale Unesco Commissie, 16-27.

Divorce and the status of women. In: M. Niphuis-Nell (ed.). *Demographic aspects of the changing status of women in Europe.* Leiden: Martinus Nijhoff, 33-47. NIDI/CGBS-Publication 7.

with G. Devel & C. Deneffe-Marcelis. *Gezinssociologische Documentatie - Jaarboek.* Leuven: Acco, 304 p., nr. 2.

with G. Devel & C. Deneffe-Marcelis. *Gezinssociologische Documentatie - Jaarboek.* Leuven: Acco, 355 p., nr. 3.

with L. Bijnens & E.J. Leemans. *Gehandicaptenproblematiek en gehandicaptenbeleid.* Nationaal Onderzoeksprogramma in de sociale wetenschappen, Onderzoeksproject 'Marginalisering en Welzijnszorg'. Leuven: K.U.Leuven, Sociologisch Onderzoeksinstituut, 6 vol.

with B. Buysse & E.J. Leemans. *Marginalisering in en rond het arbeidsproces.* Nationaal Onderzoeksprogramma in de sociale wetenschappen, Onderzoeksproject 'Marginalisering en Welzijnszorg'. Leuven: K.U.Leuven, Sociologisch Onderzoeksinstituut, 3 vol.

with R.-M. D'Hertefelt, C. De Paepe & J. Vanhoutvinck. *De een-oudergezinnen/Les familles mono-parentales.* Nationaal Onderzoeksprogramma in de sociale wetenschappen, Onderzoeksproject 'Marginalisering en Welzijnszorg'. Wetenschappelijk rapport 15 p.

with R. Renier, E.J. Leemans & F. Lammertyn. *Bejaardenproblematiek en bejaardenzorg. De bejaardentehuizen - Vlaanderen.* Nationaal Onderzoeksprogramma in de sociale wetenschappen, Onderzoeksproject 'Marginalisering en Welzijnszorg'. Leuven: K.U.Leuven, Sociologisch Onderzoeksinstituut.

with E. Samoy, E.J. Leemans & F. Lammertyn. *De algemene sociale dienst-verlening en de gezinsvoorzieningen.* Nationaal Onderzoeksprogramma in de sociale wetenschappen, Onderzoeksproject 'Marginalisering en Welzijns-zorg'. Leuven: K.U.Leuven, Sociologisch Onderzoeksinstituut, 4 volumes.

with H. Van Geel, H. Van Nuland, K. Kloeck & E.J. Leemans. *De zorg voor sociaal gehandicapten.* Nationaal Onderzoeksprogramma in de sociale wetenschappen, Onderzoeksproject 'Marginalisering en Welzijnszorg'. Leuven: K.U.Leuven, Sociologisch Onderzoeksinstituut, 4 vol.

*When two become three. Transition to parenthood.* Vienna: International Union on Family Organizations, 9-12 June 1978.

*Congres recreatie '98. Thema: Gezin/huishouding.* Noordwijkerhout: Congres van de Stichting Recreatie, 5-6 oktober 1978.

1979  with M. Matthys & C. De Paepe. *Le divorce en Europe occidentale - Divorce in Western Europe. Bibliographie annotée - Annotated Bibliography.* Paris: GIRD, 287 p.

& J. Aldous. European and United States political contexts for family policy research. *Journal of Marriage and the family, 41*(3), 497-505.

with G. Devel & C. Deneffe-Marcelis. *Gezinssociologische Documentatie - Jaarboek.* Leuven: Acco, 465 p., nr. 4.

Het profiel van het Vlaamse gezin. In: *Twintig eeuwen Vlaanderen.* Hasselt: Heideland/Orbis, 265-326. Deel 7: De Vlaamse Gemeenschap.

Sociale stratificatie. In *Twintig eeuwen Vlaanderen.* Hasselt: Heideland/ Orbis, 327-396. Deel 7: De Vlaamse Gemeenschap.

Echtscheiding in België. *Kultuurleven, 46*(1), 5-16.

De verkeersongevallen op de openbare weg. *Gezinsbeleid in Vlaanderen, 8*(1), 24-29.

The situation of children of migrants and their adaptation and integra-tion in the host society, and their situation in the country of origin. *International Migration, 17*(1/2), 59-75.

Quando due diventano tre. *Riflessi, 31*(2), 45-69.

De sociologie in België. *Sociodrome,* (5), 3-5.

*The situation of children of migrants and their adaptation and integration in the host society, and their situation in the country of origin.* Geneva: ICEM, Fourth Seminar on 'Adaptation and Integration of Permanent Immigrants', 8-11 May 1979, Paper n° 1.

*La situation des enfants de migrants, leur adaptation et leur intégration dans la société d'accueil, leur situation dans le pays d'origine.* Genève: CIME, Quatrième séminaire sur 'L'adaptation et l'intégration des immigrants permanents', 8-11 mai 1979, Communication n° 1.

*Situación de los hijos de los migrantes, su adaptación y integración en la sociedad de acogida y su situación en el país de origen.* Ginebra: CIME, Cuarto Seminario sobre 'Adaptación y Integración de los Inmigrantes Permanentes', 8-11 de Mayo 1979, Documento n° 1.

1980   with J. Aldous & K. Johnson. *The politics and programs of family policy: United States and European perspectives.* Notre Dame/Leuven: Center for the Study of Man/Leuven University Press, 289 p.

&  J. Aldous. European and United States Perspectives on Family Policy: A summing up. In: J. Aldous & W. Dumon (eds.) *The politics and programs of family policy.* Notre Dame/Leuven: Center for the Study of Man/ Leuven University Press, p. 253-276.

with G. Devel & C. Deneffe-Marcelis (red.). *Gezinssociologische Documentatie - Jaarboek.* Leuven: Acco, 532 p., nr. 5.

Kind en gezin: een sociologische benadering. In: *Wie ben ik, wie zijn jullie? Een waardevaste opvoeding in een waardenloze wereld?* Nijmegen: Katholiek Studiecentrum, 59-66.

*Family policy in Western Europe.* Loccum: International Colloquium on Family Research, 27-29 February 1980.

1981   & K. Matthijs. *Système d'observation permanente des migrations - Belgique 1980-1981.* Leuven: K.U.Leuven, Sociologisch Onderzoeksinstituut, 71 p.

&  C. De Paepe. *XIXth International CFR-Seminar on Divorce and Remarriage.* Key Papers + Addendum, Reaction Papers / Free Papers, Discussant Papers, Proceedings. Leuven: 30 August - 4 September 1981. Leuven: K.U.Leuven, Sociologisch onderzoeksinstituut, 5 vol.

with M. Verwimp & C. Deneffe-Marcelis (red.). *Gezinssociologische Documentatie - Jaarboek*. Leuven: Acco, 449 p., nr. 6.

with J. Vanhoutvinck, e.a. *Preventie van structurele marginalisering van niet-traditionele gezinnen*. Brussel: Ministerie van Wetenschapsbeleid - Nationaal Onderzoeksprogramma in de Sociale Wetenschappen, Rapport 17: 232 p.

with B. Froeyen, E. Van Wassenhove & H. van Winckel. *Preventie van structurele marginalisering van niet-traditionele gezinnen / Prévention de la marginalisation structurelle des familles non-traditionnelles*. Brussel: Nationaal Onderzoeksprogramma in de sociale wetenschappen, Onderzoeksproject 'Marginalisering en Welzijnszorg'. Wetenschappelijk rapport 17. 242 p.

with B. Froeyen, E. Van Wassenhove & H. van Winckel. *Preventie van structurele marginalisering van niet-traditionele gezinnen: survey van de huismoeders / Prévention de la marginalisation structurelle des familles non-traditionnelles: enquête sur les ménages*. Brussel: Nationaal Onderzoeksprogramma in de sociale wetenschappen, Onderzoeksproject 'Marginalisering en Welzijnszorg'. Syntheserapport 43, 30 p.

Sociologie in België. In: L. Rademaker (red.). *Sociologische grondbegrippen. 1. Theorie en analyse*. Utrecht/Antwerpen: Het Spectrum, 166-198. Aula 685.

Het gezin, de kern van de samenleving. *De bazuin, 64*(9), 5-6.

The situation of migrant women workers. *International Migration, 19*(1/2), 190-209.

La famiglia e la politica familiare in evoluniare nella societa degli anni '80. In: *La politica familiare in Europe*. Milano: Franco Arnylli, 43-52.

*The situation of migrant women workers*. Geneva: ICEM, Fifth Seminar on 'Adaptation and Integration of Permanent Immigrants', 26 p.

*La situation de la travailleuse migrante*. Genève: CIME, Cinquième séminaire sur 'L'adaptation et l'intégration des immigrants permanents', 26 p.

*La situación de las trabajadores migrantes*. Ginebra: CIME, Quinto Seminario sobre 'Adaptación y Integración de los Inmigrantes Permanentes', 26 p.

1982   *Het profiel van de vreemdelingen in België.* Leuven: Davidsfonds, 144 p.

      & K. Matthijs. *OCDE-système d'observation permanente des migrations -* Belgique 1981-1982. Leuven: K.U.Leuven, Sociologisch Onderzoeksinstituut, 15 p.

      with M. Verwimp & C. Deneffe-Marcelis (red.). *Gezinssociologische Documentatie - Jaarboek.* Leuven: Acco, 541 p., nr. 7.

1983   with C. Deneffe-Marcelis & M. Verwimp (red.). *Gezinswetenschappelijke Documentatie - Jaarboek.* Leuven: Acco, 603 p., nr. 8.

      & G.A. Kooy. *Echtscheiding in België en Nederland.* Deventer: Van Loghum Slaterus, 178 p. Sociologische monografieën.

      & K. Matthijs. *OCDE-Système d'observation permanente des migrations - Belgique.* Leuven: K.U.Leuven, Sociologisch Onderzoeksinstituut, 52 p.

      Effects of undocumented migration for individuals concerned. *International Migration,* 21(2), 218-229.

1984   with C. Deneffe-Marcelis & M. Wyns (red.). *Gezinswetenschappelijke Documentatie - Jaarboek.* Leuven: K.U.Leuven, Sociologisch Onderzoeksinstituut, 872 p., nr. 9.

      & K. Matthijs. *OCDE-Système d'observation permanente des migrations - Belgique.* Leuven: K.U.Leuven, Sociologisch Onderzoeksinstituut, 34 p.

      & A. Van Bedts. Ongehuwd samenwonen in Vlaanderen, een eerste en voorlopige verkenning. In: R.L. Cliquet & R. Debusschere (red.). *Relationeel en reproduktief gedrag in Vlaanderen.* Brussel: CBGS-Ministerie van de Vlaamse Gemeenschap, 37-62. CBGS-monografie nr. 1.

      Causes and effects of the new patterns of fertility and family formation. Sociological interpretations and expectations for the future. In: S. Feld & R. Lesthaeghe (eds.). *Population and societal outlook,* Brussel: Koning Boudewijnstichting, 159-166.

1985   with C.J.M. Corver & J.M.L. Jonker. *Primaire leefvormen, ontwikkelingen en theorieën, onderzoek en problemen in de jaren zeventig.* Amsterdam: SISWO, 180 p.

with C. Deneffe-Marcelis & M. Wyns (red.). *Gezinswetenschappelijke Documentatie - Jaarboek*. Leuven: K.U.Leuven, Sociologisch Onderzoeksinstituut, 763 p., nr. 10.

Enkele facetten inzake de ontwikkeling van de gezinssociologie in België (1975-1982). In: C.J.M. Corver, W. Dumon & J.M.L. Jonker. *Primaire leefvormen. Ontwikkelingen in theorieën, onderzoek en problemen in de jaren zeventig*. Amsterdam: SISWO, 11-33.

De demografische situatie van de vreemdelingen in België. In: A. Martens & F. Moulaert (red.). *Buitenlandse minderheden in Vlaanderen - België*. Antwerpen/Amsterdam: De Nederlandsche Boekhandel, 45-59.

Kooy's contributie buitengaats. In: *Tussen expressie en reflectie. Verzamelde opstellen voor G.A. Kooy*. Wageningen: Landbouwhogeschool, 143-145.

Kosten van kinderen. Wie zal dat betalen? *Gezinsbeleid in Vlaanderen*, *14*(1), 35-42.

1986  (red.) *Sociale (on)gelijkheid*. Leuven: Vereniging voor Sociologie/Sociologisch Onderzoeksinstituut, 217 p. Sociologische Studies en Documenten 26.

with C. Deneffe & P. Goossens (red.). *Gezinswetenschappelijke Documentatie - Jaarboek*. Leuven: Universitaire Pers Leuven, 790 p., nr. 11.

& H. Van Nuland. Family planning practices among minors in Belgium. In: H. Rodman & J.T. Prost. *The adolescent dilemma*. New York: Praeger, 5-20.

& L. Michiels. OCDE-*Système d'observation permanente des migrations - Belgique*. Leuven: K.U.Leuven, Sociologisch Onderzoeksinstituut, 85 p.

with H. Pas F. Van Mechelen & H. Deleeck (red.). *Het gezin gezien*. Brussel: Hoger Instituut voor Gezinswetenschappen, 174 p.

with V. Van Rompuy, H. Deleeck, G. De Swert, R. Savage & F. Vanistendael. Individu of gezin in sociale zekerheid en personenbelasting. Paneldiscussie. In: J. Pacolet & I. Nicaise (red.). *Draagkracht, sociale zekerheid en personenbelasting*. Leuven: Hoger Instituut voor de Arbeid, 218-220, 229-232.

& A. Van Bedts. *Ongehuwde vrouwen in Vlaanderen. Resultaten van NEGO IV (Nationale Enquête Gezinsontwikkeling, 1982-1983)*. Brussel: CBGS - Ministerie van de Vlaamse Gemeenschap, 240 p., CBGS-werkdocument 32.

Congresthema: Sociale (On)gelijkheid. In: W. Dumon (red.). *Sociale (On)gelijkheid*. Leuven: Vereniging voor Sociologie/Sociologisch Onderzoeksinstituut, 13-17.

Slottoespraak Congres Sociale (On)gelijkheid. In: W. Dumon (red.). *Sociale (On)gelijkheid*. Leuven: Vereniging voor Sociologie/Sociologisch Onderzoeksinstituut, p. 45-51.

Herinnering aan 25 jaar Hoger Instituut Gezinswetenschappen. In: H. Pas, F. Van Mechelen, W. Dumon & H. Deleeck (red.). *Het gezin gezien*. Brussel: Hoger Instituut voor Gezinswetenschappen, 15-18.

One-parent families. Conceptual and methodological issues. In: F. Deven & R.L. Cliquet (eds.). *One parent families in Europe*. The Hague/Brussels: NIDI/CGBS, 349-359.

Sociologie. In: R. De Schrijver & R. Dillemans (red.). *Wegwijs Cultuur*. Leuven: Davidsfonds, p. 445-449.

De kijk van de cliënt, gezin en familie. In: *Focus op de thuissituatie*. Brussel: VIW, 24-33.

Problems faced by migrants and their family members, particularly second generation migrants, in returning to and reintegrating into their countries of origin. *International Migration, 24*(1), 113-128.

Gezin en Kerk. Sociale verandering en spanningsveld tussen twee instituten. *Collationes, 16*(3), 285-300.

1987   (red.). *Aids: een multidisciplinaire aanpak*. Leuven/Brussel: K.U.Leuven, Sociologisch Onderzoeksinstituut/FCLG, 142 p.

with C. Deneffe & P. Goossens (red.). *Gezinswetenschappelijke Documentatie - Jaarboek*. Leuven: Universitaire Pers Leuven: K.U.Leuven, 666 p., nr. 12.

& L. Michiels (1987). *OCDE-Système d'observation permanente des migrations - Belgique*. Leuven: K.U.Leuven, Departement Sociologie, Sociologisch Onderzoeksinstituut, 88 p. SOPEMI 1987/1.

& L. Michiels. OCDE-*Système d'observation permanente des migrations - Belgique.* Leuven: K.U.Leuven, Departement Sociologie, Sociologisch Onderzoeksinstituut, 80 p. SOPEMI 1987/2.

& R. Lesthaeghe. *Generaties en gezinnen: hun reilen en zeilen sedert de jaren zestig.* Leuven: Acco, 280 p.

Concluding remarks: What is changing in the changing family? What are the alternatives in alternative patterns of family life? In: L. Shamgar-Handelman & R. Palomba (eds.). *Alternative patterns of family life in modern societies.* Rome: Instituto di Richerche sulla Popolazione, p. 503-509.

Meer staat, meer gezin? In: H. Adriaansens & P. Van den Akker (red.). *Meer staat - Meer welzijn? De verhouding tussen individu en staat bij een terugtredende overheid.* Verslag van het symposium bij het afscheid van Prof. dr. Jacques Stalpers van de Katholieke Universiteit Brabant. Tilburg: Tilburg University Press, p. 50-65.

Inleiding: Aids een taak van de federatie. In: W. Dumon (red.). *Aids: een multidisciplinaire aanpak.* Leuven/Brussel: K.U.Leuven, Sociologisch Onderzoeksinstituut/FCLG, 1-2.

La politique familiale en Europe occidentale. Une réflexion sociologique. *L'Année Sociologique,* XXXVII, 291-308.

Gezinspolitiek in België. *Tijdschrift voor Sociologie,* 8(2/3), 257-275.

1988  with C. Deneffe & P. Goossens. *Gezinswetenschappelijke Documentatie - Jaarboek.* Leuven: Universitaire Pers Leuven, XVIII + 577 p., nr. 13.

with C. Deneffe & J. Van Acker. *Gezinswetenschappelijke Documentatie 13. Seksueel misbruik van kinderen en het gezin.* Leuven: Universitaire Pers Leuven, 86 p.

with K. Matthijs & C. Sels. Gezinsarbeid. In: *Maatschappelijke uitstraling van sociale wetenschappen; vriendenboek Professor Dr. F. Van Mechelen.* Hasselt: Concentra, p. 109-122.

& L. Michiels. *Problematiek, regelgeving en praktijk van interlandelijke adoptiebemiddeling in Vlaanderen.* Leuven: K.U.Leuven, Sociologisch Onderzoeksinstituut, 257 p.

*Family and migration: effects of migration on family structure.* Geneva: ICEM, Eighth Seminar on 'Adaptation and Integration of Permanent Immigrants', 13-16 September 1988, 26 p.

Famille et migration: effets de la migration sur la structure familiale. Genève: CIME, Huitième séminaire sur 'L'adaptation et l'intégration des immigrants permanents', 13-16 septembre 1988, 30 p.

*Familia y migración: efectos de la migración en la estructura familiar.* Ginebra: CIME, Octavo Seminario sobre 'Adaptación y Integración de los Inmigrantes Permanentes', 13-16 de septiembre 1988, 32 p.

1989 *Aids: Voorlichting en preventie.* Leuven/Brussel: K.U.Leuven, Sociologisch Onderzoeksinstituut/FCLG, 62 p.

(red.) *Geweld in het gezin.* Leuven/Brussel: K.U.Leuven, Sociologisch Onderzoeksinstituut/ FCLG, 97 p.

& G. Adriaensens. *OCDE; Système d'observation permanente des migrations; Belgique 1988-1989.* Leuven: K.U.Leuven, Departement Sociologie/ Sociologisch Onderzoeksinstituut, 95 p. SOPEMI 1989/3.

& C. Deneffe. *Gezinswetenschappelijke Documentatie - Jaarboek.* Leuven: Universitaire Pers Leuven, XXII + 689 p., nr. 14.

& C. Deneffe. *Gezinswetenschappelijke Documentatie 14 - Literatuuroverzicht België-Nederland 1989.* Leuven: Universitaire Pers Leuven, 140 p.

with C. Deneffe & K. Marcelis. *Geweld op vrouwen. Verkrachting. Literatuuroverzicht 1985-1989. / Violence à l'égard des femmes. Viol. Aperçu de la littérature 1985-1989.* Brussel: INBEL, 152 p.

with C. Deneffe & K. Marcelis. *Seksuele mishandeling van kinderen. Incest. Literatuuroverzicht / Abus sexuel d'enfants. Inceste. Aperçu de la littérature.* Brussel: INBEL, 124 p.

with C. Deneffe & K. Marcelis. *Mishandeling en verwaarlozing van kinderen. Literatuuroverzicht. / Enfants maltraités et négligés. Aperçu de la littérature.* Brussel: INBEL, 174 p.

& A. Van Bedts. *Van éénoudergezin tot fusiegezin.* Leuven: K.U.Leuven, Departement Sociologie, 113 p.

Inleiding: Aids: Voorlichting en preventie. In W. Dumon (red.). *Aids voorlichting en preventie.* Leuven/Brussel: K.U.Leuven, Sociologisch Onderzoeksinstituut/ FCLG, 1-2.

Inleiding. In W. Dumon (red.). *Geweld in het gezin.* Leuven/Brussel: K.U.Leuven, Sociologisch Onderzoeksinstituut/FCLG, 1-2.

Family and migration. *International Migration, 27*(2), p. 251-270.

1990 & G.Adriaensens. OCDE; *Système d'observation permanente des migrations; Belgique 1990.* Leuven: K.U.Leuven, Departement Sociologie/Sociologisch Onderzoeksinstituut, 101 p. SOPEMI 1990/4.

*Family policy in EEC countries.* Luxembourg: Office for official publications of the European Communities, 349 p.

& J. Aldous. Family policies in the 1980's: controversy and consensus. *Journal of Marriage and the Family, 52*(4), p. 1136-1151.

Knelpunten inzake gezinsbeleid in Europa. *Gezinsbeleid in Vlaanderen/ Europees gezinsbeleid, 19*(2), p. 28-35.

with G. Adriaensens & M. Cuyvers. *Aids-preventie in Vlaanderen; een sociale kaart van de Aids-organisaties.* Leuven: K.U.Leuven, Departement Sociologie/Sociologisch Onderzoeksinstituut, 93 p.

& C. Deneffe. *Gezinswetenschappelijke Documentatie - Jaarboek.* Leuven: Universitaire Pers Leuven, XIX + 724 p., nr. 15.

& C. Deneffe. *Gezinswetenschappelijke Documentatie 15 - Literatuuroverzicht België-Nederland 1990.* Leuven: Universitaire Pers Leuven, 142 p.

1991 with F. Bartiaux & T. Nuelant. *National family policies in EC-countries in 1900. Families and policies: evolutions and trends in 1989-1990.* Brussels: Commission of the European Communities, European Observatory on National Family Policies, 269 p.

with F. Bartiaux & T. Nuelant. *Les politiques familiales des Etats membres de la Communauté en 1990. Familles et politiques: tendances et évolutions en 1989-1990.* Bruxelles: Commission des Communautés européennes, Observatoire européen des politiques familiales, 278 p.

303

& C. Deneffe. *Gezinswetenschappelijke Documentatie - Jaarboek.* Leuven: Universitaire Pers Leuven, XXI + 729 p., nr. 16.

& C. Deneffe. *Gezinswetenschappelijke Documentatie 16 - Literatuuroverzicht België-Nederland 1991.* Leuven: Universitaire Pers Leuven, 125 p.

& C. Deneffe. *Relaties en Seksualiteit - 1. - Jaarboek 1991.* Leuven: GIDS, IX + 245 p.

with H. Peeters & M. Cuyvers. *Het Aidsbeleid in Vlaanderen; een organisatiesociologische doorlichting.* Leuven: K.U.Leuven, Departement Sociologie/Sociologisch Onderzoeksinstituut, 115 p.

& R. Van Meensel. *Een permanent systeem inzake registratie van migrantenkinderen in het Nederlandstalig onderwijs.* Leuven: K.U.Leuven, Departement Sociologie, 146 p.

Politiche della famiglia e della popolazione in Europa oggi. In: P. Donati & M. Matteini. *Quale politica per quale famiglia in Europa; ripartire della comunità locali.* Milaan: Franco Angeli, p. 47-64.

The European observatory on national family policies. In: M. Ferrera (ed.). *The evaluation of social policies; experiences and perspectives/ L'évaluation des politiques sociales; expériences et perspectives.* Milaan: Dott. A. Giuffrè, p. 5-9.

Gezinsbeleid in Vlaanderen. In: F. Lammertyn & J.C. Verhoeven (red.). *Tussen sociologie en beleid. Vriendenboek Prof. Dr. E. Leemans.* Leuven: Acco, p. 187-197.

Family policy in the EEC countries. *Bevolking en Gezin,* (1), 1-16.

1992 with N. Cuvelier & A. Vansteenwegen. *Partnerrelaties.* Brussel: FCLG, 53 p.

*Report of the Conference 'Child, family and society'.* Luxemburg 27-29 May 1991. Brussels, 260 p.

*Rapport de la Conférence 'Enfant, famille et société'.* Luxembourg 27-29 mai 1991. Bruxelles, 276 p.

*National family policies in EC-countries in 1991: volume 1.* Leuven: European Observatory on National Family Policies, 158 p.

*Les politiques familiales nationales dans les Etats membres de la Communauté européenne en 1991: volume 1.* Leuven: Observatoire européen des politiques familiales nationales, 169 p.

*Nationale Familienpolitik in den EC-Länder in 1991.* Leuven: Europäischen Observatorium für nationale Familienpolitik, 158 p.

*National family policies in EC-countries in 1991: volume 2.* Leuven: European Observatory on National Family Policies, 266 p.

*Les politiques nationales dans les Etats membres de la Communauté européenne en 1991: volume 2.* Leuven: Observatoire européen des politiques familiales nationales, 287 p.

& C. Deneffe. *Gezinswetenschappelijke Documentatie - Jaarboek.* Leuven: Universitaire Pers Leuven, XIX + 691 p., nr. 17.

& C. Deneffe. *Relaties en Seksualiteit - 2. - Jaarboek 1992.* Leuven: K.U.Leuven, GIDS, IX + 235 p.

with H. Peeters & C. Deneffe. *Ongewenste zwangerschap in de landen van de EEG; een follow-up studie met geannoteerde bibliografie.* Leuven: K.U.Leuven, GIDS, 255 p.

Het hier en nu van de partnerrelatie. In: W.A. Dumon, e.a. (red.). *Partnerrelaties.* Brussel: FCLG, p. 1-4.

La politique familiale en Europe: controverses. In: Haut Conseil de la Population et de la Famille, *Actes du Séminaire du Politique et du Social dans l'avenir de la famille.* Paris, 6-7 février 1990. Paris: La Documentation française.

1993 *Scenario's voor de toekomst.* Leuven: Acco, 197 p.

& C. Deneffe. *Gezinswetenschappelijke Documentatie - Jaarboek.* Leuven: Universitaire Pers Leuven, XXIII + 749 p., nr. 18.

& C. Deneffe. *Relaties en Seksualiteit - 3. - Jaarboek 1993.* Leuven: K.U.Leuven, GIDS, X + 205 p.

Veranderende familiepatronen in West-Europa. In: *Referatenboek: Verandering in gezin en familie en in de maatschappij.* Brussel: Internationale Vrouwenraad, p. 21-35.

La situation des familles en Europe occidentale. In: *Rapport de consultant sur la situation de la famille en Europe occidenntale.* Actes de la réunion préparatoire à l'année internationale de la famille, organisée à l'intention des pays d'Europe et d'Amérique du Nord, La Vallette (Malte) 26-30 avril 1993. Nations Unies.

Mutations des modèles familiaux en Europe occidentale. In: *Familles en mutation dans une société en mutation.* Actes du colloque. Conseil International des femmes. Bruxelles, 8-10 février 1992. Paris: UNESCO, 25-33.

The European Observatory on National Family Policies. In: M. Ferrera (ed.). *The evaluation of social policies: experiences and perspectives /L'évaluation des politiques sociales: expériences et perspectives.* Proceedings of the international seminar organised at the University of Pavia, 18-21 March 1993 in collaboration with the Commission of the European Communities / Actes du séminaire international organisé par l'Université de Pavia, 18-21 mars 1993 en liaison avec la Commission des Communautés européennes, 164 p.

Childhood matters: A critique. In: J. Qvortrup (ed.). *Eurosocial. Report 47. Childhood as a social phenomenon: Lessons from an International Project.* Vienna: European Centre for Social Welfare Policy and Research, p. 45-50.

Changing family patterns in Western Europe. In: *Changing families in changing societies.* Proceedings of the International Conference in Brussels, 8-10 February 1992. Wiesbaden: Bundesinstitut für Bevölkerungsforschung, p. 16-21.

1994 with C. Deneffe & T. Nuelant. *Bibliographie des politiques familiales nationales dans les Etats membres de l'Union Européenne (1990-1993) / Bibliography on national family policies in the member States of the European Union (1990-1993).* Bruxelles/Brussels: CCE/CEC, 242 p.

& C. Deneffe. *Gezinswetenschappelijke Documentatie - Jaarboek.* Leuven: Universitaire Pers Leuven, XXI + 575 p., nr. 19.

& C. Deneffe. *Relaties en Seksualiteit - 4. - Jaarboek 1994.* Leuven: K.U.Leuven, GIDS, X + 199 p.

with C. Deneffe & T. Nuelant. *Bibliographie des politiques familiales nationales dans les Etats membres de l'Union européenne (1990-1993).*

*Bibliography on national family policies in the member States of the European Union (1990-1993).* Bruxelles: Commission européenne, DG V (Doc V/5006/95-FR-EN), 226 p.

& T. Nuelant. *National family policies in EC-countries; trends and developments in 1992.* Leuven: European Observatory on National Family Policies, 142 p.

& T. Nuelant. *Les politiques familiales nationales des Etats membres de la Communauté européenne; tendances et évolutions en 1992.* Leuven: Observatoire européen des politiques familiales nationales, 148 p.

& T. Nuelant. *National family policies in EC-countries: changes during 1992: Technical annex.* European Observatory on National Family Policies.

*Changing Family Policies in the member States of the European Union.* Leuven: European Observatory on National Family Policies, 328 p.

*Evolutions des politiques familiales dans les Etats membres de l'Union Européenne.* Leuven: Observatoire européen des politiques familiales nationales, 360 p.

*Veränderungen der Familienpolitik in den Mitgliedsstaaten der Europäischen Union.* Leuven: Europäisches Observatorium für nationale Familienpolitik, 370 p.

*Changing family policies in the member States of the European Union.* Brussels: Commission of the Eurtopean Communities DG V, European Observatory on National Family Policies, 328 p.

*Evolutions des politiques familiales dans les Etats membres de l'Union Européenne.* Bruxelles: Commission des Communautés Européennes DG V, Observatoire Européen des Politiques Familiales Nationales, 360 p.

*Veränderungen der Familienpolitik in den Mitgliedsstaaten der Europäischen Union.* Brussel: Kommission der Europäischen Gemeinschaften DG V, Europäischen Observatorium für nationale Familienpolitik, 370 p.

European Observatory on National Family Policies / Observatoire européen des politiques familiales nationales. In: *Decentralisation and gearing the various levels of the private/public divide / La décentralisation et l'articulation des différents niveaux de politique avec le clivage privé/public.*

Proceedings of the Workshop, Bordeaux 8-10 October 1993 / Actes de l'atelier de travail, Bordeaux 8-10 octobre 1993. Leuven: European Observatory on National Family Policies / Observatoire européen des politiques familiales nationales. 240 p.

National family policies in the member states. Current trends and developments. In: W. Dumon (ed.). *Changing Family Policies in the member States of the European Union.* Leuven: European Observatory on National Family Policies, p. 303-326.

European observatory on national family policies / Observatoire européen des politiques familiales nationales. In: *Decentralisation and gearing the various levels of the private/public divide. / La décentralisation et l'articulation des différents niveaux de politique avec le clivage privé/public.* Proceedings of the Workshop, Bordeaux 8-10 October 1993 / Actes de l'atelier de travail, Bordeaux 8-10 octobre 1993. Leuven: European Observatory on National Family Policies / Observatoire européen des politiques familiales nationales, 240 p.

*National family policies in the member States of the European Union in 1992 and 1993; synthesis report. / Les politiques familiales nationales des Etats membres de l'Union Européenne en 1992 et 1993.* Leuven: European Observatory on National Family Policies / Observatoire européen des politiques familiales nationales, 173 p.

*National family policies in the member States of the European Union in 1993; trends and developments; technical report. / Les politiques familiales nationales des Etats membres de l'Union Européenne en 1993; tendances et évolutions; rapport technique.* Leuven: European Observatory on National Family Policies / Observatoire européen des politiques familiales nationales, 185 p.

De plaats van het gezin in de maatschappelijke context van de jaren negentig. In: G.A.B. Frinking, e.a. *Goedgezind: Reflecties over een nieuwe werkelijkheid.* Verslag van het symposium dat op 10 december 1993 door het IVA Tilburg werd georganiseerd ter gelegenheid van het zilveren ambtsjubileum van dr. P.A.M. Van den Akker. Tilburg: IVA Tilburg, p. 25-35.

Schets van de toekomstige evolutie op het vlak van gezins- en relatievorming en de gevolgen daarvan voor kinderen. In: BGJG. *Kinderen in veranderende gezinnen. Verslagboek van de studienamiddag van 1 juli 1994,* p. 10-15.

Famiglia e movimenti migratori. In: E. Scabini & P. Donati (eds.). *La famiglia in una società multietnica. Sudi interdisciplinari sulla famiglia.* Milaan: Università Cattolica del Sacro Cuore, Centro Studi e Richerche sulla Famiglia, n.13, p. 27-53.

The European observatory on national family policies. *Social Europe,* (1), 38-41.

L'observatoire européen des politiques familiales nationales. *Europe sociale,* (1), 38-42.

Europäische Beobachtungsstelle für einzelstaatliche Familienpolitik. *Soziales Europa,* (1), 38-42.

Gezinsbeleid op het federale niveau. *Belgisch Tijdschrift voor Sociale Zekerheid, 36*(1), 17-20.

*Situation of families in Western Europe.* Consultant paper United Nations.

1995  & J. Van Acker. *Gezinswetenschappelijke Documentatie - Jaarboek.* Leuven: Universitaire Pers Leuven/GIDS, XXI + 726 p., nr. 20.

Family and work in Belgium. In: T. Willemsen, G. Frinking & R. Vogels (eds.). *Work and family in Europe: The role of policies.* Tilburg: University Press, 9-17.

Enkele kenmerken van gezinsverandering in Vlaanderen in de jaren negentig. In: W.A. Dumon, e.a. (red.). *Gezien het gezin: feiten en waarden.* Leuven: Davidsfonds/Universitaire Pers Leuven, p. 19-33.

with A. Vansteenwegen, L. Vandemeulebroecke, G. Maertens, G. De Maeyer & A. Deyaert. *Gezien het gezin: feiten en waarden.* Leuven: Davidsfonds/Universitaire Pers Leuven, 257 p.

The situation of the family in Western Europe. *Social Security, Journal of Welfare and Social Studies,* (44), 5-22.

*Gender and family policy in Europe: Recent trends.* Paper prepared for the XXXIIth International CFR-seminar Genders, generations and families. Murikka (Finland), June 19-22.

1996    & J. Van Acker. *Gezinswetenschappelijke Documentatie - Jaarboek.* Leuven: Universitaire Pers Leuven/GIDS, XX + 492 p., nr. 21.

& J. Van Acker. *Gezin, Relaties en Seksualiteit. Documentatie voor hulpverlening en vorming 5, 1995-1996.* Leuven: K.U.Leuven, GIDS, IX + 205 p.

Les incertitudes des politiques à l'égard de la famille. In: J. Commaille & F. de Singly (éds.). *La question familiale en Europe.* Paris: l'Harmattan, p. 81-119.

*De Bond van Grote en Jonge Gezinnen: Academische zitting.* Hasselt: Concentra.

1997    & J. Van Acker. *Gezinswetenschappelijke Documentatie - Jaarboek.* Leuven: Universitaire Pers Leuven/GIDS, XXIII + 510 p., nr. 22.

& J. Van Acker. *Gezin, Relaties en Seksualiteit. Documentatie voor hulpverlening en vorming 6, 1996-1997.* Leuven: K.U.Leuven, GIDS, X + 296 p.

The uncertainties of policy with regard to the family. In: J. Commaille & F. de Singly (eds). *The European family. The family question in the European community.* Dordrecht: Kluwer Academic Publishers, p. 61-78.

The situation of families in Western Europe: a sociological perspective. In: S. Dreman (ed.). *The family on the threshold of the 21st century. Trends and implications.* New Jersey: Lawrence Erlbaum Associations, p. 181-200.

*European perspectives for a family impact analysis. The family impact monitor project.* Brussels, November 28th.

1998    Recent trends and new prospects for a European family policy. In: S.C. Ziehl. *Multi-cultural diversity and families.* A collection of papers presented at the Committee on Family Research Seminar, July 1996. Grahamstown, South Africa: Rhodes University, Sociology Department, p. 276-304. Paper 11.

Family and housing: A problematic relationship. In: *Demography and housing / Démographie et logement / Demografie en huisvesting.* Brussel: Commissie voor de Gezinshuisvesting, p. 167-186.

# Tabula gratulatoria

Aldous Joan, Notre Dame (USA)
Amaro Fausto, Portela (P)
Amery-Moyersoen Frances, Winksele (B)
Avramov Dragana, Brussel (B)
Baers Joris, Leuven (B)
Bernardes Jon, Wolverhampton (GB)
Billiet Jaak, Heverlee (B)
Bundervoet Jan, Leuven (B)
Burggraeve Roger, Leuven (B)
Callebaut-Matthijs, Voorde (B)
Cantillon Bea, Antwerpen (B)
Casaer Paul, Leuven (B)
Cliquet Robert, Brussel (B)
Commaille Jacques, Paris (F)
Cooreman Rik, Heverlee (B)
De Blauwe Hugo, Oud-Heverlee (B)
De Cock Paul, Leuven (B)
Defever Mia, Leuven (B)
De Jong Gierveld Jenny, Den Haag (NL)
Dehaes Viviane, Brussel (B)
Del Campo Salustiano, Madrid (E)
Delanghe Luc, Heverlee (B)
Delva Jan, Brussel (B)
De Man Jan-Piet, Edegem (B)
Dencik Lars, Roskilde, (DK)
Deneffe-Marcelis C., Winksele (B)
Deven Fred, Brussel (B)
De Vuyst Jeroen, Diest (B)
De Wilde Hilde, Winksele (B)
Ditch John, York (UK)
Dobbelaere-Voyé Karel en Liliane, Leuven (B)
Donati Pierpaolo, Bologna (I)
Du Bois-Reymond Manuela, Leiden (NL)
Dumon Jeroen, Gruenwald (D)
Dumon Magda, Eeklo (B)
Dumon Simone, Maldegem (B)
Dumon Sonja, Eeklo (B)
Dumon Tom en Krista Olemans, Heverlee (B)
Dumon-Evers Peter en Hilde, Genève (CH)
Dumon-Ghaneie Kristoffel en Arezoo, Wayne PA (USA)

Edgar Don, Eagleton Vic (AUS)
Ellemers J.E., Groningen (NL)
Evers Diana, Kessel-Lo (B)
Eydal Gudny Björk, Reykjavik (IS)
Gerris Jan, Nijmegen (NL)
Glabeke Kathia, Heverlee (B)
Goossens Luc, Antwerpen (B)
Haavio-Mannila Elina, Helsinki (FIN)
Houtmans Tilly, Nijmegen (NL)
Hultåker Örjan, Stockholm (S)
Jansen Harrie, Rotterdam (NL)
Jennes Gaby, Berchem (B)
Jonker J.M.L. Nijmegen (NL)
Kellerhals Jean, Genève (CH)
Kiely Gabriel, Dublin (IRL)
Knipscheer Kees, Amsterdam (NL)
Korvela Pirjo, Helsinki (FIN)
Kwaaitaal-Roosen Elma, Nijmegen (NL)
Laermans Rudi, Brussel (B)
Lagrou Leo en Marie-Anne Dewulf, Leuven (B)
Lammertyn Frans, Leuven (B)
Lay Wiliam, Brussel (B)
Levin Irene, Oslo (N)
Lombaerts Herman, Leuven (B)
Loosveldt Geert, Leuven (B)
Lüscher Kurt, Konstanz (CH)
Maes Rudolf, Heverlee (B)
Marcoen Alfons, Leuven (B)
Matthijs Koen, Leuven (B)
Neyens Michel, Luxembourg (L)
Nicholls Brian Thomas, Copenhagen (DK)
Niit Helle, Tallinn (EST)
Nuelant Tanja, Brussel (B)
Nuyens Yvo, Geneva, (CH)
Oris Michel, Liège (B)
Pas Herman, Antwerpen (B)
Pauwels Koenraad, Melle (B)
Peuskens Joseph, Kortenberg (B)
Richardson Valerie, Dublin (IRL)
Roberts Ceridwen, London (UK)
Roe Keith, Leuven (B)
Roussel Louis, Paris (F)
Sabbe Maurits, Leuven (B)
Schulpen Luc, Brussel (B)
Segers Jozef, Lennik (B)

Segers Raymond, Lennik (B)
Senaeve Patrick, Leuven (B)
Sercu Lieven, Roeselare (B)
Settles Barbara, Delaware (USA)
Tolleneer Jan, Wilsele (B)
Top Stefaan, Rotselaar (B)
Trost Jan, Uppsala (S)
Van Damme B. en R., Linden (B)
Van de Kaa Dirk J., Den Haag (NL)
Vandemeulebroecke Lieve, Leuven (B)
Van den Auweele Dirk, Leuven (B)
Van den Berghe G., Leuven (B)
Vandenberghe Lieven, Brussel (B)
Van den Brande A., Gent (B)
Van den Troost Ann, Leuven (B)
Vanderleyden Lieve, Beersel (B)
Van Elslande Ria, Perk (B)
Van Houtte H., Winksele (B)
Van Houtte Jean, Berchem (B)
Van Mechelen Frans, Brussel (B)
Van Moll F. W., Breda (NL)
Van Molle Leen, Leuven (B)
Vanstallen R., Heverlee (B)
Veereman G., Leuven (B)
Verbeke Alain, Leuven (B)
Verbruggen Agnes, Melle (B)
Verhellen Eugeen, Gent (B)
Vermaerke Roger, Brussel (B)
Verstraeten Danielle, Pellenberg (B)
Vorlat Emma, Korbeek-Lo (B)
Walgrave Lode, Leuven (B)
Willems-Mallego, Oud-Heverlee (B)
Wynant-Dierickx, Outer (B)

*** 

**Brussel (B)**
Bond van Grote en van Jonge Gezinnen
Caritas Catholica Vlaanderen
COFACE
Hoger Instituut voor Gezinswetenschappen
Kind en Gezin
Vlaams Centrum voor de Bevordering van het Welzijn van Kinderen en Gezinnen

**Den Haag (NL)**
NIDI-library

**Dublin (IRL)**
Department of Social, Community and Family Affairs

**Edegem (B)**
European Institute for the Best Interests of the Child

**Leuven (B)**
Bibliotheek Psychologie, Pedagogische Wetenschappen en Antropologie, K.U.Leuven
C.O.S en Jeugdgezondheidszorg, K.U.Leuven
Departement Sociologie, K.U.Leuven
European Health Policy Forum
GIDS
Instituut voor de Overheid, K.U.Leuven
Trefpunt Zelfhulp
Vlaamse Leergangen

**Uppsala (S)**
Department of Sociology, Uppsala University